Hermes' Dilemma and Hamlet's Desire

HERMES' DILEMMA AND HAMLET'S DESIRE

On the Epistemology of Interpretation

Vincent Crapanzano

HARVARD UNIVERSITY PRESS

Cambridge, Massachusetts, and London, England
1992

Library of Congress Cataloging-in-Publication Data

Crapanzano, Vincent, 1939–
    Hermes' dilemma and Hamlet's desire : on the epistemology of
interpretation / Vincent Crapanzano.
        p.   cm.
    Includes bibliographical references and index.
    ISBN 0-674-38980-8 (alk. paper).—ISBN 0-674-38981-6 (pbk.: alk. paper)
    1. Ethnopsychology.   2. Ethnology—Philosophy.   3. Psychoanalysis.
    4. Hermeneutics.   5. Language and languages—Philosophy.   I. Title.
    GN502.C74   1992   91-15215
    305.8'001—dc20   CIP

For Jane Kramer

Acknowledgments

My thanks to many people for their help, inspiration, facilitation, and critical reading: to Lila Kalinich who organized the symposium, Language and the Unconscious, for the Columbia Psychoanalytic Center in which "Centering" was first given; George Marcus and James Clifford who asked me to participate in the seminar at the School of American Research in Santa Fe for which "Hermes' Dilemma" was written; James W. Stigler, Richard A. Shweder, and Gilbert Herdt for inviting me to contribute "Self-Characterization" to the Chicago Symposia on Culture and Human Development; Mrs. Abram Kardiner and the organizers of the Kardiner Lecture for giving me the opportunity to deliver "Talking (about) Psychoanalysis"; and to the members of the Kroeber Society at Berkeley for whom I prepared "Glossing Emotions." I am particularly grateful to Benjamin Lee for inviting me to present "The Self, the Third, and Desire" at a conference at the Center for Psychosocial Studies in Chicago, for many other invitations to the Center, and for innumerable, critical telephone discussions of many of the ideas in this book. I am also grateful to Bernard Weissbourd, the Center's President, for creating one of the most exciting intellectual fora in which I have had the privilege to participate. I owe special thanks to Tullio Maranhao and the Rice Circle for encouraging me to write "Dialogue," and to Alcida Ramos and the students and faculty in the Department of Anthropology at the University of Brasilia for patiently listening to me develop my ideas on dialogue and hermeneutics; to Vivian Garrison who edited with me *Case Studies in Spirit Possession* in which "Mohammed and Dawia" first appeared, and to the real Mohammed and Dawia and countless other Moroccan friends who graciously shared their lives with me; to Hans Peter Duerr for asking me for "Symbols and Symbolizing"; to Bryce Boyer for insisting that I write "Rites of Return"; and to Mme Claude Briquet who introduced me to Hamlet. I should also like to thank Marc Augé, Gilles

Bibeau, Ellen Corin, Michael Fischer, Stephen W. Foster, Wlad Godzich, Françoise Héritier, John Lucy, Paul Parin, Goldy Parin-Matthéy, Richard Parmentier, and Burton Pike. I am especially appreciative of the students at Princeton, Harvard, the University of Chicago, the Ecole des Hautes Etudes en Sciences Sociales, the University of Paris at Nanterre, the University of Stockholm, and the Graduate Center at the City University of New York for their critical reception of many of the ideas in this book. To Michael Silverstein I am especially indebted for his help in organizing this book and finding a title for it. His relentless analysis of language's several functions has been the source of my rather promiscuous metaphorizations of these functions for which I cannot in any way hold him responsible. To Dorothy Reisman who typed and retyped many of these essays, to Anita Safran who patiently corrected them, and to Lindsay Waters who encouraged me to collect them I am particularly grateful. To my daughter, Wicky, and my wife, Jane Kramer, I owe my greatest thanks, for they have had to live with me as I wrote and propounded.

The following is a list of the original titles, places, and dates of publication of essays that appeared elsewhere. They are listed in order of publication and are reprinted by permission of the publishers.

"Saints, *Jnun*, and Dreams," *Psychiatry*, 38 (1975): 145–159.

"Mohammed and Dawia: Possession in Morocco," pp. 141–176, in *Case Studies in Spirit Possession*, ed. V. Crapanzano and V. Garrison (New York: John Wiley, 1977).

"Rites of Return: Circumcision in Morocco," *The Psychoanalytic Study of Society*, 9 (1981): 15–36.

"The Self, the Third, and Desire," pp. 179–206, in *Psychosocial Theories of the Self*, ed. B. Lee (New York: Plenum, 1981).

"Text, Transference, and Indexicality," *Ethos*, 9 (1981): 122–148. Reproduced by permission of the American Anthropological Association.

"Einige Bemerkungen über den Symbolismus," pp. 71–81, in *Sehnsucht nach dem Ursprung*, ed. Hans-Peter Duerr (Frankfurt/Main: Syndikat, 1983).

"Hermes' Dilemma: The Masking of Subversion in Ethnographic Description," pp. 51–76, in *Writing Culture: The Poetics and Politics of Ethnography,* ed. J. Clifford and G. E. Marcus (Berkeley: University of California Press, 1986). Copyright © 1986 by The Regents of the University of California.

"On Glossing Emotions," Kroeber Anthropological Society Papers, 69–70 (1989): 78–85.

"Talking (about) Psychoanalysis," *Psychoanalysis and Contemporary Thought,* 12 (1989): 3–26. By permission of International Universities Press, Inc. Copyright © 1989 by International Universities Press, Inc.

"On Self-Characterization," pp. 401–423, in *Cultural Psychology: Essays on Comparative Human Development,* ed. J. W. Stigler, R. A. Shweder, and G. Herdt (Cambridge: Cambridge University Press, 1990).

"On Dialogue," pp. 269–291, in *The Interpretation of Dialogue,* ed. T. Maranhao (Chicago: University of Chicago Press, 1990). Copyright © by the University of Chicago.

Contents

Hermes' Dilemma and Hamlet's Desire

Introduction

The essays in this book are united by conceptual anguish. They question how the human sciences, particularly anthropology and psychoanalysis, articulate their fields of study. They note a prophetic fulfillment in the move from the initial foci of discovery to final theoretical formulation—a move that passes through the representation of findings and the interpretation of these findings, or perhaps more correctly their representation. The discursively transactional basis of the initial formulations, the representations, interpretations, and theoretical conclusions seem to be masked or denied in the interlocking of the processual stages. In complex reflexive ways, they each seem to justify an underlying vision, an *optique* that promotes and supports the masking or denial of their transactional basis.

Although I have taken advantage of the authority inherent in those peculiar genres—the papers and articles—social scientists and psychologists write, I prefer that my own writings be taken as essays in the etymological sense of the word, as attempts, trials, and probes. The essay enjoys a freedom, a tentativeness, and a speculative possibility that do not exist in the insistent paper or the determined article. Behind them lie an epistemology of certitude, a politics of final authority, and a bracketing of the ethical. (I will not comment on the aesthetic.) No doubt a case can be made for certitude, for final authority, and for the irrelevance of the ethical in some research in the human sciences, but I would be hard put to make a case for them in *all* the research in which human scientists engage.

In the last few years there has been much talk—salvationist talk—about developing experimental modes of writing ethnography (Marcus and Cushman 1982). Indeed, with a rapidity that is startling even in this "speedy" age, talk about experimental writing (less so actual writing) has become so conventional that it can no longer inspire literary experiment. We have to remember that the rhetorical force of any experimental expression is self-subverting. An experiment in writing is a one-time affair. If repeated it becomes conventional or quotational, referring back to the initial experiment so as to regain, magically, some of its force. Speaking of experimentation is of course different, for however conventional it may become, it can always suggest the *truly* experimental. In an age as clotted with self-reflection as ours—it could be characterized humorously as meta-modern, to suggest the archness of our current use of the word *modern*— only commentary holds out the possibility of the experimental. But the experimental remains, as such, an impossible possibility, for it can never be attained through commentary. We are left, no doubt for different crimes, in the position of Tantalus, and our role as commentators and meta-commentators, as Tantalus-like figures, has to be taken account of (!) in our critical self-understanding and our understanding of our commenting and meta-commenting roles. "Meta-modernity" seems to set in just as the meta-narratives of modernity lose their force.

As anachronistic as it may be, the essay is one genre that still gives us the possibility of expressing eloquently some of the thoughts, odd bits of information, epiphanous experiences, and speculative fantasies that are conventionally eliminated in the paper and the article. The freedom of the essay permits, without sacrificing rigor of thought, a play, an irony, a critical awareness that is for me at the heart of the human sciences. Of course most human scientists would take offense at the very suggestion that play, irony, and critical awareness are at the heart of their disciplines.[1] (In retrospect I take offense at that notion of "a heart of the discipline.") Have we assumed for too long now that play and seriousness are opposites? Have we forgotten our childhood when we knew how to play seriously? Or our flirtations when we knew how to be serious playfully? We are concerned here with values that even the most relativistic of us would prefer to ignore.

Hermes was a messenger and a trickster. In several of the essays in this book, I liken the anthropologist to him. All truly informative messages have a puckish dimension that jolts us from our ordinary expectations. The messenger has power only if he is heard. To be heard, in Heidegger's sense (1967), to be harkened to, demands all the rhetorical artifice the messenger can command. He must disrupt the prejudices and pre-understandings of his interlocutors and break the frames in which these prejudices and pre-understandings are held. Paradoxically, the messenger must first create disbelief and then destroy it without destroying the anguish and concern the disbelief triggered, for without anguish and concern the message cannot be heard. This is one way of describing Hermes' dilemma.

The messenger is always in a precarious position. Caught between two worlds—that of the message giver and that of the message receiver—he is caught between two desires. The message giver wants the messenger to convey his message and the message receiver (despite himself) wants to receive the message he desires. Each attempts to seduce the messenger. (Any adequate theory of the message, information theorists notwithstanding, has to take account of desire and power.) Where does the messenger stand? He himself is not without desire. He is not without power. He lives in a world charged with value, with loyalties, and with animosities. He cannot simply repeat the message he has heard. (Even direct quotation requires reframing.) He has to understand the message, to interpret it, translate, contextualize, and elaborate it, and he has to justify all these procedures. He has responsibility! The messenger is not an automaton—that fictitious role—in which he is socially cast *per necessitatem.*

Like Hermes, the anthropologist brings a message from those with whom he has worked. He describes their world. He may become their *porte-parole,* but, ironically, they have not sought him out. He has sought them out. He is a messenger seeking a message, and when he finds it he appropriates it, translates it, and makes it "relevant" to those to whom he delivers it. He distorts the message or, perhaps more accurately since desire is at play, perverts it. He betrays the message givers (if they are not wise enough to appreciate his dilemma) and insofar as they harken to the message, he betrays the message receivers. They get more than they sought—or perhaps less. Unlike the message giver, who even in his refusal to give a message gives one through his silence, the message receiver can refuse the message. But as every trickster knows, and every real messenger, there is something insinuating about the unheard message, if only the knowledge of its existence. Here is the messenger's ultimate power. Few of us are willing to assume it fully and take the responsibility it imposes. We shield ourselves with a determined scientism, or we indulge ourselves with the anguish of our dilemma. We seek salvation in new methodologies, new modes of analysis, new ways of conveying our messages.

I have pushed this conceit far enough. The anthropologist is obviously more than a messenger, and we are all messengers in one way or another. I wish to call attention to the moral and political consequences of the anthropologist's role as messenger. Insofar as we are shielded by fictions of objectivity, neutrality, and distance, the moral and political consequences of our role provide the determining undersong of our investigations.

Concern for the subversive effect of the *heard* message is of particular importance today. I studied anthropology in the 1960s when the privileged and the not so privileged in America and Europe and occasionally elsewhere seemed to hold two contradictory positions: an anything-goes relativism and a revolutionary dogmatism. When I left to do fieldwork in Morocco in 1967, hippie relativism was in the ascendancy—it was the time of the great be-ins—and when I returned almost two years later, after 1968, revolutionary dogmatism, political protest at least, was at its height. I saw the contradiction between relativism and dogmatism everywhere. Though one dominant stance had replaced another, the values of the former were not abandoned. Both positions shared a deep discontent with the way the world was and a sometimes overenthusiastic appreciation of otherness, be it exotic or utopian. (Often the two were romantically blended.) There was a sense of the possible and a faith in its attainment. And then the faith began to crumble. The world diminished. The self-indulgent, promiscuous mysticisms of the love generation gave way to a self-seeking speculation. The enthusiasm of the militants yielded to an egoistic accommodation.

Since then the notion of otherness has become more and more abstract—bloodless—and has been renamed: the Other, *l'autre*, alterity. With this transformation the often silly delight the flower children took in the people who embodied otherness has gone, as has the militants' faith in them. In the 1960s anthropologists were the bearers of exotic wisdoms. They described other social and political arrangements: extended families, primitive communisms, the spirit of communitas. Today the anthropologist's message of otherness is perceived as a threat to a stable and complacent order. Or it is selfishly appropriated without even the hippies' delight in otherness by New Age cultists and survivalists. Otherness raises the specter of relativism, and relativism, as even the most superficial readings of Allan Bloom, Alain Finkelkraut, and William Bennett reveal, is only a rhetorical ploy for affirming the status quo or inspiring a nativistic return to "tradition." They confuse for obvious political purposes an anything-goes relativism with what should properly be understood as a heuristic relativism. A heuristic relativism recognizes that in order to understand the other creatively and thereby oneself and one's world, one has to take the part of the other. This does not mean to switch allegiance, for then the other would no longer afford a vantage point for self-viewing and discovery—for challenging ones assumption. What the "antirelativists" choose not to understand is that without self-questioning and self-doubt one is left with only repetition, however elaborated, and with a morally and politically convenient traditionalism.

Through its engagement with the other, with people of often dramatically different values, cultural orientations, and social arrangements, anthropology has a potentially privileged position among the human sciences, in society at large. It is a role that it has not played for years, at least not actively, but it can and ought to once again. By forcing us to assume different perspectives, the anthropologist *can* lead us to question the basic assumptions we make about ourselves and others and about the nature of our worlds. He provides us with an "external" vantage point the way the philosophical traveler once did (see Chapter 4). (This way of thinking has not lost its appeal as the current boom in serious travel literature indicates.) Despite his often long sojourns among others, despite his intimate knowledge of their folkways, the anthropologist can never fully convey the alterity of the people with whom he has lived and worked, for he can never rid himself completely of his own cultural assumptions. His external vantage point forces him to stress difference—a difference that demands a translation which, paradoxically, affirms that difference.

The vantage point the anthropologist provides is, like all vantage points, never stable though it may be conventionally fixed.[2] It is the vantage point of an ever shifting interlocutor with whom one is dialogically engaged. Dialogues, I suggest, are never dyadic. Each partner in a dialogue is simultaneously participating in what I call shadow dialogues with absent (though significant) interlocutors who change as the primary dialogue changes. Like the figures of transference and countertransference psychoanalysts talk about, these absent interlocutors are subject to the complex play of desire and power. I spell all this out in Chapters 3, 4, and 8. Here I want to stress that the conventional fixity of a vantage point is the product of a struggle between (socially determined) desire and (socially effective) power within the confines of a tradition that can be subverted.

In offering at least the illusion of a radically external vantage point, the anthropologist finds himself in a doubly subversive position. If he takes the alterity he posits seriously and if he is committed to conveying it so it can be *heard*, he does violence to the assumptions of his society. He also does violence to his discipline, for it is very much a product of those culturally and historically determined assumptions. Built into anthropology's project is its own subversion. Like the trickster the anthropologist risks tricking himself. Tikoloshe, the African trickster, had a giant penis which he slung over his shoulder. One day, as he was chopping wood, he accidentally (so we must assume) chopped it off. Anthropology's project, which I articulate in strong male imagery—for it has grown out of and reflects a predominantly male orientation—is governed by this subversion.

I do not want to exaggerate the role of the anthropologist in changing social and cultural values and orientations. Despite the occasional James Frazer or Margaret Mead, the anthropologist is—he certainly has been—a marginal figure both in the academy and publicly. Stanley Tambiah (1985:341) notes that planning and development experts do not view anthropology as "the queen of the social sciences" but as "the mother of low status servants and handmaids fitted for the labor-intensive job of pitching tents in the outbacks and wildernesses," useful to collect information that can be converted into such variables as "the cultural factor" or "the psychic components of income and consumption" in their macromodels. Until recently, when historians, literary critics, a few philosophers, and a handful of political scientists have taken up "structuralism" and "interpretive anthropology," the same could be said, with appropriate modification, about the attitude of hardline social scientists, economists, and psychologists.

Anthropologists are certainly not immune to the spirit of their times. Ernest Gellner (1988), carrying out a long polemic against hermeneutics (Clifford Geertz) and relativism, argues that just as American Indians are susceptible to strong drink (a point that can be contested) so "ordinary Americans, culture-blind by background, are specially vulnerable to the ideas of culture and hermeneutics, to the intoxicating ideas that systems of meaning differ profoundly, are justified by their own distinct standards, and are separated by profound gulfs, the crossing of which is an arduous and perhaps even perilous performance." American cultural blindness apparently leads "to an unduly reverential, rather mystical explication of 'meanings' in lieu of more ordinary styles of social description and explanation" and to a race of "anthropological Hamlets" who suffer the "hurt" of broken categories, and though rewarded by "transcendental insights of great depth," are punished by a style that precludes "limpid lucidity."

What is troubling here is not the polemicist's shaky footing but its consequences. "Cultures are not cognitively equal, and the one within which alone anthropology is possible cannot really be denied a special status. The nature and justification of that pre-eminence is a deep and difficult matter. But it springs from something far more important than the arrogance of an imperial class. It is linked to the very possibility of *reason*" (Gellner 1988:29). With these words Gellner wipes out the very possibility of anthropology, for an anthropologist has to begin his research with an openness—a bracketing off, however unsuccessfully, of his prejudices—and pre-understandings. Gellner even cuts himself off from other anthropologies, coming from other societies with other values. And he implies that such societies lack *reason,* that hallmark of the West, without speci-

fying what he means by "reason." What most anthropologists
have learned and tried to convey is that reason cannot be easily
separated from value; that reason has to be distinguished from
reasoning; and that the members of even the most primitive
societies are not deprived of reason though they may evaluate
it differently and distribute their reasoning differently.

Few anthropologists would of course publicly subscribe to
Gellner's views, but unfortunately they are implicit in much of
what they say and write. (I worry that his viewpoint will win
adherents as Western anthropologists, still in a dominant position, are forced to listen to their non-Western colleagues who
struggle to develop their own anthropologies.) We should not be
surprised. The anthropologist is no less subject to his culture's
assumptions than anyone else. But as an anthropologist, I believe, he has to question these assumptions and to force others
to question them. Like the critical philosopher, I would situate
anthropology in that Kantian tradition, he ought to remind us of
the limits of our understanding. Paradoxically, a certain cultural
confidence is required to maintain that stance. When it is lacking, as among white South Africans, the perception of others
becomes rigidly stereotyped, the behavior intolerant, and the
appreciation of other social and cultural arrangements empty
(Crapanzano 1985). Put no doubt too simply, certainly too opti-
mistically, one of anthropology's missions is to cleanse our assumptions of their presumption. And, I would add, any engaged
anthropology— call it applied, participatory, or clinical—has to
address the same problems among its subjects. Otherwise it remains patronizing and simply manipulative.

As I was preparing this book I awoke one night from a dream
that may be related to the anxiety I felt in looking back at what
I had written. All I could remember of it was a voice saying, "the
I of the now is not the I of the now," and seeing the equation "I
$\neq$ I." Half asleep, I added, "by the breath of a word." There is
in any collection of essays a biographical dimension. Certainly
they inspire the author to autobiographical reflection—to a sum-
ming up. To discuss the essays produces an embarrassment, a
longing to change them and a resistance to changing them, a
need to justify them, and a desire to paraphrase them in terms

of one's present sophistication. They call attention to the presumption in even one essay of a single "editorial" vantage point, one that denies precisely "the breath of a word." We write as though we had a single, controlling voice, and expect to be read as such. We are distressed by changes of voice, changes in attitude, contradictory stances, which announce the inconstancy of the self and the instability of our vantage point. One purpose of our rhetoric is to mark us as constant throughout our writing, to fix our perspective. We are taught to read accordingly—to perpetuate an author's illusion of singularity, coherence, and constancy, and in our engagement with him our own illusions of singularity, coherence, and constancy.

Reading, like writing, is a social activity—a response to particular social arrangements. We do not read generally but rather in genre-specific ways, and if we fail to read in these ways, we are considered bad readers, tactless readers (yes, tact plays an important role in reading), or, like the deconstructionists' reading of philosophy, blasphemously brilliant readers. A brilliant misreading is a breach of the unstated pact between writer and reader to preserve the conventionality of reading and thereby the writer's self and the intentional edifice he has constructed. When we read an ethnography, for example, we are meant to pay attention to its descriptions, to the quality of the ethnographer's interpretations, and to the significance of the theories he develops. We are not to pay attention, at least explicitly, to the way the ethnographer constitutes himself through his ethnography or the way he constructs his arguments rhetorically. Such considerations would be tactless because they would be evaluative of the author's person, his competence as an ethnographer, and his talent as a writer.

The power of the deconstructionists—and the threat they pose—lies in their refusal to read texts as they were conventionally meant to be read: for their context, the story they have to tell, their manifest argument, what the author intended. Deconstructionists do violence to convention; they call attention to the rhetorical dimension of the texts that is masked by an ideologically justified conventional focus on the text's informational— its semantico-referential—dimension. It is no accident that the deconstructionists were inspired by four brilliant "misreaders" (or shall I say tactless readers?): Marx, Nietzsche, Freud, and Lévi-Strauss. Certainly the deconstructionists have made an art of what the anthropologist does and usually prefers not to acknowledge (except for that small and most probably ephemeral group of ethnographers who are reading ethnographies deconstructively). Wittingly the deconstructionists read the way anthropologists unwittingly have "read" what the people they study say. When Derrida reads Rousseau or de Man Nietzsche, they commit a "blasphemous" act similar to that of Evans-Pritchard when he listens to what the Azande have to say about witchcraft or of Lévi-Strauss when he analyzes a Bororo myth. In their different ways, they are concerned not with the intentional message of what they read (though they have to take that into account), but with the way the messages are constructed and made persuasive. Where the anthropologist and the deconstructionist differ is in their particular intention. The deconstructionist seems content with revealing the construct and its hidden rhetoric. Their exposure is an end in itself though it may be justified, at some level, on pedagogic grounds or as a contribution to an understanding of construction, rhetoric, and *literaturnost*. The anthropologist tries to relate construct, rhetoric, and literariness to social and cultural arrangements, which may be reflective of "more basic" political and economic ones. He faults the deconstructionist for failing to situate the texts he deconstructs as well as his own deconstructions. Deconstructive readings are for him mere exercises, displays of virtuosity, games in a decadent world. The deconstructionist finds the anthropologist's commitment to discovering the social, cultural, political, and economic underpinnings naive; for him, the anthropologist fails to realize the complex textual construction of these "basic" arrangements, the arbitrariness of their relationship to the texts and discourse (the "saying" the anthropologist is trying to locate), the desperate rhetoric of contextualization and explanation. Though anthropologists and deconstructionists share the intellectual inspiration (Nietzsche notwithstanding), they have different intentions, certainly different interpretive moralities.

Reading and writing are complex social transactions and relate to other transactions and their glosses in the community of readers and writers. The embarrassment—the editorial push—

we (Americans and Europeans) feel when we discover changes in *our* voice and stance reflects our obsessive concern with the self, with its singularity, its constancy, its coherence, and our apperception of its fragility, and artifice.

All the essays in this book question at some level our basic assumptions and presumptions in thinking about and representing the self, its incarnate transactions, and its social and cultural environment. My concern with the self is certainly a reflection of my culture and my biography. It is also a product of my anthropological research and a deepening awareness of how the notion of the self and its representation have changed in Western thought and literature.

Although I had read accounts of how notions of the self, its experience even, vary from society to society, I did not fully appreciate these variations until I had done extensive fieldwork in Morocco with people possessed and obsessed by demons. I was prepared for differences, but I suppose I expected them to be in style rather than in experience (insofar as I could appreciate it) and grounding organization. I went to the field with a strong though skeptical interest in psychoanalysis and presumed, if not its present universality, then, with modification, its potential universality, and I returned from the field with discomfort. Yes, it was possible to apply psychoanalytic understanding to what I observed, but doing so seemed reductive and culture-specific. Much of the subtlety I observed in the way Moroccans articulated and explained their experiences was lost. Moreover, the philosophical-psychological challenge that other modes of articulation and explanation posed was side-stepped. Gradually, as should be evident in the development of my essays, I moved away from a primary—a potentially reductive— psychoanalytic understanding to an ironic one that recognizes the cultural and historical specificity of psychoanalytic understanding and acknowledges our—the Westerner's, my own— entrapment in the idiom from which that understanding derives. It seems to me that such an ironic stance is properly anthropological. It recognizes the self-reflective, the reflexive, nature of any ethnographic understanding and the limits of any cross-cultural translation. It does not presume universality but does not deny its possibility *at some level.*

Although I did not formulate my position this way when I wrote on psychoanalysis, I believe all the essays reflect it. I have tried in many of them to elaborate a "pre-psychological" theory, based *arbitrarily* on the primacy of language in both psychoanalytic and anthropological practice, representation, and understanding. In part it derives from the belief that the study of language has a rigor that permits a meta-language, as far removed from the "psychological" as any we have that can do justice to it. I am not promoting a nominalism here; I am not denying the importance of other modes of communication, appreciation, and understanding. I am using language here tactically, as a way of questioning our psychological presumption, which others, perhaps more soberly, would call our psychological assumption. (Ethnographers have certainly shown, as I have tried to show with respect to spirit possession, that experiences we understand in psychological terms can be understood in other ways in other cultures and in other ways at other times in our own culture [see Chapter 7].) I must confess I am seduced at times by my linguistic tactic and at other times viscerally disturbed by it. So strong is my attachment to my psychology; so strong is my commitment to a critical epistemology.

My approach to the self is dialectical. I am concerned with the transactions out of which self-awareness develops, the discursive practices that articulate the self, and the social, political, and economic forces that lead to the hypostatization, the essentialization, and the perpetuation of the self. (I discuss these processes in chapters 3 and 4.) I lay particular stress on the way in which a regnant linguistic ideology can help to mask the transactional basis of the self and supports its hypostatization, esentialization, and perpetuation.

By *linguistic ideology* I mean the assumptions, often implicit, we make about language and its use (Silverstein 1979). The term has both a cognitive and an evaluative—an axiological—dimension, for an ideology of language determines how we perceive and describe a language and how we evaluate it. Language may be viewed as transparent or opaque, limiting, even recalcitrant. It may be the subject of considerable speculation. I have observed, for example (1985), that English-speaking South

Africans take language in a generally utilitarian and instrumental fashion, while Afrikaans-speakers take it—the *tal*—substantively as a carrier of culture, tradition, religion, and national identity. Priority may be given to the spoken or the written (Derrida 1967; Tylor 1987) or to a particular signifying practice such as "prose" or "poetry" (Kittay and Godzich 1987). In some societies, as among Calame-Griaule's (1965) Dogon, language and its indigenously understood operations may serve as metaphors for describing reality; in others it may have little metaphorical scope. Often, in literate societies, linguistic ideology is given more or less systemic expression in grammars, style manuals, and philosophical discussions of language. I am tempted to say, as is conventional in anthropological-linguistic circles, that a linguistic ideology comprises all the assumptions about language and language-use a people make without taking account of other languages or linguistic possibilities, but *that* would be too facile. A comparative perspective can be incorporated into any linguistic ideology. Think, for example, of all those stereotypes Europeans make about each other's languages. They range from comparative word counts to, say, an English speaker's assertion that syntax is the principal carrier of nuance in French. They would include the usual cliches about French as the language of love, Italian of passion, Spanish of honor, German of philosophy, and Russian of soul—*dusha*. These comparative stereotypes do not alter a people's conception of language.

Is linguistic ideology rooted in the "grammar" of its language? A Whorfian would insist that it is an inevitable refraction of the language, while a Marxist might dismiss grammatical determination as bourgeois mystification. Certainly a number of linguists see an intimate relationship between grammar and categories of thought. Emile Benveniste (1966; see also Chapter 6) argues, for example, that Aristotle's categories are derivative of ancient Greek grammar, but he fails to add that these categorical refractions can be—and are—used to discuss language.

Arguments tend to be circular, for it is never quite clear how one can attain an ideologically free grammar and thereby demonstrate its relationship to categories of thought. Ann Banfield (1985) suggests, for example, that *écriture*, as it is used in contemporary French criticism, is related to two features of French grammar: the aorist (*le passé simple*), which is used only in writing and is "a pervasive sign of literacy itself," and the peculiar use of the third person singular in novelistic narratives. Unlike the "je" which creates (an illusion of) an ordering by a transcendant subjectivity, the "il" carries the action of the narrative. Both the aorist and "the third person of the novel," as Barthes (1953) calls it, produce (the illusion of) an absolute distance between the writing and the narrated events, an independence from the narrator, a sort of depersonalized or impersonal, a "mythic" time (*le temps d'histoire*), an order of reality which appears to transcend all subjectivity or being. In this way a writing independent of the narrator can be invoked, or, as in Lévi-Strauss, an authorless and timeless mythology be conceived. However illuminating, Banfield's discussion of the semantics of *écriture* is for our purposes unsatisfactory, simply because she bases her analysis on what ideologically implicated critics—Roland Barthes, Michel Butor, Maurice Blanchot, and Michel Foucault—have to say about the "grammar" of the aorist and the novelistic third person. Their grammar is of course a prop for their understanding of *écriture*. The circularity of Banfield's (perhaps anyone's) discussion of the relationship between language and thought categories is already in evidence in her initial hypothesis: "I want to argue that [why the notion of *écriture* emerged specifically in French thinking[has something to do with the French language itself and with a French—it is not Continental—attitude to language, an attitude which might be called a grammatical way of thinking" (1985:2).

In the West we have tended to view language unifunctionally, in essentially semantico-referential terms, and to understand other functions of language as derivative of language's referential function (Derrida 1972; Silverstein 1979). (Think of some of the arguments advanced by the logical positivists.) It is not clear, however, that other functions of language can be derived from the semantico-referential. Silverstein (1979:87), stressing the pragmatic and the meta-pragmatic functions of language, has argued against the priority we give to the semantico-referential. I have also discussed the role of priority placed on the semantico-referential function in making pragmatic and meta-pragmatic operations. (A similar case, in more restricted circumstances, can be made for what Jakobson (1960) calls the poetic function—the way in which words refer back or direct attention to themselves.)

By semantico-referential I mean that (intensional) dimension or function of an utterance where meaning is in all but a trivial fashion independent of its intra- and extra-linguistic context. It is the aspect of language that has received the greatest attention by philosophers and linguists (Bar-Hillel 1970) and provides the basis for our folk models of language. This privileging of semantic meaning ties in well with an "otherworldly," epistemological tradition, going back at least to Socrates, which gives preference to decontextualized or decontextualizable—pure—knowledge.) The pragmatic or indexical refers to the (extensional) dimension or function of an utterance where meaning depends on its intra- and extra-linguistic context. If we contrast a proposition like "ice floats on water" with an ordinary conversational remark like "I couldn't abide that man's arrogance" we immediately see the difference. The meaning of the first proposition remains constant despite virtually all the contexts in which it might be said. The meaning of the second remark can only be understood fully when we know (or imagine) its context of utterance. Otherwise, how would we identify the *I*, the putatively arrogant man, and the time of not abiding? Deictics like "this" and "that," honorifics like "madame" and "boy," first and second person personal pronouns, and verb tense are all pragmatic in function. They are both context-reflective and context-creative. Some indexicals, the deictics, *here* and *there*, for example, have referential content—Silverstein (1976) calls them "referential indexes"—or they may be devoid of referential content, Silverstein's "pure" or "non-referential" indexes. A shift from "here" to "there" in response to the question "Where is the key?" changes the referential content of the utterance "Here is the key" in a way in which a change from "O moço" to "O Seu" (from a vocative expression used to address in Brazilian Portuguese a man inferior to the speaker to one denoting equality or superiority) does not involve a change in referential content. The same man is being addressed though the social context of the utterance is dramatically altered. Such pure indexes are very context-creative.

Indexicals also call attention to a particular functional modality of an utterance and thereby mask its other functional modalities (Silverstein 1987). As such they regiment conventional interpretation. I should add that no utterance, even the most context-independent proposition, is devoid of a pragmatic dimension, for minimally it marks its semantico-referentiality and in practice it articulates, if only through contrast, its intra-linguistic environment. It may also serve to index the parties to the encounter in which it occurs.

In Chapter 5, I consider the implications of the basic asymmetry between meta-referential and meta-pragmatic statements. Meta-referential statements refer to the semantic meaning of an expression: "'Sydenham's chorea' is yet another name for an infectious encephalitis of the cortex and basal ganglia"; "'By those others' he meant the possessing spirits he could not name without endangering himself." Meta-pragmatic statements refer to the pragmatic features (or use) of an expression: "'Here' like 'there' is a spatial deictic"; "Whenever that old peasant wants something from him she calls him 'sua eccellenza.'"[3] In a meta-referential utterance the *Einstellung,* to use Jakobson's (1960) term, the dominant functional orientation or modality of the primary utterance and the meta-statement, is the same: semantico-referential. (It also has a pragmatic dimension, as should be clear from the examples I have given—examples that cast me in a certain way.) In the meta-pragmatic utterance the *Einstellungen* are different: pragmatic at the primary level and semantico-referential at the meta-level. I argue that interpretations of transference and countertransference are based on the pragmatic features of therapeutic exchanges—particularly pragmatic locutions through which the analyst and the patient cast themselves and their various transferential personae. I argue further that the language in which transference and countertransference—the pragmatics of the exchange—is discussed (that is, the semantico-referential meta-pragmatic language) is the same as the semantico-referential meta-referential language in which, for example, the analyst discusses the symbolism of dreams and the configurations of past behavior described by the patient. I suggest that the identity of the two meta-languages obscures their different functional bases, creating a closed hermeneutical system. I believe that in societies that give priority to the semantico-referential function, the obscuring of the pragmatic function at the referentially expressed meta-pragmatic level is characteristic of all closed hermeneutical systems, that is, of all systemic, totalizing ideologies. It is at least one process of mystification, one process of repression.

We have to examine carefully how mystification and repression are produced and how the interpreter uncovers them. We have to ask how mystificatory and repressive processes are related to the priorities granted particular *Einstellungen* and their distribution wtihin the genres and styles of any language. Are the processes of mystification and repression the same in speech communities that stress other *Einstellungen*? Do these relate to questions of literacy? And how? Can such priorities be related to socio-economic and socio-political arrangements? We have to recognize that our notion of ideology (including, circularly, linguistic ideology) relates to the assumptions we make about and the attitudes we take toward language, discourse, and text. Our descriptions of ideology, like those of culture and worldview, stress their semantic content. (I include the ideological construction of our own ideology.) They tend to be pictorial, monolithic, "logical," coherent, and, though recognized as subject to change, also somehow timeless, certainly static. They presume a notion of constant truth. Like texts (as we understand "texts"), ideologies are decontextualized, though we may deny their being decontextualizable, and in many political analyses, once descriptively decontextualized, they are *mirabile dictu* recontextualized in accordance with the analyst's own theoretical disposition. For us, ideology is both a native category and an analytic one. As for other such duplex categories—they are characteristic of our sociologies and psychologies—this doubling (I am tempted to write this duplicity) permits all sorts of rhetorical manipulations that confirm a particular, an interested, ah! an ideological view of the world. Certainly we have to be careful when we describe the ideologies of other people who share neither our notion of ideology nor our assumptions about language, text, and discourse.

In a very speculative and no doubt premature way, I would like to consider the implications of the asymmetry of meta-linguistic statements for the human sciences.[4] I suggest that in the West the language in which pragmatic features of any verbal exchange are discussed is seldom linguistic or communicational. It is metaphorized.[5] Freud did not discuss transference in linguistic but in psychological terms. Marx did not discuss class relations in terms of language but socio-dramatically, at times militaristically.

I have observed that middle-class white Americans talk about the pragmatic features of their exchanges in characterological and socio-dramatic terms. Obviously the way they talk about them varies with the occasion, the oral and written genres at their disposal, and the quality of their dialogical engagement. When asked about a particular exchange, Americans will often paraphrase it briefly, in terms of its content ("We talked about love"; "John said that Mary assumed the stock market would crash"), and then go on to describe the pragmatic features either in characterological or socio-dramatic terms or in a mixture of them.[6] Often the discussion is supplemented by examples that are given to illustrate the pragmatics of the encounter—and not the lexical meaning. The manifest lexical meaning in these paraphrases frequently illustrates the pragmatics of the encounter as well. The lexical message is set up to function pragmatically.

A letter F. Scott Fitzgerald sent to Edmund Wilson in February 1933 (Fitzgerald 1956:277) illustrates my point. Fitzgerald apologizes for his behavior at a meeting he had with Wilson and Hemingway.

> We had a most unfortunate meeting. I came to New York to get drunk . . . and I shouldn't have looked up you and Ernest in such a humor of impotent desperation. I assume full responsibility for all unpleasantness—with Ernest I seem to have reached a state where when we drink together I half bait, half truckle to him . . . anyway, plenty of egotism for the moment.

Note that not a word of what was said is mentioned. (Admittedly Wilson, Fitzgerald's correspondent, was present and knew what had been said, but *that* would not necessarily preclude its mention.) Fitzgerald talks around the offense by describing his own psychological condition: drunkenness, "a humor of impotent desperation," "plenty of egotism."

> Dos [Passos] was here, and we had a nice evening—we never quite understand each other and perhaps that's the best basis for an enduring friendship. Alec came up to see me at the Plaza the day I left (still in awful shape but not conspicuously so). He told me to my amazement that you had explained the fundamentals of Leninism, even Marxism the night before, and Dos tells me that it was only recently made plain thru the same agency in the *New Republic*. I little thought when I left politics to you and your gang in 1920 you would devote your time to cutting up Wilson's shroud into blinders. Back to Mallarmé.

This passage has to be understood in terms of what preceded it. In describing his meeting with Dos Passos, Fitzgerald does not say what they talked about. He only refers to their happy failure of communication. His descriptions of his talk with Alec and later again with Dos Passos mention the subject matter in so truncated a manner that it indicates primarily how Alec, Dos Passos, and Fitzgerald characterized Wilson. It is important to note here the pragmatic function of the paraphrase of the encounter itself. It is clearly the secondary dialogue in which the paraphrase occurs that governs the elaboration of the paraphrase, despite its purported realism.[7]

The dialogical determination of the embedded descriptions of an encounter is illustrated in a second example—an oral one. Again the pragmatic features of the encounter are described metaphorically. John meets Harry on the street. Harry has just run into Pete whom he has not seen since Pete ran off with Joan. Harry and Joan had been living together. Pete is starting a disco which he refers to as "the club."

> Harry: Jesus, you'll never guess who I just ran into.
> John: It must've been a ghost. You look awful.

Harry: Pete.
John: Oh!
Harry: You said it.
John: It had to happen. This ain't the Big Apple, you know.
       What'd he say?
Harry: You wouldn't believe it. He acted like nothing had
       happened. He just talked about that damned club. He
       plans to open in September.
John: That soon?
Harry: Yeah. "Things are looking good, ole buddy," he said.
       You know the way he talks. "Ole buddy," my eye! He
       was real high. He'd just seen the lighting engineer. He
       came in under estimate.
John: Some guys have all the luck.
Harry: You can say that again.
John: Well, I meant . . .
Harry: He promised to invite me to the opening. It was weird.
       He could've been talking to anyone. You'd think Joan
       didn't exist. I didn't exist.
John: Maybe he was nervous.
Harry: Oh, no. He was real smooth.
John: Yeah. He's pretty smooth.
Harry: You never liked him. I guess I was kinda taken in.
       Jesus, I've known the guy forever. We were . . .
John: Did you mention Joan?
Harry: Naw. I was tempted to, and then I thought, "Fuck it."
       She's outta my life.
John: Yeah.
Harry: I broke off real quick. The bastard would've invited
       me to lunch, and I probably would've ended up
       paying.

Here we have the report of a very tense scene. Clearly, the
relations between Harry and Pete override the content of their
conversation. We do not know whether John's interest in what
they said was simply a tactful way of finding out how they got
on without pressing his friend. To John's question, "What'd he
say?" Harry responds by describing *how* Pete talked and acted.
He condenses what was presumably a longer conversation into
"He just talked about that damned club." He then adds a bit of
information about the opening of the club. Is this a surrender

to John's question—a way of perpetuating his conversation with John? Harry quotes Pete and comments on Pete's way of talking. "You know how he talks." This observation turns Harry's attention to Pete's state of mind. "He was real high." He describes the meeting. "It was weird." "He could've been talking to any one." Are they reflective of Pete's earlier verbal qualifiers: "He acted like nothing had happened. He just talked about . . ."? These socio-dramatic qualifiers lead Harry (through John's "He must have been nervous") to characterize Pete as "smooth" and himself as a dupe. John returns to the content of the encounter: "Did you mention Joan?" The way has been prepared for this potentially indiscrete question. Harry says he hadn't and describes how he ended the conversation. He uses the figure of hypothesis ("If I'd gone on, the bastard would have . . ."). The figure also serves to end—one presumes—a chapter in Harry's conversation with John.

Few of the lexical messages that passed between Harry and Pete are given in this paraphrase. What little content is reported functions primarily to perpetuate the exchange between John and Harry. It has, I suggest, a phatic function, which can be described in psychological terms as "supportive." Unlike many reports of discursive exchanges, Harry refers specifically to the way Pete speaks. His meta-linguistic observations are immediately related to socio-dramatic and ultimately to characterological ones. Does the characterological function as a full stop to descriptive inquiry in Harry and John's set? Is it genre-specific?

I doubt that the pragmatic features of exchanges are described metaphorically in characterological and socio-dramatic terms in other speech communities. My impression is that even in the West there are important differences. In France, for example, if I may generalize, such descriptions, when expressed in characterological terms, are less personality-oriented than in the United States. They usually refer to the moral condition of the characterized. Often they are cast in proverbial terms, referring to something that may have been learned in one of those *leçons de morale* that Wylie (1964) described in his book on the Vaucluse, or to some literary-philosophical aphorism.

I am suggesting here that in speech communities which stress the semantico-referential function of language, the pragmatic function tends to be masked by the semantico-referential. When the pragmatic features are discussed, they are not ordinarily discussed in linguistic terms but metaphorically. As I noted, the principal *Einstellung* of meta-pragmatic language, whether expressed directly in linguistic or in metaphorical terms, is semantico-referential. Its pragmatic function is considered irrelevant to its interpretation. It can be read as though it were removed from its *own* situational and dialogical environment. This gives to meta-pragmatic statements, particularly those metaphorized into highly valued idioms, a timeless, an essential quality. In "Chapter 4" I suggest that characterizations of the self and other are essentializations of pragmatic *Gestalten* whose dialogical foundations are denied. Here I propose that the characterological and socio-dramatic language with which we describe metaphorically pragmatic features of discursive encounters ground our folk psychologies and our folk sociologies. In other words, folk psychologies and sociologies are meta-pragmatic refractions of the pragmatic features of discursive encounters. These characterological and socio-dramatic meta-pragmatic languages are, in inevitable circular fashion, valorized by the precipitated folk psychologies and sociologies. It is precisely at the nexus of pragmatics and meta-pragmatics (and not, I believe, at the semantico-referential level) that we have to look if we want to relate our ideological formations and folk sciences to socio-discursive forms, indeed, to socio-economic and socio-political arrangements. We have of course to ask how our purportedly scientific psychologies and sociologies relate not just to folk sciences but to the pragmatic basis of these folk sciences.

In his description of civil war in Corcyra, Thucydides (1954) observed that as the strife intensified, savage passions were unleashed, fathers killed their sons, men were butchered at sacred altars, revenge became more important than self-preservation, and words had to change their "usual meaning" to fit the new circumstances.[8] "What used to be described as a thoughtless act of aggression was now regarded as the courage one would expect to find in a party member; to think of the future and wait was merely another way of saying one was a coward; any idea of moderation was just an attempt to disguise one's unmanly character; ability to understand a question from all sides meant that one was totally unfit for action. Fanatical enthusiasm was the mark of a real man" (p. 209).

Thucydides' observation about meaning merits consideration. Can words so radically and so rapidly change their meaning? Can they lose their meaning? The poet says so. Words "strain," "crack," and "decay with imprecision," Eliot (1952) wrote in "Burnt Norton." They do "not stay in place." Can language lose its conventional (as opposed to its symptomatic) communicative capacity? We tend to isolate language, understood in the broadest sense, from other social and cultural institutions. Though I make reference in *Hermes' Dilemma* to the relationship of language to other institutions, I have also treated language autonomously. As such, language becomes simply an instrument, a sometimes recalcitrant instrument, in the struggle between differently empowered desires, however they are founded, determined, legitimated, passed even "through the defiles of the signifier" (Lacan 1966). (We can never, it seems, escape circularity.) But language should not be reduced so easily to mere instrumentality. Whatever its instrumental role, whatever its reflexive capability, whatever (illusion of) transcendence, removal, and distance it gives, language articulates in complex ways with the sources of desire and power in any social formation.

Given the complexity of language, its many functions, its reflexivity, its cover stories, it probably makes little sense to discuss the relationship between language (except as a cultural category) and the sources of desire and power and their conventionalization and institutionalization. It does seem, however, that the (institutionalized sources of power and desire can affect the meaning-generating and context-calling capacity of language. If, as I believe, there is in language, taken multifunctionally, an inherent, ideologically supported, masking process (that is, as one function or *Einstellung* is conventionally highlighted, others, always effective, are masked) then one of the ways in which power and desire, in whatever institutional form, affect language is by determining, metapragmatically, the priority given a particular function or *Einstellung*. Put another way: one of the stakes in the play between desire and power is the control of how language can be read—of the pragmatic regimentation of an "appropriate" hermeneutic. It is at this level, as I hope these essays will demonstrate, that the negotiation of meaning and relevance between speakers occurs. They do not usually negotiate consciously, for they are ideologically blinded to the pragmatics of their discourse by their commitment to its semantico-referential meaning. (Is it possible that what we call "unconscious" is that which is masked in any communicative exchange and *placed*, for whatever reasons, somewhere, in the psyche?)

Speakers do not of course negotiate freely but from within the tradition in which they find themselves or strive to locate themselves when the tradition is in doubt. When the traditional communicative conventions are undermined through civil strife, as in Corcyra, or through rapid social change, as in so much of the world today, or at the height of revolution before conservative forces gain or regain the ascendancy, or through fundamental breaches in the ritual and moral order of society, as in Hamlet's Elsinore, then the negotiations of meaning and relevant context break down. Society finds itself in an evidential crisis. No one knows, no one can really know, anything. The play of the empowered desires becomes extravagant, savage, and promiscuous, and can only be controlled, if at all, by an even more savage empowered desire. Or it ends, as at Elsinore, with the slaughter of the players—more often than not, I suspect, without a Horatio, a Hermes, or even an ethnographer to tell the tale.

· I ·

THE TEXTUALIZED SELF

1.
Centering

Turning and turning in the widening gyre
The falcon cannot hear the falconer;
Things fall apart; the center cannot hold;
Mere anarchy is loosed upon the world.
The blood-dimmed tide is loosed, and everywhere
The ceremony of innocence is drowned;
The best lack all conviction, while the worst
Are full of passionate intensity.

—Yeats, "The Second Coming"

"During the summer of 1895 I had been giving psychoanalytic treatment to a young lady who was on very friendly terms with me and my family. It will be readily understood that a mixed relationship such as this may be a source of many disturbed feelings in the physician and particularly in the psychotherapist." With words reminiscent of the opening of a romantic novel, something by Lermontov, Gottfried Keller, or perhaps Victor Hugo, Sigmund Freud (1954a:106; 1983:97)[1] begins his account of a dream he had on July 23–24, 1985, known as the dream of Irma, which launched a new approach to the study of dreams. Freud refers to the dream as a *Traummuster*, which his English translator, James Strachey, anxious, one supposes, to preserve the scientific tone of Freud's project, translates as a "specimen dream." *Muster* can also mean a model, a pattern, a standard, or a sample. All of these meanings suggest the exemplary, centering, quality of the dream for Freud's new science.

The rhetorical strategy I call *centering* plays, I believe, an important role in the ongoing transactions that occur in the psychoanalysis, certainly in the reports and interpretations of such transactions. It also plays an important role in other exchanges, including the ethnographic. I will discuss this strategy in Freud's presentation of the dream of Irma.

By a center I mean an image, an event, or even a theoretical construct functioning as a nucleus or point of concentration that holds together a particular verbal sequence. The center gives coherence, a semblance of order at least, to what would otherwise appear to be a random, meaningless sequence of expressions. Centering functions both pragmatically and metapragmatically in any *interlocution.* (I stress "interlocution" because even in the monologue—in autobiographies and in treatises like *The Interpretation of Dreams*—there is always, at some level, an interlocutor, a reader, for example, who even through silence affects the course of the monologue [Bakhtin 1977; 1981; Todorov 1984].) Centering is both recursive and precursive. It gives meaning and order to those utterances that precede it and to those that will follow it; that is, until a new center is formed. Strictly speaking, there are always centers embedded within centers—within larger "centered" and "centering" units of discourse. The center's force lies in its ability to call forth the legitimation of its own dominant linguistic function (Jakobson 1960; 1987): informative, emotive, pragmatic, aesthetic. It legitimates, in other words, its symbolic reference, its connotative resonances, its precipitation of relevant contextual features, its rhetorical and stylistic conventions. Centering appears always to exceed itself by referring itself to what lies outside the interlocution to be centered. Figuratively, it is possible to say that centering stops discursive time, at least the discursive display of meaning. Time past folds forward; time future folds backward—into the center from which meaning and order spring.

Let me give an example of centering from one of Henry James's (1983:1187–1188) earliest novels, *Confidence.* Bernard and Angela, two lovers, are recalling one of their earliest meetings, at Baden.

"How did you know, at Baden, that I didn't like you?" he asked, as soon as she would allow him.

She smiled very gently. "You assured me yesterday that you did like me."

"I mean that I supposed I didn't. How did you know that?"

"I can only say that I observed."

"You must have observed very closely, for superficially I rather had the air of admiring you," said Bernard.

"It was very superficial."

"You don't mean that; for, after all, that is just what my admiration, my interest in you, were not. They were deep, they were latent. They were not superficial—they were sub-terranean."

"You are contradicting yourself, and I am perfectly consis-tent," said Angela. "Your sentiments were so well hidden that I supposed I displeased you."

"I remember that at Baden you used to contradict yourself," Bernard answered.

"You have a terrible memory!"

"Don't call it terrible, for it sees everything now in a charm-ing light—in the light of this understanding that we have at last arrived at, which seems to shine backward—to shine back on those Baden days."

"Have we at last arrived at an understanding?" she asked . . .

This passage is particularly interesting because it serves both to center, through memory/"memory," the relationship between Bernard and Angela (or, more accurately perhaps, to give Ber-nard the illusion of having centered the relationship) and to describe the effects of such centering: "in the light of this under-standing that we have at last arrived at, which seems to shine backwards." Much of the novel that preceded this conversation is in fact a preparation for the "understanding" or Bernard's presumption of understanding (that the narrator manages to make so confident and yet so vulnerable through an ironic play with distance), and much that follows is an undoing of this "understanding"—an unmasking, at times cruel, of Bernard's presumption. I should add, for those familiar with the novel, that this particular centering relates back to an earlier one, at the very beginning of the book, when Angela and Bernard meet for the first time, and Bernard presumes to sketch Angela with-out really obtaining her consent. ("'Is she posing—is she attitu-dinizing for my benefit?' [Bernard] Longueville asked of him-self. And then it seemed to him that this was a needless assumption" [James 1983:6].) This first centering is grounded, so to speak, by a nonverbal (though, insofar as it is textually created, verbal) icon. Such "media-switching" is one important centering strategy.

Traumatic events such as childhood seductions (the "Turk's" attempted rape of the young Rousseau), the death of a parent or spouse, or the loss of a home (*The Cherry Orchard*), religious conversion (St. Augustine's being one of the most exemplary), objectifying events (Jean Genet's getting caught stealing—in Sartre's [1964] version), a pilgrimage, a first love, are all possible centering events in the articulation of biographical or social experience. Dreams, particularly in societies like Morocco, where they are given a privileged status, are often centers (see Chapter 11). Rites of passage, like other rituals, center experience; they become reference points for retrospective understanding and for the interpretation of future events. Examples of centering events in psychoanalytic literature include the wolf dream in Freud's Case of Wolf Man (1959a) and the rat punishment in his Case of Rat Man (Freud 1959b).

In ethnographic and other cross-cultural encounters where the conventions of centering are not necessarily shared by the parties to the encounter, the negotiation of a "meaningful" center plays an important role. Each party attempts to center the relationship—the conversation—in terms of his own concerns and conventions: the ecological anthropologist, for example, by stressing environmental conditions that are validated by his training and research interests, his informant by talking about earth spirits that are of religious importance to him. There are, of course, coincidences of interest that can become centers, but though the interest is shared, its personal and cultural significance may not be. I remember spending the better part of an afternoon talking to a Moroccan school teacher about how men and women visitors walk around the saint's tomb in a sanctuary. I was interested in the negative connotations of left (the side from which women begin their circumambulation) and the positive connotations of right (the side from which men begin theirs), and I wanted to explore the ramifications of these evaluations in Moroccan culture. The schoolteacher was anxious to demonstrate, with resigned irony, that women end up on the right and men on the left. His interest was in the wheedling ways of women—in fatality, in the contradictions we humans see, from our lowly perspective, of God's determination of earthly life. What the teacher wanted to talk about, and what we did ultimately talk about, was a religious tract he had read about the failings of human understanding.[2]

Characteristic of centering events, images, or constructs, at least in the Western World, is that they are understood symbolically. They demand interpretation, and interpretation involves the discovery of their often hidden referent or referents. It is the referent—the deeper and further from consciousness the better—that empowers, *pari passu,* the centering image. This is of course particularly true in psychoanalysis (but by no means restricted to psychoanalysis). There, such centering events may refer to repressed desires: Freud understood the dream of Irma in terms, among others, of his desire not to be held responsible for the persistence of Irma's pains—to make his colleague Otto responsible for them. Or the centering events may stand for events barred from consciousness: Wolf Man's "witnessing" his parents' intercourse *a tergo.*

But, aside from these internal referential props for establishing a center, there are many external ones, and these vary from culture to culture. Framing an event by labeling it, as Freud does with his dreams in *The Interpretation of Dreams,* discussing it, highlighting it phonologically through alliteration, intonation, or rhyme, or calling attention to it through jokes, puns, and other word plays may also support a centering image. In discussing *Confidence,* I suggested, for example, that an allusion to an object in another dominant medium could empower a center. Or, as we shall see in the dream of Irma, an event may be centered by calling attention to it without naming or describing it—through *praeteritio.* Often support is found through reference to paradigmatic stories, from mythology, from Scripture, within literature from antecedent texts. Such stories may be institutionally valorized—through education, ritual, art, theoretical performance, or adoption by a socially significant figure. Moroccans with whom I worked would refer a sudden paralysis, understood in terms of being struck by a demon, back to the first time they had been demonically attacked. A son whose father has put him in danger might understand his plight in terms of Abraham's sacrifice of Isaac, if he should be a Christian fundamentalist. Afrikaners frequently support the way they center their relations with the English by alluding to the "wounds" their grandfathers suffered during the Anglo-Boer war (Crapanzano 1985). In the sciences, theoretical principles and interpretive paradigms serve similar functions. In psychoanalysis, the Oedipal complex is such a paradigm; the conflict between the pleasure principle and the reality principle, a theoretical orientation.[3]

Now all of this may sound so obvious as to merit no comment. After all, symbolic centers exist in all narratives. I do not deny this; I do not want to privilege psychoanalytic discourse. I want to stress a dynamic that has important implications for understanding how these events become potent centers in psychoanalysis (and by extension in other conversations) and how, at the same time, they mask the very strategies that centered them. I suggest that the symbolic understanding of such events (however valuable such understanding may be therapeutically or theoretically) conceals a second process, in linguistic terms a pragmatic process (roughly reducible in psychoanalysis to transference and countertransference [see Chapter 5] that articulates discursive contexts.[4] So long as the pragmatic centering strategies are masked by the sheer symbolicity of the centered and centering images, the falconer is under the illusion that the falcon hears him; that order prevails over anarchy; that innocence and conviction are protected from mere passion.

The Dream of Irma

A large hall—numerous guests, whom we were receiving.—Among them was Irma. I at once took her on one side, as though to answer her letter and to reproach her for not having accepted my "solution" yet. I said to her: "If you still get pains, it's really only your fault." She replied: "If you only knew what pains I've got now in my throat and stomach and abdomen—it's choking me"—I was alarmed and looked at her. She looked pale and puffy. I thought to myself that after all I must be missing some organic trouble. I took her to the window and looked down her throat, and she showed signs of recalcitrance, like women with artificial dentures. I thought to myself that there was really no need for her to do that.—She then opened her mouth properly and on the right I found a big white patch; at another place I saw extensive whitish grey scabs upon some remarkable curly structures which were evidently modelled on the turbinal bones of the nose.—I at once called in Dr. M., and he repeated the examination and confirmed it . . . Dr. M. looked quite different from usual; he was very pale, he walked with a limp and his chin was clean-shaven . . . My friend Otto was now standing beside her as well, and my friend Leopold was percussing her through her bodice and saying: "She has a dull area low down on the left." He also indicated that a portion of the skin on the left shoulder was infiltrated. (I noticed this, just as he did, in spite of her dress.) . . . M. said: "There is no doubt it's an infection, but no matter; dysentery will supervene and the toxin will be eliminated." . . . We were directly aware, too, of the origin of the infection. Not long before, when she was feeling unwell, my friend Otto had given her an injection of a preparation of propyl . . . proprionic acid . . . trimethylamin (and I saw before me the formula for this printed in heavy type) . . . Injections of that sort ought not to be made so thoughtlessly . . . And probably the syringe had not been clean. (Freud 1954a:107)[5]

You may well ask why I have chosen to discuss this dream rather than a centering event in a case history. When we read a case history, we are reading a highly conventionalized report of what transpired during the therapeutic sessions—a report with its own style, rhetoric, and literary antecedents. The centering that occurs in such case studies is complex. We have the report of what transpired and the centering that occurred therein, and we have centering in the report itself. The latter inevitably affects the way the former is presented. However accurate the presentation, it can never do justice to the transactions being presented. (We may be able to repeat an utterance but we can never repeat its pragmatic entailments if only because we are repeating.) The pragmatic processes that centered the event in the primary discourse (itself at some level a fiction) can only be described referentially.

I hope to side-step some of these problems by looking at the way in which the dream of Irma becomes a center for Freud's readers. In other words, I take Freud's text as primary discourse. Such an analysis should point to some of the ways in which an event is centered and its centering concealed. It is limited, however, because it refers to a "monologic" text. Freud does all the talking. Unlike the patient, or the analyst, the reader does not respond (except at the level of phantasm) at the moment of utterance or writing, but such a monologic pretense should not blind us to its inevitable interlocutory affect (Bakhtin 1981; Tedlock 1983). I should add that my analysis will suggest, inevitably, an intentionality that even in a written and edited text is never so conscious.[6]

The dream of Irma is reported in Chapter 2 of Freud's *Interpretation of Dreams*.[7] Chapter 2 is preceded by a long, and to most readers uninspired, review of the scientific literature on dreams. (It is curious that an author of such breadth of knowledge and interest as Freud should have systematically avoided considering the dream as it occurred in nineteenth-century philosophical and imaginative literature. Dreams, and all sorts of dream theories, were important to the German and French Romantics—Carus, Novalis, Nerval—with whom Freud was presumably familiar [Béguin 1939].) This first chapter does mark *The Interpretation of Dreams* a scientific work and its author a scholar and a scientist—statuses which were important to Freud and figure in *his* understanding of the Irma dream (Schorske 1980:183).

Chapter 2 begins with Freud's contrasting the scientific—the somatic—view of dreams with the popular view that holds that they are interpretable. After discussing two popular methods of dream interpretation, the symbolic (*die symbolische Methode*) and the decoding (*die Chiffriermethode*), Freud (99–100; 91–92) declares himself a partisan of the interpretive school.

It cannot be doubted for a moment that neither of the two popular procedures for interpreting dreams can be employed for a scientific treatment of the subject . . . Thus one might be tempted to agree with the philosophers and the psychiatrists and, like them, rule out the problem of dream interpretation as a purely fanciful task.

But I have been taught better. [*Allein ich bin eines Bessern belehrt worden.*] I have been driven to realize that here once more we have one of those not infrequent cases in which ancient and jealously held popular belief seems to be nearer the truth than the judgment of the prevalent science of today.

Having marked himself as a scientist, a special one who is willing to pay attention to popular wisdom, Freud (100; 92) switches
register completely—to the autobiographical, the confessional,
telling us how he learned to interpret dreams. "My knowledge
of that procedure was reached in the following manner. I have
been engaged for many years (with a therapeutic aim in view)
in unravelling certain psychopathological structures—hysterical
phobias, obsessional ideas, and so on." Freud's style here anticipates the novelistic opening to his Preamble to Irma's dream
("During the summer of 1895 I had been giving psychoanalytic
treatment to a young lady") and subsequent autobiographical
intrusions into this purportedly scientific text.[8] He (100–101;
93) goes on to discuss how he learned that "a dream can be
inserted into the psychical chain that has to be traced backward
in the memory from a pathological idea." He outlines his
method of self-observation, relating it to Schiller's discussion of
poetic creation in *On the Aesthetic Education of Man,* and
claims that he himself (like the poet) has little difficulty in such
self-observation.

After informing us that in the course of his practice he has
analyzed over a thousand dreams, Freud explains why he will
have to interpret a dream of his own. He cannot treat the dreams
of a neuropath because they may be atypical and because they
would require distracting background material. "Each dream
would therefore necessitate a lengthy introduction and an investigation of the nature and aetiological determinants of the psy-
choneurosis. But these questions are in themselves novelties
and highly bewildering and would distract attention from the
problem of dreams" (104; 96). (Later in *The Interpretation of
Dreams,* quite oblivious to the contradiction, he does make use
of his patient's dreams.) He cannot discuss dreams of normal
people he has heard because he does not have sufficient, presumably non-distracting, background material. "My procedure
is not so convenient as the popular decoding method which
translates any given piece of a dream's content by a fixed key"
(105; 96). He has no choice then but to consider one of his own
dreams. "Thus it comes about that I am left to my own dreams,
which offer a copious and convenient material derived from an
approximately normal person [*von einer ungefahr normalen
Person*] relating to multifarious occasions of daily life."

He argues that in the case of dream interpretation, self-observation may prove more revealing than the observation of others. But it has its difficulties: "the natural hesitation about revealing so many intimate facts about ones mental life" (105; 96).[9] Here Freud alerts his readers to the inevitable confession he is about to undertake for scientific reasons (it is the same gossip's trick we find in the Case of Rat Man [see Chapter 9]). There is no way he can safeguard what he has to say from misinterpretation by strangers, but he will sacrifice himself ("But it must be possible to overcome such hesitations"). He quotes Dalbeuf who argues, in Rousseau's fashion, that every psychologist is under an obligation to confess even his weaknesses if they may shed light on some obscure, psychological problem.[10] And then, for the first time, Freud (105–106; 97) addresses his readers directly. "And it is safe to assume that my readers too will very soon find their initial interest in the indiscretions which I am bound to make replaced by an absorbing immersion in the psychological problems upon which they throw light." He lays the burden of discretion on his readers, but in a footnote (105,n.2; 97,n.1) he undermines their very discretion. "I am obliged to add, however, by way of qualification of what I have said that in scarcely any instance have I brought forward the *complete* interpretation of one of my own dreams, as it is known to me. I have probably been wise in not putting too much faith in the readers' discretion."

Freud establishes an agonistic, if not an antagonistic, relationship with his readers—one that anticipates the competitive relationship he has with his colleagues, as revealed in the dream of Irma itself. (Are his readers his colleagues?) He puts the reader in a bind. You should resist paying attention to my indiscretions. You should be absorbed in my scientific method of interpretation. I have faith in you. You are not capable of ignoring my indiscretions. You are not able to lose yourself in my scientific endeavor. I have no faith in you. Despite my scientific aims, despite my sacrifice, therefore, I will not reveal all I should. It is your fault. There will be ellipses—holes—in what I am about to report. The reader is asked, nevertheless, to make Freud's interest his own and *in nomine scientiae* "to plunge along with [Freud] into the minutest details of [his] life, for a transference of this kind is peremptorily demanded by our interest in the hidden meaning of dreams" (105–106; 97).

Set apart as it is by title, italics, and style, the dream text is nevertheless embedded in Freud's monograph. It is preceded by a Preamble (*Vorbericht*), which relates to it explicitly, and by earlier sections, which relate to it implicitly. Several different stylistic registers—the scientific, the confessional, and the novelistic—are intertwined in the discussion that precedes (and follows) the dream. This range helps center the dream by appealing to various interests. By giving us, in the Preamble, what background he thinks necessary for understanding the dream, Freud directs our reading of the dream. Like all descriptions of context, the Preamble has an imperative as well as an informative function. We learn that Freud has doubts about the success of his treatment of Irma, that he has experienced mild reproof from Otto, a friend and junior colleague, and that although he was not clear about the disagreeable impression his friend's reproach made, he wrote Irma's case history that night in order to justify himself to Dr. M., a leading figure in his circle.

Just as Freud's Preamble begins in novelistic fashion, so his report of the dream begins like a stage description. "A large hall—numerous guests, whom we were receiving. Among them was Irma." We move into a new, theatrical register. It reflects the peculiar ontological status we give the dream and facilitates the theatrical metaphors Freud so often uses to describe the unconscious, as *ein anderer Schauplatz,* for example. In the original German Freud recounts the dream in the present tense, thereby promoting an immediacy and a timelessness that is not carried by Strachey's translation of the dream into the past tense (Maloney 1977). The dream takes place timelessly on a stage where it can be viewed with (timeless) fascination. The reality of its actors, as dream people and real people, "Freud" and "Irma" and Freud and Irma, parallel those of actors playing a role and yet identifiable as everyday people. (A similar double role occurs in transference, where the analyst is at once both doctor and, say, "mother.")

Although the dream text begins theatrically, it continues narratively, in a realistic fashion, interspersed with quotations, suggesting a dialogue between intimates. (Both Freud and Irma use the informal, second person personal pronoun, *du*.) Were it not for its title, we would not at first know we were reading a dream.

> A large hall . . . I at once took her to one side, as though to answer her letter and to reproach her for not having accepted [my] solution yet. I said to her: "If you [*du*] still get pains, it is really your own fault." She replied: "If you [*du*] only knew what pains I've got now in my throat, stomach and abdomen—it's choking me."—I was alarmed and looked at her. She looked pale and puffy. I thought to myself that after all I must be missing something organic.

Unless we assume Freud to have been completely tactless, it is only with the following sentence that we realize that we are reading an exceptional text—a dream, a story, from Kafka perhaps.

> I took her to the window and looked down her throat, and she showed signs of recalcitrance [*Dabei zeigt sie etwas Strauben*], like women with artificial dentures.[11]

Yet even this sentence and the ones that follow it, in which Freud describes the "white patches" and "whitish grey scabs" he saw in her throat, are written in a realistic style. He calls over Dr. M., who confirms his findings. Dr. M. looked different: pale, limping, clean-shaven. The narrative style shifts (marked by suspension points).[12] A more or less continuous narrative gives way to a fragmentary one just as the events described become more improbable. Doctors—Otto and Leopold who percusses Irma through her bodice (*Leibchen*, literally, "little body")—appear without explanation. Leopold notes "a dull area low down on the left" and indicates a portion of Irma's skin that is infiltrated (just as Freud notices it, despite her dress). Dr. M. declares that dysentery will supervene and eliminate the toxins. The language is medical. Freud notes, after an ellipsis, that "we were directly aware of the origin of the infection." Otto had given Irma an injection "of propyl, propyls . . . proprionic acid . . . trimethylamin," and Freud sees the formula for this printed in heavy type. He concludes, critically, moralistically, "Injections of that sort ought not be made so thoughtlessly . . . And probably the syringe had not been clean."

Despite Freud's claim that "no one could have the slightest notion of what the dream meant," it is clearly about his doubts regarding his medical competence and his relations with his colleagues. And yet there is something uncanny about the dream—something *overly* intimate, erotically so: the doctors all peering down Irma's throat. There are intimations of fellatio, of venereal disease, of pregnancy, suggested perhaps by "receiving," *empfangen,* in "whom we were receiving"; for *empfangen* means not only to receive or to welcome but also to conceive (Maloney 1977; Erikson 1954).[13] Through hypotyposis— through vividness of description—the reader is put into the position of a voyeur (a position, since Freud, that is not uncommon when one listens to someone telling a dream).[14]

Questions of Freud's medical competence, of his relationship with his colleagues, and though played down, sexuality, are raised again and again in the next section of the chapter called "Analysis," in which Freud gives his associations to the dream. The narrative movement of the associations, again written in the present tense in the German, is reflexive: segments of the dream are repeated and then followed by associations which ostensibly relate back to the dream, embroidering it, to earlier associations and to the Preamble. The text of associations would resemble an ordinary *explication de texte* were it not granted the freedom of association—a freedom, I should add, that is always grammatically restrained.[15] Freud associates in well-formed sentences! At one level, the associations add to what we already know about Irma, Freud, Otto, Dr. M., Leopold . . . At another, they add to the context. Just as the Preamble, the *Vorbericht,* provides an anticipatory context for the dream, so the text of associations provides an anastrophic—a retrospective—context, a *Nachbericht.* Between the two the dream is centered—and both the Preamble and the Analysis pull in centripetally larger and larger contexts, first from within *The Interpretation of Dreams*—Freud refers to the dream in later chapters—and then from Freud's biography.

The associations not only elaborate but also subvert the manifest meaning of the dream. They suggest another, deeper, inner meaning. The dream becomes a riddle. Freud has of course already suggested this. Not only are dream characters like Irma identifiable with real people in Freud's circle so that the dream becomes a sort of *rêve à clef*, but they allude to still others—a governess, one of Irma's friends, Freud's wife, a patient named Mathilde who died in Freud's treatment, and Freud's eldest daughter. (Suggesting a hidden identity is always powerful centering strategy.) Through suggestions, questions, stylistic innuendos, and the raising of suspicions—often melodramatically— through ellipses, the manifest meaning is undermined. "Could it be that the purpose of the dream lay in this direction [to relieve him of responsibility for Irma's pains]" (109; 99)? "I wondered why I had decided upon a choice of symptoms in the dream but could not think of an explanation at the moment" (109; 99). "I began to suspect that someone else was being substituted for her" (109; 99). "Frankly I had no desire to penetrate more deeply at this point [the meaning of 'in spite of her dress']" (113; 103).[16]

Many of the associations are confessional, having to do with Freud's medical incompetence, to his *Kunstfehler*, as the Germans say euphemistically. At one level, they attest pragmatically to Freud's honesty—to the sacrifice he is prepared to make for his scientific psychology. At another level, they provide background for what he refuses to acknowledge overtly, rendering it, whatever it is, even more damning—his erotic feelings for Irma, perhaps. He relates Irma's widowhood—and availability—to her friend's status, but he does not relate it to his own wife's availability. The associations suggest deeper and deeper meanings. Freud himself acknowledges this in a key passage. He supposes that Irma's friend would have yielded (*nachgeben*) sooner to his solution of her illness—a solution, incidentally, he never reveals. She would have opened her mouth properly and have told him more than Irma did. He (111, n.101, n.2) adds a footnote. "I had a feeling that the interpretation of this part of the dream was not carried far enough to make it possible to follow the whole of its concealed meaning. If I had pursued my comparison between the three women [Irma, Irma's friend, and Freud's wife] it would have taken me far afield.—There is at least one spot in every dream at which it is unplumbable—a navel as it were, that is its point of contact with the unknown."

Freud repeats this theme later in *The Interpretation of Dreams*. "The dream thoughts to which we are led by interpretation cannot, from the nature of things, have any definite endings; they are bound to branch out in every direction into the intricate network of our world of thought. It is at some point where this meshwork is particularly close that the dream wish grows up, like a mushroom out of its mycelium" (525; 428). These images of the navel, of a mushroom growing, of fertility and reproduction, cover metaphorically the unplumbable, the *unergründlich* (metaphorized perhaps by the female sexual organ) in any interpretation. I suggest that such images of and for the unplumbable, the unknown, refer to the limits of any referential interpretation which, when cut off from its pragmatically constituted, interlocutory context, is subject to infinite regression. I suggest further that this regression is masked by conventional full-stops often expressed in mythological form—the Oedipal myth—or in physiological metaphors—the navel.[17] But more important for our purposes, the unplumbable, the *unergründlich,* the unknown becomes the rhetorical center of the centering—the point of gravity to which everything is pulled.

Freud concludes Chapter 2 with a general discussion of dreams and asserts climactically that dreams are wish fulfillments. He notes (118,n.2; 107,n.1) that he has completed the interpretation of the dream and immediately informs the reader (in a footnote added to the 1909 edition) that he has not reported everything that occurred to him during the process of interpretation. He again spices the readers' imagination—our interest in precisely what Freud the scientist declares uninteresting: indiscretions, personal revelations, autobiography. He argues that, through the dream, he is able to bring about revenge on Otto both for his reproof and for the bottle of bad liquor he had brought him that was responsible for his dreaming of propyls. He declares Otto's competitor more trustworthy. He also takes revenge on Irma by substituting a wise, less recalcitrant patient and on Dr. M. by declaring him an ignoramus. He appeals to a higher authority—a friend (Fliess, we now know) who suggested that trimethylamin is a product of sexual metabolism. (This association led Freud to Irma's widowhood.) Ultimately, he asserts (119; 108) that the dream is a wish not to be blamed for the continuation of Irma's pains. "I was not to blame for Irma's pains, since she herself was to blame for them by refusing to accept my solution. I was not concerned with Irma's pains, since they were of an organic nature and quite incurable by psychological treatment. Irma's pains could be satisfactorily explained by her widowhood (cf. the trimethylamin) which I had no means of altering." Didn't he? He blames Otto for using a dirty needle to treat her.

But here I myself am falling into Freud's trap. I am considering the content—the symbols—rather than the construction of the dream. So powerful is Freud's rhetoric! What should be apparent by now is that Otto, Leopold, Dr. M., Fliess, Freud's wife and daughter perhaps—Irma herself—are all potential readers, reader-phantasms, for Freud. They and other readers (including myself) become agonistically engaged in Freud's text. After repeating yet again that he could have gone on with the interpretation—"I myself know the points which further trains of thought could have followed"—like a cranky Rousseau he challenges his readers directly. "If anyone should feel tempted to express a hasty condemnation of my reticence, I would advise him to make an experiment of being franker than I am" (121; 109). So now the dream centers not only Freud's theory of dream interpretation and a period in his life, but also his relationship to his colleagues—ultimately to his readers. It is they as well as Freud (for, despite my intentionalizing language, he too is subject to the constraints of interlocution) who are inevitably drawn in and forced to accept the challenge of the dream as a text to be interpreted, as a riddle to be symbolically solved. And thereby they succumb to the masking of the pragmatic processes by which the dream is centered and Freud's wished-for relationship with his colleagues, his readers—with us—is established.

2.
Hermes' Dilemma

"All translation," Walter Benjamin (1969:75) wrote, "is only a somewhat provisional way of coming to terms with the foreignness of languages." Like translation, ethnography is also a somewhat provisional way of coming to terms with the foreignness of languages—of cultures and societies. The ethnographer does not, however, translate texts the way the translator does. He must first produce them. Text metaphors for culture and society notwithstanding, the ethnographer has no primary and independent writing that can be read and translated by others. No text survives him other than his own. Despite its frequent ahistorical—synchronic—pretense, ethnography is historically determined by the moment of the ethnographer's encounter with whomever he is studying.

The ethnographer is a little like Hermes; a messenger who, given methodologies for uncovering the masked, the latent, the unconscious, may even obtain his message through stealth. He presents languages, cultures, and societies in all their opacity, their foreignness, their meaninglessness; then, like the magician, the hermeneut, Hermes himself, he clarifies the opaque, renders the foreign familiar, and gives meaning to the meaningless. He decodes the message. He interprets.

The ethnographer conventionally acknowledges the provisional nature of his interpretations. Yet he assumes a final interpretation—a definitive reading. "I have finally cracked the Kariera section system," we hear him say. "I finally got to the root of all their fuss about the *mudyi* tree." He resents the literary critic's assertion that there is never a final reading. He simply has not got to it yet.

The ethnographer does not recognize the provisional nature of his presentations. They are definitive. He does not accept as a paradox that his "provisional interpretations" support his "definitive presentations." (It is perhaps for the reason that he insists on a final reading.) Embedded in interpretation, his presentations limit reinterpretation. Ethnography closes in on itself. It is even possible that the more general theories the ethnologist generates from ethnography are only refractions, distored repetitions in another register of the provisional interpretations that support the presentation of data. The possibility must be entertained. Hermes was the tutelary god of speech and writing, and these, we know, are themselves interpretations.

Hermes, etymologically "he of the stone heap," was associated with boundary stones (Nilsson 1949; Brown 1969). The herm, a head and a phallus on a pillar, later replaced the stone heap. The ethnographer, if I may continue my conceit, also marks a boundary: his ethnography declares the limits of his and his readers' culture. It also attests to his—and his culture's—interpretive power. Hermes was a phallic god and a god of fertility. Interpretation has been understood as a phallic, a phallic-aggressive, a cruel and violent, a destructive act, and as a fertile, a fertilizing, a fruitful and creative one. We say a text and even a culture are pregnant with meaning. Do the ethnographer's presentations become pregnant with meaning because of his interpretive phallic fertilizations? (I have insisted here on using the masculine pronoun to refer to the ethnographer, despite his or her sexual identity, for I am writing of a stance and not of the person.)

The ethnographer is caught in a second paradox. He has to make sense of the foreign. Like Benjamin's translator, he aims at a solution of the problem of foreignness, and like the translator (a point missed by Benjamin) he must also communicate the very foreignness that his interpretations (the translator's translations) deny in their claim to universality. He must render the foreign familiar and preserve its very foreignness at one and the same time. The translator accomplishes this through style, the ethnographer through the coupling of a presentation that asserts the foreign and an interpretation that makes it all familiar.

Hermes was a trickster: a god of cunning and tricks. The ethnographer is no trickster. He, so he says, has no cunning and no tricks. But he shares this with Hermes: *he must make his mes-*

sage convincing. It treats of the foreign, the strange, the unfamiliar, the exotic, the unknown—that, in short, which challenges belief. The ethnographer must make use of all the persuasive devices at his disposal to convince his readers of *the* truth of his message, but, treating these rhetorical strategies as though they were cunning tricks, he gives them scant recognition. His texts assume a truth that speaks for itself—a whole truth that needs no rhetorical support. His words are transparent. He does not share Hermes' confidence. When Hermes took the post of messenger of the gods, he promised Zeus not to lie. He did not promise to tell the whole truth. Zeus understood. The ethnographer has not.

The following reading of three ethnographic texts, only one of which was written by an anthropologist, will show some of the ways the ethnographer tries to make the message convincing. One is George Catlin's (1841; 1867) account of the Mandan Indian's O-Kee-Pa ceremony; the second is Johann Wolfgang von Goethe's (1976a; 1982) description of the Roman carnival in his *Italienische Reise* of 1789; and the third is Clifford Geertz's (1973) study of the Balinese cockfight. The events as described are explosive, teasing if not the performers' then the authors' assumptions of meaning and order. The authors are challenged, and all three make use of many different rhetorical strategies for convincing the reader, and presumably themselves, of the accuracy of their descriptions (see Marcus 1980).

Foremost among these strategies is the constitution of the ethnographer's authority: his presence at the events described, his perceptual ability, his "disinterested" perspective, his objectivity, and his sincerity (see Clifford 1983a). In all three cases, the ethnographer's place in his text is purely rhetorical. It is constructed deictically, or perhaps it is better to say pseudo-deictically. It is impossible to fix the ethnographer's vantage point. His is a roving perspective, necessitated by his "totalistic" presentation of the events he is describing. His presence does not alter the way things happen or, for that matter, the way they are observed or interpreted. He assumes a Hermes-like invisibility that of course he cannot have. His "disinterest," his objectivity, his neutrality are in fact undercut by his self-interest—his need to constitute his authority, to establish a bond with his readers (more accurately, his interlocutors), and to create an appropriate distance between himself and the "foreign" event he witnesses.

Aside from the devices the ethnographer uses to constitute his authority, he uses others to establish the validity of his ethnographic presentations directly. I single out three of these, which are used to various extents and with variable success by Catlin, Goethe, and Geertz. In Catlin it is a hypotyposis that predominates. In Goethe it is an external (nonmetaphorical) theatrical narrativity. Geertz depends primarily on interpretive virtuosity. In all three cases the very figures the authors use to convince their readers—and themselves—of their descriptions in fact render them suspect, and in all three cases this failure to convince is covered by an institutionally legitimated concern for "meaning." Catlin and Goethe give the ceremonies they describe an allegorical (moral) significance. Geertz claims a phenomenological-hermeneutical perspective on meaning that is, at least rhetorically, insufficient. His essay becomes exemplary, and the cockfight itself takes on not only metaphorical but methodological significance. The O-Kee-Pa, the carnival, and the cockfight all become figures of disorder—of arbitrary violence, unruliness, and meaninglessness—in a transcending story in which precisely this disorder, this violence, unruliness, and meaninglessness are overcome. The ceremonies are shown to have, if not order and meaning, then at least significance. But, ironically, as figures that mask an initial rhetorical subversion—a failure to convince—the descriptions are again subverted. The O-Kee-Pa, the Roman carnival, and the Balinese cockfight become the "O-Kee-Pa," the " Roman carnival," and "the Balinese cockfight."

> With this very honorable degree which had just been conferred upon me, I was standing in front of the medicine-lodge early in the morning, with my companions by my side, endeavouring to get a peep, if possible, into its sacred interior; when the *master of ceremonies*, guarding and conducting its secrets, as I before described, came out of the door and taking me with a firm *professional* affection by the arm, led me into this *sanctum sanctorum*, which was strictly guarded from, even a

peep or a gaze from the vulgar, by a vestibule of eight or ten feet in length, guarded with a double screen or door, and two or three dark and frowning centinels with spears or war clubs in their hands. I gave the wink to my companions as I was passing in, and the potency of my *medicine* was such as to gain them quiet admission, and all of us were comfortably placed on elevated seats, which our conductor soon prepared for us.

With these words George Catlin (1841:161–62), the romantic-realist painter of the American Indians, describes his entrance into a medicine lodge in which he was to witness what is surely one of the most sanguinary rites in the annals of ethnography, the Mandan O-Kee-Pa—"an ordeal of privation and torture" in which young Mandan men, "emaciated with fasting, and thirsting, and waking, for nearly four days and nights," were hung by rawhide passed through the skewered flesh of their shoulders and breasts from the lodge's roof until they were "lifeless." The O-Kee-Pa was celebrated annually, according to Catlin, to commemorate the subsiding of a great flood that the Mandan believed once covered the world, to ensure the coming of the buffalo, and to initiate the young men of the tribe into manhood through an ordeal "which, while it is supposed to harden their muscles and prepare them for extreme endurance, enables the chiefs who are spectators to the scene to decide upon their comparative bodily strength and ability to endure the extreme privations and sufferings that often fall to the lots of Indian warriors" (1841:157).

It was the summer of 1832—six years before the Mandan were devastated by an epidemic of smallpox. Catlin had spent several weeks with them. He found that "they are a people of decidedly a different origin from that of any other tribe in these regions," and later he argued that they were descendants of Welsh sailors who under the direction of Prince Madoc had set sail in the fourteenth century (actually in the twelfth century) and were thought to have settled somewhere in North America (Catlin 1867; Ewers 1967). The day before his admission to the medicine lodge Catlin painted a picture of the master of ceremonies, and so pleased was this great magician with his portrait—"he could see its eyes move"—that he and the other "doctors" unanimously elevated Catlin to a "respectable rank in the craft" of magic and mysteries and gave him the name "White Medicine Painter." It was this honor that allowed him to enter the lodge with his three companions. They were apparently the first white men to witness the O-Kee-Pa, and Catlin was the first to describe it: on January 10, 1833 (though written on August 12, 1832), in the *New-York Commercial Advertiser;* in 1841 in his *Manners, Customs, and Conditions of the North American Indians;* and finally in 1867 in a little book (with a *Folium Reservatum* for scholars) entirely devoted to the ceremony.

Catlin asserts melodramatically that he shudders and even shrinks from the task of reciting what he has seen.

> I entered the *medicine-house* of these scenes, as I would have entered a church, and expected to see something extraordinary and strange, but yet in the form of worship or devotion; but, alas! little did I expect to see the interior of their holy temple turned into a *slaughter-house,* and its floor strewed with the blood of its fanatic devotees. Little did I think that I was entering a house of God, where His blinded worshippers were to pollute its sacred interior with their blood, and propitiatory suffering and tortures—surpassing, if possible, the cruelty of the rack or the inquisition; but such the scene has been, and as such I will endeavor to describe it.   (1841:156)

Despite all of Catlin's shuddering and shrinking, he and his companions managed to watch the spectacle from the seats they were assigned. "We were then in full view of everything that transpired in the lodge, having before us the scene exactly, which is represented in the first of the four pictures [that Catlin painted of the ceremony and that illustrated his second and third accounts]. To this seat we returned every morning until sun-down for four days, the whole time which these strange scenes occupied" (1841:162). They were not even permitted to move from their assigned places. Once when Catlin got up to take a closer look at what he calls the central mystery of the rite—"the *sanctissimus sanctorum,* from which seemed to emanate all the sanctity of their proceedings"—he was sent back to his seat.

> I started several times from my seat to approach it, but all eyes were instantly upon me, and every mouth in the assembly sent

forth a hush—sh—! which brought me back to my seat again;
and I at length quieted my stifled curiosity as well as I could,
upon learning the fact, that so sacred was that object, and so
important its secrets or mysteries, that not *I* alone, but even
the young men, who were passing the ordeal, and all the village, save the conductor of the mysteries, were stopped from
approaching it, or knowing what it was.　(1841:162)

Like an artist standing before his easel, Catlin's vantage point
is fixed. So at least he asserts. *And yet* he is in fact no objectivist,
no Robbe-Grillet describing the ceremony laboriously, metonymous step by metonymous step, from the fixed position of
his consciousness. His vision is larger, constructed, exaggerated,
uneven—metaphorical. His eye constantly betrays itself. He describes the arrival of the evil one, O-Kee-hee-de.

But alas! in the last of these dances, on the fourth day, in the
midst of all their mirth and joy, and about noon, and in the
height of all these exaltations, an instant scream burst forth
from the tops of the lodges!—men, women, dogs and all,
seemed actually to howl and shudder with alarm, as they fixed
their glaring eyeballs upon the prairie bluff, about a mile in
the west, down the side of which a man was seen descending
at full speed toward the village. This strange character darted
about in a zig-zag course in all directions on the prairie, like
a boy in pursuit of a butterfly, until he approached the piquets
of the village, when it was discovered that his body was entirely naked, and painted as black as a negro, with pounded
charcoal and bear's grease.　(1841:166)

Catlin rambles, repeats, generalizes, simplifies, exaggerates,
and embellishes. He refers indiscriminately to what he has seen
before or learned afterward. Amidst a purportedly realistic description, masked here as elsewhere in *Manners, Customs, and
Conditions* by measurement ("about a mile in the west," a vestibule of eight or ten feet"), are metaphorical turns of phrase,
similes in the above example ("like a boy in pursuit of a butterfly," "painted as black as a negro") that seem as inappropriate
to the event he describes as the colors—Baudelaire (1846)
called them terrifying, mysterious—of his Indian paintings.[1]
They ring true neither to his presumed experience of the event
nor to that of the Mandan participants. The two experiences

are stylistically blurred—sacrificed ultimately to the experience Catlin wishes to engender in his readers. This pathopoetic sacrifice of the participant's subjectivity to that of his readers occurs even when Catlin claims to take the participant's point of view. He describes, for example, one of the hanging victims of torture, a composite of several.

> Surrounded by imps and demons as they appear, a dozen or more, who seem to be concerting and devising means for his exquisite agony, gather around him, when one of the number advances toward him in a sneering manner, and commences turning him around with a pole which he brings in his hand for the purpose. This done in a gentle manner at first; but gradually increased, when the brave fellow, whose proud spirit can control its anger no longer, burst out in the most lamentable and heart rendering cries that the human voice is capable of producing, crying forth a prayer to the Great Spirit to support and protect him in this dreadful trial; and continually repeating his confidence in his protection. In this condition he is continued to be turned, faster and faster—and there is no hope of escape from it, and his struggling ceases, and he hangs, apparently, a still and lifeless corpse!   (1841:171)

Here Catlin moves from his (objectifying) metaphorical perspective to that of the tortured; despite this move, his intention is not phenomenological but rthetorical: he does not describe either the Indian's or his own experience of the torture. The "imps and demons as they appear" (to whom? to Catlin? to the Mandan?) is stylistically equivalent to "there is no hope of escape from it." They are directed to the reader, and it is the reader's reaction that will guarantee Catlin's perceptions.

In these passages and throughout his *Manners, Customs, and Conditions of the North American Indians*, Catlin's principal stylistic figure is hypotyposis. His aim is to impress his experience of what he has *seen* so strongly, so vividly, on his readers that they cannot doubt its veracity. It is the visual that gives authority. The realistic tradition, Alexander Gelley (1979:420) observes, "sought to reinforce the description of things and places by making the object of the description coincide with the object of a specular act, image, or process." Catlin's assertion of a fixed vantage point, of an assigned seat—there are similar assertions elsewhere in *Manners, Customs, and Conditions*—must be understood rhetorically. It attests deictically to his presence. It gives him the authority of the painter before his easel. It enables him to lead his readers into the visualized scene and to convince them (and himself) of its truth.[2]

Catlin's vision is not, however, secure. Unlike today's social scientists whose theories (regardless of their merit) serve their ethnographic credibility, Catlin's credibility has ultimately to rest on the power of his descriptions. Just as his painting is not particularly believable, neither is his prose. It undermines itself. His intention is realistic, but his style is romantic. Through metaphor, often extravagant metaphor, ecphonesis, the promiscuous use of the vocative, hyperbole, pathopoeia, apoplanesis, interruption, suspense, subjectivism—to name only a few of his stylistic strategies—Catlin tries to give to his descriptions a compelling veracity, but in the end these very strategies subvert his intention. Realism demands stylistic sobriety. For Catlin such sobriety precludes the hypotyposis upon which his credibility rests.

In *Manners, Customs and Conditions* he begins the letter in which he describes the O-Kee-Pa ceremony with these words: "Oh! *'horrible visu—et mirabile dictu!'* Thank God, it is over, that I have seen it, and am able to tell it to the world" (1841:155). But why see it? Why tell it to the world? Catlin has no framework for his experience—no justification for his reportage. His intention is documentary, but does this intention justify witnessing and describing a "shocking and disgusting custom" that "sickens the heart and even the stomach of a traveller in the country" (182–83) and yet that fills such a traveler with pity?

Catlin rationalizes his description in a confused manner. (He was never a systematic thinker.) He writes that the ceremony "will be new to the civilized world, and therefore worth knowing" (157). He suggests that parts of the ceremony are grotesque and amusing and others, having to do with the deluge, are "harmless and full of interest" (177). He has no theoretical justification. Native exegesis is not satisfactory. The ceremony cannot be historically situated. He argues that even if he had time to elaborate a disquisition on the ceremony, he would probably fail because simple people like the Mandan "have no history to save facts and systems from falling into the most absurd and disjointed fable and ignorant fiction" (177).

Catlin shares here the distinctly nineteenth-century conviction that explanation is embedded in origin. In *Manners, Customs, and Conditions* he relates Mandan beliefs and tales to Biblical stories of the flood, Eve's transgression, and the birth and death of Christ. (Such an equation puts a stop fundamentalistically to the quest for both origins and meaning.) Noting the Mandans' distinctive ("white") appearance, noting too that their culture hero is white, Catlin assumes Christian contact, and, as we have seen, twenty-six years later, he argued that the Mandan were descended from the Welsh. But to acknowledge Christian influence or, for that matter, Welsh descent hardly explains the O-Kee-Pa tortures. Catlin shifts abruptly—his informal letter style permits this[3]—and he discusses the Mandans' potential for salvation. "I deem it not folly nor idle to say that these people *can be saved,*" he concludes his letter,

> or officious to suggest to some of the very many excellent and pious men, who are almost throwing away the best energies of their lives along the debased frontier, that if they would introduce the ploughshare and their prayers amongst these people, who are so far separated from the taints and contaminating vices of the frontier, they would soon see their most ardent desire accomplished and be able to solve to the world the perplexing enigma, by presenting a nation of savages, civilized and Christianized (and consequently *saved*) in the heart of the American wilderness.   (1841:184)

Catlin's ultimate justification—a justification that runs through American anthropology—is pragmatic; applied, as we say; evangelical in the case in point. The pragmatic, the applied, and the evangelical must also be understood rhetorically.

Despite his figurative language, his speculations about meaning, and his concern for the Indians salvation, Catlin was in fact haunted by this problem of credibility. "I took my sketch-book with me," he writes toward the beginning of his description of the O-Kee-Pa ceremony,

> and have made many and faithful drawings of what we saw, and full notes of everything as translated to me by the inter-

preter; and since the close of that horrid and frightful scene, which was a week ago or more, I have been closely ensconced in an earth covered wigwam, with a fine sky-light over my head, with my pallette and brushes, endeavouring faithfully to put the whole of what we saw upon canvas, which my companions all agree to be critically correct, and of the fidelity of which they have attached their certificates to the backs of the paintings. (1841:155)

Acting with foresight, Catlin also had his companions Kipp, Crawford, and Bogard attach a certificate of authenticity to his account of the ceremony in *Manners, Customs, and Conditions;* for his report was to be questioned by no less a figure in American ethnology than Henry Rowe Schoolcraft. In the third volume of his *Historical and Statistical Information Respecting the History, Condition and Prospects of the Indian Tribes of the United States,* Schoolcraft (1851–1857) included a two-page article on the Mandan by David D. Mitchell, then superintendent of Indian affairs in St. Louis, who had been in the Indian trade in Mandan territory in upper Missouri in the 1830s. Mitchell's article concluded: "Information about their (the Mandans') peculiar customs can be found in the Journal of Lewis and Clark. The scenes described by Catlin, existed almost entirely in the fertile imagination of that gentleman" (254). When he was in South America, Catlin learned of Schoolcraft's and Mitchell's repudiation of his work in a letter from Alexander von Humboldt, who urged him to write to Prince Maximilian of Neuwied, who had also spent a winter among the Mandan. Before Catlin was able to obtain a letter of vindication from the prince—he eventually did in 1866—both Schoolcraft and Mitchell died. Although Catlin's description is now more or less accepted as an accurate portrayal of the O-Kee-Pa ceremony (Bowers 1950; see also Matthews 1873), Catlin himself was plagued by the doubt cast on the accuracy of his accounts for the rest of his life.

On February 20, 1787, Ash Wednesday, Goethe wrote: "At last the foolishness is over. The innumerable lights last night were another mad spectacle. One has only to see the Roman carnival to lose all desire ever to see it again. It is not worth writing about. If need be, it might make an amusing conversation piece"

(1976a:228).[4] Ironically, a year later Goethe saw the carnival again, and in 1789, upon his return to Weimar, he published an account of it with colored engravings. He later incorporated this little book, *Das Römische Karneval*, into his *Italienische Reise*, which is essentially an arrangement of letters and diary entries the poet edited twenty-five years after his Italian trip.[5]

Goethe only loosely follows the chronological order of the Roman carnival, which begins gradually with the opening of the theaters in Rome after the New Year and culminates on Ash Wednesday. He stresses the fact that the carnival fits naturally with the Roman lifestyle. It is really not that different from Sunday and holiday merriment in Rome.[6] Even the costumes and masks are familiar sights, Goethe argues, citing the hooded monks who accompany funerals throughout the year. He carefully locates the carnival, at least the parts he thinks worthy of describing, on the Corso. (Like Catlin, he is careful to give precise measurements of the location of the ceremony.)

This Corso becomes the carnival's theater. The stage is the street itself. The audience stand or are seated along its sides, on the sidewalk, on balconies, and on window sills. Goethe describes the costumes, masks, carriages, horses (for the race with which the carnival ends each evening), as though he were describing costumes and props for a theatrical production. The characters—guards, Pulcinelle, *quaccheri* ("quakers") in old-fashioned, richly embroidered clothes, sbirri, Neapolitan boatmen, peasants, women from Frascati, German baker apprentices with a reputation for drunkenness—are like characters from the *commedia dell'arte*. (The *quacchero*, Goethe himself remarks, is like the *buffo caricato* of the comic opera; he plays either a vulgar fop or the silly, infatuated, and betrayed old fool.) The characters have no depth. They are emblematic, as are their skits. The overall movement—the action—of the carnival leads each day to a mad, riderless horse race, and the carnival itself ends dramatically on the evening before Ash Wednesday. Everyone carries a lighted candle. Everyone tries to blow out other people's candles, shouting, *sia ammazzato chi non porta moccola* ("death to anyone who is not carrying a candle"). Every one tries to protect his or her own candle. "No one can move much from the spot where he is standing or sitting; the heat of so many human beings and so many lights, the smoke from so many candles, blown out again and again, the noise of so many people, who only yell all the louder, the less they can move a limb, make the sanest head swim. It seems impossible that no accident will occur, that the carriage horses will not go wild, that many will not be bruised, crushed, or otherwise injured" (1976a:675).

The crowd finally disperses, the common people to relish their last meat dish before Lent, the fashionable to the last performance of the theater. The "madness" ends on Ash Wednesday. "How happy I shall be when the fools are silenced next Tuesday," Goethe writes in a letter on Feburary 1, 1778. "It is terribly annoying to watch others go mad when one has not caught the infection oneself" (1976a:681). As we shall see, Ash Wednesday gave Goethe occasion to contemplate the meaning of this folly, this Saturnalian merriment, with its role reversals, its vulgar gestures, its transvestitism, its libertinism, and what offended him most, its disorder.

In contrast to Catlin's account of the O-Kee-Pa ceremony, with its subjectivism, its metaphors and hyperboles, and indeed in contrast to Goethe's own *Sturm und Drang* writings, with their exuberant subjectivism and insistent concern with *Innerlichkeit*, innerness, the *Italian Journey,* including *The Roman Carnival,* treats the external, *das Aussere,* with an emotional calm that must surely have been disappointing to the readers of *Werther.* (There are in fact few "extravagant" metaphors in Goethe's text, and the few there are do not subvert his "realism" as Catlin's do.) On November 10, 1786, Goethe wrote from Rome: "I live here now with a clarity and calm that I have not felt for a long time. My habit of looking at and reading all things as they are, my conscientious [effort] to keep my eyes open, my complete renunciation of all pretension again stand me in good stead and make me privately very happy. Each day a new remarkable object; daily, vast singular new pictures—a whole that, however long one thinks and dreams, is never accessible through the imagination" (1976a:178–179).

There is something salubrious in Goethe's "new" approach to reality. It should be remembered that his Italian trip had the therapeutic purpose to reanimate him, and that he often spoke of it as a rebirth (Fairley 1947). "In this place," he writes on the same day, "whoever looks seriously about him and has eyes to see must become strong; he is bound to acquire an idea of strength that was never so alive for him" (1976a:179). He insists on seeing things again and again to avoid the mixture of truth and lies that make up first impressions (Goethe 1976b:86; Staiger 1956:14). Under the tutelage of Angelica Kauffmann he draws, to deepen his perception of the objects around him. As Emil Staiger (1956:15–16) shows, it is the idea ("Begriff," "anschauender Begriff," "lebendiger Begriff" in Goethe's writing) that unites the changing and the unchanging, the multiple perceptions of an object. Goethe's objectivity remains always the objectivity of a subject. His objective is not the opposite of the subjective. According to Staiger (1956:18), the contrast is between inner comprehension of the thing ("ein 'innerliches' Erfassen der Dinge") and its objective (*sachlich*) comprehension. Distance, understood both literally and figuratively, is necessary for this objectivity, but as Staiger (1956:18) notes, Goethe is less concerned with a specific perspective than with showing an eternal truth.[7]

Although Goethe, like Catlin, occasionally situates himself as if before an easel in his descriptions in the *Italian Journey* (for example, 1982:30), he does not assume a fixed perspective in *The Roman Carnival*. Indeed, in the very first paragraph of his work he writes conventionally of the impossibility of describing the carnival and thereby turns the carnival itself into a figure of madness and disorder.

> In undertaking to write a description of the Roman Carnival, we must fear the objection that such a festivity cannot really be described. A huge, lively mass of sensuous beings moves immediately before one's eyes and will be seen and grasped by everyone in his own way. The objection is still more serious when we admit that the Roman Carnival gives neither a whole nor pleasing impression; neither particularly delights the eyes nor gratifies the mind of the foreign spectator who sees it for the first time and wants only to watch, indeed can only watch. There is no overview of the long and narrow street in which innumerable people move about; one hardly distinguishes in the midst of the tumult anything the eye can grasp. The move-

ment is monotonous, the noise is deafening, the end of each day unsatisfactory. These doubts alone are soon raised when we examine the matter more closely; and above all the question will be whether or not any description is warranted. (1976a:639)

The absence of a single perspective over the carnival is associated with tumult (*Getümmel*), deafening sound (*der Lärm betäubend*), masses of sensuous beings, (*eine so grosse lebendige Masse sinnlicher Gegenstände*), undifferentiated movement, ultimately with an unpleasant and unsatisfactory experience—at least for the foreign observer. (Throughout the *Italian Journey* Goethe refers to the foreigner, the foreign observer, as though there were a single "foreign" vantage point on Italy and its carnival.)[8] It will be Goethe's task to bring order to this disorder through his description—a description, he says, that will convey the enjoyment and tumult (*Freude und Taumel*) of the occasion to the readers' imagination.

Goethe himself does not take a specific spatial vantage point—always a possibility even when there is no overview, no *Ubersicht,* no cathedral tower, which played such an important role in his student days in Strasburg (Lewes 1855:67). He moves indifferently up and down the Corso. He moves equally indifferently through time. With the exception of the lighting of candles on the evening before Ash Wednesday, the only nonrepetitive event in Goethe's carnival, he does not specify the time of the events he describes. He writes in the "present" tense, which serves at once to give a feeling of timeless flow and to permit generalizations. Like Catlin, Goethe conflates and generalizes characters and events, and only rarely, to add life and authenticity to his descriptions, does he specify his relationship to particular events and characters. "We remember among others one young man who played perfectly the part of a passionate, quarrelsome, and in no way to be calmed woman. He argued the length of the Corso, grabbing everyone while his companions appeared to be taking great pains to calm him down" (1976a:647). Describing a battle of confetti, he writes: "We ourselves saw one such battle at close quarters. When the combatants ran out of ammunition, they threw the little gilded baskets at one another's heads" (1976a:660).

More often, however, Goethe does not indicate his relationship to the event through the first person pronoun ("we remember"; "*we* ourselves saw") but by means of various spatial and temporal deictic locutions that give the event and characters an illusory specificity. In a section in which he describes the masks and fancy dresses of the carnival generally, he writes, for example: "*Here* a Pulcinella comes running along with a large horn dangling from colored strings around his waist . . . And *here* comes another of his kind . . . more modest and more satisfied" (1976a:647; emphasis mine).

Despite the repeated "here" (*Hier kommt ein Pulcinell gelaufen; Hier kommt ein anderer seinesgleichen*) we have no coordinates other than our general knowledge that we are "with Goethe" somewhere along the Corso during the carnival. Goethe in fact begins this part of his description with the ringing of the noonday bells on the Capitol, which announces the period of license, but we do not know which day of the carnival it is. In other sections he uses temporal deixis. He begins a description of evening, before the races: "Now as evening approaches" (*Nun geht es nach dem Abend zu* [1976a:664]). Again we have no idea which evening. And at still other times, in the midst of a generalized, spatially and temporally decontextualized description of an event, he will suddenly make use of a "meanwhile," an *inzwischen,* that has no coordinates. As I have said, the function of these deictics is purely rhetorical, to add life to his descriptions and make them more convincing. They attest to Goethe's presence and appeal to the reader to "join" him. There is an appellative dimension to Goethe's deictics, perhaps to all deictics. He draws his readers into a seemingly real moment of observation that is in fact only an artifice of his text. He offers them the security of his presence as they witness the tantalizing disorder of the events that take place in the Corso.

Goethe becomes the reader's mediator and a sort of tour guide to the carnival. He stands outside it, though, particularly outside the tumultuous crowd—the common people—milling up and down the Corso. He is aloof, a foreigner, at times condescending. He sees little joy in the carnival and, like Hawthorne and Henry James after him, he does not share in any of its merriment. He preserves his distance, an order-bestowing theatrical distance, and only occasionally does he identify with the spectators—not with the huge lively mass of sensuous beings, but with an elite who watch the crowd from their benches and chairs. He describes the homey feeling produced by the rugs hanging from balconies and windows, by the embroidered tapestries draped over the stands and by the chairs brought out from inside the houses and palaces along the Corso. "When you leave the house, you do not believe you are outside, among strangers, but in a room full of acquaintances" (1976a:646). He does not abandon his class. He does not phenomenologically or rhetorically assume the subjectivity of the participants. Indeed, in his first mention of the carnival the year before, he was more sensitive to the participants' experience: "What one finds unpleasant about it is the absence of inner gaiety in the people, who lack money to gratify the few desires they may still have . . . On the last days the noise was incredible, but there was no heartfelt joy" (1976a:228–229).

Although Goethe is interested in display, in what he can see and not in the *Innerlichkeit* of the participants, it is precisely with the "inner meaning" of the carnival that Goethe concludes his essay. It passes like a dream or a fairy tale, he says, leaving perhaps fewer traces on the souls of the participants (*Teilnehmer*) than on Goethe's readers. He has brought to their imagination and understanding a coherent whole (*vor deren Einbildungskraft und Verstand wir das Ganze in seinem Zusammenhange gebracht haben*). Is Goethe suggesting that for an experience to be more than ephemeral it must be described with coherence and order? He goes on to observe that "the course of these follies" draws our attention to the most important stages of human life, "when a vulgar Pulcinella indecently reminds us of the pleasures of love to which we owe our existence, when a Baubo profanes the mysteries of birth in public places, when so many lighted candles at night remind us of the ultimate ceremony" (1976a:676). He sees the Corso itself as the road of earthly life where one is both spectator and actor and where one has little room to move freely because of external forces. The horses racing past are like fleeting delights "that leave only a trace on our soul." Carried away by the force of his imagery, Goethe remarks "that freedom and equality can only be enjoyed in the intoxication of madness and that the greatest desire rises to its highest pitch when it approaches close to

danger and relishes in voluptuous, sweet-anxious sensations"
(1976a:677).

Reminiscent of his unrestrained *Sturm und Drang* period,
these last observations seem removed from any specific referent
in the carnival. The carnival is an excuse for Goethe's meditation. His concern is with its meaning not for the participants,
but for himself and his readers. Ignoring the historical and the
collective, the link, as Bakhtin (1965) stresses, between popular
destiny penetrated by the comic principle and the earth, Goethe
reduces the carnival to a conventional allegory of individual
destiny. Its meaning lies in a transcendent story—the kind Catlin sought for the O-Kee-Pa ceremony but could never really
find. Through Goethe's allegory, the individual is, so to speak,
resurrected from the milling, seething, tumultuous—the
unindividuated—crowd.[9] Goethe, a kind of trickster, a magician
of words, a Hermes reporting the carnival to those up north,
across the border, restores order at this reflective level to an
event that, despite the expository, the theatricalized order he
has already given it in his description, must rhetorically remain
a symbol of madness and disorder. Like Catlin, Goethe seeks
moral significance (albeit trivial) in ceremony—in the carnival.
"And so without even thinking about it, we have also concluded
with an Ash Wednesday meditation, which we trust has not
saddened our readers. Rather, since life as a whole remains
like the Roman Carnival, without an overview [*unübersehlich*],
unsavory, and precarious, we wish that through this carefree
crowd of maskers everyone will be reminded with us of the
importance of every one of the momentary and often seemingly
trivial pleasures of life" (1976a:677). With this conventional Ash
Wednesday meditation, Goethe's conclusion marks a return to
contemplation, introspection, and concern for the meaning of
what we do.[10] His "return" parallels a return in the ceremony
he describes. During the carnival there is no reflection, just
play, masquerading, and, as we say nowadays, acting out. With
Ash Wednesday begins a period of penitence, and, we must
presume, a return to introspection, order, and individuality.

The title of Clifford Geertz's (1973) "Deep Play: Notes on a
Balinese Cockfight," written about the time the film *Deep*

Throat was all the rage, announces a series of erotic puns—puns, Geertz maintains, the Balinese themselves would understand—throughout his essay. Puns are frequent in ethnography. They position the ethnographer between his world of primary orientation, his readers' world, and the world of those others, the people he has studied, whom at some level, I believe, he is also addressing (Crapanzano 1977c). Through the pun he appeals collusively to the members of one or the other world, usually the world of his readership, thereby creating a hierarchical relationship between them. He himself, the punster, mediates between these worlds.

Geertz's essay is divided into seven sections, and the titles of these sections—"The Raid," "Of Cocks and Men," "The Fight," "Odds and Even Money," "Playing with Fire," "Feathers, Blood, Crowds, and Money," and "Saying Something of Something"—are all suggestive of a distinctly urban environment, of a sex-and-violence whodunit, something out of Mickey Spillane perhaps, which, unlike Geertz's erotic puns, the villagers could not possibly have understood, at least not in 1958. The titles do little to characterize the ethos of a Balinese village or cockfight, but, like puns, they create a collusive relationship between the ethnographer and his readers. They also attest to the ethnographer's stylistic virtuosity. He and his readers come out on top of the hierarchy of understanding.

Geertz's essay begins with a humorous tale of entry—by now, in its own right, a genre or subgenre of ethnography. The anthropologist-hero is cast stereotypically as a *naif*, an awkward simpleton, not at all sure of his identity, often suffering from some sort of exotic malady, caught in a betwixt and between world. We could see him at Goethe's Roman Carnival. He is no longer in his own world, and he has not yet mastered the new world he will constitute through his ethnography.

> Early in April of 1958, my wife and I arrived, malarial and diffident, in a Balinese village we intended, as anthropologists, to study. A small place, about five hundred people, and relatively remote, it was its own world. We were intruders, professional ones, and the villagers dealt with us as Balinese seem always to deal with people not part of their life who yet press themselves upon them: as though we were not there.

For them, and to a degree for ourselves, we were nonpersons, specters, invisible men.   (1973:412)

Here in the first paragraph of "Deep Play" Geertz establishes an opposition between himself and his wife and the Balinese who live in their own remote little world. Geertz and his wife are "anthropologists," "professionals," and "intruders." The tale of entry is, as I have noted, called "The Raid," referring manifestly to a police raid of a village cockfight. It may also reflect Geertz's attitude toward his and his wife's presence, their mission, in the village. He claims dramatically that he and his wife were "nonpersons, specters, invisible men" for the villagers and "to a degree for ourselves"—that is, until like the other villagers attending the cockfight, they fled the police. Then they were recognized. Geertz offers no evidence for this contention, and in the very next paragraph he contradicts himself.

But except for our landlord and the village chief, whose cousin and brother-in-law he was, everyone ignored us only as the Balinese can do. As we wandered around, uncertain, wistful, eager to please, people seemed to look right through us with a gaze focused several yards behind us on some more actual stone or tree. Almost nobody greeted us; but nobody scowled or said anything unpleasant to us either which would have been almost as satisfactory . . . The indifference, of course, was studied; the villagers were watching every move we made, and they had an enormous amount of quite accurate information about who we were and what we were going to be doing. But they acted as if we simply did not exist, which, in fact, as this behavior was designed to inform us, we did not, or anyway not yet.   (412–413)

There is of course a difference between being a nonperson, a specter, an invisible man—a collection of nonequivalent statuses in any case—and being treated with "studied indifference." The Geertzes may have been treated as though they were not there, but they were surely there. How else could they be informed of their "nonexistence"?

I call attention here to what might simply be dismissed as a not altogether successful storytelling ruse, were it not indicative of a more serious problem that flaws Geertz's essay. Here, at a descriptive level, he blurs his own subjectivity—his experience of himself in those early Balinese days—with the subjectivity and the intentionality of the villagers. (His wife's experience presents still another problem as well as something of a conceptual embarrassment: she is dismissed from this tale of men and cocks—a dismissal already heralded in the first paragraph by the use of "men" in the phrase "invisible men.") Later, at the level of interpretation, we discover the same confusion (see Crapanzano 1981; Lieberson 1984). We must ask whether this interpretive confusion is facilitated by Geertz's particular descriptive tack.

Through puns, titles, subtitles, and simple declarations, the "anthropologist" and his "Balinese" are separated from one another. In the opening section of "Deep Play" Geertz and his wife are cast, however conventionally, as individuals. The Balinese are not. They are generalized. Turns of phrase like "as Balinese always do," reminiscent of superficial travel accounts and "national character" studies, run through "Deep Play": "in a way only a Balinese can do" (412); "the deep psychological identification of Balinese men with their cocks" (417); "the Balinese never do anything in a simple way when they can contrive to do it in a complicated way" (425); "the Balinese are shy to the point of obsessiveness of open conflict" (446). The "Balinese"—surely not the Balinese—become a foil for Geertz's describing, interpreting, and theorizing—for his self-presenting.

Geertz likens his nonpersonhood to being "a cloud or a gust of wind": "My wife and I were still very much in the gust of wind stage, a most frustrating, and even, as you begin to doubt whether you are really real after all, unnerving one" (413). And he goes on to describe the police raid through which he achieved his "personhood." This passage is significant not so much because of what Geertz has to say about himself and his wife, as because of a pronoun switch from "I/we," or more accurately from "I plus noun" ("my wife and I"), to "you." This switch anticipates his disappearance in the sections to come. The "you" serves, I suggest, as more than an appeal to the reader to emphathize with him. It decenters the narrator in the space of intersubjective understanding. He engages in a different sort of dialogue with his reader than with the Balinese. *They* remain cardboard figures.

Despite popular grammatical understanding that a pronoun is simply a noun substitute, there is, as Emile Benveniste (1966b) and others have observed, a fundamental difference between first and second person personal pronouns ("I" and "you" and their plurals) and third person pronouns ("he," "she," "it," "they"). The first and second are properly indexical: they "relate" to the context of utterance. The third person pronouns refer back anaphorically to an antecedent, a noun, often enough a proper noun, in the text. They are liberated, so to speak, from the context of utterance, but they are embedded in the textual context. They are intratextual and derive their meaning from their textually described antecedents. In Geertz's essay, and in most ethnography, the I-you of the ethnographer and the I-you of the ethnographer's interlocutors in the field are converted asymmetrically into an anaphorically free I and an anaphoric—a cumulative—they. Indeed, in most ethnographic texts including Geertz's the I itself disappears except in conventional tales of entry or in text-evaluative shifters and becomes simply a stylistically borne "invisible" voice.[11] Symptomatically, "we" seldom occurs in ethnography.

"The Raid" represents a delicate, unstable moment. Geertz, the author/narrator, is an "I." The Balinese are referentially described: a "they." Just as the Balinese recognize Geertz as a person after his flight from the police, he, as the I narrator, flees from the text in a section revealingly entitled "Of Cocks and Men." Does the lingering I of "The Raid" compensate for Geertz's nonpersonhood in those first days of field work he is describing?

Throughout the remainder of "Deep Play" there is a continual blurring of Geertz's undertanding and the understanding of the Balinese as he describes them. Without any evidence he attributes to the Balinese all sorts of experiences, meanings, intentions, motivations, dispositions, and understandings. He writes, for example:

In the cockfight man and beast, good and evil, ego and id, the creative power of aroused masculinity and the destructive power of loosened animality fuse in a bloody drama of hatred, cruelty, violence, and death. It is little wonder that when, as is the invariable rule, the owner of the winning cock takes the carcass of the loser—often torn limb from limb by its enraged owner—home to eat, he does so with a mixture of social embarrassment, moral satisfaction, aesthetic disgust, and cannibal joy. (430–431)

We must not be carried away by Geertz's Grand Guignol sensibility. We must ask: on what grounds does he attribute "social embarrassment," "moral satisfaction," "aesthetic disgust" (whatever that means), and "cannibal joy" to the Balinese? to all Balinese men? to any Balinese man in particular? Clearly Geertz's aim, like Catlin's, is to render the moment vivid, but unlike Catlin, who makes no pretense of uncovering the subjective meaning—the experience—of the O-Kee-Pa ceremony for the Mandan, Geertz does make such a claim of the Balinese.

Toward the end of his essay Geertz suddenly declares the cockfight to be an art form, which he understands in a very Western way: "As any art form—for that, finally, is what we are dealing with—the cockfight renders ordinary, everyday experience comprehensible by presenting it in terms of acts and objects which have had their practical consequences removed and been reduced (or, if you prefer, raised) to the level of sheer appearance where their meaning can be more powerfully articulated and more exactly perceived" (443). We must ask: for whom does the cockfight articulate everyday experience and render it more perceptible? After likening the cockfight to *King Lear* and *Crime and Punishment*, Geertz goes on to assert that it

catches up these themes—death, masculinity, rage, pride, loss, beneficence, change—and ordering them into an encompassing structure, presents them in such a way as to throw into relief a particular view of their essential nature. It puts a construction on them, makes them, to those historically positioned to appreciate the construction, meaningful—visible, tangible, graspable—"real" in an ideational sense. An image, fiction, a model, a metaphor, the cockfight is a means of expression; its function is neither to assuage social passions nor to heighten them (though, in its playing-with-fire way it does a bit of both), but, in a medium of feathers, blood, crowds, and money, to display them. (443–444).

We must ask: who is historically positioned to appreciate the construction? Geertz completely ignores the fact that *King Lear* and *Crime and Punishment* are culturally and linguistically marked as a tragedy and a novel; as representations of a particular order; as fictions to be read in a special way—indeed, to be read. He offers no proof anywhere that the cockfight is so marked for his Balinese. Piling image on image—"image," "fiction," and "metaphor"—may assuage Geertz's own theoretical anxiety, but it hardly gets rid of the problem. (Image, fiction, model, and metaphor are of course no more equivalent than nonperson, specter, and invisible man.) Cockfights are surely cockfights for the Balinese—not images, fictions, models, and metaphors. They are not marked as such, though they may be read as such by a foreigner for whom these terms have interpretive value.[12] It is perhaps no accident that in a following paragraph Geertz describes the cockfight as "disquietful": "The reason it is disquietful is that, joining pride to selfhood, selfhood to cocks and cocks to destruction, it brings to imaginative realization a dimension of Balinese experience normally well-obscured from view" (444). We must ask yet again: for whom is the cockfight disquietful?

In the final pages of "Deep Play" Geertz likens the cockfight to a text. He also refers to it as "a Balinese reading of Balinese experience," "a story they tell the natives about themselves," a "metacommentary." "It is a means of saying something about something." It requires the anthropologist to "penetrate" it, just as a critic "penetrates" a text. For Geertz the interpreted text, the cockfight, is a drama of status hierarchy, and in blatantly intentional language he suggests that is why Balinese go to cockfights. "Balinese go to cockfights to find out what a man, usually composed, aloof, almost obsessively self-absorbed, a kind of moral autocosm, feels like when, attacked, tormented, challenged, insulted, and driven in result to the extremes of fury, he has totally triumphed or been brought low" (450).

Elsewhere, he asserts Balinese subjectivity at cockfights.

> Enacted and re-enacted so far without end the cockfight enables the Balinese, as read and reread, Macbeth enables us, to see a dimension of our own subjectivity. As he watches fight after fight, with the active watching of an owner and a bettor (for cockfighting has no more interest as a pure spectator sport

than does croquet or dog-racing), he grows familiar with it and what it has to say to him much as the attentive listener to a string quartet or the absorbed viewer of still life grows slowly more familiar with them in a way which opens his objectivity to himself.   (450–451)

Who told Geertz? How can a whole people share a single subjectivity? Are there not differences between texts, commentaries, meta-commentaries, dramas, sports, string quartets, and still lifes? Has Geertz abandoned all of the analytic distinctions that have characterized the success (and the failure) of his civilization? Like Catlin's colorful, concrete metaphors, Geertz's colorless, abstract metaphors subvert both his description and his interpretation. Indeed, they subvert his authority. His message is simply not convincing.

"Deep Play" offers no understanding of the native from the native's point of view. There is only the constructed understanding of the constructed native's constructed point of view. Geertz offers no specifiable evidence for his attributions of intention, his assertions of subjectivity, his declarations of experience. His constructions of constructions of constructions appear to be little more than projections or blurrings of his point of view with that of the native, or, more accurately, of the constructed native.

Finally, as if to give his, or any anthropologist's, constructions a certain substantialized authority, Geertz refers in "Deep Play" to culture "as an ensemble of texts, themselves ensembles, which the anthropologist strains to read over the shoulder of those to whom they properly belong" (452–453).[13] The image is striking: sharing and not sharing a text. It represents a sort of asymmetrical we-relationship with the anthropologist behind and above the native, hidden but at the top of the hierarchy of understanding. It reflects, I believe, the indexical drama of "The Raid" in which the parties to the ethnographic encounter are brought together in the narration as they are separated through style. There is never an I-you relationship, a dialogue, two people next to each other reading the same text and discussing it face-to-face, but only an I-they relationship. And eventually even the I disappears, replaced by an invisible voice of authority who declares what the you-transformed-to-a-they experience.

In traditional ethnography the ethnographer's encounter with the people he has studied is rarely described. Often, as in the case of Geertz's "Deep Play," hardly a traditional ethnography, even the activity that is described and interpreted—a cockfight, a carnival, a test of prowess, or, for that matter, the weaving of a basket or the preparation of a meal—is not presented in its particularity as a single, and in some ways unique, performance. We are usually given a general picture. Presumably many observations, taken from many vantage points, are conflated into a single, constructed performance, which becomes a sort of ideal Platonic performance. Catlin and Goethe describe a single performance, but, despite deictic and other particularizing locutions, they do it in a generalizing way. Geertz, who apparently attended many cockfights, never describes a specific cockfight. He constructs the Balinese cockfight and interprets his construction: "the Balinese cockfight." His conventional tale of entry serves a deictic function not that different from Catlin's "assigned place" or Goethe's repeated "here" and "now." It gives the illusion of specificity when there is no specific temporal or spatial vantage point. It attests to the ethnographer's having been there and gives him whatever authority arises from that presence.

In "Deep Play" the problem of the ethnographer's authoritative constructions is further complicated by the author's phenomenological and hermeneutical pretensions. Neither Catlin nor Goethe make any sustained effort to describe the experience for the participants of the ceremonies they observed. Catlin assumes the perspective of the Mandan only rhetorically. For him, the O-Kee Pa was a "shocker" ("This part of the ceremony [the torture], as I have just witnessed it, is truly shocking to behold, and will stagger the belief of the world when they read of it" [1857:157]); and he struggled unsuccessfully to give it meaning. He could find no familiar story in which to fit it in more than a fragmented way. The Roman carnival became for Goethe an allegory of individual destiny. It was of course not that unfamiliar. He was able to organize it along familiar theatrical —*commedia dell'arte*—lines and to synchronize his descriptive rhythm with the carnival's rhythm. We may find Goethe's allegory arch, moribund even, but it is subsuming. For Geertz, the cockfight itself becomes a grand metaphor for Balinese social organization, and it therefore closes in on itself. His essay is less a disquisition on Balinese cockfighting, subjectivity or objectively understood, than on interpreting—reading—cultural data. His analysis is exemplary, and this exemplary quality, Geertz's interpretive virtuosity, helps render it ethnographically convincing. Its ultimate significance is not moral but methodological. Catlin makes a plea for the salvation of the Mandan; Goethe for the full appreciation of fleeting moments of joy; Geertz for hermeneutics. In all three instances the events described are subverted by the transcending stories in which they are cast. They are sacrificed to their rhetorical function in a literary discourse that is far removed from the indigenous discourse of their occurrence. The sacrifice, the subversion of the event described, is in the final analysis masked neither by rhetoric, hypotyposis, theatricality, and interpretive virtuosity nor by their metaphorization—salvation, life, society—but by the authority of the author, who, in much of ethnography, stands above and behind those whose experience he purports to describe. All too often, the ethnographer forgets that the native, like Eduard in Goethe's *Elective Affinities,* cannot abide someone reading over his shoulder. If he does not close his book, he will cast his shadow over it. Of course, the ethnographer will also cast his shadow over it. It is perhaps for this reason, if I may conclude with the conceit of my own tale of entry into this chapter, that Zeus understood what Hermes meant when he promised to tell no lies but did not promise to tell the whole truth.

3.
The Self, The Third, and Desire

> I have the intention of carrying out a particular task and I make
> a plan. The plan in my mind is supposed to consist in my seeing
> myself acting thus and so. But how do I know that it is myself
> that I'm seeing? Well, it isn't myself, but a kind of a picture.
> But why do I call it the picture of *me*?
>
> "How do I know that it's myself?": the question makes sense
> if it means, for example, "how do I know that I'm the one I see
> there?" And the answer mentions characteristics by which I
> can be recognized.
>
> But it is my own decision that makes my image represent my
> self. And I might as well ask "how do I know that the word 'I'
> stands for myself?" For my shape in the picture was only an-
> other word "I."
>
> —Wittgenstein, *Philosophical Grammar*, 62

"The fact that the dreamer's own ego appears several times, or
in several forms, in a dream," Freud wrote in his 1925 revision
of *The Interpretation of Dreams* (1954a: 12), "is at bottom no
more remarkable than that the ego should be contained in a
conscious thought several times or in different places or
connections—e.g., in the sentence 'when I think what a healthy
child I was.' "[1] Implicit in his rather unwieldy sentence is a
"psychology" that is neither immediately nor necessarily associated with Freud's explicit psychology.[2] This implicit psychology serves as the ground for his thought. It serves, too, I suggest,
as the ground for my own thought here.

Freud presupposes a fundamental distinction between dream
and conscious thought. The dream is where *apearances* occur;
conscious thought *contains*. In its ordinariness, conscious
thought apparently has a certain priority over the dream. Freud
assumes also a particular spatialization and temporalization of
both mental phenomena. The ego can "appear" several times
in "several forms" in a dream and is "contained" several times
"in different places or connections" in conscious thought. (One

wonders whether or not transformations of the ego can occur in conscious thought as well as in the dream.) What exactly does Freud mean by the "ego" here?[3] I should point out that it is not the ego of his typology "id, ego, and superego." It is the ego of "egotistical." ("Dreams are completely egotistical," he writes at the beginning of the paragraph which ends with the sentence I have quoted.[4]) It appears to be synonymous with, or a referent of, the repeated I in the final phrase "when I think what a healthy child I was."[5]

Freud is calling attention to the identity of the ego over time—and not to its linguistic determination. He is not interested, in this context, in the fact that the continuity of the ego is brought into question through a language which has a particular, by no means universal, orientation toward time. Would the same observation arise in Whorf's Hopi? The ego of the past or past tense and the ego of the present or present tense are, paradoxically, both one and the same and yet different. They are one and the same, to use William James's (1890) metaphor, in the stream of thought or consciousness, in its nonreflexive moments. They are different in those reflexive moments when the stream (to pursue the metaphor) is turned back upon itself. Time is arrested; identity becomes problematic, differences can become paramount. The ego, or the self, becomes the object of scrutiny. With a certain surgical incisiveness, Flaubert (Steegmuller 1972) articulates this temporal arrest and objectification of the self, this schism between the ego then and now, when he writes in his notes on the Orient: "Between myself of that night and myself of tonight, there is a difference between the cadaver and the surgeon doing the autopsy." He had been rereading an unsent letter of departure to his mother.

My aim in quoting Freud here is twofold. On the one hand, I simply want to emphasize the degree to which our explicit psychologies are founded on the implicit psychological assumptions of our idiom. To what extent is our subject matter—the self and the congeries of associated concepts: "person," "personage," "personality," "consciousness," "psyche," "subject," and "ego"—a precipitate of our particular cultural idiom? To what extent does it make sense to talk of the self in other idioms? These questions are of course fundamental to all anthropological considerations. They have perhaps greater weight (illusory to be sure) in the consideration of "psychological" concepts which, as Peter Berger and Thomas Luckmann (1967) have noted, tend to realize themselves in the phenomena they purport to describe.

On the other hand, I want to raise the question, implicit in Freud's sentence, of the relationship between an idiom (language, understood broadly in the sense of the German *Sprache* or the French *discours*) and the self (Crapanzano 1977a). I argue that the "self" is an arrested moment in the ongoing dialectical movement between self and other; that this arrest depends upon the typification of self and other through language; that the typification of other depends upon a Third—a guarantor of meaning that permits the play of desire.

I have chosen to present my argument in a blatantly unconventional fashion. I speak not directly but instead rhetorically—through some of the writers who have determined my thoughts about the self, language, and its ideology. Although they use different theoretical models that are by no means consistent with one another, they are, I believe, all subject to similar idiomatic determinants. Even as I pass the reader (to use one of Jacques Lacan's figures) through the "defiles" of these others, I realize I am not escaping the determinants of my/their language. I can hope only to call attention to some of these determinants, embedded as they are in the particular genres and conventions at our disposal that produce "information," speed-reading, and naive empiricisms, and to suggest that all anthropological writing is, despite its pretense, metacommentary. Ironically, given the discipline's focus on the primitive, there is no single primitive text. "In the beginning was the word"; and yet to be "the word" (*logos*), the understanding, the evaluation of the word *logos* has to be presupposed.

My argument, but obviously neither its language nor its approach, has been inspired by A. I. Hallowell's (1967) observation that the self is both a social and a cultural product. It seems to me that this dual origin of the self (grounded, of course, in an idiomatically determined analytic distinction) has been one of the sources of the very considerable confusion, at least in anthropological theory, about the genesis and nature of the self.[6]

Hallowell—who is rather more careful than some writers to distinguish between self-awareness and self-conceptualization—takes self-awareness to be a generic human trait which cannot, however, be regarded as an isolated psychological phenomenon. "For it is becoming increasingly apparent that this peculiarly human phenomenon is the focus of complex, and fundamentally dependent, sets of linguistic and cultural variables that enter into the personal adjustment of human beings as members of particular societies" (1967:75). Among these "linguistic and cultural variables" are man's reflections about himself and his relationship to the world—his concepts of the self, the world, and the relationship between them. An individual's self-image and his interpretation of his own experience, Hallowell suggests, "cannot be divorced from the concept of the self that is characteristic of his society" (1967:76); self-awareness has then a conceptual as well as a perceptual aspect. Concomitant with it is the "awareness of a contrasting world of articulated objects, experienced as 'other-than-self'." What Hallowell does not make clear is exactly how self-concepts and other symbolic means of representation and reference function in self-awareness and the awareness of a contrasting world that is other-than-self.

If the symbolically mediated concepts of the self affect self-awareness and if these concepts vary from society to society, then it follows that modes of self-awareness will vary from society to society. Although this argument seems to follow from Hallowell's position, he himself is unwilling to accept all of its implications. He prefers to talk loosely in terms of selves and, at times, of self-images. He is critical of the suggestion that self-awareness is less developed among primitive peoples, and he attributes the not infrequent observation that "primitive man is unable to distinguish clearly between the 'subjective' and the 'objective' " to differences in our and their behavioral field. "Since the self is also partly a cultural product, the field of behavior that is appropriate for the activities of *particular* selves in *their* world of culturally defined objects is not by any means precisely coordinated with any absolute polarity of subjectivity-objectivity that is definable" (1967:84). Hallowell admits, nevertheless, that the line between subjectivity and objectivity is at times blurred. This results in part, he argues (1967:85), from the fact that the polarity cannot be adequately conceived in linear terms but "only with reference to the total pattern of the psychological field." He quotes MacLeod's (1947) observation that "subjectivity and objectivity are properties of an organized perceptual field in which points of reference are selves (subjects) and objects, and the 'degree of articulation' in this dimension may vary greatly"; and he suggests that variations in the degree of articulation are due to cultural factors "directly relevant to the psychological field of the individual." Hallowell's argument is circular, and we are left with no reason to assume that self-awareness and the line between subjectivity and objectivity cannot vary from society to society.

To speak far too simply, there is a contradiction between two prevalent Western positions regarding the self which is reflected in anthropological treatments of the subject, including Hallowell's. (I am using "self" here loosely—for so it has been used—to refer not only to the self, self-awareness, self-image, self-conception, but also to that congery of related concepts that include the personage and the person.) In the first view the self is regarded as a fundamental category of human thought; in the second, the self is seen to evolve (to individuate) over time.

The first position has its roots in Aristotle, is brought into question by Kant, and is established by Fichte (Mauss 1973). (In contemporary Anglo-American philosophy, Strawson [1959] argues that the "person" is a logically primitive, presumably universal concept.) The second position is deeply rooted in Western mythology and is explicitly articulated within Romanticism, Symbolism, and the evolutionary theories of the second half of the nineteenth century. Do these two positions reflect a "tension" between the stationary, Parmenidian position, supported by an ideology of reference, and the processual, Heraclitian position, which is masked by an ideology of reference?

An influential partisan of the evolutionary approach, Jacob Burckhardt, wrote (1867) that "at the close of the Thirteenth century Italy began to swarm with individuality."

In the Middle Ages both sides of human consciousness—that which was turned within and that which was turned without—lay dreaming or half-awake beneath a common veil. The veil was woven of faith, illusion, and childish prepossession [*Kindesbefangenheit*] through which the world and history were seen clad in strange hues. Man was conscious of himself only as a member of a race, people, party, family, or corporation—only through some general category. In Italy the veil first melted into air; an *objective* treatment of the State and of all the things of this world became possible. The *subjective* side at the same time asserted itself with corresponding emphasis; man became a spiritual *individual* and recognized himself as such. (1955:81; 1926:119)

Explaining the birth, or rebirth, of the individual in terms of the political circumstances in Italy, Burckhardt noted that a similar individuation had taken place in Greece (the Greek distinguishing himself from the barbarian) and among the Arabs.

A more systematic, developmental history (*Entwicklungsgeschichte*) of the self was elaborated by the controversial German historian Karl Lamprecht (1900; Weintraub 1966). The *Seelenleben* (the psychic life) of a people (*Volk*) was said to pass through two basic modes of existence: the fettered and the unfettered, each of which was divided into specific phases. In the first phase of the fettered mode man was immersed in his environment and had no awareness of himself as a separate individual. In the final phase of the unfettered mode of existence, man is fully an individual and imposes himself on an external reality to which he is strikingly sensitive.

Literary historians have noted a similar movement—whether in a single literature (usually ancient Greek) or in the entire course of Western literature. The gradual alienation of the individual from his environment, in these evolutionary approaches, appears at times to be a "historicized" version of the flight from the Garden of Eden, with "primitive" or "early" man and woman cast as Adam and Eve before they partook of the fateful fruit of the Tree of Knowledge. They enter the world of time and mortality; their identity falls in question; and referentiality itself becomes problematic.

The contradiction between the universal and the evolutionary approach to the notion of the self is found in Marcel Mauss's 1938 Huxley Memorial lecture, "Une catégorie de l'esprit humain: la notion de personne celle de 'moi','' which has inspired a number of subsequent studies (see Dieterlin: 1973). Mauss and his colleagues were interested in preparing a social history of the categories of the human mind (*esprit humain*). These categories are taken *tout simplement et provisoirement* from Aristotle. In this lecture Mauss exemplifies a certain evolution in the category *personne-moi*—from Zuni, Northwest Coast Indians, and Australian aborigines to nineteenth-century Western philosophical theories. He is careful to state that his study is neither linguistic nor psychological (though in fact both approaches are implicit in it) but conceptual. The ambiguous phenomena he calls *personne* and *moi* (person and self/ego/me)— the ambiguity is marked in the title by the lack of a comma between *personne* and *celle de 'moi'*—evolve from the personage (*de rôle rempli par l'individu dans ces drames sacrés comme il joue un rôle dans la vie familiale*) through the person seen as a mask, a name, a moral but nonmetaphysical entity, to a moral and metaphysical entity, the *moi*, a conscious self-reflective ego.

> However, the notion of the person [*la notion de personne*] had still to undergo another transformation to become what it has become in less than a century and a half, *the category of the self* [*la catégorie du moi*]. Far from being a primordial innate idea, clearly inscribed since Adam in the innermost depths of our being [*au plus profond de notre être*], it continues here slowly, almost up to our time, to be built upon, to become clearer and more specific, to be identified with self-knowledge [*la connaissance de soi*] and psychological consciousness [*la conscience psychologique*].   (Mauss 1973:359)

The movement here—explicitly conceptual—includes a turning inward, a reflexivity, a self-consciousness, and an emphasis on inner space that is clearly related to the emphasis on self and subjectivity in Romanticism, and which serves as the ground, as Foucault (1966) might well observe, for the development of psychology and phenomenology and the other human-centered sciences of the nineteenth century. Did earlier man, without a concept of the *moi*, lack self-awareness? Was his self-awareness differently articulated? Mauss ignores these questions, at least explicitly.[7]

Mauss's Huxley lecture is less bound by the social determination of the categories of the mind than is his earlier work with Durkheim (Durkheim and Mauss 1903) and Durkheim's own work (1914; 1915). In these writings "society" is the mediator between the universality of the categories of the mind and their varied expression or representation (between the universal and the particular, between essence and appearance, between the named and that which resists naming). In the Huxley lecture, the Aristotelian categories serve rather as guides for potential research; they are nevertheless, Mauss assumes, to be found, at some primordial level, in all cultures.[8]

Maurice Leenhardt (the missionary-anthropologist who succeeded Marcel Mauss to the chair of History of Primitive Religions at the Ecole Pratique des Hautes Etudes) accepts somewhat ambivalently an evolutionary approach to the study of the self—in his terms (1953), the *person*. In his work on the Canaque of New Caledonia, with whom he spent the first two and a half decades of this century, he raises the problematic of the person and challenges the usual anthropological presumption of a center of identity (an ego) which is reified in the personage (or the person, the self, personality, or character) and is located in the body. In *Do Kamo* (1979), his most mature work, a sweeping study of what might be called the ethnophilosophy of the Canaque, he lays out (not always very consistently) the parameters of the Canaque's notion of the person.

Leenhardt approaches the notion of the person in two principal and not necessarily coordinate ways: the relational and the existential (Crapanzano 1979). Both rest on the notion of *kamo*, literally the "which living" (*le qui-vivant*)—the "personage," as Leenhardt translates it. *Kamo*, "the living human ensemble," indicates life but implies neither contour nor nature. It is flexible, and it enables the Canaque to follow "the living" through its various metamorphoses. Animals, vegetables, and mythological subjects can be taken for *kamo* provided they are invested with humanity. The personage "is not perceived objectively, it is felt."

Existentially, Leenhardt (1979) attempts to relate the Canaque to his environment. In a manner reminiscent of Burckhardt and Lamprecht, and of course his friend and mentor Lucien Lévi-Bruhl, he argues that the (pre-contact) New Caledonian was not individuated; he was not a person but a personage, still embedded in his mythically determined surroundings. Self and other, self and environment—like subject and object and word and thing—were not sharply differentiated for him. His world was one of participation. It was *cosmomorphic*. He did not spread out over nature, but was invaded by nature. There was no distance between people and things. In the eyes of the Canaque, Leenhardt tells us, "rocks, plants, and the human body originate in similar structures; and identity of substance blends them in the same flux of life." From the cosmomorphic stance toward the world, the individual moves through anthropomorphism (already self-centered) to more analytic and empirical stances toward the world. The movement is one of individuation.

In the relational approach to the person, Leenhardt suggests, the Canaque knew himself only through the relations he maintained with others. The *kamo* was poorly defined for self and other; he was aware of his body only as a support and not a source of identity over time. (For Leenhardt, as for Mauss— both, in this respect, well within the Cartesian tradition—the body is a source of personal identity.) There was no center that could be marked by a fixed ego, but rather a series of relations that surrounded an empty space. One personage could be substituted for another like it. The personage had no single name, but a manifold of ancestral names that accorded with his relations. His participation in the personality of these ancestral names, Leenhardt suggests, implied identity and repetition. They enabled him to participate in the lived myth, a sort of unspoken cognitive-affective paradigm that grounded his reality.

In *Do Kamo* and other writings Leenhardt frequently confused the phenomenological and conceptual approach to the study of the person. In part this confusion is a result of his refusal to grant the personage, insofar as it is nonreflexively embedded in its surroundings, the privileged, transcendental locus that enables world-construction. The New Caledonian *kamo*, was, so to speak, truly a personage in a textless script, the *mythe vécu*, which he did not create but only lived. The reciprocal relationship between man and world, between subject and object (as determinants of each other), that enables the differentiation of experience and concept, of self and "self," were absent in the cosmomorphic stance, in the *mythe vécu*. This myth did not mediate subject and object as symbols are said to do; it was the coalesced reality in which experience and concept were one and the same. It was rather like the Symbolist poets' longed-for unity of symbol and symbolized, if I understand Leenhardt correctly.

Leenhardt's position is radical, and he cannot fully sustain it. (Is this a result of his idiom?) "The human awareness of 'being there'," the Dutch philosopher-anthropologist Wilhelm Dupre (1975:124) notes, "is an indefinite experience that becomes definite through the particular situation in which we live, and that defines the same situation by the modality of its presence." Not only is human existence (insofar as its presence is total and universal in outlook) total and universal, but "since it achieves this totality and universality only in company and union with definite and particular beings, it is equally a heterothetic existence, an existence that is real by 'positing' (Gr. *thesis*) an other (Gr. *heteron*) against itself as the limitation of an otherwise undetermined modality" (1975:121). It is not, however, the discovery of otherness that causes the person to emerge from the personage, I would argue, but the discovery of *his own otherness*.

Hallowell, Leenhardt, and Burckhardt (where he remarks that the ancient Greeks discovered *themselves* through the barbarian) all recognize an awareness of some sort of otherness for the emergence of the self (of the person, in Leenhardt's terms). They conceive of the relationship between self and other in static terms, rather like the figure-ground relationship in a perceptual field. They cannot, I believe, account for reflexivity. The notion of the self requires, as I observed, not simply an awareness of a contrasting world but a recognition, to speak awkwardly, of *one's own otherness* in that world. It requires a particular notion of possession.

George Herbert Mead's dialectical approach to the self addresses itself to the problem of reflexivity. The self for Mead

(1934) is a social product. It "has the characteristic that it is an object to itself, and that characteristic distinguishes it from other objects and from the body" (1934:136). The individual experiences himself as a self "not directly, but only indirectly from the particular standpoints of other individual members of the same social group, or from the generalized standpoint of the social group as a whole to which he belongs" (1934:138). Why the individual must take only the standpoint of "other individual members of the same social group" is not, however, clear.

For Mead, the development of the self proceeds in two stages.[9] First, one responds "to one's self as another responds to it, taking part in one's own conversation with other, being aware of what one is saying to determine what one is going to say thereafter" (1934:140). Conversation—communication "which is directed not only to others but also to the individual himself"—plays a paramount role here (1934:139). "The vocal gesture gives one the capacity for answering to one's own stimulus as another would answer" (1934:66). For there to be a unity of self, a "full self," the individual must also take the part of the whole community, of the *generalized other.*

> He must also, in the same way that he takes the attitudes of other individuals toward himself and toward one another, take their attitudes toward the various phases or aspects of the common social activity or set of social undertakings in which, as members of an organized society or social group, they are all engaged; and he must then, by generalizing these individual attitudes of that organized society or social group itself, as a whole, act toward different social projects which at any given time it is carrying out, or toward the various larger phases of the general social process which constitutes its life and of which these projects are specific manifestations. (1934:154ff)

Mead (1934:154) notes, in an interesting footnote, that "it is possible for inanimate objects . . . to form parts of the generalized and organized—the complete socialized—other for any given human individual insofar as he responds to such objects socially or in a social fashion." The "organized set of attitudes of the others" is incorporated into the self, Mead suggests somewhat obscurely, as the *me.* This *me,* which seems to correspond at times to the object of self-reflection and at other times to the incorporated generalized other, contrasts with the *I* which is the immediate "response of the organism to the attitudes of the others" (1934:175). The response of the I is always uncertain. "There is a moral necessity but not a mechanical necessity for the act" (1934:178). The I reflects a certain freedom the individual has.

If the dialectical movement that generates the self is continuous, it follows that the self is continually being created or recreated in accordance with its "conversations" with others. (Mead's behavioral approach to language always stresses its evocative function at the expense of the informative.) The self appears to be in continual flux, in this view. It is subject to the contingencies of the individual's life and the whims of those he encounters. Obviously such a view is neither phenomenologically "realistic" (we do usually perceive a certain permanence, a unity and continuity—a resistance even—in our selves), nor is it socially "realistic." It is the generalized other (and its incorporation as the me) that serves, for Mead, to give the self unity and continuity.

It is not exactly clear how the generalization and organization of the attitudes of the other, of the community that produces the generalized other, comes about. How are the attitudes symbolized or typified? What is the status of the generalized other? Mead moves here, as elsewhere in his writings, from high, theoretical abstraction to oversimplified, concrete examples (for example, a political party) which do not do justice to his theoretical position. The notion of the generalized other, or even a hierarchy of such others, is at any rate too simple. It demands a social homogeneity, I would insist, that is not to be found in even the "simplest" of societies. In Mead's argument, the generalized other functions as an anchor for the self and provides a *constant* in different social situations. Mead is, therefore, unable to grant it rhetorical flexibility. As the me (insofar as it is the me), the generalized other represents the unity of the self, its constancy and continuity, and is set against the I, the representative of uncertainty. In Mead's schema there is no explanation for the uncertainty of the I.

Mead's approach may account for the reflexivity that is necessary for the emergence of the self, for what Hallowell would call the social production of the self. It does not account, though, for its cultural production. The social-behavioral approach to symbolism (the symbol being a stimulus to the individual as well as a response)—to conversation and communication more generally—is not, in my estimation, sufficient. Conversation and communication may well be necessary for the possibility of reflexivity, but they alone cannot account for the emergence of the self.

With the possible exception of the mirror—and this is rather more dubious than Mead appears ready to admit—it is only through language that the individual reaches the position "where he responds to his own gestures as other people respond" (Mead 1934:66; compare Lacan's [1966] mirror phase). It is of course not altogether clear why Mead insists that the individual respond to his vocal gestures, or his image in the mirror, as others do (except to maintain a particularly homogeneous vision of social life and a peculiarly simplistic view of human personality). The individual, I would suggest, need only have the illusion—indeed, such an illusion may be a social inevitability—that he is responding as his counterpart responds. Together they negotiate a reality and accommodate to each other; they enter a conspiracy of "understanding." They generate the selves they chose by choosing their counterparts; that is, they typify the others, label them, name them, characterize them, take possession of themselves. The individual and his counterpart become rhetorical figures for each other.

It is this play, this casting the other to cast oneself (to use a theatrical metaphor), that Mead cannot explain. Nor can he account for those forays into fantasy, those *folies-à-deux*, those multiple follies that characterize so much of social life. Nor finally—and this is most important—can he account for the absence of lucidity, for those blind spots in consciousness that we have come to identify with that late nineteenth-century invention, the unconscious. It is with good reason that Lacan has aphoristically declared the unconscious "the discourse of the other."

Emile Benveniste adopts a dialectical-dialogical approach to the constitution of the subject. His argument has considerable bearing on our discussion of the self.[10] He (1971:224; 1966:259) writes: "It is in and through language that man constitutes himself as a *subject,* because language alone establishes the concept of 'ego' in reality, in *its* reality which is that of the being." (*C'est dans et par le langage que l'homme se constitue comme* sujet; *parce que le langage seul fonde en realité, dans* sa *realité qui est celle de l'être, le concept d' "ego.")* This sentence is significant for what it states, its argument; and for what it reveals, shows (in Wittgenstein's sense of the word). It states that the subject is constituted in and through language. It reveals that the constituted subject (I accept for the moment *sujet* as a primitive appellation) is immediately named, however obscurely, by a foreign nominalized pronomial locution that is, Benveniste would argue, essentially indexical in function— namely, *ego.*

Subjectivity is, for Benveniste (1966:259), the ability of the speaker to posit himself as "subject." (*La subjectivité, dont nous traitons ici, est la capacité du locuteur à se poser comme "sujet."* N.B. the reflexive *se poser!*) Subjectivity is defined not by the feeling (*le sentiment*) of being oneself, but as the psychic unity which transcends the totality of actual experiences of consciousness (*conscience*). *This subjectivity is nothing more than the emergence in a being of a fundamental property of language.* "*Est 'ego' qui dit 'ego' "* (1966:260).[11] Subjectivity is determined by the linguistic status of the person.

Whence the person? However labeled, it seems for Benveniste (1971:225; 1966:260) to emerge through dialogue. "Consciousness of self [*conscience de soi*] is only possible if it is experienced by contrast. I use *I* only when I am speaking to someone who will be a *you* in my address. It is this condition of dialogue that is constitutive of the *person* [*personne*], for it implies that reciprocally I become *you* in the address of the one who in his turn designates himself as *I.* Here we see a principle whose consequences are to be spread out in all directions." The speaker's I becomes the listener's you. As such, he is rendered external to himself—objectivated, we might say—capable finally of being named (whether specifically or as a generality) as person, ego, or self. This naming, I suggest, is supported by the ideological priority given to reference.[12]

The polarity between the I and the you, Benveniste notes, is unique. It signifies neither equality nor symmetry. Ego is always in a position of transcendence with respect to you. But neither I nor you can be conceived of without the other. They are complementary, opposed as interior to exterior, reversible, and reflected in such dualities as "self" and "other" or "individual" and "society." It would be erroneous, Benveniste insists, to reduce the duality to a single, original term: the ego.[13] And yet—a point Benveniste does not take up—within the language and thought of the West (we must always note Leenhardt's Canaque) primacy is always given to one of the terms: the I.

Seemingly oblivious to the implications of what he himself has written, Benveniste goes on to note that the I and the you (not the he and she) must be distinguished from all other linguistic designations. They refer neither to a concept nor to an individual. They are linguistic forms which indicate "person" (1971:276; 1966:262).

> Then what does *I* refer to? To something very peculiar which is exclusively linguistic: *I* refers to the act of the individual discourse in which it is pronounced, and by this it designates the speaker. It is a term that cannot be identified except in what we have called elsewhere an instance of discourse and that has only a momentary reference [*référence actuelle*]. The reality to which it refers is the reality of the discourse. It is the instance of the discourse in which *I* designates the speaker that the speaker proclaims himself as the "subject." And so it is literally true that the basis of subjectivity is in the exercise of language.

Subjectivity rests then in the instance of the discourse. The I does not name the subjectivity which it constitutes through discourse. It refers simply to the speaker in a specific utterance.

Taken as indices of the instance of discourse, the first and second person personal pronouns are themselves, albeit functionally significant, referentially hollow. They demand, if you will, nominalization; and Benveniste inevitably provides such nominalization—immediately by the very terms he seeks to account for (*sujet* and *subjectivité*), and mediately with ego and those other terms (person and self) which are the subject of our consideration.

But we must ask: is there any sense in asking to whom an I refers? Can we point to an I? Or are we already pointing to a me? Can we point to a subject, a person, a personage, a self in certain of their noncorporeal acceptations? Do our questions posit an illusory reality?[14] Is the "reality" not an artifact of our language? Of any language? Is it not supported by the stress we lay, ideologically, on the nominal and its peculiar relationship to an object? We have insisted for centuries now that a pronoun is a substitute for a noun—a noun's name.

Although the first and second person pronouns are indexical, they are not necessarily *understood* as such. They are understood as extending beyond the instance of discourse to other previous and future discourses; they are somehow transcendent.

Without wishing to deny the indexical function of the I and you, I would like to suggest that they also have—or are given—an anaphoric potential. They refer not just to the speaker and hearer, the addressor and addressee, of a particular utterance; they also refer back to other instances of the I (and you) uttered by the same speaker (or interlocutor). They are, in Halliday's and Hasan's (1976) sense, endophoric. (Their final reference may be conceived of as a noun, even a proper noun. Consider the special status of such nouns in our language and its grammar!)

It is precisely this anaphoric potential (which some linguists, given to taking the sentence or the repartee as their largest units of analysis, have been all too ready to dismiss) that permits, in the constitution of the self, the play both with the other—the you—and with the retrospective I (embodied in previous utterances by the speaker) and the prospective I (yet to be embodied). We must not forget the function of suspense in the constitution of the self, and the anxiety that accompanies such suspense. Narrative suspense and (conventionally) dialogical suspense are constrained suspenses which create an already mastered anxiety, although the mastering is (conventionally) denied or ignored by the interlocutor. The I retrospectively and prospectively is an other. (Or are these "I"s already "me"s?) The anaphoric potential of the first and second person pronouns enables self-constitution, transference phenomena (or at least their analyses, implicit and explicit, licit and illicit), discussions of identity, and the autobiographical enterprise itself. It permits the cohesion of a single speaker's, a single I's utterances—and the possibility of neuroses.

We should note the rarity of playing with the homonymity of the "I" and "you" of two speakers. We should note too that when such word-games occur in the West, they are frequently between a child learning to speak and an adult; and they are stopped not when the child grows tired or confused but when the adult suffers a semantic vertigo. Finally, we should note the *terror* of regarding these most sacred of designations, the I and the you, as only indexical. And we must ask, nevetheless and despite that terror, whether the anaphoric potential of which I write is a reaction to precisely that terror. (Note that I have, in my discussion of this potential, switched from an analytic modality to a hermeneutical one: "although the first and second person pronouns are indexical, they are not necessarily *understood* as such.") Am I not succumbing to an ideology that insists that I and you, like he and she, are noun-substitutes with determinant antecedents? Am I not rendering them a "one" (French *on* or German *man*)? We do make such transformations and must account for them.

The individual is born into a world of words—into the Symbolic order, as Lacan would put it—which makes him what he is. "Man speaks but it is because the symbol has made him a man" (Lacan 1966:276). Here, in language, as Lacan understands it, "What dominates is the unity of signification which establishes itself as never becoming resolved into a pure indication of the Real, but always as referring to another signification. This is to say that if the signification 'grasps' the things, it is only by constituting their set by enveloping it in the signifier" (Wilden 1968:12n). Lacan's approach to meaning is radically diacritical, and, despite occasional protestations to the contrary, essentially referential in orientation.[15] Words do not necessarily signify what they are thought (conventionally) to signify. There is, as Lacan would have it in his play on the Saussurian algorithm, a bar or barrier between the signifier and the signified. Words, signs, may serve as symbolic substitutes for that which resists signification—the repressed (structured as it is by language). They may, I suggest, also give the illusion of reference where there is no reference, or only an attenuated referential potential (as in the case of the pronominal indexicals of which I have been writing). They enable man to typify and symbolize (in ways in which he may not even be aware) the other and thereby him-*self;* they enable him to generalize these others and incorporate their responses in what Mead would call his *me*—and Freud, in a different sense, his superego. This same world of words gives order to his typifications, generalizations, and incorporations. It is systemic—governed, Lacan maintains, by the relations between signifying elements and antecedents to his significations. (It is reinforced in every act of signification.) It both deprives the individual of his unbounded freedom and gives him the only *meaningful* kind of freedom: that is, freedom within an order. The signifying chain, the Symbolic order, culture, and grammar, serve to stabilize the relations between self and other by functioning as a Third.

According to Lacan (1966:93–100), a child's entry into the Symbolic order occurs not with the first babbling, naming, or sentence-construction (however "correct") but during the Oedipal phase. It is preceded by the development of a primordial reflexivity during the mirror stage—the stage at which the child, between his sixth and eighteenth month, "discovers" himself in his mirror image, in his counterpart, his *semblable.* It is during the Oedipal phase, if I understand Lacan correctly, that the name-of-the-father[16]—his verbal authority or, perhaps better, his authority through the word—fixes the child's relationship to the word; he is "grasped" by the word. Through the primordial reflexivity of the mirror phase and the entrance into language in the Oedipal stage (and the reflexivity granted thereby), the child—the individual—becomes inevitably alienated, Lacan suggests, from himself. He discovers himself as an other in the mirror; he loses himself in language (*langue*) like an object. He can *picture* himself and *name* himself. But he is, so to speak, doubly alienated from himself. This alienation of the "self" from the self or subject is repeated, I would suggest, in our every self-reflection.

What is of interest to us here is not Lacan's approach to the genesis of the self but a particular movement in the development of the self that is given "mythical" expression in Lacan's work. It is implicit in Mead's as well. It is the movement from a dual relationship between self and other to a triadic relationship which is achieved in and through language. In psychoanalytic developmental terms, it is the movement from the symbiotic mother-child relationship to the triadic relationship of mother, father, and child. The father-qua-symbol (Lacan's name-of-the-father) is himself the symbolic matrix[17] for a series of other symbols (such as authority, law, and God, as Freud noted, and language, culture, and convention). He represents the locus of meaning and truth. This Third may be the voice of conscience (the incorporation of the father's authority, in Freud's scheme); of various demons who may be "present" at any human interchange: of God, in his omniscience and omnipotence; of the community, the party, and the cause; and most interestingly, of the other as the subject of transference.

There is of course an instability in any triadic relationship, as Sartre (1945; 1956) brilliantly showed in *No Exit* and as is constantly exemplified in familial Oedipal dramas. There is a constant shifting of alliances and objectifying gazes. There is a splitting of symbolic functions. In analyzing my use of a field assistant in some of my work in Morocco, I (Crapanzano 1980) found that my assistant was the controller of the word. He could mediate between me and my informant—and became, thereby, a symbol of constancy and continuity. He was not, however, the initiator of the word; that lay with me. Nor was he the giver of the word; that lay with my informant. (I am obviously simplifying here.) The three functions of the Oedipal father—the initiator, the giver, and the controller of the word—were split among us. (Compare the trinitarian conception of the Christian God.) Of course, there was in our relationship a certain stability, for it was framed by our intention. We three had accommodated to one another and developed our own idiosyncratic conventions, which were supported by our self-interests.

It is precisely convention, a determining frame, that is missing from Sarte's *No Exit* (and from his *Being and Nothingness* as well) and its absence produces the "hell" of instability. There are thirds but no Third in Sartre's Godless hell. The Oedipal crisis itself can be viewed, I suppose, as a struggle for a determining frame, convention, law, grammar, and authority—

all symbolized by the "father." Convention, Law, Grammar, and Authority become the Third; they stabilize the dual relationship, much as Mead's generalized other stabilizes the relationship between self and other.[18]

The Third permits a certain freedom in any dual relationship.[19] This need no longer be a life-and-death struggle, as in Hegel's (1807) depiction of the master-slave relationship. Within certain limits prescribed by the Third, self and other are able to cast each other in order to cast themselves *as they each desire*. And this is most important: the Third affords the space of desire. What is sadly lacking in Mead's approach is a dynamic that can explain the freedom of the I. Desire, too, is lacking in Leenhardt's personage who follows by rote his textless script. He cannot take possession of it. Then, perhaps, the personage would become a person.

Desire, Lacan has written, is "an effect in the subject of that condition which is imposed upon him through the defiles of the signifier" (Wilden 1968:185). Need is directed toward a specific object, is unmediated by language, and, unlike desire, can be satisfied directly. (Desire must always be satisfied, insofar as it can be satisfied, by symbolic substitutes for that which it can never possess [Crapanzano 1978].) To become a self, the individual must seek recognition by demanding the other to recognize him-self, or his desire[20]—to acknowledge at least the noun (his name) as a (grammatically) legitimate *Anlage* for the I and the you. The individual must take possession of his own otherness and not be aware simply of the otherness about him.

A possessive reflexivity, one mediated by desire, and not simply by a mechanical reflexivity, is required for the emergence of the self and indeed of self-awareness. "The Empirical Self of each of us," William James (1890:291) observed a century ago, "is all that he is tempted to call by the name *me*. But it is clear that between what a man calls *me* and what he simply calls *mine* the line is difficult to draw." And Burckhardt, it will be remembered, referred to the "veil" of pre-Renaissance man as woven of "childish prepossession" (*Kindesbefangenheit*).

It is only after we have recognized the fundamental role of desire in the genesis of the self that we can begin to explain the positing of those others: the primitive, the fettered, the personage, and that host of slightly less stereotyped others to which anthropologists and psychiatrists refer—those others against whom or at least through whom we constitute our own highly "individuated" selves. (Is the discovery of those others not one of the anthropologist's and the psychiatrist's unspoken functions?) It is only after this recognition of desire that we can begin to appreciate our occasional (if not permanent) nostalgias for Edenic conditions—or our ruthless denial of Edens. Only then can we begin to understand why Freud used the phrase (so revealing really) "when *I* think what a healthy child *I* was" to illustrate his point about the continuity of the ego, or why Flaubert chose to write "Between myself of that night and myself of tonight, there is the difference between the cadaver and the surgeon doing the autopsy." It was less to emphasize his own discontinuity than to scandalize his reader, and perhaps even himself. To coin a proverb: *Il faut un bourgeois pour s'épater.* Is that bourgeois our Third?

4.
Self-Characterization

The finished man among his enemies?—
How in the name of Heaven can he escape
That defiling and disfigured shape
The mirror of malicious eyes
Casts upon his eyes until at last
He thinks that shape must be his shape?
And what's the good of an escape
If honour find him in the wintry blast?

    —Yeats, "A Dialogue of Self and Soul"

The ideas I want to develop here about the self, the other, and their characterizations received preliminary formulation in the last chapter (see also Chapter 5 and Crapanzano (1977b; 1980) where I favored a radically dialectical approach to the self. I maintain that the dialectical movement of self formation is continuous; that the characterizations or typifications of the other are subject to conventional constraints embedded in language, to desire (itself articulated through and constrained by language), and to the resistance of the other, resistance being understood in phenomenological terms as the most elementary criterion of the real. I argue that the arrests of the dialectical process through desired characterizations and typifications of the other (and therefore the self) mask the continuous, complexly circular movement of self-and-other constitution. Any description of it, whether expressed in narrative form (as in Hegel's [1977] tale of the master and the slave or Sartre's [1964] of Jean Genet) or theoretically (in Mead [1934; 1964], Sartre [1956; 1964], or Lacan [1966]), suggests, inevitably, a determinable beginning to the movement and a *reality* to the arrests. In other words, exposition confirms the ideological masking of circularity and the play of desire and language with resistance—the real.

I do not deny the existence of arrests in the dialectical process. They may be understood in terms of an internalization of significant figures or images in the subject's biography; they may also be conceived in terms of more or less culturally sensitive maturation processes of the inevitable emergence of archetypical orientation points, of a response to conditioned typifications and generalizations of the other, or of some sort of psycho-physiological entropy. Such formulations—we recognize them as *our* psychologies—serve to reinforce our own cultural understanding of the self as having evolved or developed into a more or less consistent, particular, perduring entity, which may yet be subject to conflict, splitting, and fragmentation as well as to amalgamation, cohesion, and growth. Here I am striving to discuss the self at what can be called, *faute de mieux*, a pre-psychological level; that is, I am seeking a formulation that will enable us to understand the grounding of our psychologies and provide, if not a meta-language, then a nonpsychological vantage point for their viewing.

Strictly speaking, I can only evoke the possibility of such groundings, vantage points, and meta-languages; for insofar as I write in the same language as the psychologies, I am bound to fail. My horizon is as encompassed by the same language as the psychologies themselves. There can, in my view, be no truly external vantage point, no transcendental ego, no real possibility of a transcendental reduction, or epoché. There can only be the evocation of such transcendencies, which have themselves, ironically, to be seen as possibilities within our encompassing language. Such possibilities are facilitated by our peculiar narrative conventions (the omniscient narrator or, for that matter, reader), by our theologies (an omniscient deity, itself perhaps a refraction of our narrative presumption), and by such long-standing tropes as the traveler.

The traveler, today embodied with suspiciously forceful empirical certainty in the anthropologist (more accurately, in the "anthropologist"), has had very considerable philosophical currency (van den Abbeele 1984). (How often do we read, say, Lévi-Strauss' *Tristes Tropiques* as though we were reading about Lévi-Strauss and not about "Lévi-Strauss," the character that Lévi-Strauss creates in his tale?) Spanning worlds, translating without *really* translating, explaining without *really* explaining, describing without really describing, doomed less tragically than comically to failure, the traveler may be from the West—the hero who bursts forth—or like Montesquieu's Usbek or our "man-from-Mars," he may be from some imaginary exotic place. The traveler, the anthropologist, the man-from-Mars and what they purportedly said provide at least the illusion of a transcendent vantage point for self-reflection (Crapanzano 1987a).

Although dialectical models of self-constitution conceptualize the process in dyadic terms, as between self and other, I believe it has (regardless of the actual number of participants) to be understood in triadic terms (see Chapters 3 and 8). Insofar as the self is an arrested moment in a continuous dialectical movement, and insofar as such arrested moments depend upon language, the constitution of "self" requires a guarantor of meaning, or at least of the conventions of meaning, a Third, that permits, within limits, the play of desire. It is not a real or imaginary being but a function that can be embodied in real or imaginary beings, in king or fetish, in even their anatomical parts (the eye, for example, as in Victor Hugo's "La Conscience": "Il vit un oeil, tout grand ouvert dans les ténèbres, Et qui le regardait dans l'ombre fixement"), indeed, in conscience itself. More abstractly, the function of the Third may be symbolized by such notions as the law, convention, reason, culture, tradition, language, or tact. It may be conceived as the (absent) interlocutor in those silent but forceful secondary, or shadow, dialogues that accompany any primary dialogue (for example the dialogue between the student of anthropology who engages silently with his mentors back home and all they symbolize as he converses with his friends in the field [see Chapter 8].[1] The institutionalization, ritualization, and internalization of the representations—the embodiments and symbolizations—of the Third mask their instability and project an illusory stability that is now perhaps shaken in our "post-modern" era. The representations of the guarantor of meaning are themselves implicated in the dialectical play of desire, convention, and resistance, becoming the ultimate stake in the negotiations between ego and alter. Who has the fetish has the power!

The Western propensity to confuse the experience of the self, the notion of the self, and self-characterization reflects the structure of our languages, then at least the assumptions we make about them. I refer specifically to our ambivalent, referential view of language in which the word may be taken to be either "true to" a reality out there, say the self, or to be creating, delineating, or in some other way determining that reality (Silverstein 1976; 1979; 1985). We have, accordingly, an empiricist view of the self, as existing independently of its linguistic designation or a linguistically determined, a naively Whorfian, view of the self.

It is tempting to assert that through the arrests in the dialectical processes the self is transformed into a "self," but such an assertion oversimplifies a much more complicated linguistic and interpretive process. The arrests would then simply afford an act of self-nominalization from the vantage point of a fixed alterity supported by a monumental guarantor of meaning. The self, like the other, would become an object of reference—labeling or typification—without regard to the dialogical context in which the referencing and the rhetorical and pragmatic features of that dialogue occurred. Berger and Luckmann (1967:30–31) write, for example: "The reality of everyday life contains typificatory schemes in terms of which others are apprehended and 'dealt with' in face-to-face encounters. Thus I apprehend the other as 'a man,' 'a European,' 'a jovial type,' and so on." Such typifications are thought to be diagnostic: that is, to be based on "inherent" referentially describable—essential(-ized)—features of the typified individual and consequently subject to empirical verification. Consider the diagnostic criteria for Martland's Traumatic Encephalopathy, that is, for being punch drunk. They are described in a standard psychiatric textbook (Noyes and Kolb 1963:190) as follows:

> The patient shows an insidious impairment of skill, a slowing of muscular action, a little uncertainty in equilibrium, slight confusion, and deterioration in attention, concentration, and memory. Speech becomes thick and hesitating. The patient "continuously simulates a person who is just a little drunk." Most patients are voluble and euphoric. Confusion and defects of memory become more marked, and intellectual impairment

continues to a disabling degree. The tremor, propulsive gait, and mask-like facies of parkinsonian syndrome appear.

Similar criteria can be elicited for any role player, personality type, or character.

I suggest that the criteria upon which typifications or characterizations of self and other are based refer less to inherent, referentially describable and essentialized features or traits of the individual to be typified than to pragmatic features of the verbal transactions (and their accompanying behavior), in which the typifier is engaged with the typified. (See the introduction for a discussion of the semantico-referential and pragmatic functions of language.) In other words, typifications and characterizations are essentializations of pragmatic features or *Gestalten* of the encounter that are ascribed to the individual to be typified.[2] They are meta-pragmatic ascriptions; they are not expressed, however, in linguistic terms but metaphorically, in highly conventionalized socio-dramatic or characterological terms. I shall be concerned here with those meta-pragmatic ascriptors that "describe" pragmatic features in characterological terms.[3] Like all meta-pragmatic characterizations, they are formulated, inevitably, in referential terms that are organized into (folk) psychologies and characterologies that ignore, if they do not deny, their pragmatic basis.

Such psychologies promote the illusion of a primary, referentially describable basis for their attributions, and as such they not only ground a static, naively empirical view of their subject (one that denies the "creative" dimension of the word), but they also support the conventional arrests, the hypostasizations, and the reifications of individual self-articulations.[4]

Meta-pragmatic ascriptors express in referential language pragmatic features of verbal transactions. Such features are "summarized" meta-pragmatically in socially conventional, more or less precise characterological and psychological terms. They make use of scientific or scientistic terms: "John is an introvert"; "Susan is paranoid"; "Peter is schizy." Or they may make use of more common folk psychological expressions: "John's not much of a joiner"; "Susan sees herself as a victim"; "Peter is timid"; "Susan is suspicious"; "Peter is distracted."

More often such characterizations are imprecise, discursive, and shift from idiom to idiom. They may have what I would call a referential-pragmatic lead-in: "John, well, he doesn't say much; he kind of keeps to himself; I guess he's real timid." "Susan thinks everybody hates her. You smile at her, and you'd think you'd stabbed her in the back; she's a real creep." "Now Peter, you got to understand him; he's real hard to know—kind of unpredictable; sometimes he's with you and sometimes he's way off in left field; yeah, I guess you'd have to say he's got a screw loose; he's a real nut, but likable." Often such characterizations are accompanied by examples of behavior that support the characterizations. Such examples are conventional paraphrases of events that occurred or are likely to have occurred; pragmatically, they serve to support the ultimate, referential characterization. (I should add that such characterological summations, referential as they are, may serve, pragmatically, to put a stop to the characterizing discourse or to shift it to the interlocutor.) Rarely in such characterizations are ego's self-characterizations accepted as referentially adequate.[5] Notions of character, personality, and self are, I believe, meta-meta-pragmatic. They are referential abstractions of referentially expressed and pragmatically persuasive meta-pragmatic statements. Hence when we talk about the notion of self prevalent in a particular society, we are talking about abstractions of meta-pragmatic ascriptions and descriptions, which, if current in the society and not just an outsider's abstraction, feed back on the meta-pragmatic vocabulary and indeed highlight those pragmatic features of the primary discourse that are ideologically relevant.

The illustration of this process presents us with considerable, possibly insurmountable, difficulties. Much of the characterization that takes place is articulated silently, in shadow dialogues. They afford the vantage point for the reflective stance required for such a characterization. (Most often such characterizations are not only *post dictionem* but occur in another conversation with another interlocutor.) Of course such reflective moments may well be triggered by various rhetorical strategies within the primary discourse. Among these are meta-linguistic and what, for want of a better term, I call quasi-meta-linguistic locutions, hedges such as "as it were," "so-to-speak," "if I may say"—expressions that cause a pause in the primary discourse without the speaker's actually making an explicit meta-linguistic comment ("Oh dear, what nonsense I am talking") but rather suggesting a reflective understanding of the meaning of what follows that is left to the interlocutor to determine (Sweetser 1987; Kay 1987). They serve as well to cast the speaker as someone "sensitive to the nuances of language," "cautious," "bright," or "indecisive," and his interlocutor as someone capable of appreciating his sensitivity, caution, brightness, or indecision. They create a complicity between the speaker and his audience.

If characterizations are made in the primary discourse, they often change the direction or the level of discourse. They draw attention in characterological or personality terms to the self-constituting dimension of the primary discourse, and—this is most important for it is a source of very considerable rhetorical power—they evoke the existence of other possible, more privileged, "truer" understandings (rooted, I would argue, in the secondary dialogues) that are somehow external to, and conventionally masked by, the primary discourse. These understandings are placed, in our culture, in that always mysterious and potentially threatening place, the mind of the other. Characterizations can shift the established hierarchical or egalitarian relationship between the speaker and his interlocutor in dramatic ways that may require some sort of redressive maneuvering to restore the "original" relationship. They may, of course, be redressive of some previous disturbance in the established relationship.

To illustrate this process of characterization I will quote from *Alice in Wonderland*. Alice has come to the little house where the Duchess lives. She approaches the door timidly and knocks. The Frog Footman, who is sitting at the door, tells her it is no use knocking because there is too much noise inside for anyone to hear her knock.

"Please, then," said Alice, "how am I to get in?"
"There might be some sense in your knocking," the Footman went on, without attending to her, "if we had the door

between us. For instance, if you were *inside,* you might knock, and I could let you out, you know." He was looking up into the sky all the time he was speaking, and this Alice thought decidedly uncivil.

"But perhaps he can't help it," she said to herself, "his eyes are so *very* nearly at the top of his head. But at any rate he might answer questions.—How am I to get in?" she repeated, aloud.

"I shall sit here," the Footman remarked, "till tomorrow—"

At this moment the door of the house opened, and a large plate came skimming out, straight at the Footman's head: it just grazed his nose, and broke to pieces against one of the trees behind him.

"—or next day, maybe," the Footman continued in the same tone, exactly as if nothing had happened.

"How am I to get in?" asked Alice again, in a louder tone.

"*Are* you to get in at all?" said the Footman. "That's the first question, you know."

It was, no doubt: only Alice did not like to be told so. "It's really dreadful," she muttered to herself, "the way all the creatures argue. It's enough to drive one crazy!"

The Footman seemed to think this a good opportunity for repeating his remark, with variations. "I shall sit here," he said, "on and off, for days and days."

"But what am *I* to do?" said Alice.

"Anything you like," said the Footman, and began whistling.

"Oh, there's no use in talking to him," said Alice desperately: "he's perfectly idiotic!" And she opened the door and went in. (Carroll 1865:80–82)

This playful passage is deceptively simple. The Footman does not seem to engage Alice as a person (despite his "you know's," impersonal and conventional as they are). At first he is caught up in the logic of knocking and entering and then in his stubborn assertion of remaining seated. He shows no wonderment; he makes no characterizations; he seems oblivious to their very possibility. Alice is, however, immediately disturbed by his "uncivil" manner as she calls his behavior, and although she tries to justify it (as a civil person might when confronted with incivility) on the basis of his anatomy ("his eyes are so *very* nearly on the top of his head"), she cannot excuse his refusal "to answer questions." Note that Alice does not say "to answer my questions," but more impersonally "to answer questions." Is the "my" precluded by the Footman's contextual disengagement, his indifference to Alice, leaving her no choice but to re-assert her *I* in repeating, "How am I to get in?" Have we here, incidentally a pun, on the eye of the Frog Footman and Alice's pronominal "I"? Clearly, if the Footman's eye/I is on top of his head, he cannot relate—see/speak—to Alice. Alice's repetition of the question produces a stubborn, almost echolalic "I" in the Footman: "I shall sit here till tomorrow." So caught up is he in this pronouncement, so unmindful of his situation, that the progression of his pronouncement is unaffected even by the plate thrown from the house that grazes his nose. He continues to speak "exactly as if nothing had happened." Finally, after Alice asks yet again how she is to get in (is she only referring to the Duchess's house or also to the Footman's discourse, mind, attention, or engagement?), the Footman answers her in an altogether unpleasant manner: "*Are* you to get in at all? That's the first question, you know." (The narrator chooses, for the first time in the passage, to characterize Alice's feelings rather than to allow her to express them: "Alice did not like to be told so.") Muttering to herself, she characterizes the Footman: he is dreadfully argumentative. Note the partially communicative externalization of this first characterization. A response follows impersonally—from an unclear vantage point—Alice's? the narrator's? It is a semi-objective entry into the mind of the Footman: "The Footman seemed to think this a good opportunity for repeating his remark." Alice asks (Lewis Carroll stresses Alice's I): "But what am *I* to do?" The Footman responds indifferently and begins to whistle. Whistling is a sort of analogue to his previous disengaged utterance. Alice is left desperate. "Oh, there is no use in talking to him. He is perfectly idiotic." And she opened the door and went into the Duchess's house.

We can read this entire passage as a play on the gap between conventional behavior and talk—the signifying chain—and reality—the signified—or as a display of the failure of the pragmatic features of an utterance to engage with its context, creating thereby the highly impersonal, autonomous, dream-like quality of Alice's wonderland. But for our purposes, what is important is the pragmatic basis for Alice's characterizations. They result from a failure in the self-constituting process. Alice is never really acknowledged by the Frog Footman in her particularity; at most she is a stimulus for his cogitations and his willfulness. She herself is unable to address the Footman with the indexical second person pronoun, a "you," but has to refer to him with the third person, anaphoric pronoun, a "he." She seems to be conversing with another (who may just happen to be embodied in the Footman if he should happen to overhear her mutterings) in another dialogue, just as the Footman's "you" in his "you know" could be addressed to anyone, not Alice in particular. Her verbal transactions with the Footman become a text for her that serves (one hopes) to engage another interlocutor (the reader perhaps) in her self-constitution—in a pragmatically resonant dialogue.

Before pursuing the implications of such secondary dialogues that are embedded in a literary text that is written in the third person, affording, thereby, certain meta-pragmatic—psychological or characterological—possibilities not afforded in everyday discourse, let me give a second example, this time an ordinary conversation between two teenage girls whom I will call Christine and Peggy.

C. You know it was really weird. Here I was in this scary movie with Tommy. He was practically a stranger. I couldn't keep my eyes open, but he just sat there—so cool. I really hated him.

P. Yeah, I know what you mean. He isn't fazed by anything.

C. He's really cool.

P. Antarctic.

C. No, he's really a nice guy—kind of sweet. I didn't really know him until then. I got so worked up. I kept seeing the hitcher behind every parked car we passed.

P. Oh, God.

C. Well, I'm not really the scared type, but I kept shutting my eyes in the movies and then . . .

P. Peeking. Yeah, I know what you mean. I do it all the time. It's like cheating but . . .

C. Anyway I got myself so hyper that Tommy had to calm me down—until two in the morning.

P. What'd your father say? He's so strict.

C. He didn't say anything. He must have fallen asleep.

P. Ooh, fresh. Are you going to see him again?

C. Maybe.

P. Come on.

C. Well, maybe on Friday. It's not sure yet. Come on, you've got Rob.

P. Yeah, but . . .

c. Well, Tommy's not your type. You need someone more outgoing. Me, I like the quiet type—cool and confident.

P. Rob's cool and confident.

C. Yeah, but he's outgoing. You need that kind of guy. You're his type. He's got such awesome eyes. Do you think Tommy's my type?

P. You're both kind of . . . Well, you're like, wild, and he's calm and cool.

C. Yeah, I got you. I guess I am kind of wild.

We see in this exchange dramatic, at times almost desperate shifts in alignment—in what Erving Goffman (1983) would call footing—as Christine and Peggy choreograph their relationship—their identities. The stakes are high and, in contrast to Alice's abortive attempts to "reach" the Frog Footman, the two girls are fully engaged. Peggy and Christine as well as Tommy, Rob, and Christine's father are all characterized at some point. Tommy is the central figure. Christine casts him as "practically a stranger," "cool," "a nice guy," "kind of sweet," "quiet," "cool and confident." Peggy repeats Christine's characterizations. She says Tommy "isn't fazed by anything." When she exaggerates Christine's characterization of Tommy as "cool" with an "Antarctic," however, Christine immediately corrects her: "No, he's really a nice guy—kind of sweet." Christine is, from the start, in the dominant position. She speaks more and continually centers the conversation on herself. (She uses a total of twenty-two first person locutions, "I," "my," "mine," and "me," to Peggy's four; she uses five second person locutions to Peggy's four.) Peggy can do little more than echo her. When Peggy tries at one point to turn the conversation to herself—"Peeking . . . I do it all the time. It's like cheating but . . ."—Christine immediately refocuses the conversation on herself and (her) Tommy. She characterizes herself both directly, "I'm not the scared type," and indirectly, "I couldn't keep my eyes open." Peggy never characterizes herself and she accepts Christine's characterization of her. When Peggy does ask Christine directly whether or not she is going to go out with Tommy again, Christine hedges. Why? We do not know. Did Tommy ask her out? She does use the hedging, however, to her advantage. She points out Peggy's possible envy. (We do not know how Peggy looked; she may of course have stimulated such a remark.) "You've got Rob" Christine says, and tells Peggy that Tommy is not her type, restoring thereby her dominant footing. (Peggy may have initiated this through her expression.) Peggy needs someone outgoing, according to Christine; Christine herself needs someone "quiet," "cool," and "confident." Hurt, Peggy insists that Rob is "cool and confident." A serious break between the two girls is imminent. Christine quickly restores the relationship by telling Peggy that Rob, outgoing and with "awesome eyes," is her type, and then with vulnerable hesitation, she asks Peggy if Tommy is her type. Peggy's answer is a stroke of diplomatic genius. She hesitates (complementing Christine's hesitation), she calls Christine "wild" (a term of flattery here), and partially echoes Christine's characterization of Tommy as "cool and confident" with "cool and calm." Christine has no choice but to agree to Peggy's characterization of her. "I guess I am kind of wild." Despite Peggy's dominant position as characterizer of Christine at this moment, Christine remains the center of conversational attention. Does Peggy's characterization of Christine as "wild" reflect the "wildness" of her conversation—in the absence of a cooling and calming Tommy?

With varying degrees of intensity and articulation the constituting of self and other occurs in all verbal transactions. Alice's encounter with the Frog Footman comes as close to being a limiting case as do some of the conversations that occur, or perhaps do not occur, in Beckett's novels, plays, and monologues. (Conversation, it should be remembered, comes from *versari*, to be situated or occupied, and *cum*, with.) Self-characterizations and characterizations of one's interlocutor, however, are not all that frequent in most ordinary conversations, and when they occur, they usually involve some sort of change in the level of discourse and in the footing of the participants. Alice characterizes the Footman in the third person; Christine's self-characterization "I'm not the scared type,"—and her demand to be characterized by Peggy are complex strategies for focusing the exchange. It would seem that their pragmatic function here, as in many similar conversations, overrides whatever semantic value the characterizations have. Indeed, we often ignore a person's self-characterizations, particularly when they are expressed in the present tense, or regard them not as accurate descriptions but symptoms of the person's character.[6]

Characterizations occur in various types of psychotherapy (to produce, for example, insight or abreaction), in certain job interviews (particularly those that measure stress: "You are a bitch"), in amorous conversations ("You're a love"), and in auditions ("You'll never be a Hamlet"). Often the characterizations are given to produce an effect (insight, catharsis, stress, anger, humility, delight, love). There may of course be a good deal of characterizing third parties. Here too these third party characterizations, however accurate diagnostically, serve pragmatic purposes. They may figure in a drama of self-constitution as they did for Christine and Peggy.

Retrospective and third party characterizations demand a level of articulation that does not necessarily occur in the shadow dialogues—the mentation and cogitation that take place alongside the primary self-constituting discourse. Indeed, many of the retrospective and third party accounts describe or conventionally paraphrase these secondary dialogues. Narratives, in the third person, for example, have conventions for describing these (usually immediately reflective) co-occurring thoughts and perceptions. These conventional descriptions, which often obscure even the retrospective dimension of immediate reflection, are not particularly well developed in the passage from *Alice in Wonderland* we have considered, but they are there. "Alice did not like to be told so." "The Footman seemed to think this a good opportunity for repeating . . ." Such descriptions, at least in the realist novels of the nineteenth century (but also in Virginia Woolf and a good deal of Joyce), are expressed in well-formed sentences—descriptions that promote an *interiority*, an independence of mind, and an articulateness of thought that seems co-ordinate with an ideology of individualism. Often, particularly in Trollope, the early George Eliot, and even Jane Austen, such descriptions promote an illusion of an omniscient capacity ironically undermined by a failure of (moral) character that hides its ignorance from itself or presumes an unrealistic extension of its knowledge. Later in the nineteenth century, novels like Eliot's *Daniel Deronda* and in *Doppelgänger* tales probe the limits of lucidity. The moral-and-cognitive (literary) self is sundered, and the resultant point of nonlucidity, located now within the self, is given an institutionalized expression (and the possibility of at least partial correction) in the development of psychoanalysis and its "discovery" of the unconscious. Such a view articulates an individuality that is somehow "independent" of the dialogical—the transactional—dimension of human social life, though, I hasten to add, some privileged (most often parental and sometimes traumatic) transactions from early childhood are incorporated, in a primitive, petrified, form, within the individual's character or self.

Jane Austen's (1816) heroine Emma Woodhouse, "handsome, clever, and rich, with a comfortable home and happy disposition," meets Mr. Frank Churchill. He is the son, by a previous marriage, of a Mr. Weston who has recently married Emma's former governess, Miss Taylor. Emma had a hand in arranging this marriage. Unlike Jane Austen's other heroines, Emma has shown little concern for her own marriage. She is, in Sir Walter Scott's (1815) words, bent "on forging wedlock-fetters for others." Although Frank Churchill is unknown in Highbury—he was taken in by Mr. Weston's wealthy in-laws when he was a child—he is the subject of considerable speculation in this quiet community whose members, at least those of the middle class of whom Austen writes, escape through "the little event" from what seems to be a life of consummate boredom. Frank has been expected for a considerable time, so considerable a time that to some of Emma's set his failure to visit his father and his father's new wife intimate a flaw in his character. Mr. and Mrs. Weston do not conceive of this possibility. They should like to engage

Frank's interest in Emma and Emma's in Frank. Despite herself, Emma is curious about Frank.

Emma opens the door to the parlour and discovers two gentlemen sitting with her father. They are Mr. Weston and his son. Frank had arrived earlier than expected, and Mr. Weston hastened to bring him to visit Highbury's most distinguished family.

> The Frank Churchill so long talked of, so high in interest, was actually before her—he was presented to her, and she did not think too much had been said in his praise; he was a *very* good looking young man: height, air, address, all were unexceptionable, and his countenance had a great deal of the spirit and liveliness of his father's; he looked quick and sensible. She felt immediately that she should like him; and there was a well-bred ease of manner, and a readiness to talk, which convinced her that he came intending to be acquainted with her, and that acquainted they soon must be.   (128)

Emma is pleased with Frank's "eagerness to arrive, which had made him alter his plan, and travel earlier, later, and quicker, that he might gain a half a day" (128). Mr. Weston is, of course, exultant at his son's early arrival, remarking that an early arrival gives such pleasure that is worth the little extra exertion needed. Frank gently corrects his father's observation: "It is a great pleasure, where one can indulge in it, though there are not many houses that I should presume on so far; but in coming *home* I felt I might do anything" (128).

> The word home made his father look on him with fresh complacency. Emma was directly sure that he knew how to make himself agreeable; the conviction was strengthened by what followed. He was very much pleased with Randalls [the Westons' house], thought it a most admirably arranged house, would hardly allow it even to be very small, admired the situation, the walk to Highbury, Highbury itself, Hartfield [the Woodhouse home] still more, and professed himself to have always felt the sort of interest in the country which none but one's *own* country gives, and the greatest curiosity to visit it. That he should never have been able to indulge so amiable a feeling before, passed suspiciously through Emma's brain; but

still, if it were a falsehood, it was a pleasant one, and pleasantly handled. His manner had no air of study or exaggeration.
He did really look and speak as if in a state of no common
enjoyment. (128)

After talking about "subjects in general" that "belong to an
opening acquaintance," Frank "contrived to find an opportunity, while their two fathers were engaged with each other, of
introducing his mother-in-law, and speaking of her with so
much handsome praise, so much warm admiration, so much
gratitude for the happiness she secured to his father, and her
very kind reception of himself, as was an additional proof of his
knowing how to please—and of his certainly thinking it worth
while to try to please her" (129). Frank Churchill's praise continues; he comes near to "thanking Emma" for Miss Taylor's
merits, "without seeming quite to forget that in the common
course of things, it was rather to be supposed that Miss Taylor
had formed Miss Woodhouse's character, than Miss Woodhouse
Miss Taylor's" (129).

> "Elegant, agreeable manners, I was prepared for," said he;
> "but I confess that, considering every thing, I had not ex-
> pected more than a very tolerably well-looking women of a
> certain age; I did not know that I was to find a pretty young
> woman in Mrs. Weston."
>
> "You cannot see too much perfection in Mrs. Weston for my
> feelings," said Emma; "were you to guess her to be *eighteen*,
> I should listen with pleasure; but *she* would be ready to quar-
> rel with you for using such words. Don't let her imagine that
> you have spoken of her as a pretty young woman."
>
> "I hope I should know better," he replied; "no, depend
> upon it, (with a gallant bow), that in addressing Mrs. Weston
> I should understand whom I might praise without any danger
> of being extravagant in my terms."
>
> Emma wondered whether the same suspicion of what might
> be expected from knowing each other, which had taken strong
> possession of her mind, had ever crossed his; and whether his
> compliments were to be considered as marks of acquiescence,
> or proofs of defiance. She must see more of them to understand
> his ways; at present she only felt they were agreeable. (129)

Emma notices the attention Mr. Weston is paying to her exchange with Frank Churchill, and she is "most comfortable" in
her father's "perfect exemption" from any penetration of what
may be transpiring between them. (He is, again in Sir Walter
Scott's words "a silly valetudinarian.") The two visitors soon
leave, Mr. Weston for the local inn where he has some business
and his son to visit Miss Jane Fairfax whom he feigns to know
but slightly. "Emma remained very pleased with this beginning
of the acquaintance, and could now engage to think them all at
Randalls any hour of the day with full confidence in their comfort" (131).

This passage is more complex than the two others we have
considered. The novel's "every sentence, almost every epithet,"
Reginald Farrer wrote in the *Quarterly Review* in 1917, "has its
definite reference to equally unemphasized points before and
after in the development of the plot." The passage I have chosen
is, in fact, pivotal in the unfolding of both plot and character.
There are intimations of Frank's (for want of a better word)
duplicity and Emma's misapprehension—her *méconnaissance*
that, ironically, like all *méconnaissance*, requires a *connais-
sance,* a subliminal knowing of Frank, herself, and her relationship to Frank that is self-masked in her exquisitely commanded
characterization of Frank, Mr. Weston, and her father as well as
in her studied self-observation. What is of interest to us, however, is the manner in which the characterizations are conveyed.
The novel is written in the third person but, as Wayne Booth
(1961) has observed, written largely, though not completely,
through the eyes of Emma herself. The passage contains direct
and indirect quotation as well as free-form quotation (*erlebte
Rede*) of conversation and thinking. At the simplest level this
narrative technique permits the expression of the (putative) simultaneity of Emma's (silent) perception and thought and the
discourse she is participating in or witnessing. Thus as Emma
hears Frank Churchill use the word "home" for his father's
house Randalls ("but in coming *home* I felt I might do anything") we follow Emma's contemporaneous, though silent, observation of Mr. Weston ("his father looked at him with fresh
complacency") and Emma's conviction (a characterization) that

Frank "knew how to make himself agreeable." There are numerous instances of this technique throughout the passage, and they make use, as we shall see below, of complex shifts of sometimes ambiguous vantage points.

What is striking about Emma's or the narrator's observations that lead to explicit or implicit characterizations is that they are less concerned with the referential function of the discourse, quoted or paraphrased, than with its context-producing, its self- and other-constituting effectiveness. Emma's interest in Frank's use of "home" is not referential—he could have used any number of other terms for Randalls—but has to do with its pragmatic implication. "Home" operates here rather like an honorific; it is a meta-pragmatic shifter that gives a certain intimate and personalized quality to Randalls and to Frank Churchill a certain filial sensitivity that produces in his father "a fresh complacency." For Emma, it renders Frank "agreeable"; certainly it shows him capable of making himself agreeable. Emma's characterization of Frank is based here on the pragmatic function of "home" and her characterization is meta-pragmatic. Her conviction is strengthened, we are told, by what follows. Frank professes an exaggerated admiration for Randalls, Highbury, and Hartfield as well as that interest "in a country which none but one's *own* country gives." (The author emphasizes "own.") It is again, I submit, the pragmatic features of Frank's descriptions that lead Emma to a passing "suspicion" that he might have indulged himself in the pleasures of home and Highbury earlier if his feelings were so heartfelt, and to her dismissal of that suspicion: "but still if it were a falsehood, it was a pleasant one, and pleasantly handled." Emma makes similar observations on the basis of Frank Churchill's "handsome praise" and "warm admiration" for Mrs. Weston and the gratitude he claims to have "for the happiness she secured to his father, and her very kind reception of himself." He understood what would be welcome: he could be sure of little else. When Frank speaks of his stepmother's youth, however, Emma corrects him sharply ("Don't let her imagine that you have spoken of her as a pretty young woman"), forcing him to take account of himself ("I hope I should know better") and to extricate himself from this indiscretion through a gallant bow and an ever more gallant bit of flattery: "No, depend upon it, that in addressing Mrs. Weston I should understand whom I might praise without any danger of being thought extravagant in my terms." Such flattery, which calls attention, implicitly, to its own artifice, risks drawing Emma into an intimate but always insecure complicity—a sort of doublebind of the sophisticate—that can only perpetuate the artifice (and ultimately the insecurity) upon which it is built. Emma wonders—she can no longer be sure—"whether the same suspicion of what might be expected from their knowing each other, which had taken strong possession of her mind, had ever crossed his." She wonders whether "his compliments were to be considered as marks of acquiescence, or proofs of defiance." Caught in this hermeneutic impasse, Emma, rather more practical than she sometimes lets on, concludes that "she must see more of them to understand his ways." (The "them" refers back to "compliments.") But she finds his ways agreeable.

Much that transpires in Emma's Highbury is seen through Emma's eyes. Jane Austen's narrative technique permits her, as I have noted, to report conversations and to describe the accompanying thoughts and perceptions of her heroine. A *simultaneity* is conventionally produced that is internal to the narrative and does not seem to be disturbed by the temporal progression, the sequentiality, of the narrative itself. In the passage we have been discussing, many of the paraphrases of Emma's thoughts and perceptions appear to arise from Emma's own unmediated vantage point. "Emma was directly sure that he knew how to make himself agreeable." "He did not advance a word of praise beyond what she knew to be thoroughly deserved by Mrs. Weston; but undoubtedly he could know very little of the matter." "Emma wondered whether the same suspicion of what he expected . . ." (All of these examples are or approximate indirect discourse.) Other paraphrases, however, seem to arise from an external, objectivistic—the narrator's— vantage point, giving the distance that Wayne Booth maintains keeps Emma a sympathetic figure. "Their subjects in general were such as belong to an opening acquaintance." "But when satisfied on all these points, and their acquaintance proportionately advanced, he contrived to find an opportunity, while their two fathers were engaged with each other, of introducing his mother-in-law . . ." The objectivity of such passages—their apparent source in a distinct and separate narrator—is suggested less by grammar than by a coloring, a tonality (through choice of words and turns of phrase) that does not fully coordinate with the coloring and tonality we would expect from Emma as we come to know her. (We should note that the novel begins from the perspective of the narrator and only slowly introduces Emma's perspective.) When we read these objectivistic passages, carefully, however, we often find it difficult to determine exactly where Emma's consciousness ends and the narrator's begins. There is here, as in other novels and stories, I believe, a blurring that has been denied all too frequently by critics who insist upon neat and discriminate vantage points. They fail to take into account the submerged dialogical relationship between a character's vantage point and that of the narrator—and the blurrings that can, and do inevitably, occur.

Such a dialogical relationship is apparent in the following lines.

(1) That he should have been able to indulge so amiable a feeling before, passed suspiciously through Emma's brain;

(2) but still if it were a falsehood, it was a pleasant one, and pleasantly handled.

(3) His manner had no air of study or exaggeration.

(4) He did really look and speak as if in a state of no common enjoyment.

The passage begins from the vantage point of the narrator as indicated by "passed suspiciously through Emma's brain." The Emma we have come to know (stylistically at least) would not be given to such a neuroanatomical figure to describe her own thoughts and perceptions. The second sentence places us within Emma's purview. (Its transitional status, bridging the objectivism of the first sentence with the subjectivism of the third and fourth sentences, is suggested both by the use of the argumentative "but still" and by the semicolon that divides it from the first but not the third sentence.) The third and fourth—declarative—sentences are clearly articulated from Emma's perspective. They state a fact—a characterization—with certainty. There is within this sequence of sentences, I submit, a submerged dialogical progression. From the vantage point of an absent interlocutor, expressed through the objectivistic language of the first sentence, Emma is made to perceive something not particularly agreeable. The second sentence is a response to this undesirable perception. It is argumentative, with its "but still." The third and fourth sentences are assertions that conform less to the "objective fact" (the facts described from a narrator's point of view) of Frank Churchill's duplicitous flattery than to Emma's desired picture of Frank Churchill. But even in these two sentences there is a responsive dimension indicated by the negatives ("no air of study or exaggeration," "no common enjoyment," as well as by the "really" in the fourth sentence: "He did really look and speak as if").

Similar, submerged dialogical progressions can be seen in other passages. Let me quote, once more, the following one: "Emma wondered whether the same suspicion of what might be expected from their knowing each other, which had taken strong possession of her mind, had ever crossed his; and whether his compliments were to be considered as marks of acquiescence, or proofs of defiance. She must see more of them to understand his ways; at present she only felt they were agreeable." Here, the dialogical progression appears to be internal. Caught in a hermeneutical impasse, Emma converses with herself, or more accurately, with a sort of internalized interlocutor—an alter ego. She affirms her stance in the last two sentences in response to a not fully articulated perception of a possibly undesirable aspect of Mr. Frank Churchill. But even in this "internal dialogue" we recognize at least a vestigial identification of the silent, internalized dialogical partner with the narrator; this is suggested, again, by a neuroanatomical figure, "which had taken strong possession of her mind."

It is ironic that the very figures "brain" and "mind" that reveal the submerged dialogue between Emma and the narrator are precisely the figures that serve to mask the dialogical nature of the self. "Brain" and "mind" are, in the West, two of the most preeminent *loci* of the self. They connote independence, autonomy, particularity, originality, individuality, and thinghood. Like mind and brain, the self is conceived as somehow independent of the other, of social transactions; and yet, as we know, this independence is always in question. Psychologies, like the psychoanalytic, have to be conceived as compromises between two contradictory ideological positions: the self (psyche, soul, mind) as somehow independent—a position symbolically affirmed by a series of often crude physical and physiological metaphors—and the self as a product of social interaction. In psychoanalysis, social interaction is primarily restricted to the internalization of parental norms and values during a relatively short period in the individual's development; thereafter, barring traumatic and other exceptional experiences, the individual's self, now formed, seems removed from the influences of social interaction.[7] Such a position conforms, I believe, to a prevalent ideology of individualism that has yet to take account of human sociality.

· II ·

THE DIALOGIC SELF

5.
Text, Transference, and Indexicality

In the "Postscript to the Case of Dora," *Fragment of an Analysis of a Case of Hysteria,* written shortly after *The Interpretation of Dreams* but published five years later in 1905, Freud (1959b, 1942a) considers Dora's transference and his failure to detect it or at least perceive its consequences in the course of her treatment and its abrupt termination. He (Freud 1959b:141, 1942a:281) notes that "psychoanalytic treatment does not create transferences, it merely brings them to light, like so many other hidden psychical factors." He (1959b:139–140, 1942a:280) stresses the extreme difficulty of detecting the transference: "Transference is the one thing the presence of which has to be detected almost without assistance and with only the slightest clues to go upon, while at the same time the risk of making arbitrary inferences has to be avoided."

Freud calls attention here to one of the most ticklish problems of psychoanalysis at both the clinical and the theoretical levels: how do the participants in the psychoanalytic encounter come to understand the complex symbolic nature of the encounter? And how does the analyst make use of that understanding therapeutically? Indeed, is such understanding ever possible? Does it demand a lucidity that, despite years of training, can never be fully achieved by either party to the encounter insofar as both are embedded in that encounter? In psychoanalytic theory the dynamics of the psychoanalytic encounter are understood in terms of transference, that is, of the way the patient and the analyst project onto each other feelings, thoughts, and wishes that relate to some other significant figure, usually a parent or a sibling, in their respective biographies. Understanding of the transference comes through psychoanalysis itself; circularity is avoided through serialization. Having been analyzed, the analyst is, within limits, able to appreciate the role of his own countertransferential relationship to the patient in interpreting the patient's transference to him.

Indeed the "Case of Dora," in which Freud first addresses himself to the phenomenon of transference, attests to the difficulty of detecting and interpreting transference. Freud's own failure to appreciate the role of Dora's transference has been attributed to his failure to understand his own response to Dora—to his own countertransference. The *Fragment* itself has been seen as a product of his countertransference (Lacan 1966; Marcus 1974; Gearhart 1979). The message is clear. Psychoanalysis cannot proceed successfully without an understanding of the dynamics of the encounter. Such an understanding must include not only the patient's experience of the analyst and his expression of it, but also the analyst's experience of the patient and its expression.

The theory of transference and countertransference embedded in Freudian psychology is a refraction of the encounter itself, and thereby conforms to, indeed confirms, its own explanatory ground. We have to ask whether or not the theory of transference and countertransference is a product of the dynamics of the psychoanalytic encounter. Despite meta-psychological claims, there can under such circumstances be no truly metapsychological understanding since there can be no external vantage point from which to view—to question—the theoretical frame itself of transference and countertransference. Like other totalizing systems of interpretation, the Freudian hermeneutic is closed in upon itself.

In this chapter, I will consider Freud's understanding of the dynamics of the psychoanalytic encounter, "the talking cure" as one of his patients dubbed it, and attempt precisely through the consideration of "talk"—reported talk in the case in point—to arrive at a theory of transference and countertransference that is "external" to the Freudian project. My aim is not to offer another explication of Freud's thought but, *through the consideration of Freud's thought,* to examine the nature of such understanding. My concern is hermeneutical. I am less interested in the encounter (except as an occasion for interpretation) than in the interpretation of its dynamics. My use of Freud's texts is ethnological and implies neither acceptance nor rejection of

Freud's thought. It is, however, motivated by the importance of Freud's thought in Western thinking. Freud has not only contributed to that thinking but is very much its product. His work is grounded in, and limited by, a particular epistemological configuration, an episteme (Foucault 1966) which has been determined at least in part, as Jacques Derrida (1967a, 1967b) points out, by writing. Freud's interpretation of the dynamics of the encounter is facilitated by this episteme, specifically by the (derivative) ideological priority given the semantico-referential function of language (Silverstein 1976, 1979)[1] and to the text understood as an objectification of that function. Freud's thought exemplifies essential features of recent Western hermeneutical thought. Whether or not these features are universal is a question that demands comparative study. I hasten to add that such a comparative study will be limited, inevitably, by the same epistemological configuration that has grounded Freud's thought and my own understanding.

The Analogy with *the Interpretation of Dreams* Texts

In the *Fragment* Freud (1959b:139, 1942a:280) contrasts the difficulty of detecting the transference with the ease of interpreting dreams. "It is easy to learn how to interpret dreams, to extract from the patient's association his unconscious thoughts and memories, and to practice similar explanatory arts [*Ubersetzungskunste*]; for these the patient himself will always provide the text."

The text—a written document, a record—gives interpretive certainty.[2] Put into words the dream can be transcribed into a text. In *The Interpretation of Dreams* Freud (1954a:514, 1942b:518) writes with respect to dream texts: "In short, we have treated as Holy Writ what previous writers have regarded as an arbitrary improvisation, hurriedly patched together in the embarrassment of the moment." The distortions that occur in putting the dream into words, Freud argues, are not arbitrary but are as determined as any of the distortions produced by the dreamwork. The dream text may be treated, therefore, as Holy Writ (*Heilige Schrift*). In his 1912 paper "Recommendations to Physicians on the Psychoanalytic Method of Treatment, Freud

(1959h:326) excludes dreams, dates, and "single incidents of a noteworthy kind which can easily be detached from their context to serve an independent purpose as examples" (are there any?) from his general suggestion that notes not be taken during psychoanalytic sessions. In the Case of Dora he (Freud 1959b:24, 1942a:166) writes that the analyst "cannot make notes during the actual sitting with the patient for fear of shaking the patient's confidence and of disturbing his own view of the material under observation." Note-taking focuses attention and promotes selective hearing.

Transference produces no such Holy Writ. Transferences are described by Freud (1959b:138, 1942a:279) in the Case of Dora as "new editions of facsimiles of the tendencies and fantasies which are aroused and made conscious during the progress of analysis." (*Es sind Neuauflagen, Nachbildungen von den Regungen und Phantasien, die wahrend des Vordringens der Analyse erweckt und bewusst gemacht werden sollen.*) Freud also likens them to "new impressions" (*Neudrücke*), "reprints" (*Neuauflagen*), and "revised editions" (*Neubearbeitungen*). He (Freud 1959a, 1945b) uses similar metaphors in "The Dynamics of Transference," which was written in 1912, seven years after the Case of Dora was first published, and in his 1915 paper, "Observations on Transference-Love," he (1959d:387, 1946a: 317) refers to love, and not just transference-love, as "reprints of old traces" (*Neuauflagen alter Zuge*). Transferences are repetitions of past experiences now directed toward the person of the physician.

To put it another way: a whole series of psychological "experiences are revised, not as belonging to the past, but as applying to the person of the physician at the present moment" (Freud 1959b:139). Tranferences extend, Freud adds in "Recollection, Repetition, and Working Through," to all other aspects of the current situation. The primary text of which the transferences are new editions must be inferred from these new or revised editions. Such inferences are supported by Freud's psychology, including his theories of memory, repetition, and the determining influence of the past. Freud does not appear to doubt the existence of an original text. In "Recollection, Repetition, and Working Through," he (1959e:371, 1946b:131) asks what it is the patient in fact repeats during transference: "The answer is that he reproduces everything in the reservoirs of repressed material that has already permeated his general character—his inhibitions and disadvantageous attitudes of mind, his pathological traits of character. He also repeats during the treatment all his symptoms."

The Ideology of Texts

Freud's metaphor of the text and those derived from printing reflect not only the importance of the word, especially the written word, in psychoanalytic understanding (as well as in Freud's own life), but also a particular approach to language and interpretation that stresses the symbolic (the semantico-referential). In the analysis of dreams, as Freud carries it out, the primary focus is on what symbols stand for, refer to, or denote in and of themselves. In the analysis of transference the focus is, I believe, on the pragmatic or deictic, the *indexical*, function of language.[3]

It is important to remember that the same verbal material, say a dream text, can and does carry both functions, and that any stretch of language can carry several, possibly contradictory, indexical functions. Freud's textual or symbolic model of language did not permit him to appreciate fully the difference between the indexical and symbolic function of language. His blindness to the effects of transference cannot be understood solely in terms of countertransference. Conceptual problems also played a role.

To argue that the text gives interpretive certainty is to engage in a mode of concrete thinking—to take solace in the substance, the materiality, of the written word. (*Text* is derived from the Latin *textus*, "something woven," the past participle of *tegere*, "to weave.") Text, as I am using it here, must not be confused with "Text" as it has been used by Roland Barthes (1977) and other structuralist and post-structuralist critics who define Text as a "methodological field," "a process of demonstration," or "an occasion for reading" from the work—"a fragment of substance occupying a part of space of books (in a library for example)." Here I insist on the ambiguous nature of the text as both a methodological field and a fragment of substance. It is this (traditional) ambiguity, rooted in the Western episteme, in the double-face of the sign (or better, of the conception of the sign as double-faced) that permits the play with interpretation. In its work aspect, which, according to Barthes (1977), "closes on the signified" and is only "moderately symbolic," the text offers the comfort and security of the immediate, concrete presence of a single, durable, legitimate, or authoritative—a best—reading. In its methodological aspect as Text, whose field is that of the signifier—open, plural, radically symbolic—it permits the pleasures associated with play and the distinctly bourgeois flirtations with nihilism, iconoclasm, meaninglessness, and chaos that have characterized so much recent literary criticism. It denies the possibility of a best reading. What mediates between the possibility and impossibility of a best reading is the notion of depth: a plunge "downward" to some "arch-text," "deep structure," "unconscious significance," or "true meaning." The metaphor of depth is compelling. Reading, interpretation, and understanding become archeology or philology. Think of the ambiguity of archeological and philological imagery in Freud's writings. In any case, "depth" permits the gathering together and the ranking of multiple, even contradictory readings. Hierarchy is preserved in an egalitarian set. We must recognize the function of courtesy even in our most theoretical endeavors.

Freud (1954a, 1942b) recognizes that the text bears several meanings, even more than are indicated by the all too simple dichotomy between manifest and latent. In his discussion of dream texts and their determination, cited above, Freud (1954a:515, 1942b:519) writes: "The modifications to which dreams are submitted under the editorship of waking life are just as little arbitrary. They are associatively linked to the material which they replace, and serve to show us the way to the material." Note the use of the word *material* in the English translation. The German is *Inhalt*, literally, "content," "tenor," "purport," "subject matter," not "material." The modifications lead, in any case, to new *material* or *contents*. But Freud does not stop with this. With what can be regarded almost as Nietzschean irony (or perhaps it is just a slip of the pen), he concludes the last quoted sentence with "which may in turn be a substitute for something else" (*der selbst wieder der Ersatz eines anderen sein mag*). The dream text leads associatively to other material, to other contents, which replace it, but even these substitutes are substitutes for something else.[4]

Is there a something else? Or are there just other things? Is there no end to interpretations and readings? Freud seems to suggest an infinite interpretive regress here. The problem is by no means unique. All hermeneutical systems are threatened with an interpretive swirl and must provide ideologically supported conventions that arrest it. Such conventions, as Nietzsche (1965:510) points out extravagantly, require a forgetting. "Only by forgetting that primitive world of metaphors, only by the congelation and coagulation of an original mass of similes and percepts pouring forth as a fiery liquid out of the primal faculty of human fancy, only by this invincible faith, that *this* sun, *this* window, *this* table is a truth in itself: in short only by the fact that man forgets himself as subject, only by all this does he live with some repose, safety, and consequence." We can well appreciate Freud's search for certainty in the text. Such certainty was, after all, supported by a venerable philological and hermeneutic tradition itself rooted in the Holy Writ. Psychoanalysis was at the time in its infancy and its ideological props to conventional arrests of the interpretive regress were less than certain. Think of the apologetic tone of many passages in both *The Interpretation of Dreams* and the *Fragment of an Analysis of a Case of Hysteria.*

There is a remarkable irony in Freud's search for certainty: the medium in which he sought certainty—the text, the written word or its possibility—was in fact responsible for the very uncertainty he sought to escape. "In literate culture," Walter Ong (1970:32) writes, "the illusion is widespread that if one has the exact words someone has uttered one has by that very fact his exact meaning." Repetition is possible. One can return to the exact words—to the identical text. Implicit in what Ong calls our chirographic-typographic culture is a whole metaphysics of repetition and identity, of origin and presence, indeed, of possession and meaning.[5] Ong goes on to argue that all interpretation of written records is finally dependent on *present vocal exchange,* whereas we (in the West) feel the spoken word to be "a modification of something which normally is or ought to be written." We fail to preceive that "the word as record depends for its meaning upon the continuous recurrence of the word as event" (Ong 1970:32–33). It is not a record at all but "something that happens, an event in the world of sound through which the mind is enabled to relate actuality to itself" (1970:32). In nonliterate cultures, the word is one with its context. Truth is felt as an event in its immediacy. Repetition and memory, popular opinion notwithstanding, are thematic and not verbatim as in literate cultures. Verbal learning, Ong claims, is celebratory: play and not work. Without records there is no history as we understand it. In literate cultures words, reduced by writing to objects in space, are, despite their quality as object, always removed from actuality. They are "less real (although more permanent) than when they are spoken" (1970:114). They are at a remove from their life-situation, their context of utterance. Their object-ness offers only false security.

We need not accept Ong's portrayal of oral word culture or his idealization of the word. Derrida (1967b:11–12) would probably see in Ong's argument an eloquent statement of the Western "logocentric-phonocentric" heritage in which "absolute proximity of voice and being, of voice and the meaning of being, of voice and the ideality of meaning" is proclaimed. The very idealization of the spoken word, masked on occasion by the idealization of the written word, would itself be seen as a consequence of writing. Language, as Derrida (1976:52) maintains in a brilliant if scandalous conceit, is "a species," "a general possibility" of writing; through writing, taken not altogether metaphorically, the (unity of the) sign is sundered. "The exteriority of the signifier is the exteriority of writing in general . . . Without that exteriority, the very idea of the sign falls into decay" (1976:14). The sign and language generally are constituted by a radical alterity—by "differance" (*differance*) understood both as a sort of temporal deferment, "by the time of a breath," of the signifier from signified, and as the relation of opposition (differences) that obtains among the elements in any linguistic system (1976:18). Alterity within unity, difference within identity, absence within presence—Derrida's Hegelianism is apparent—are constituted by writing and "deseminated" in such notions as the psyche and as conscious/unconscious.[6] Ong's emphasis on decontextualization through writing (the removal of the word from its actuality) is of particular significance. The wrenching of the word from its context, the possibilities of reconstruction, and those of the exploitation of an utterance are of a magnitude that is unattainable in a purely oral culture. (I am writing again within the confines, the *clôture,* of a metaphysics that postulates the possibility of a purely oral culture— within the confines of our unregenerate, though self-conscious, anthropological discourse.) Memory is extended. The chain of quotation, of interlocutors reporting what they heard, is depersonalized. Quotation becomes possible even when the original context of utterance is completely lost, where only fragments remain. Scholarship, Talmudism, and textual criticism become realities. Utterances are given a political dimension and a textual authority they never had before, and this dimension, this authority, affects all social discourses, especially ones that, like the psychoanalytic, aspire to authenticity and fullness.

To assume as Ong does that the context of the spoken word (even in nonliterate cultures) is "furnished ready made" is to fail to grasp the creative function of pragmatic expressions (Silverstein 1976, 1979). They do not simply refer to the context of utterance, they precipitate it. The context of utterance, and the meanings that obtain therein, are always negotiated by the parties to the utterance according to certain conventional rules. There is probably never full agreement about the context and its meanings (if for no other reason than the existence of differing perspectives imposed by the "I" and the "you" which are also embedded collusively in the "we"),[7] but accommodation or acquiescence to a version may be determined by power or, as we might say, "pragmatic considerations." Such a version belongs to none of the parties to the encounter, but it is usually presumed to be the reality of one's counterpart to which one has acquiesced to expedite the matter at hand. This presumption, which is rarely articulated in most ongoing social transactions, gives one the comforting illusion of knowing one's counterpart and his or her reality. Expressed in pragmatic terms, it permits a certain disengagement from the reality of the transaction. The disengagement helps to insulate the participants from the repercussions of failure. It preserves the "I" and the "you" within the "we." The "we," Jean-Paul Sartre (1956:414) notes, "is experienced by a particular consciousness." The acquiescence permits, too, a superior stance in the inevitable jockeying for power in such negotiations.

The Limits of Decontextualization

Deixis does serve at any rate to set at least illusory limits to the possibility of decontextualization, and thereby it limits the indiscriminate politicizing of discourse. It is interesting to recall that in the quotation from Nietzsche's (1965, 1966) posthumous essay, "Truth and Falsity in an Ultramoral Sense," cited above, he made use of the deictic demonstrative adjective "*this*"— "*this* sun, *this* window, *this* table"—in his contention that only by forgetting themselves as "artistically creating subjects" do individuals "live with some repose, safety, and consequence."[8] In this essay Nietzsche (1965:507) is particularly concerned with the distortions through generalization that come with naming and the formation of ideas. "Let us especially think about the formation of ideas. Every word becomes at once an idea not by having, as one might presume, to serve as a reminder for the original experience happening but once and absolutely individualized, to which experience such word owes its origin, no, but by having simultaneously to fit innumerable, more or less similar (which really means never equal, therefore altogether unequal) cases. Every idea originates through equating the unequal." Nietzsche goes on to show how this equation leads to the idea, say, of a leaf. By disregarding the "individual and the real" we are left with idea and form.

Whatever we may think of Nietzsche's insistence on the distortion inherent in the production through words of ideas, we must grant that much of what transpires during psychoanalysis and in the course of ethnographic research is an attempt to reproduce the *original,* the *real,* the *individual* (even where there was no "original," "real," or "individual"). The patient works to overcome the generalizing power of words and the analyst's freedom to construct or reconstruct the events indexed as having occurred elsewhere and in the past, through the assertion of the here-and-now. Analysts, too, in their reconstructions (think of Freud's insistence on the *reality* of Wolf Man's primal scene) insist on the original, the real, and the individual, but, ideally, unlike the patient caught within the transference, only assert a *relationship* between the original event and the present.[9] Put perhaps too simply: through the transference the patient attempts to bring the past in all its originality into the present: to declare, and not just in memory as did Augustine, the present-ness of past relationships.[10] Whether through verbal or nonverbal means, the patient attempts to index a past relationship or event as present: to render the time referred to in an utterance the same as the time of the utterance, to confuse narrative time with the time of narrative performance.

In my field research in Morocco with the members of a religious brotherhood, the Hamadsha, who specialize in the cures of the demon-struck and the demon-possessed, I found that certain members of the brotherhood frequently confused narrative times with the time of performance. One man in particular, Tuhami, about whom I (1980; see also Chapter 11) have written extensively, would attempt to revivify his past and even modify it through his stories. In recounting a movie he had seen, he would insert himself in it, adopt it, and confirm his adoption through his narrative. Such subterfuges are not unknown to the psychiatrist. They are also part of everyday life and its evocative expressions and vicarious participations. They reflect the conventions of narrative operative in a particular culture and the participations permitted therein. Maurice Leenhardt (1979) reported that the natives of New Caledonia would be carried away by their language to the very spot where the story they were recounting took place. If storytellers happened to forget the name of a place in their story, they would refuse to—they could not—continue their narration. "He feels himself inexact; he is really lost in the geographical area of his story" (Leenhardt 1979:84). Similar participations by storytellers and their listeners, by actors and their audiences, have been reported elsewhere in the ethnographic literature. They seem to parallel ritual identifications and possessions. They are not unfamiliar to the Westerner carried away by a particular tale, and they have been sought—and experienced—by Western writers.

Dora

In the Case of Dora, however condensed and subject to Freud's conscious and presumably unconscious selection, it is still possible to perceive something of the indexical assertion of past into present. This case history, Freud (1959b:16–17, 1942a:166–167) tells us, was "only committed to writing from memory, after the treatment was at an end," but while his "recollection of the case was still fresh" and was "heightened" by his "interest in publication."[11] "Thus the record [*Niederschrift*] is not absolutely—phonographically—exact, but it claims to possess a high degree of trustworthiness" (1959b:17).

Freud (1954b, 1950) conceives of the *Fragment* as a practical extension of *The Interpretation of Dreams* and organizes his presentation around two of his patient's dreams. At eighteen, Dora was brought against her will to Freud by her father. Since childhood she had suffered from a number of "hysterical" symptoms which had recently intensified. These included dyspnea, migraine, nervous coughing accompanied by a loss of voice, a pseudo-appendicitis, a periodic limp, and vaginal catarrh. (Dora had seen Freud two years earlier because of her cough and hoarseness, but as her symptoms went quickly into remission, she received no prolonged treatment.) At the time of her second visit to Freud, she was on bad terms with her parents and chronically depressed, had lost consciousness in an altercation with her father, and had written a suicide note. Dora's family circumstances are reminiscent of one of Schnitzler's *Kamerastücke.* She lived with her parents in a health resort to which her father had retired twelve years earlier because of tuberculosis. There, her family had become the intimate friends of Herr and Frau K. Frau K had nursed Dora's father during his illness and apparently became his mistress; Dora cared for the Ks children and had become "almost a mother to them"; she took long walks with Herr K, who, according to Dora, had approached her sexually on two occasions. She rebuffed him, and on the second occasion reported his overture to her mother, an apparently obsessive *Hausfrau,* who told Dora's father. Confronted with Dora's accusations Herr K denied them adamantly, suggesting that they were a product of her imagination. Dora's father believed Herr K's story and refused to break off with the Ks as his daughter wished. Freud remarks at one point that Dora's father had handed her over to him for psychotherapy just as her father and Frau K had handed her over to Herr K. A detailed consideration of Freud's analysis is beyond the scope of this paper. The reader should remember, however, that although Freud recognized in Dora's first dream her desire to give up treatment, he was startled when she did in fact break it off.

The Past in the Present

Let me cite two examples from the *Fragment* of the indexical assertion of the past into the present. They both concern Dora's first dream.

> A house was on fire. My father was standing beside my bed and woke me up. I dressed myself quickly. Mother wanted to stop and save her jewel-case; but Father said: "I refuse to let myself and my two children be burnt for the sake of your jewel-case." We hurried downstairs, and as soon as I was outside I woke up. (Freud 1959b:8)

> [In einem Haus brennt es, *erzählte Dora*, der Vater steht vor meinem Bett und weckt mich auf. Ich kleide mich schnell an. Die Mama will noch ihr Schmuckkästchen retten, der Papa sagt aber: Ich will nicht, dass ich und meine beiden Kinder wegen deines Schmuckkästchens verbrennen. Wir eilen herunter, und sowie ich draussen bin, wache ich auf]. (Freud 1942a:225)

It should first be noted that although the German text of the dream was written in the present tense, it has been inexcusably translated by the Stracheys into the past tense. The dream, a recurrent one, first occured after Herr K's second attempted seduction of Dora. Dora associates its recent recurrence to an argument between her father and mother over locking the dining room. In discussing the jewel-case, which Dora relates to a gift Herr K gave her a short time before and which Freud sees as a symbol of female genitals, Freud (1959:85–86, 1942a:232) explains that the dream means Dora is ready to give Herr K what his wife has withheld from him.

The dream confirms once more what I already told you before you dreamed it—that you are summoning up your old love for your father in order to protect yourself against your love for Herr K. But what do all these efforts show? Not only that you are afraid of Herr K, but that you are still more afraid of yourself, and of the temptation you feel to yield to him. In short, these efforts prove once more how deeply you loved him.

[Wie ich's Ihnen schon vor diesem Traume gesagt habe, der Traum bestätigt wieder, dass Sie die alte Liebe zum Papa wachrufen, um sich gegen die Liebe zu K. zu schutzen. Was beweisen aber alle diese Bemühungen? Nicht nur, dass Sie sich vor Herr K. furchten, noch mehr fürchten Sie sich vor sich selber, vor Ihrer Versuchung, ihm nachzugeben. Sie bestatigen also dadurch, wie intensiv die Liebe zu ihm war.]

After this quotation of himself, Freud (1959b:86, 1942a:232) adds, in a footnote, that he told Dora:

Moreover, the reappearance of the dream in the last few days forces me to the conclusion that you consider that the same situation has arisen once again, and that you have decided to give up treatment to which it is only your father who makes you come.

[Ubrigens muss ich aus dem Wiederauftauchen des Traumes in den letzten Tagen schliessen, dass Sie dieselbe Situation für wiedergekommen erachten, und dass Sie beschlossen haben, aus der Kur, zu der ja nur der Papa Sie bringt, wegzubleiben.]

There is a warmer, more colloquial, certainly more paternal tone in the original German than in the English translation of this passage. Dora does not readily accept Freud's suggestion, and Freud himself, as we know, ignores his own insight. In the next session Freud relates the dream back to Dora's early childhood, to bedwetting. Just as Freud thought his interpretation of the dream complete, Dora adds that when she wakes up from the dream, she always smells smoke and, at least according to Freud, relates the dream to one of his rejoinders, "There can be no smoke without fire" and to his being a passionate smoker (as were Herr K and Dora's father). Dora, Freud (1959b:90, 1942a:236) suggests, would like to have had a kiss from him.

This would have been the exciting cause which led her to repeat the warning dream and to form her resolution of stopping treament; but owing to the characteristics of "transference" the validity is not susceptible to definite proof.

[Dies war für sie der Anlass, sich den Warnungstraum zu wiederholen und den Vorsatz zu fassen, aus der Kur zu gehen. So stimmt es sehr gut zusammen, aber vermoge der Eigentümlichkeiten der "Übertragung" entzieht es sich dem Beweise.]

From even this paraphrase of Dora's sessions with Freud it is clear that Dora insists on "the present" of the dream and that Freud seems anxious to relate it back to Dora's childhood, except when he considers the transference. Certainly by bringing up the smell of smoke after Freud thought his interpretation complete, Dora renders the past present.

The second example, in fact a continuation of the first, involves Dora's playing with a small reticule—opening it, putting her finger in it, and shutting it—at the session following her denial of ever having masturbated. The theme of masturbation was brought up by Freud in his discussion of bedwetting. He does not consider its significance for the tranference but sees it only as a symptomatic act (*Symptomhandlung*) confirming his interpretive insight.

Self-Constitution in Discourse

The temporal movement in psychoanalytic discourse, taken in its fullest sense to include both verbal and nonverbal communications, is considerably more complex than a simple indexical assertion—a repetition—during the transference of past into present (or at times, as in Freud's analysis of Dora's dream, of present into past). The movement is, as Lacan (1966:215–226) notes, dialectic—in the sense of dialogue—and has, despite the analyst's silences, to be understood as such.[12] The patient's narration, including the recounting of dreams and their associations, is in response to the analyst's presence, interpretations, constructions and reconstructions, as well as silences—just as the analyst's words are a response to the patient's presence, words, and silences.[13]

Dialogues, whatever their subject matter, are always dramas of self-constitution. The psychoanalytic dialogue includes (and this renders the drama even more complex) the interpretation of transference and countertransference. The interpretations themselves serve to arrest, perhaps more accurately to support theoretically the arrest, of the self-constitutive process. Directed toward the other, the transferences are paradoxically lodged in the self by the other, in the patient by the physician. (The case of countertransference is more complex because it is mediated by the analyst's own analyst or some other significant person.) As "new editions," "revised editions," "facsimiles," "new impressions," and "reprints," transferences are metaphorically objectified and given, to speak figuratively, a life of their own. In "Recollection, Repetition, and Working Through," for example, Freud (1959e:374, 1946b:135) writes: "The transference thus forms a kind of intermediate realm between illness and real life, through which the journey from the one to the other must be made." Similar locutions occur elsewhere in Freud's writings and in the writings of other analysts: Transferences are situated, possessed even, and they enter the drama of self-constitution. Theory cannot be divorced here from practice.

Transference and countertransference can readily be interpreted in terms of the drama of self-constitution. Self and other, patient and analyst, are constantly indexing each other as they would themselves. There is in this drama minimally a double set of indexical possibilities for the two participants. On the one hand, there is the set of the socially typified physician and patient between whom there is said to be a "working relationship" or "therapeutic alliance," and, on the other hand, there is the set of transference and countertransference figures between whom the transference and countertransference operates. To separate these two sets, as some theorists have attempted to do (Zetzel 1956; Greenson 1965, 1967; Greenson and Wexler 1969), or to merge them as others have tried to do (Klein 1932; Rosenfeld 1965), is to oversimplify the psychoanalytic encounter. Both sets of possibilities are essential to analysis and cannot be understood in isolation. Much of what transpires during analysis can be understood as indexical switching from one set to the other.[14] Freud was both physician and father/lover to Dora, and

Dora was both patient and daughter/lover to Freud.[15] Consider, for example, the way in which Freud uses the formal German "you," (*Sie*)[16] to address Dora—the pronoun is perhaps appropriate for a physician addressing a patient of Dora's age and social status—and *Papa* (unfortunately translated as "father") when he talks about Dora's own father. "Papa" tends to infantilize Dora. Dora's discourse must be understood as both a stimulus and a response to Freud's words. Dora, it will be remembered, referred to her own parents in recounting the dream as *der Papa* and *die Mama.* Both sets of identities are indexed within the utterance and permit thereby the play between past and present that we have noted. Given the patient's talk and the analyst's silence and controlled interventions, the patient's transference is always more apparent than the analyst's, but, as we have been assured, with care the analyst's transference can also be read.

Reading a Transference

What does it mean to read, to interpret, a transference? Lacan (1966:225), whose view of language is essentially referential, answers revealingly: "Nothing other than to fill this dead point with a decoy." *Le vide de ce point-mort*, literally, the emptiness of neutral (in a car's transmission), refers to a stagnant moment in the analytic dialectic in which the appearance/ghost (*l'apparition*) of permanent modes by which the subject constitutes objects occurs. Lacan's imagery here, like Freud's printing imagery, reflects the insufficiency of their models of language. We have, as Freud continually points out, no transference text in the way we have a dream text. We have "new and revised editions" from which, like an archeologist or philologist, the analyst reconstructs the original text. Unlike the dream text, these secondary texts do not offer the same (however illusory) certainty and security. Why? I believe the answer lies in the fact that there is not and never was a primary text, nor, for that matter, new and revised ones, *that in any way resemble the understood dream text.* I am not denying here that the indexical play interpreted in terms of transference is a repetition of past behavior. It may well be. Analysts, who, under most circumstances, have access *only* to the patient's present behavior, can neither prove nor disprove their biographical reconstructions. These—and the fact of repetition—must remain hypothetical. The same argument, a little more complex, holds for the interpretation of countertransference. What I am stressing here is that dream interpretation in *The Interpretation of Dreams* and in the Case of Dora is based on semantico-referential function of language, and the interpretation of transference on the indexical function. The dream text, a concatenation of symbols (of distinct grammaticality: primary process), is to be understood symbolically. The transference is detected not from the symbolic features of language but from the indexical (understood both narrowly and broadly). The dream text can of course (and does) give clues to the transference, for it too serves inevitably an indexical function.

A primary text, the dream text, is the object of the semantico-referential, the symbolic, interpretation. It is embedded in a specific context, its context of utterance, and in a secondary context—the context of associations that are elicited. Through a series of interpretive operations analysts produce a secondary text ("the latent content"), which they assert to be the meaning of the primary dream text ("the manifest content"). This second text is itself symbolically understood. (Like the primary dream text, the secondary one carries certain indexical possibilities which figure in the ongoing psychoanalytic dialogue.) Like all symbolically understood discourse, the dream text, particularly the secondary dream text, is considered to be more or less independent of context. The integrity of its meaning survives subsequent quotation. It has, or is assumed to have, a certain truth. For our purposes the important point is that the meta-language by means of which the dream texts, primary and secondary alike, are described and understood is semantico-referential. Moreover, the meta-language of the semantico-referential function of language is, as Silverstein (1976) notes, itself semantico-referential. The semanticity (the symbolicity) of the meta-language of the symbolic replicates the semantico-referential function of the described texts, the primary and secondary dream texts. Given the "scientific" status of the meta-language, it legitimates and confirms the symbolic understanding of these texts.

Conversely, the interpretation of transference and counter-transference yields no text that in any way resembles the symbolically understood dream text. The clues for transference are indexical; having no independence, they relate the utterance immediately to a presupposed or created context. They embed the utterance—its "truth"—in that context. There is—and this is most important—no indexical meta-language for describing the indexical function of language. There can therefore be no replication of function in the meta-language of the described function. The semanticity of the meta-language of indexicality does serve, I believe, if only by analogy to the semanticity of the meta-language of the symbolic, to mask the indexical status of the indices—the clues for transference. There is, as Silverstein (1979) observes, a "tendency to rationalize the pragmatic system of language, in native understanding, with an ideology of language that centers on reference and prediction." The structure of indexical functions "is understood and represented in meta-pragmatic ideology as a kind of *metaphorical transfer* (analogy) from the structure and asymmetric symbolism of semantico-referential categories, particularly as embedded in lexical form" (Silverstein 1979). By extension, the meta-language used to describe and interpret transference and counter-transference is the same meta-language that is used to describe and interpret the dream text or perhaps more accurately the dream work.

This point should be stressed, for the symbolic nature of the meta-indexical language facilitates the (illusion of) consistency and coherence in psychoanalytic understanding and, I believe, in other similarly constituted hermeneutical systems. These would include both interpretive systems studied by anthropologists and those of which anthropologists themselves make use. Mystification (or at least a certain species of mystification) can perhaps be understood as a "cover-up" of the potential *décalage* between the way an event or set of relations is symbolically constructed and the way it is indexed. As a corollary, demystification (or a certain species of demystification) is an uncovering

of the *décalage*. The uncovering, in certain Marxist interpretations and in psychoanalytic interpretations of nonpsychoanalytic
situations (for example, transference and countertransference
in the ethnographic encounter), may involve the use of an extra-
systemic ("nonnative") symbolic meta-language—the interpreter's—to describe intrasystemic (the participants') indexical
process. This indexical process is granted a kind of existential
priority legitimated by the "scientific" or other privileged
status of the interpreter's hermeneutic. The intrasystemic indexical process, understood in terms of the interpreter's privileged meta-language, reflects, then, the "real" relations or the
"real" nature of the event. Entrapped within their own language, the participants are precluded understanding of the
"real" nature of the relations or events. Any demystification,
any interpretation, involves a one-upmanship which is always
illusory, for the interpreter's interpretation is always subject to
one-upmanship by another, outside interpreter equipped with
yet another "authoritative" hermeneutic.

When Freud attempts to construct the original transference
text, he is, I fear, only historicizing the symbolic meta-language
of the ongoing indexical drama of self-constitution, which is
misleadingly metaphorized as a new or revised edition. The
printing metaphor conceals the indexical nature of the "clues"
(*Anhaltspunkte*) to transference by relating them to dream and
similar texts. In fact, text is to symbol as edition is to index, in
Freud's metaphorical usage. As historicized constructions or,
less accurately, reconstructions of the ongoing symbolically understood indexical drama of self-constitution, the constructions
and reconstructions support both the symbolic interpretations
of the dream text and other privileged communications and the
momentary arrests in the ongoing process of self-constitution.
Through the interpretation of transference and countertransference, "the moments of stagnation in the analytic dialectic"
are privileged (Lacan 1966). The subjects, *les sujets*, the subjec-
tivities, constituted in and through the analytic discourse are, as
in any self-reflective movement including those that occur in
the ethnographic encounter, rendered objects unto themselves
and their counterparts—objects which conform to a particular,
desired view of human beings.[17] Paradoxically, the symbolically

facilitated dialectical arrests and objectifications of the participants to the analytic dialectic lead (so it is argued in other terms)
to patients' liberation from the constraints of their own (symbolically understood) biography. Psychoanalysis can be understood,
though it need not be so understood, as a drama of self-
constitution, masked symbolically by biography and revealed
indexically by, among other things, the assertion of the past into
the present. Only by remembering himself as an "artistically
creating subject," to use Nietzsche's words, can the patient
escape the hold of these congealed and coagulated metaphors
that give him—we may now say—*illusory* repose, safety, and
consequence.

6.
Talking (about) Psychoanalysis

At the beginning of *The Psychological Frontiers of Society*, Abram Kardiner (1945:1) wrote: "There is today no discipline which can be called a science of society; there is only a group of social sciences, each of which has been isolated and self-contained as regards the subject matter." Today, more than forty-five years after Kardiner wrote these words, they still hold true, despite efforts to achieve a unified social science or, as the French would prefer, a unified science of man. There may be even less unity in the sciences today than there was at the time Kardiner was writing. Indeed, the very notion of unity has been questioned. Postmodernist critics see unity as an artifice—an arbitrary conventional narrative that is no longer compelling (Lyotard 1979; Tyler 1986; 1987). Kuhnian romantics would maintain that traditional notions of unity break down anyway in a world like ours, whose paradigm or paradigms of knowledge are shifting (Kuhn 1970). More conservative critics would argue that there can be no notion of unity in a world in which political confidence, moral certainty, and epistemological cohesiveness have been shattered.

Certainly in anthropology today, in psychoanalysis, and, I suspect, in the other social sciences, there is (and I pun) an apprehension of immanent, radical change, the nature and consequences of which are not yet clear. There is a sense that the assumptions and methodologies upon which these sciences are based are no longer (and have never really been) particularly adequate. They have been called a fiction that has sustained a picture of the world, a social philosophy, and an ideology of individualism and materialism that no longer seem morally or psychologically satisfactory.

Kardiner (1945:1) observed that "There has been more agreement in respect to techniques largely through the influence of the natural sciences. The result was that only those data were considered relevant for the social sciences that could be treated by the proofs and quantitative procedures so successful in the natural sciences." Today there is far less agreement about techniques and methodologies in the social sciences than when Kardiner was writing. In anthropology an important split separates those who continue to align their science with the natural sciences—their opponents call them "positivists," somewhat pejoratively—from those who see their discipline as essentially interpretive and align themselves with the humanities, history, and philosophical hermeneutics. I have heard their opponents call them "intellectuals" with all the derogation an anti-intellectual can muster. What is striking is that the purview of anthropology, so divided, is no longer restricted to data "that could be treated by the proofs and quantitative procedures so successful in the natural sciences." Similar splits rend psychoanalysis—a discipline certainly with a fissiparous history—between practitioners who stress causal models for psychological expression and those who emphasize *the* interpretation of psychological expression in its own right.

Given these internal schisms, the relationship between anthropology and psychoanalysis, which has always been uneasy despite the efforts of men like Kardiner, becomes all the more problematic. In the guise of one intellectual argument or another, a good deal of jockeying for priority takes place between the two disciplines. Anthropologists have been markedly ambivalent about psychoanalysis. Many, the majority perhaps, have rejected its utility for anthropology. They see psychoanalysis as a culture-specific psychology whose universalist claims are blatantly reductionist. Others acknowledge the utility of psychoanalytic techniques for the collection of data but are reluctant to accept, except in the most superficial way, psychoanalytic explanation. And still others—the psychoanalytic anthropologists—argue that not only psychoanalytic techniques but psychoanalytic interpretations and explanations, *with appropriate modification,* offer a key to ethnographic understanding. As a group, they resent the failure of psychoanalysis to integrate their findings in any serious way into its theory and, where appropriate, its practice. It must be admitted that despite years of interest, at least since the publication of *Totem and Taboo* in 1913, psychoanalysts have used the findings of ethnographers in a rather *ad hoc* way to support rather than to challenge their given theories. Consider—and I make no academic judgment here about the worth of their contributions—how seldom the works of Geza Roheim, George Devereux, Paul Parin, Kardiner himself, Melford Spiro, or Robert LeVine are debated in psychoanalytic circles! I am not keening the unheard voices of psychoanalytic anthropologists—of anthropologists generally—but simply noting a fact that has to be accounted for in terms of the structure of the two disciplines and their respective position in our society.

Anthropology and psychoanalysis differ not only in terms of their purview but also, perhaps more significantly, in terms of their structure as disciplines.[1] Psychoanalysis has what can be called, not pejoratively, a theological structure. It has a privileged body of texts, essentially the Freudian corpus, that determine its boundaries, ground its therapy and research, and limit what might otherwise be an infinite interpretive regress. There are, of course, other texts of varying authority that may elaborate the primary corpus (within limits that are never so fully elaborated as to avoid some negotiation), but ultimate authority lies with the primary texts. Too great a deviation from what is taken to be the meaning of these primary texts usually leads to denunciation, cries of heresy, and excommunication. There are institutions that support the discipline's structure by providing initiatory procedures, standards of membership, channels of publication, a tribunal, and, as in the case of the expulsion of Jacques Lacan, procedures of excommunication.[2] Members of the institutions, the majority of whom are in private practice, do not form as institutionalized a community as the academic scholars, who are bound to their universities and restricted by limited financial means. Heretical groups have tended to organize themselves along these same institutional lines. Attempts to mend rifts and breaches have rarely succeeded. The "closed" structure of the discipline has been masked more or less successfully by an open-ended, progressivistic ideology that is shared with other contemporary sciences.

In contrast, anthropology has no central text, though there

have been frequent attempts to put forward some texts, those of Boas, Malinowski, and Radcliffe-Brown, for example. There is, in fact, little agreement on the subject matter of the discipline. Anthropological practice is restricted at least symbolically to fieldwork, and despite numerous accounts of the field experience and several methodological treatises on the subject, the nature of fieldwork is still conventionally described by the all but meaningless phrase "participant observation." Without a central, authoritative text, interpretation is always uncertain. Reference may be made to the "canon," but as there is little agreement about the canon, such reference is rhetorical and does little to assuage the anguish of interpretive uncertainty. Reference to authoritative texts in other disciplines is no more efficacious, because anthropology does not share the cultural assumptions and institutional features of these other disciplines. Anthropology has a much looser institutional structure than psychoanalysis. There are no set initiatory procedures; standards of membership are ethical rather than theoretical; there is no tribunal and no procedures for excommunication other than for ethical reasons. Under such circumstances there can be no official heresies, only contesting schools of thought. The recent proliferation of associations reflects differences in theoretical orientation but these are not, to my knowledge, exclusive.

José Ortega y Gasset (1961) claimed that "The choice of a point of view is the initial act of any culture." I believe the same can be said for any scholarly or scientific endeavor, *but* for that endeavor to continue in a serious scholarly or scientific way, the point of view always has to be challenged. Otherwise, we risk taking repetition for innovation, ideology for knowledge. Of all scientific disciplines, anthropology is unique in that *up to a point* it has incorporated that challenge to its own vantage point in its very stance (Crapanzano 1987). The anthropologist has to listen to those whom he studies; he has constantly to relativize his own position, to question his most basic assumptions about himself and the nature of the world in which he lives and to contemplate, with requisite courage and irony too, the always somewhat terrifying possibility of otherness.

In other words, inherent in the ethnographic stance is a subversion of that stance. The anthropologist is at risk. The way in which anthropology's knowledge is constituted, interpreted, and preserved is unstable. One consequence is a compensatory, sometimes irritable (if I may speak figuratively) clinging to a particular model, metaphor, or theoretical construct that is often borrowed uncritically from another authoritative discipline and legitimated thereby. A further consequence of this inherent instability is a marked tendency to reduce the challenge to perspective to mere rhetoric and to retreat into a sort of ethnographic hermeticism. In fact, anthropologists are known in and out of university circles to be closed in upon themselves and to avoid any *real* intellectual engagement with representatives of other disciplines. Anthropology's relationship to psychoanalysis, even with the qualifications I have made, is somewhat of an exception.

The uncritical acceptance of "outside" models, metaphors, and theoretical constructs, the hermeticism, and the failure to engage with other scholarly disciplines are a great pity, for anthropologists eschew thereby a certain intellectual responsibility. The challenge they present to their own vantage point and assumptions, through harkening to the word of the other, can and ought to be extended to other disciplines. I have likened the anthropologist to the trickster—to Hermes the messenger god whose messages toppled the worlds of many to whom they were delivered. He can also be likened to a gadfly who constantly irritates the intellectually complacent by reminding them of the possibility of other ways of articulating and understanding the world and themselves. I am not promoting the destructive pleasures of iconoclasm or of extreme relativism. I am simply suggesting that the anthropologist, not as some omnipotent hero but as an ordinary man or woman who has seen and had to reckon with the radically different, conveys this experience to those who might otherwise remain unchallenged—or, perhaps more accurately, challenged within the conventions of the endeavor. In this respect the anthropologist offers the reader at least the illusion of an external vantage point on his world and the possibility of viewing that world differently, critically, and hopefully creatively.

In this spirit, and contrary no doubt to Kardiner's hope for a unified social science, I suggest that it is *precisely* conflict between anthropology and psychoanalysis that can be most creative. Nowadays, we often speak of dialogue between two disciplines, and when we do so, we usually use "dialogue" rhetorically to refer to some sort of merging of perspectives—what Hans Georg Gadamer (1975) calls a *fusing of horizons*—and we risk denying the agonistic dimension of dialogue. For any communication to occur, as anyone who has had experience with schizophrenics knows, some common ground must be shared by the parties to the communicative act, if only the desire to communicate. But to assume that these grounds and assumptions remain fixed (as so many models of communication suggest) is to fail to take into consideration the temporal dimension of communication that affords agonistic possibility (Veltrusky 1976). It is to freeze discourse, or more accurately, to freeze our understanding of discourse in a manner that is familiar to everyone who has worked with obsessive-compulsives, the severely depressed, the paranoid, and the panicked.

How then does an anthropologist talk about psychoanalysis? He is confronted with the same problems he confronts whenever he talks about any culture, particularly his own. The problem is to find an appropriate vantage point. Is it possible for a Western anthropologist to find a completely external vantage point on psychoanalysis? Is it possible to talk about psychoanalysis without talking psychoanalysis? It is this problem—the problem of a fully independent but adequate meta-language—that led to the parentheses around "about" in the title of this chapter.

Insofar as we use the same language to talk about psychoanalysis as psychoanalysis uses in its own practice and its own meta-psychological discussion of its practice, it would seem that we can achieve neither a fully external vantage point nor a fully independent yet adequate meta-language. We are caught in an hermeneutical circle. We can achieve internal distance, but not a fully external perspective.

Let me illustrate. Several years ago I met a middle-aged woman who had been in analysis for many years and had finally stopped—I do not say completed—her analysis. She explained that she had stopped when she suddenly realized that *personality*—she had apparently been much concerned about personality—was an assumption. At one level, her realization has to be understood in terms of those tales we tell about how we stopped or completed our analysis. (Have these tales ever been studied?) At another level, it indicated a perhaps profound insight or a perhaps even more profound evasion that came with an external vantage point. The woman I am referring to had become a serious student of Buddhism, and it was through Buddhism that she came to understand personality as an assumption. She did not, however, question the notion of "assumption." That was taken for granted and gave her a footing in her own culture. Obviously, if she had questioned "assumption"—the assumption of assumption—she would then have had to ground herself in yet another concept or orientation.

Strictly speaking we can only evoke the possibility of external vantage points and independent meta-languages. Our horizon is encompassed by the same language as psychoanalysis itself. There can, in my view, be no truly external vantage point, no transcendental ego. There can only be the evocation of such transcendencies, which have themselves to be seen as possibilities within our encompassing language. Such possibilities are facilitated by our peculiar narrative conventions (the omniscient narrator or, for that matter, reader), by our theologies (an omniscient deity, itself perhaps a refraction of our narrative presumption), and by such tropes as the traveler and the anthropologist.

The anthropologist interested in the ways in which what *we* would call psychological reality is articulated in other cultures is confronted with one of the most ticklish of ethnographic problems. For much of what we in the West call psychological and locate in some sort of internal space ("in the head," "in the mind," "in the brain," "in consciousness," "in the psyche") is understood in many cultures in manifestly nonpsychological terms and located in other "spaces" (Lienhardt 1961; Crapanzano 1977a; Fajans 1985). The symbols, metaphors, and other figures that are used to describe that reality are different from those in our own culture, and they hang together differently. To declare such articulations inadequate, as some Western thinkers (Hallpike 1979, implicitly) have done, is, in my view, an act of intolerable cultural arrogance. To reduce such articulations, as many psychoanalysts have done, to some sort of projective

♦

mechanism of the established givens of psychological makeup is to perpetuate a closed system of thought and to ignore, if not the real possibility of human variation, then variations in human expression. To accept the possibility of such difference does provide, I believe, a *provisional and always incomplete* ground for self-reflection that cannot be obtained internally.

Let me give an example from my research in Morocco (Crapanzano 1973a; see also Chapters 7 and 11). There I was working with spirit-possessed individuals who, when "possessed" or "struck," exhibited dramatic symptoms of the sort that Charcot, Richer, Bernheim, and Freud himself would have found familiar but would seem exotic to today's psychoanalysts. I speak of sudden blindness, mutism, and paralysis, aphonia, tics, and other motor disturbances, anaesthesias and paraesthesias, glossolalia and echolalia, mimetic behavior, all accompanied by a *belle indifférence*. For all of these a demon (with a particular character and desires) was held responsible. Cures were spectacular: communal exorcisms with elaborate trance dances, possession crises, and acts of self-mutilation.

To classify these as symptoms of hysteria, to see the demons as projections of internalized psychic content, and to understand the behavior as some sort of acting out of the repressed is to surrender too quickly to the complacency of a familiar psychology. To recognize that the demonic idiom is a *given* in the world of the Moroccans and provides them all—patients, exorcists, and bystanders—with an interpretation of experience and a "means" (at some level) for escaping from, modifying, or coming to terms with that experience is to recognize another possible—a puzzling and therefore epistemologically disturbing—ground for framing, articulating, and transforming reality.

From the point of view of diagnosis, I found that the hysteriform symptoms of possession were by no means restricted to what the Western diagnostician would call hysteria. The demons provided a means for articulating what in the West would have been understood as symptoms of depression, panic, schizophrenia, as well as hysteria. Given the status of demons in the Moroccan world, the location and treatment of the illness were evaluated differently. *But*, more important for our purposes, our notions of internalization and projection—and of mind, psyche, and self—become problematized. Put in extreme fashion: the Moroccan would find the psychoanalytic theory of internalization and projection, the priority of the psyche, puzzling and presumptuous. For him we have got it all backward. It is the external (the really real) and its introjection (if that is the right word)—the demons and the demonic—that have priority.

I do not want to argue one "psychology" against another. I want to suggest that through the serious (though obviously provisional) taking the part of the other, we come heuristically to relativize our own position. We have to ask why something that we see as projection of endopsychic contents is seen by the Moroccan as a really real externality that can at times, in some way, enter the human body. Does the location of such "processes" in the psyche, in the demonic, elsewhere, relate to particular social arrangements? Is the priority we give the psyche (carried, as it is, to the extreme by Jung and his followers as well as by his romantic predecessors) really a precipitate of these arrangements and not a reflection of the essential make-up of the human being? Are the processes "described" by the Moroccan and the psychoanalyst at some level, regardless of location, isomorphic? Is there some way of getting behind these "psychologies" and "demonologies" to some underlying ground shared by the two? These are the questions that anyone seriously interested in human and cultural variation has to ask.

The comparativist is, of course, confronted with many difficulties. These include the status, the contextualization, and the framing of the material upon which he bases his comparisons, indigenous theories about and attitudes toward that material, his own theoretical and axiological presuppositions about it, and problems of elicitation, translation, interpretation, and exposition. I should add to this list symbolic-emotional reactions to the material of the sort George Devereux (1967) called attention to in *From Anxiety to Method in the Behavioral Sciences.*

My own particular tack has been to bracket off the "psychological" (insofar as that is possible) and to look at psychoanalytic and other (folk)-psychological formulations of "psychological" processes from the point of view of language. Psychoanalysis is, of course, a "talking cure," and we need not invoke Lacan to recognize Freud's own interest in language as a key to psychological understanding. I should add that many therapies in other cultures as well as our own are talking cures. I think, for example, of Eskimo confessions described by Rasmussen (1929), the dream therapies—theatricals really—of the seventeenth-century Iroquois (Wallace 1958) as well as shamanistic rites that talk the patient through to cure (Lévi-Strauss 1958:63–74). Insofar as the glosses—the descriptions, interpretations, and explanations—of the talking are in the same language as the talking, they, the meta-psychologies and, if you will, the meta-demonologies—refract that talk.

Wittgenstein (1971) among others asserts that a psychology is embedded in language (*Sprache*). Lacan (1966) pointed out that the analyst does not analyze a dream but a dream text. Distortion (*Entstellung, transposition* in French) is, for Lacan, a sliding, a *glissement* of the signified under the signifier, the concept under its acoustic image. Displacement and condensation are *homologues* (Lacan used the term evasively) of metonymy and metaphor—according to Roman Jakobson (Jakobson and Halle 1971), two of the most basic linguistic operations. Emile Benveniste (1966:75–87) has noted a parallel between style and the properties that Freud found to be characteristic of dream language. "The unconscious makes use of a veritable 'rhetoric' which, like style, has its figures, and the old catalogue of tropes furnishes an inventory appropriate to both registers of expression" (Benveniste 1956:86). The substitutions engendered by taboo, Benveniste maintained, can be likened to such rhetorical figures as euphemism, allusion, antiphrasis (that is, expression by its opposite), praeteritio (that is, a purposeful passing over the significant in order to emphasize it), and litotes, and he too signaled the importance of metaphor and metonymy. But, lest we be too arrogant in our assumption of cultural superiority, let me refer to my late friend Moulay Abedsalem, an old, illiterate Moroccan pallbearer and shroud maker (Crapanzano 1988). Moulay Abedsalem once explained that what one dreams is what the soul has witnessed. Dream distortion results, he said, from the mind's (*'aqel*) inability to translate accurately what the soul has experienced. Insofar as mind has to make use of words to convey dreams, it is words that distort them. How else, Moulay Abedsalem asked with terrible irony, would we know our dreams?

It is my assumption that language precipitates our psychologies and facilitates our (theoretical) understanding of them. There are, of course, many ways of understanding language and, therefore, of posing the question of the relationship between language and psychology. Lacan and his followers, with some discomfort, accepted an essentially Saussurian model of language. Benveniste (1966:63–74) argued that the grammatical categories are refracted, for example, in Aristotle's list of categories: substance, *ousia*, with the substantive; quantity and quality with quantitative and qualitative adjectives; place and time with adverbs of place and time; disposition with the middle voice; state with the perfect; action with the active voice; and so on. And, by extension, we can argue that the categories of psychology are also refractions of grammar—perhaps glosses of such performatives as "I think," "I apologize," "I repent," "I am revolted by," or "I am guilty about" (Lee 1985). We have of course to distinguish between language and its spoken manifestation, speech, and what we have to say explicitly or implicitly about language and speech (Silverstein 1979).

In the last few years both anthropology and psychoanalysis have turned toward interpretation—a turn, I should add, that has been critically questioned by many practitioners in both fields. According to the defenders of this view, the two disciplines are not, and cannot be evaluated in terms of, the hard sciences. Rather they have to be understood as exercises in interpretation. I use the word "exercises" here in order to stress one result of this interpretive turn: an emphasis on process or strategy of interpretation, and the recognition, however reluctant, that even the most fundamentalistic of interpretive systems offer no final interpretation or reading, though they may provide authoritative interpretations or readings. (The authority of such interpretations is external to the interpretive strategy itself.) If they have no extrinsic goals such as cure—goals that can be somehow measured or evaluated—the exercises of interpretation risk becoming interpretations-for-interpretation's sake. At best they become exemplary and programmatic; at worst, attestations of the interpreter's virtuosity (see Chapter 2). From the point of view of the relationship between psychoanalysis and anthropology, interpretation, more correctly "interpretation," becomes a bridge between them. It serves this function well: if not actually then symbolically.

The interpretive turn in both anthropology and psychoanalysis has deep roots in Western thought, extending back at least to Aristotle's *Peri Hermeneias*—a work in which Aristotle dealt with the grammaticality of predication—but it is not until the Renaissance, with the rediscovery of classical learning, and the Reformation, with the reevaluation of Holy Writ, that hermeneutics, the science of interpretation, comes into being.[3] (I should add a third important source of hermeneutics: the renewed interest in Roman law in twelfth-century Italy.) As Hans Georg Gadamer (1975) has remarked, all three sources of modern hermeneutics begin with the awareness of a *gap* between the object to be interpreted—one of Cicero's orations, for example, a book of the Old Testament, or the Code of Justinian—and the cultural assumptions of the interpreter. The gap can of course be understood in temporal or spatial terms, that is, historically or ethnographically. It results from a certain opacity—an intransigence—discovered in the object, which therefore can no longer be taken for granted. In Heidegger's (1967) terms (though not necessarily as Heidegger meant them) the object of study is no longer *zu-handen* (ready-at-hand) but *vor-handen* (present-to-hand). "The modes of consciousness, obtrusiveness, and obstinacy all have the function of bringing to the fore the characteristics of presence-at-hand in what is ready-at-hand" (Heidegger 1967:104). It is the intransigence of the object to be understood that problematizes the worldview of the interpreter, creating a peculiar sense of time ("history"), a peculiar sense of space ("ethnographic"), and a peculiar relationship which contemporary theorists of interpretation have likened to dialogue. The "historic," the "ethnographic," and the "dialogical" mediate the distance—or perhaps better, they "justify" it in almost the printing sense of the word.

A certain vulnerability characterizes all acts of interpretation. It does not, however, result from the confrontation with the opaque, the intransigent, and the obtuse, but from problematizing the taken-for-granted world of the interpreter. (Relativism is one mode of this problematizing.) *And* with this vulnerability comes a danger: a potential surrender to an authoritative, unquestioned position that incorporates the intransigent in an interpretation that does away with its intransigence arbitrarily, without even acknowledging its possibility. Examples of this surrender are legend in cross-cultural encounters: the assumption that they are just like us or, more often, that because they are different (primitive, Black, Hopi, heathen) they must be thus and so. The rise of Protestant hermeneutics itself grew out of the Reformers' refusal to accept the Roman Church's authority in understanding Scripture. That authority rested on "a grandiose *petitio principii*," since the basis for Rome's interpretive authority was an interpretation of the very book to be interpreted—of those Biblical passages that were understood as a demonstration of how God had instituted the Holy Catholic Church with St. Peter and his successors as heads and authoritative interpreters (Burckhardt 1968). Early Protestant theologians stressed the principle of perspicuity (*perspicuitas*) and the self-sufficiency of Holy Writ. They laid the basis for an intrinsic interpretation that accepted no external worldly authority, although in pietistic circles divine guidance was sought even through vocalization. Matthis Flacius Illyricus, one of the earliest of these Protestant hermeneuticists, argued in 1567 in his *Clavis Scripturae Sacrae* that Scripture had *not yet* been understood correctly and that true understanding did not—could not—proceed from external authority (Mueller-Vollmer 1985). It required careful linguistic and hermeneutical preparation.

The object of hermeneutical speculation has been the *text,* and insofar as the interpretive turn in the social and psychological sciences rests upon the hermeneutical tradition as filtered through Heidegger, Gadamer, and Ricoeur, it has adopted, implicitly if not always explicitly, a text metaphor. Culture, society, and psyche are all metaphorized as texts—texts to be read and interpreted. In anthropological circles the text metaphor has received its most explicit if uncritical expression in the writings of Clifford Geertz (1973:452): "the culture of a people is an ensemble of texts." Now, without denying the illuminating capacity of the text metaphor—it has certainly enabled many anthropologists to present, in often enlightening ways, aspects of culture that had to be ignored by those of a more positivistic bent—it does require critical regard. We have to ask: why is the text metaphor so popular today? Why is any one of several understandings of "text" given to the text metaphor? For, obviously, more than one understanding of text is possible.

I do not propose to answer these questions here. I only want to point out the need to raise them if any critically reflective anthropology, psychoanalysis, or psychoanalytic anthropology is to be established. I do want to suggest, however, that the prevalent text metaphor in these disciplines can serve to block such questions. The reduction of the human and its products to a text can produce political and ethical complacency. Put simply: if we are treating texts, we don't have to bother ourselves terribly about people. Text metaphors seem also to refract the very process that produces their tenor, literally the collecting of texts of one sort or another; that is, the reducing of complex multidimensional exchanges to relatively simplified and highly conventionalized renditions—recordings, paraphrases, and other types of reports. Insofar as they are written, the complex exchanges are thus decontextualized and subject to ever greater decontextualizations. Descriptions of the circumstances in which such exchanges occur—of what Henry James (1984) called the medium—as well as descriptions of behavior and environment are also highly conventionalized and subject to similar chains of decontextualization and recontextualization.

More important, a text can be internally reflexive (as, for example, through the use of shifters and other meta-locutions) and this "internal" reflexivity, read as self-reflection, critical self-reflection even, can cover for the absence of an "external" vantage point of any sort for reflection. In other words, self-reflection occurring in a frame can hinder the questioning of the frame itself by creating the illusion of critical reflection. We see, for example, a great deal of self-reflection in psychoanalytic theory and therapy—the discussion of transference, of memory lapses, of slips of the tongue, of changes in style and tone, of accompanying emotion—and in anthropological studies of fieldwork if not in the actual field encounter—discussions about *rapport* or, on rare occasions, discussions in the field with one's informants about the nature of the encounter (Dwyer 1982).

Such discussions do not raise, however, the role of psychoanalysis in Western political arrangements or of anthropology—of rapport—in a specific social context. Discussions of the hierarchical relationship between doctor and patient in the psychoanalytic hour, even if they touch upon social and political implications of such hierarchical relations, are immediately "internalized" in the psychoanalytic frame. Why, asks the analyst, are you projecting *our* relationship onto the social? What are the transferential implications of such a political discussion? (There are moments when this "incorporation" can become downright obscene as, for example, in Argentina during the military dictatorship, when at least one analyst attempted to reduce the fear of male authority expressed by a political victim of torture to castration anxiety resulting from an unresolved Oedipal conflict.)[4] In anthropology there are, to be sure, moments in which the social and the political implications of the field situation (and the relations that transpire therein) are brought up, alas, rather more conventionally (as self-indices: "I am appropriately liberal, leftist") than self-critically. But in these examples, the significance of their very discussion is not questioned. And certainly if such discussions occur in the field, they are immediately reduced (by the anthropologist at least) to data!

In contemporary hermeneutics, inspired by Heidegger (1967) and elaborated by Gadamer (1975), dialogue has become a regnant metaphor for describing—indeed prescribing—the relationship between the interpreter and the text (see Chapter 8). The dialogue model evokes the "mutually" lived experience of the oral encounter that is lost in the asymmetrically lived experience of textual interpretation. Here Hermes, the messenger god and progenitor of interpretation, leads the dead (another of his tasks) backward from Hades to the quick world of the interpreter. Ironically, the dialogue having passed through the Stygian defiles of the text in historical and literary hermeneutics, is restored to its original context—the live, oral encounter between two or more conversationalists in the hermeneutically understood encounters of contemporary anthropology and psychoanalysis. Such a passage is not without peril. The lived encounter is textualized: its mutuality is, through the metaphor, deadened. A distance between speakers is created, at least inter-

pretively, and decried in such confessional modes as the anthropologist's or psychoanalyst's memoir. The interlocutor may as
well be dead. Speaker A is to Speaker B as Interpreter is to Text
as Live is to Dead.[5] The dialogue model comes to resurrect that
which has been declared dead by the power of an inappropriate
metaphor, while all the time it was live and well. I speak of
course of the patient and the informant. No wonder Hermes
was—and is—a trickster. Or am I now talking about Christ before Lazarus?

Distance, death, Hermes, and Christ aside, an important consequence follows the passage of the dialogue through the defiles
of the text: an attitude toward language—toward communication—that ignores if it does not deny the pragmatic (the rhetorical or paralexical) dimensions of the lived encounter (Silverstein
1976; 1979). Insofar as a dialogue is an active exchange between
two or more parties, it is a continual and responsive negotiation
of the reality of the encounter: how it is framed, how it is to be
discussed, understood, and interpreted, and how the parties to
it—and their relationship as both part and creator of the reality,
the context—are themselves to be constituted. Through the acceptance of the text metaphor and the model of the dialogue for
its interpretation (at least as they have been articulated in today's hermeneutical thought) the pragmatic features are drastically reduced by the very metaphor and model. Culture, society,
and psyche, so reduced, are to be understood in essentially referential terms; that is, in terms of that (at least through our granting agencies) fetishized commodity called data.

In anthropology, interpretive strategies have been founded
on the intensional and extensional notions of symbolic meaning,
on system-determined meaning, and on use-meaning (see Chapter 9). Often, as in the writings of Victor Turner (1967), several
different, often inconsistent approaches have been used in a
sort of hip-shooting sort of way. For other anthropologists, most
notably Geertz (1973), the symbol is understood less in a denota-
tional than in a presentational manner, making it difficult to
determine for whom the symbol presents—the native, the anthropologist, or the reader. In psychoanalysis, the dominant interpretive mode, well delineated in Freud's *The Interpretation
of Dreams* (1954), is also referential. The aim of psychoanalysis

is to uncover the hidden meanings of dreams and other symbols that give masked expression to desires or their objects that are barred from consciousness. Through free-association, through the creating of a countertext, the psychoanalyst is able, in ways that are not clearly spelled out, to discover those hidden symbolic referents. The correctness of interpretation, which arises out of the montage of text and countertext, of dream and associations, is justified intuitively; on admittedly circular theoretical grounds; and in terms of therapeutic efficacy. In both anthropology and psychoanalysis the mode of interpretation is archeological. Its predominant metaphor is "depth."[6] The "deeper" the meaning the "truer" the meaning. The deepest referents, particularly in psychoanalysis, are few in number. This reductive tendency is not corrected by an elaborated theory—and a methodology for the study—of symbolic hierarchy. In psychoanalysis and in anthropology (at least where it assumes presentational symbols), symbolic interpretation, understood referentially, covers pragmatic processes that are not understood as such (see Chapter 5).

Anthropologists and other social scientists have, I believe, accepted an overly simplified role model for describing human transactions. This model may give a certain conceptual elegance to our descriptions of such transactions but does not do justice to the "play" that occurs in them. Although role theorists have recognized that people may have more than one role and that these roles are often in conflict—in the office romance, for example—they do not have an adequate way of conceptualizing the play among multiple roles that are rarely articulated as such—named and discussed. I doubt whether the play even reaches awareness most of the time. Roles are constantly being negotiated pragmatically, played up and down. Think of a job interview between a man and a woman. Think of the mild (or heavy) flirtation, of expressions of seriousness, of attestations of expertise, of leadership, of the ability to follow instructions—all of which occur simultaneously or seriatim and are conflated into a single event, the job interview, with one party to it simply known as the applicant and the other as the employer.

Freud's discussion of transference alerts us, in a very special context, to the interdependent play of multiple, articulated, quasi-articulated, unarticulated, and inarticulable role modalities in any transaction.[7]

The constituted role of doctor and patient, pragmatically marked and remarked, permits the play, the indulgence, of acting out other roles (understood here conventionally in terms of the individual participant's biography). If we look carefully at the transactions between doctor and patient, we see that despite the intensity of the transference, the "doctor" and the "patient" are always there, as it were, behind the scene. Indeed, they enter into the defenses and counterdefenses of the two. One moment the patient plays daughter, for example, and the next, perhaps having gone too far, eliciting too intolerable a "paternal" response from the analyst, she becomes patient, prompting a more distant, a more professional response (see Chapter 5).

Any social transaction involves an attempt to negotiate (not explicitly) a common understanding of what is transpiring: that is, an attempt to determine pragmatically how the transaction will be referentially read—named, paraphrased, interpreted, and incorporated into larger understandings—without exposing the pragmatic determinants of such a reading. Traditional hermeneutical approaches which focus on the symbolic significance of such transactions support this masking. They legitimate our propensity to essentialize the pragmatic *Gestalten* of exchanges, to detemporalize perduring transactions, to permit, in often morally and politically compromising ways, decontextualizations and recontextualizations, and to perpetuate thereby cultural and psychological pictures that do not threaten the complacency with which we have come to accept notions of otherness.

It is here that a pragmatically sensitive, relativizing perspective of the sort I have been advocating, however incomplete, can be salutary—particularly in an era as conservatively smug and as culturally arrogant as the one in which we are living. Relationships between individuals, institutions, or disciplines that surrender the agonistic approach to facile affirmations of harmony and accord are in danger of losing the vigor, critical reflection, and creativity that come with the disquieting knowledge that the world may indeed appear differently to those with whom we engage. Even more disquieting is the knowledge that there is no knowledge complete in and of itself, but only a think-ing that aspires to a knowing. Such, I like to think, was Freud's project; such is the project of any psychoanalysis; and such is the project of an anthropology that has the courage to accept its own mission. It is in terms of this thinking that any meaningful engagement between disciplines or people has to occur.

7.
Mohammed and Dawia

For the possessed, possession is real. However it manifests itself—in trance, acute hysterical dissociation, schizophrenic reactions, multiple personality, tantrums, or love—possession provides an existential validation for the belief in a class of spirits able to enter and take control of a human being or animal. The belief that one has been or can become possessed is an important determinant of the subjective life of the individual and of his behavior. The state of possession itself enables the possessed to express and communicate, in a symbolic fashion, a range of subjective experiences or psychological dispositions, and to demand an appropriate response. It allows people to explain certain life experiences that extend beyond the limits of the "possession state."

The spirits or demons capable of entering and seizing control of an individual serve more than an explanatory function.[1] They enable the person possessed to articulate a range of experiences which the Westerner would call "inner," "psychological," or "mental." Spirits in this case can be called symbolic-interpretive elements (Crapanzano 1973a; see Chapter 11). They, like feelings of helplessness or being overwhelmed, symbolize certain psychological dispositions and offer immediately an interpretation in a manifestly nonpsychological idiom. They may even evoke the dispositions, as T. S. Eliot's (1960) objective correlatives evoke the feelings and emotions associated with them. They are not projections in the psychoanalytic sense of the word but givens in the world of those who believe in them. Insofar as these symbolic-interpretive elements are part of a system—demonology—they are subject to the logical constraints and evaluations of that system and thus serve to structure and evaluate (the articulation of) the dispositions accordingly. The dispositions are articulated, if not actually cast, on a stage external to the individual in a collective rather than an individual idiom.

That the dispositions are articulated on an external rather than an internal stage in collective terms has certain important consequences. Insofar as subjective experience is expressed in terms of external spirits subject to systemic constraints accepted by the individual and those around him, the locus of the individual's selfhood appears differently oriented and the dimensions of individuality differently determined for him than they would be for the Westerner (see Chapters 3 and 11). We might expect, for example, that the individual's sense of personal responsibility would be different. Psychological dispositions associated with a breach in the individual's moral code, which the Westerner would express in terms of guilt, might well be articulated in terms of spirits (Crapanzano, 1972). The individual does not chastise himself, as the Western depressive does, but is chastised by the spirit.

The articulation of psychological dispositions in terms of symbolic-interpretive elements also affects the relations that obtain between the possessed and those around him. The possessing spirit serves as a mediator, a *tertium quid*, between the possessed and the other (Girard, 1961). Dyadic relations become triadic, and there is a consequent depersonalization and generalization of these relations. They are removed from the idiosyncratic plane of reality and "projective reality," subject to the constraints of language, to another plane (*der andere Schauplatz* in Freud's sense), the demonic subject to the constraints of the demonology (Mannoni, 1969). The interplay between self and other is cast not in the *real* but in the *imaginary* (Lacan, 1966). The symbolism differs essentially from the symbolism of the neurotic or psychotic in that it is collective rather than individual. Relations so articulated persist where, were they articulated on the plane of reality, they would perish.

The role that possessing spirits and possession play in the articulation of life experience will be illustrated through the life histories of Mohammed, a Moroccan Arab man possessed by a she-demon named 'A'isha Qandisha, and Dawia, Mohammed's wife, possessed by the he-demon Shaykh al-Kanun, believed to be 'A'isha Qandisha's husband. I will be concerned specifically with one sequence of events that are associated in their minds and form an episode in their lives: the death of their son Gueddar and Dawia's entry into the Hamadsha brotherhood. 'A'isha Qandisha and Shaykh al-Kanun play an important role in the couple's present-day articulation of the events.

The material is biographical. My analysis is based on Mohammed and Dawia's recollection of these events about fourteen years after their occurrence. Belonging to the past, the events speak to the present (van den Berg 1955). Their expression is determined by the present-day situation of the participants, including the other—my wife and myself—whom they address. It is shaped by that "conversation," described by Peter Berger and Hansfried Kellner (1970:62), which sustains the shared world of a married couple.

> Furthermore, it is not only the ongoing experience of the two partners that is constantly shared and passed through the conversation apparatus. The same sharing extends into the past. The two distinct biographies, as subjectively apprehended by the two individuals who have lived through them, are overruled and reinterpreted in the course of their conversation. Sooner or later, they will tell all—or, more correctly, they will tell it in such a way that it fits into the self-definitions objectivated in the marital relationship. The couple thus constructs not only present reality but reconstructs past reality as well, fabricating a common memory that integrates the recollections of the two individual pasts.

I will argue that it is precisely Mohammed and Dawia's present-day articulation of the events, if not their past articulation of them, in terms of 'A'isha Qandisha, Shaykh al-Kanun, and possession that enables them to construct a world in which the maritally disruptive effects of the death of a son and the birth of an unwanted daughter are mollified. The events are mediated by the presence of the tertium quid, the demons, who are external to the participants but impose their will on them. These demons and the relations they impose not only structure the marital situation, past and present, but also fit within the participants' articulation of the remainder of their biographical experience. They serve then as biographical orientation points and correlatives for feelings and emotions that extend beyond the situation at hand. In this fashion, they may be said to symbolize these feelings and emotions.

'A'isha Qandisha, Shaykh al-Kanun, and the Hamadsha

'A'isha Qandisha and Shaykh al-Kanun are *jnun* (*jinn* in the masculine singular; *jinniya* in the feminine singular), a class of spirits created before man and composed of vapor and flame. 'A'isha Qandisha is famous throughout northern Morocco; Shaykh al-Kanun and the fact of his marriage to 'A'isha Qandisha are not so well known. Although the jnun are usually imperceptible to man's ordinary senses, they may render themselves visible in a variety of forms. They have names and sexes, but the names of only a few are commonly known. Although the jnun are not necessarily evil or harmful, they are usually avoided because they are whimsical and arbitrary, capricious and vengeful, quick-tempered and despotic, and therefore potentially dangerous at all times. If they are wounded or insulted, they are quick to retaliate by striking their adversary or taking possession of him. (The symptoms of the victims of the jnun range from feelings of general malaise and mild depression to sudden blindness and complete paralysis of the limbs and face.) Most often the man or woman who has injured a jinn is quite ignorant of his or her misdeed. Men and women who are angry or frightened or in a liminal period associated with a change in social status are particularly liable to attack. Treatment of a jinn's victim may aim at its permanent expulsion or, as in the case of the victims of 'A'isha Qandisha and other named jnun, at a symbiotic relationship in which the jinn is transformed from a malevolent into a benevolent spirit (Crapanzano 1971; 1973a). The jinn's victim becomes a follower *(tabi)* of the jinn and is said to lean on *(muttakil)* him. The jinn may require the follower to obey seemingly arbitrary commands—wearing certain colors, burning special incense, or performing a trance dance *(hadra)* to a specific musical phrase or melody *(rih)*. The cures are performed by members of such popular Islamic brotherhoods as the Hamadsha, of which Mohammed and Dawia are devotees *(muhibbin)* (Crapanzano 1973a:157–168; Herber 1923, Jeanmaire 1949; Westermarek, 1926: vol. 1, 262–413).

The character and attributes of Shaykh al-Kanun and of most other male jnun are not elaborated, while those of 'A'isha Qandisha are well developed. She is said to appear either as a beauty or a hag but always with the feet of a camel or some other hoofed animal. In her ugly aspect she is black and has long, straggly hair, pendulous breasts, and elongated nipples. She likes red and black, black benzoin *(jawi khal)*, and the music of Hamadsha. Lalla 'A'isha, as she is sometimes called, inspires fear in all Moroccans who are familiar with her. She is always libidinous, quick-tempered, and ready to strangle, scratch, or whip anyone who insults her and does not obey her commands. She demands absolute and unquestioning obedience from her followers, who are often called her slaves. I have heard them refer to her as "our mother." 'A'isha Qandisha is also said to enter into marriage with men by seducing them before they discover her identity.[2] She may require her "husbands" to wear old and dirty clothes and never cut their fingernails; she often restricts their sexual activities. A man's only safeguard against 'A'isha is to plunge an iron or steel knife into the earth before succumbing to her. Like other jnun, Lalla 'A'isha appears in dreams and visionary experiences, often as a woman familiar to the dreamer or visionary, but always named 'A'isha.

The Hamadsha, who specialize in the trance cure of 'A'isha Qandisha's victims, trace their spiritual heritage back to two Moroccan saints of the late seventeenth and early eighteenth century, Sidi 'Ali ben Hamdush and Sidi Ahmed Dghughi. They may be divided into three principal groups: the descendants of the saints, who do not usually dance; the professional Hamadsha, who perform the cures; and the devotees who attend their ceremonies. The Hamadsha are notorious for slashing their heads with knives and halberds or bashing them with jugs of water and iron balls during their trance dances. Their trances are not to be understood in terms of some sort of mystical union with the Divine, but in terms of the jnun, most frequently 'A'isha Qandisha, and of the saints they venerate. The blessing or *(baraka)*, of the saint enables the Hamdushi[3] to enter trance; the violent, frenetic phase of the trance, called *jidba*, in which the acts of self-multilation occur, is usually interpreted as pos-

session by 'A'isha Qandisha or another jinn. The trancer mutilates himself to please the she-demon and to force her to leave
him. The cures involve an intricate restructuring of the relationship between the she-demon and her victim (Crapanzano 1971).
'A'isha is transformed from a malevolent into a benevolent spirit
who keeps her victim in good health and fortune as long as
he follows her commands. The breach of these commands is
associated with a breach in the victim's moral code, with an
inability (in the case of a man) to live up to the ideal standards
of male behavior.

The Episode

Mohammed and Dawia's versions of the episode differ in a number of significant details, although both include the following
important facts. Dawia left Mohammed to watch over their
eighteen-month-old-son, Gueddar. Gueddar knocked over a kettle of boiling water and was burned so badly that he died three
days later. Mohammed invited the Hamadsha and slashed his
head violently; he continued to dance with them very often.
Dawia disapproved of Mohammed's head slashing. After Gueddar's death, a scorpion stung her on her way home from one of
the dances at which Mohammed mutilated himself. A few
months later Dawia gave birth to Khadija, a daughter. Mohammed, who had wanted a son, was disappointed. Dawia threw
water on a fire five days after Khadija's birth and was struck
by a jinn. Mohammed slashed his head on Khadija's name-day
celebration. On the Feast of Sheep ('ayd l'kabir) Dawia was
struck again. She fell to the ground, talked nonsense, and either
refused to nurse Khadija or nursed her feet. She did not respond
to the treatment of a fqih, or teacher-magician. The leader of a
Hamadsha team was called in, and he played different melodies
on a guitar (ganbri) for three days until he was able to find
the one to which Dawia's jinn responded. The Hamadsha were
summoned, and a black he-goat was sacrificed. Dawia was made
to drink the goat's blood. She danced the trance dance for the
first time in her life, and was cured. She claims to have been
struck by Shaykh al-Kanun, the Shaykh of the Brazier.

Mohammed's Account

Although Mohammed mentioned the death of his son at one of our first meetings, he did not tell me that he had been looking after the baby at the time of the accident. Even after I had known him for more than six months, Mohammed was very evasive: "I cried once when I lost my son. In 1952, a child was born after Fatna [his eldest daughter]. He was next to the boiling water. It fell over him and burned him, his whole right side. We took him to the hospital, but there was nothing to be done. He was one-and-a-half years old." I had asked Mohammed if he had ever cried as an adult. We had been talking about men and women who cry in trance. Mohammed had explained that this was a style of trance for those who do not slash their heads. "It is like hitting the head for them." Later in the interview he told me that Dawia had nursed Gueddar when she was pregnant. "His mother was pregnant and nursed him. She did not tell this to the doctor. The milk is poison then. A month after conception, the milk becomes poison." Mohammed was referring to the prevalent belief that the milk of a pregnant women is poison to her children.

Mohammed often confuses the first time he slashed his head, probably after his discharge from the army in 1944, with his performance of the trance dance after his son's death. He remembers the performance as the one when he slashed more violently than he had ever done before or since. He associates this performance, and others after Gueddar's death, with Dawia's illness.

> The first time Dawia danced, she was sick for three months. I used to dance the trance dance, but Dawia didn't. There was a saint called Sidi M'hamed. When Dawia was sick, I took her there. We found a team [of Hamadsha] there—about sixty people. There was a ball game. I heard the trance dance as I was playing and went to it. I danced with the halberd *(shaqria)*. I hit my head very hard, and my whole body was covered with blood. Dawia refused to go with me or wash my clothes. We had a mule. I climbed on the mule. I told Dawia to climb on too, but she refused because I was all covered with blood.

She walked, barefoot, and was bitten by a scorpion.[4] I said, "Well, here is your blood. Why did you laugh at me?" She was sick for three days from the scorpion. I had to take a razor blade and scratched the place where she was bitten . . . One day the village headman *(muqaddim)* called out that there should be no fires outdoors. He saw Dawia had already lit a fire in the oven. She tried to put it out. Something hit her. I didn't think that she was sick, but during the Feast of the Sheep we sacrificed our sheep, and the moment she took a piece of meat she threw herself against the wall. Something had taken her. Then I knew something was wrong. Khadija was three months old. I went to get a fqih. He found Dawia hidden under the covers. He began to read the Koran. He saw Dawia get up and thought he was reading the right passage. But Dawia slapped him.[5] He left right away. I looked for another fqih. Dawia told him to leave or she would slap him too. Then I knew that she was possessed *(maqiusa)*. I went to Moha. He is dead now. He was an oboe player *(ghiyyat)*.[6] He came with his guitar. He looked for a Koran. When he went in to the room, he put it at Dawia's feet. She could not have seen it, but she cried out: "Take your book away. Take your book away." Then he knew she was possessed.

Moha played the guitar for Dawia until he found her melody. He invited his team, and Dawia danced. "Since then," Mohammed said proudly, "she dances the trance dance and is possessed."

Mohammed describes his condition at this time. We were discussing dreams about 'A'isha Qandisha and his problems with her:

[When did you first have problems with her?] I dreamed a lot about a woman called 'A'isha and others who were probably 'A'isha. [Cuts off conversation.] [What happened then?] I had to sponsor nights [ceremonies]. If I didn't something would happen. She is in all houses. [Indicates with a gesture that she is in his house.] There are some houses where she always is. Others, only sometimes. [When were your first problems?] "In 1954 *[sic]* when Khadija was born. At that time Dawia took sick. Each night 'she' came to me. I sent someone to Moha. He stayed with Dawia for three days. Dawia dances to his air. I dreamed of 'her.' A night was necessary. I made two nights for 'her.' " [Mohammed appears confused and very nervous.]

Dawia's Account

Dawia, a more consistent informant, does not appear to have the same need to preserve the episode's symbolic superstructure.

> There was a boy, Gueddar, who died. He came after Fatna. He was cross-eyed. When he was born, he was born in a caul . . . His eyes were crossed, and his pupils were white. He grew quickly. Once, his father took him to be registered—he was one-and-a-half and looked four. Once we went to Meknes [they were living in the country] to live but we didn't stay. I wanted to return to my village. We stayed only three months. It was harvest time. I left Gueddar with his father. "Watch the child," I said. "I am going to get water at the fountain." Mohammed was making tea. The kettle was on the brazier, full of boiling water. The boy did not see well. Mohammed was not paying attention. Gueddar knocked over the kettle. The boiling water spilled all over him, from shoulder to foot. The child had neither finger- nor palmprints. When we were in Meknes, a woman gave him some cake and then kissed his hand. The moment she took his hand, she took away his blessing. Three days later he was burned, and three days after that he died. We had gone to the doctor.

Dawia explained that children born without finger- and palmprints are considered to have a lot of baraka; people who are cross-eyed are said to be able to find buried treasure. The woman in Meknes had wanted Gueddar's baraka. Gueddar also had bad luck because they had abandoned the family custom of shaving a child's head and leaving his pigtail in the saint's tomb. They had Gueddar's head shaved in Meknes. At his burial, near their ancestral saint's tomb, Dawia found a ten-franc piece and two beads from a necklace—an indication that the next child would be a girl. She says that she was not pregnant at the time of Gueddar's death but conceived six months later.

Dawia claims that Mohammed had frequently slashed his head before they were married, but that only after Gueddar's death did he first extend an invitation to the Hamadsha. He hit his head with particular violence on that occasion. Dawia also stresses that Mohammed did not report Gueddar's death to the authorities because he did not want to lose the dependent child allowance from the French government.

Mohammed's head-slashing reminds Dawia of how she became a Hamdushiyya.

We were at Sidi M'hamed. Mohammed, my sister, and I were eating. There was a team there. Mohammed saw the team and left his meal and went to them, and I was angry. It was the *musem* [annual pilgrimage to a saint's tomb]. The team was big, very big. There was a crowd of people, men and women, performing the trance dance. They touched shoulders [when they danced]. I didn't like that. I went over to watch. There was a Khalifi [a member of a saintly lineage from the Gharb]. They have pigtails. He pulled me into the dance. He made me lie on my stomach, and he walked on my back [to give me baraka]. He said, "Dawia get up. That which you have long sought from Allah you will receive today." When I got up, I saw Mohammed hitting his head with a halberd. I was upset after the Khalifi made me fall. I insulted him. I said to my sister, "Look at the people! What do they do? They are stupid. They are crazy *(hummaq)*."

Dawia watched the Hamadsha all day. When it was time to leave, she refused to get on the mule with Mohammed because he was all covered with blood.

There were many girls and women, walking and dancing. Each time Mohammed saw me tired, he stopped and said. "Come, get on." I walked. I didn't want to get on. I was barefoot. Suddenly a scorpion gave me a terrible bite on the foot. I was nearly dead. Mohammed and my sister stopped. They tied my leg so that the poison would not rise, and they took a razor blade and scratched a little on the spot where the scorpion had bitten me. Mohammed said, "Now, you will get on the mule." I still refused. My sister carried me on her back . . . We walked a little, and then my sister got tired. Mohammed got off the mule, and I got on. We arrived home. I was unable to eat for three days. My foot was swollen. When I was sick, my mother said, "Well, it is your fault. Why didn't you listen to Mohammed? If you continue to refuse, perhaps you will die." Since then I have always feared Mohammed and I began to love the Hamadsha. Every time Mohammed invited them, I made good meals, but I still didn't dance. Soon, after the birth of Khadija—I was already pregnant at the pilgrimage—two months later, after the harvest, Khadija was born. She was

five days old, and my mother, who was a midwife, was not at
my house. It was very hot and the wind was strong. The village
headman called out, "If anyone starts a fire outside, he'll have
a year of prison." Mohammed had brought a bucket of water.
When I heard the headman, I threw the water on the brazier.[7]

It was two days before the Feast of the Sheep.[8] We sacrificed
a sheep. I washed up all the blood. I was a little sick and
didn't eat anything until nightfall. Then we prepared skewers
of meat. We began dinner. I was alone with Khadija and Mohammed. I took a piece of bread to pick up the meat, and my
hand stopped on the plate. I do not remember what happened.
Mohammed said later that I fell and talked to myself and tried
to cry "tai bah bah" [nonsense syllables]. Mohammed was
afraid. He went to get my mother. My mother came and saw
me. My eyes were popping out to here. [Points to cheeks.]

Mohammed brought one fqih, who stayed the night, and then
in the morning a second. "He came and read the Koran, but I
gave him a slap. I said, Will you go? Or do you want me to
scratch out your eyes?" The fqih left, and Dawia began to nurse
Khadija's feet. Mohammed got Moha. "I do not remember his
coming. Mohammed was afraid of me. Ever since I threw water
on the fire, he thought that as the jnun attacked me, they would
perhaps attack him." Moha played for Dawia for three days and
then she was taken to her mother's house, for fear that there was
a jinn in her own.[9] She was made to drink the blood of a goat
sacrificed for her, a common Hamadsha practice. "The moment
I drank the blood, I saw 'A'isha and her husband dancing the
trance dance. He spoke to me in Jews' language. 'A'isha looked
like a Muslim but she also spoke to me in the Jews' language.
He sang my trance *(hal)*, but I did not understand . . . They
were happy because they had drunk some blood and felt good."
Dawia claims that with the exception of 'A'isha's hands, which
were like camel's feet, the she-demon looked just like her. "If
you had shown me a picture of 'A'isha at that moment, I would
have said it was Dawia."

Dawia was then given unsalted meat *(massus)*.[10] She ate half
and Moha left the rest where she had thrown the water. "There
was a friend, a true Hamdushiyya, in the team. She took water
and threw it on the ground and then led me to the trance dance.

She threw the water because 'A'isha is always in the ground and loves water and mud. She did this so that 'A'isha would leave the ground." The Hamdushiyya helped Dawia dance. " 'A'isha and her husband were on each side of me. I was afraid they would enter me again." Then, after a break for tea, Dawia danced alone to the music of the guitar. She saw 'A'isha and her husband as Muslims.[11]

"They were dancing in front of me. They were both in blue jallabas. They were happier as Muslims. When they were Jews they were happy, but they always had their eye on me—the illness." On a later occasion Dawia describes Mohammed's reaction to Khadija's birth in the following manner:

> When I was pregnant with Khadija, I knew I should have a boy, but I did nothing because it comes from Allah. When she was born, Mohammed came in and was a little sad but said nothing. On the seventh day, at the name-day celebration, he slashed his head. Mohammed, at Khadija's birth, as is our custom, kissed Khadija and touched my cheek and said O.K. During the first seven days, I was a little sick. I threw water on the fire before the seventh day. I was hit by a jinn then, but it [the sickness] came little by little. I had a fever. I was sicker then than after the birth of my other children. After the seventh day, Mohammed said, "I am sorry we had a daughter. Now we have a problem." When Khadija was twenty-five days old, Mohammed declared her birth and the death of his son. He did not say exactly that it was my fault but he suggested it. "If it had been a boy, we would not have had any problems." [Mohammed refers here to the fact that he had not declared Gueddar's death.] He did not hit me, but he often said, "Ah, I am sorry." Even now he says it. He bothered me a lot. "I do not like this," he screamed at me. He got very angry. It was true he went to other women. He told me so, laughing. It was true. I was hit by the jinn three weeks after the birth of Khadija. When I was possessed *(maqiusa)*, Mohammed no longer talked about the problem of Khadija. He was much gentler. He came to me and said, "Ah, I'm sorry that I screamed at you, that I bother you." He kissed my cheeks and said, "Do not suffer. You will be cured." He knew it was because of his yelling that I was sick. And he cried and wept next to me. Even though I was sick, even though he yelled, I think that all he says is not from his heart.[12]

The Characters: Mohammed

In 1968, at the time of my research, Mohammed was living in a shantytown on the outskirts of Meknes with his wife and their seven children. (His eldest son, a child by his first wife, lived in the Rif.) He is in his late forties, a thin, coffee-colored man with exceptionally bright brown eyes. His bearing is military, and he frequently makes use of military expressions in his conversation. He is nicknamed "the sergeant." Mohammed spent nearly two years in the French army during World War II before he was discharged because of an injury suffered on the Tunisian front. One of his fingers was blown off and a second paralyzed. He does not seem much concerned about his injury but he does take particularly good care of his fingernails.[13] They are a sign that he does not have to work. He lives on a pension from the French government. (He bought his present house with compensation money for his war injury, which he finally received in 1966; it is one of the better houses in his neighborhood). Although he occasionally seems embarrassed by the fact that he lives in a shantytown, he has never seriously considered working to improve his situation. His embarrassment may be on account of his daughter Fatna, a primary school teacher, who keeps nagging him to move to a more fashionable part of Meknes.

Mohammed's military bearing is really the only thing about him that suggests a soldier. He does not impress one with the strong and aggressive, the decisive and disciplined character of a military man. He is in fact a cautious, somewhat indecisive, usually gentle man of moderate intelligence who is immediately likeable. Like many Moroccans, he is quick to form dependency relations with people in superior positions and feels betrayed when his needs are not met. Occasionally he falls into an exceptionally violent tantrum and beats his wife and children.[14] Once, just before he moved to Meknes, he was arrested because of a fight in which he bit off his opponent's nipple. Unlike other Moroccan men, he takes an active part in the tantrum fights that many of his female neighbors have over their children. He and his family joke about his extreme rage, in which he forgets himself. This rage, they claim, is produced by the swelling of a vein, the *hasham*, which causes the rage in the blood, the *hasham-*

iyya, to mount to the head. It is the hashamiyya, not the man, that is responsible for acts committed during rage. Note the shift of responsibility from the self: "the hasham does not like anything that is not just."

Mohammed was born in a small village in the Gharb in 1924 or 1925. His parents were fellahin who trace their ancestry back through a local saint, Sidi Gueddar, to Sidina Omar, the prophet's caliph. When Mohammed was about six, his father, Hassan, divorced his mother, Dawia. Mohammed finds the subject of his father's divorce almost too painful to talk about and is not sure exactly when it took place. He knows only that it was before his circumcision at seven. His mother remained in the village until the war. Then she disappeared. "I have no idea if she is alive or dead," Mohammed said once with tears in his eyes. "My mother went away after my father divorced her, and I went into the army. I put a request for information about her on the radio. They asked for her twice, but we never heard a thing. My mother comes from Fez. She is not here. I do not know if she is alive or dead." Mohammed does not resent his father for divorcing his mother. Divorce is a man's prerogative.

After his divorce Hassan married 'A'isha, a divorced woman with one son, and subsequently had four sons and two daughters by her. Mohammed did not, and still does not, get along with either his stepmother or her sons. 'A'isha appears to have favored her own children at Mohammed's expense. "[How did you get on with your step-mother?] I was never in agreement with her. There were always problems. She did not want me in the house because I was not her son. [Did you ever want to hit her?] [He laughs.] She used to make me do woman's work." 'A'isha apparently used to report his disobedience to her husband, who beat Mohammed violently, often throwing him to the ground. On at least one occasion Hassan tied Mohammed up before beating him with a stick. Mohammed's father, now senile, appears to have been dominated by 'A'isha, who even now does not let him eat at Mohammed's house. Mohammed's present relations with his half-brothers and sisters are as bad as those with his stepmother. He does not admit to any jealousy or resentment, but he gossips about them and complains about their treatment of his father. He is proud that he became a Hamdushi before they did. He claims to have cursed his eldest brother over money matters, and he holds this curse responsible for his brother's illness.

Mohammed spent his childhood in the country. He slept in the same room with his mother and father until their divorce, and then in a room with his paternal grandmother. He remembers his father beating him once when he wet his bed. He was circumcised comparatively late.

> I remember when I was circumcised. I did not think it was going to happen. I thought I was the favorite son and was going to a feast . . . I was given a good *jallaba* and a *burnous*, and was put on a horse and led around the village. I was taken to the mosque, and then home. The barber was hidden in the room so that I wouldn't see him. When I was brought in, two men held me tightly. The barber came and sharpened his scissors. [Demonstrates.] He took the foreskin and put a little bit of sheep manure under and twisted the foreskin around it. This was to protect the head *(ras)*. He cut it with a single stroke. And the skin jumped off, and I jumped. I cried terribly. A woman put me on her back and danced in front of the oboes. The woman danced with me a little. She did this so that I would forget the pain. The barber had put on medicine [had, in fact, pushed the bleeding penis into a freshly cracked egg to which a little rabbit dung had been added]. I stopped crying. They sacrificed a bull for me. They made a lot of bread and invited a lot of people and had a feast. I sat in a corner. The guests gave me money: one thousand francs, five hundred francs, two hundred francs, one hundred francs. [He is very nervous and is beginning to free associate.] The feast lasted all day. On the second day they put medicine on me. I remained in bed all day. The third day I walked a little. If a woman is menstruating, she is not clean and cannot look at the boy because then the wound will not heal. The scissors were really hard. When he cut, I jumped in the air. I thought I would kill him. I thought that had I been big, I would have killed him. Who can look at a person who has caused you blood and pain? No one can take that. There are people who are not circumcised until they are big and then they run away. I thought at the beginning that he had cut if off.[15]

Mohammed played with other boys at the river and attended the traditional village school for a short time—he is able to sign his name—and then became a shepherd.

Like many other country boys, he masturbated and indulged in homosexual play, mutual masturbation, and anal stimulation without penetration, and acts of bestiality with goats, mares, mules and cows. "There were times we wanted to take a cow without its calf. We would take off our clothes. One boy gets under the cow, he rubs a little manure on himself, and knocks at the cows udders. The cow thinks it is its calf, and then the rest of us can go in." Mohammed is not particularly ashamed of either his homosexual or bestial relations. They are expected of adolescent boys, especially in the country.

When Mohammed was still in his early teens, his family moved to Meknes. He held several odd jobs, but was never apprenticed to a master artisan. In 1942 he joined the army— "My father was poor so I joined up"—and was wounded nearly two years later. After his discharge in 1944, he returned to the country. His first sexual experience with a woman was in the army.

It was in Meknes. It was Sunday. The company went to the brothel. I watched my buddies go in with the whores but I couldn't. I was alone. I was fixed to the spot like a tree. There were two women, a Muslim and a French one. They came to me, and each one pulled at me. It was the French one who won out. "Come, come, you have nothing to fear," she said. I had confidence in her but not in the Muslim women. She put me to bed. She took off all my clothes. She put my penis in her mouth. I was scared. I though she'd bite it off. The moment I saw my penis in her mouth, I was scared. When she saw my penis was hot, then she took me in the Muslim way. She kept saying, "Come! Come!" I was afraid, but the moment I saw my penis in her vagina, I began to move. After I finished, she gave me one hundred francs." Mohammed had intercourse with other prostitutes and with fellow recruits during his military service, but he never again had fellatio. "I felt cornered," he said. "It was like a second circumcision. I bit myself on the arm." Moroccans of his background do not practice oral intercourse. Fellatio is considered French, and not Muslim; there are many jokes, suggestive of castration, about it.[16]

Upon his return to the country, Mohammed was married to Zahara but divorced her as soon as she was pregnant. "When she got pregnant, she didn't like me any more. This often happens to women who are pregnant for the first time. She wouldn't even stay in my house. I waited two months because I thought that she might change her mind. She didn't so I went to the judge and got divorced . . . I was tired of her behavior. I didn't get the bride price back." The child, a son, lived with his mother until he was five and then with Mohammed's maternal grandfather.

Mohammed had not wanted to marry Zahara. He wanted Dawia, whom he had known since she was born, but Dawia's father had refused him on the grounds that she was too young for marriage. After he divorced Zahara, Mohammed ritually shamed Dawia's father into accepting his proposal by publicly sacrificing a sheep for him. They were married in a year, when Dawia was twelve. Three years later, Dawia gave birth to Fatna. While she was pregnant, Mohammed left her and— apparently without divorcing Dawia—married a third woman, lived with her three months, divorced her and returned to Dawia. A year later Dawia gave birth to Gueddar and then to Khadija. The family moved to Meknes where the other children were born. When I last saw Mohammed, in the summer of 1973, he said that now he would have no more children, and this saddened him.[17] He dotes on his grandchildren.

In recounting his personal history, Mohammed first refers to 'A'isha Qandisha after describing Gueddar's death. His relationship with the Hamadsha, however, goes back to the time he was a shepherd in the country, lost several animals in his charge, and fell sick. He recovered after dreaming that a saint saved him from demonic attack, and dancing a few days later with the Hamadsha (see Chapter 11 for details of the dream).

Since Gueddar's death Mohammed has been a regular devotee of the Hamadsha. Although he claims to have powers of curing victims of the jnun, he has consistently refused to become a member of a team. "I wouldn't be a member. I don't want to leave my house empty and not know what is happening to my children." Mohammed attends the annual pilgrimage to the Hamadsha saints, and he visits their shrines and the shrine to

'A'isha Qandisha when there is an illness in the family. On these pilgrimages he is relieved of depression, paresthesia, chest pains, and difficulties in breathing. He is also relieved by the trance dance. Unlike some Hamadsha, Mohammed had considerable difficulty in entering trance. His melodies must be played perfectly. If they are not, he becomes irritable and is not satisfied. His body becomes sore, his limbs stiff, and he feels very depressed until he has another opportunity to dance. He usually does not remember his trance experience. "I see nothing in front of me but the oboe *(ghita)*, the drum *(tabil)*, and the recorder *(nira)*.[18] When I dance I listen to what the oboe and the drums are saying." It is my impression that he usually does not mutilate himself until another dancer does so first.

Mohammed tries to invite the Hamadsha at least once a year, but he often does not have enough money to do so. During the nine months I spent with him, however, he did invite them twice: once because Dawia had fallen sick and once to celebrate the recovery of his abducted daughter (Kramer 1971). He performs the trance dance more frequently—at least once a month and on occasion two or even three times a week—and usually he slashes his head. Like other devotees he is compelled (by 'A'isha Qandisha) to dance whenever he hears his special melody. Mohammed responded to three melodies in 1968 and to four by 1973.[19] I have noticed that he usually manages to attend ceremonies when he is anxious or depressed. He is very offended by the suggestion of a relationship between the trance dance and sexual intercourse.

Mohammed considers himself *maqius* by 'A'isha Qandisha. "Maqius" may be translated as either possessed or struck by a jinn. According to Mohammed, the jinn may enter the body but need not always be there. "Sometimes she squeezes my knees or my back or my shoulders. She moves all the time." For Mohammed "maqius" seems to mean that he is in intimate association with 'A'isha Qandisha, who may either protect him, strike him, or possess him. He holds her responsible for feelings of sudden dizziness, headaches, difficulties in breathing, depressions, the success of his curse on his eldest stepbrother, inconsequential chance events, his curing ability, and certain dreams. 'A'isha Qandisha, he claims, has recently given him the power to see the jnun.

Three years ago I started to see them. I see them like I see
people. I see them everywhere, even next to cars.[20] The first
time I saw them, I saw . . . people flying and then I saw that
they were different . . . [What happened that day?] The night
before I had danced the trance dance and had not had
enough,[21] and then in the morning I took a walk and saw them.
Even now sometimes they punch me in the shoulder. I see
them all the time. When? Even at night. I have told you this
because I see them and I am not a seer *(shuwwaf)*. I have been
friends [with the jnun] ever since I first saw them. Perhaps if
I keep trying to be friends, they will give me my bread [the
ability to become a seer].[22] I can feel them. They are always
next to me. [Even today?] Today I smelled incense when I
was still in bed. I asked my wife if she smelled it. She did too.
So we looked around and could find nothing. [I don't under-
stand]. They were the ones who burned it. Are they all the
same? They change their faces all the time. They have many
different colored bodies and eyes, mouths, wings, and horns.
Sometimes their faces are like men and at other times like
dogs. [Are they men or women?] I can't tell. There is always
one tight against the right and another tight against the left.[23]
There are big ones and small ones. Old ones and young ones.
Each person has two. The one on the right is like a man. He
is big and you see from heaven to earth. The one on the left
is not so big. Only their faces are like people's.

Mohammed does not deny the role of 'A'isha Qandisha in his
first attack by the jinn, and he holds her directly responsible for
his condition since his son's death. He sees her during trance,
and when he slashes his head, he sees her slashing her own
head. He claims that he can see her not only in dreams but at
other times as well.

Even without the trance, I see her next to me. Even now—in
the air, not on the ground. [What does she look like?] She
is difficult to describe. She changes. Sometimes she is red.[24]
Sometimes she is black. I see two of her. If I look carefully, I
see more than ten. [When did you see her for the first time?]
I saw her about four in the morning, and the second time at
four in the afternoon. It is difficult to talk about her because
she told me not to say anything. It is possible that she will sit
down now on your notebook, and you will not see her. Most
Hamadsha who say they see her are lying. They can only see

her when they're asleep. If they tell you they see her when they're asleep, they're telling the truth. I see her often. I'd be able to see her on an airplane. She is always next to me.

Mohammed is often reluctant to talk about 'A'isha for fear of punishment. One night, after a discussion with me, he was "almost strangled by her."

The Characters: Dawia

Dawia is a handsome, articulate woman of thirty-six. She is proud of her marriage to Mohammed, and one senses in their presence unusual warmth and intimacy. Dawia was born in Mohammed's village. Her father was a fellah, and her mother bore twelve children, of whom six boys died at birth. Dawia is the third eldest of her five sisters; her surviving brother is the youngest child.

Dawia's life, as she tells it, begins with her marriage to Mohammed. Her earlier memories concern Mohammed's visits and his first proposal. Her saddest childhood memories are of being sent out by her mother in a thunderstorm to bring in the sheep, and of being beaten by her father when she had cooked a meal badly. Her happiest memories are of receiving new clothes for the Festival of Sheep and for a pilgrimage to Sidi Gueddar. "My mother gave me new clothes. She said, 'Come, we will go to the pilgrimage.' I was not married yet. When I heard there would be a pilgrimage, I was very happy. Also very free. I walked all around near the trance dance. I ate candy and walked as long as I wanted to. I had never been so free." Dawia immediately relates this event to "an even happier one": the day Mohammed asked for her in marriage. She remembers being her father's favorite; her mother was cruel to her; especially after the birth of a long-awaited son. She fought with her eldest sister until her father knocked their heads together; then they stopped fighting. She also fought with her second sister, and still does. That sister is always telling her to divorce Mohammed.

Dawia's family invited the Hamadsha at least once a year to glean their baraka, but no one in the family performed the trance dance.

I saw people dance the trance dance and hit their heads even with jugs, halberds and stones. The first time I saw someone hit his head—he was called Hassan—it was at my parents', and Mohammed also hit his head with a jug. I was very little, and he, Hassan, hit first with a jug and then with a pot. There was a lot of blood. I was frightened. I ran away, and so do most girls when they see that. I came back when the Hamadsha had stopped. My mother took me in her arms and said, "Don't be afraid. They are only dancing the trance dance. It is not serious." My oldest sister put me on her back.

Dawia remembers imitating the Hamadsha after their dances. "We let our hair down[25] and danced like the women, and the boys took little sticks and pretended they were knives."

Dawia recounts her life, from the time of her marriage to the present, in terms of Mohammed. The principal events are her pregnancies, sickness in her family, the move to Meknes, occasional pilgrimages, the trance dance, and her relationship with the jnun.

Mohammed first asked for Dawia in marriage when she was about ten. "When he left the army and returned to the village, he saw me. He loved me. He wanted to marry me. I did not know what to think about it. I did not even know what marriage was. I liked him very much. He always brought me candy. He was always there between my eyes." After he married Zahara, Mohammed continued to visit Dawia's family, and he always brought her gifts, clothes, and toys. He said that he had been forced into marrying Zahara by his father. Zahara was so jealous of Dawia that on one occasion she tried to poison her. Mohammed noticed in time, and hit Dawia so that she would not come back to visit Zahara. "He hit me because he loved me so much and had seen that I was almost killed." When Dawia was a little older, her father started to arrange a marriage for her with another man. "I was there. I knew what was going on. I wanted to marry Mohammed but couldn't say anything. It would have been shameful. I loved Mohammed but could not tell the truth. Mohammed was nearly raised in our house, among the five girls. He was always fair. There were never any stories with him." When Mohammed learned of this, according to Dawia, he threatened to kill her rather than let her marry another man.

Dawia's father and mother did not approve of Mohammed because he slashed his head and because he had left his first wife when she was pregnant. When he took a second wife during Dawia's first pregnancy, Dawia's father would not let her return to him until he had divorced the other woman.

Dawia learned about marriage from her two older sisters. Whenever she saw Mohammed after his second proposal was accepted, she ran away and cried. She cried throughout her wedding. On the last night of the wedding: "I was in the room with a lot of women. Outside there was dancing and much noise. The women bothered me. They said, 'Oh, he is coming. He is coming. He will put himself inside you.' Mohammed came in and sat down and made tea. I still had the wedding hood on. I would not take it off. Mohammed gave me tea, and I refused it. He ate some bread and asked me to eat some. I said no. It was two in the morning. He took off my hood. I cried. I screamed." Mohammed tried to be gentle with Dawia, but finally had to force her onto the bed. He took off all her clothes except a white chemise. "He kissed me. I cried. He caressed me, and I pushed him away. He said, 'I am only going to laugh with you. Don't be scared.' When I saw his penis. I was scared. Then he made love to me. There was such pain. I cried. I cried. The pain was terrible. He tried many times. It took a long time." Mohammed wrapped Dawia up, threw some candy into the room, as is the custom, and left. "Then the women entered. My sister took the [blood-stained] chemise and put it on her head and took it outside to dance with [in order to show all the guests that Dawia was a virgin]. The other women were next to me. They were eating the candy. They said, 'Well, you guarded it well, but he succeeded in the end.' They laughed and I cried. My mother found me crying and hugged me and said, 'Now your problems are over. Let us hope it will last all your life.'" For over a month, Dawia was in pain every time Mohammed made love to her. She remembers these first weeks of marriage as the most terrible in her life.

Shortly after her menarche, and two years after her marriage, Dawia conceived Fatna. "I didn't know what was wrong. I vomited all the time. I couldn't drink tea. I went to my mother and asked what was wrong. 'Perhaps you are pregnant,' she said.

Then I didn't love Mohammed any more. Each time he spoke to me, I cried. I thought of what would become of me: living in the country with all those children." Dawia refused to sleep with Mohammed, fearing that she would conceive again each time he made love to her, and have a multiple birth. But she remembers him as gentle with her, even though he left her during that pregnancy.

Dawia and Mohammed's relationship seems to have remained fragile until Gueddar was born. Mohammed frequented other women. The family moved to Meknes after Gueddar's birth—Mohammed began to smoke *kif* then[26]—but returned to the country before his death. Dawia, far from her family, was not happy in Meknes. She is still suspicious of city life and its effect upon children. "They depart from the tradition," she says of city people. "They are not as close to their families. They marry different people because they are educated." But after Khadija was born the family moved back to Meknes, and Dawia now considers herself a permanent resident of the city. Her primary identification, however, is still with her village, which she visits whenever she can. She claims that the fight in which Mohammed bit off his opponent's nipple was responsible for their move to the city. The French civil administrator put pressure on them to leave the village by threatening to block their compensation money if they did not send their children to city schools.

Dawia has been an active devotee of the Hamadsha ever since her first performance of the trance dance. Although she dances as frequently as Mohammed, like most female devotees she does not mutilate herself. Her feelings after a good trance dance are like the feelings she has after making love well. She visits the Hamadsha saints and 'A'isha Qandisha's shrine during the annual pilgrimage, and whenever anyone in the family is ill. When her son, Abderrahim, was sick—he was suffering from convulsions—she took him to the saints' villages and promised them, and 'A'isha Qandisha, a sacrifice if he got better. She and Mohammed danced on this trip and invited the Hamadsha when Abderrahim recovered. Dawia performed the trance dance seven days after each of her children (since Khadija) was born because the dance relieves her depression. "A woman who has the jnun inside her," she explains, "is depressed because she does not like blood." Dawia also danced when a daughter, Hadda, died five days after birth. She holds herself responsible for Hadda's death. She had eaten butter. "The followers of Sidi 'Ali do not eat butter.[27] So my daughter was strangled. He who is in me was not satisfied with me. To avenge himself, he killed my daughter. 'A'isha does not like butter." Dawia acknowledges the fact that sometimes, after a misunderstanding with Mohammed or a neighbor, she becomes sick. "I take a little henna[28] and mix it with water and drink it like soup," she says. "If the henna does not work, then I call in the Hamadsha."

Dawia has in fact only been struck once since her initial attack after Khadija's birth, in March 1968. She had dusted a mat into a drain. (Drains are a favorite spot for the jnun.) "I went into the kitchen. Someone grabbed my left big toe. I felt as though my foot was asleep. I could not move it. In the kitchen, there was a tea tray, a kettle of boiling water, and a brazier. Mohammed was praying. I cried. I fell. Mohammed caught me just in time, before I upset the kettle of boiling water. I was in bed for two hours. My foot was still asleep. My last thought before falling—I saw a snake pass in front of my eyes. I woke up." Dawia explained that the snake was a jinn. The next day she was attacked again, this time by something that looked like a dog. "Perhaps it was Shaykh al-Kanun disguised as a dog." Mohammed called the fqih who could do nothing for her. That evening Mohammed fell sick. "He was hit by the same thing that hit me. He was hit in the eyes. He trembled with cold from eight until eleven-thirty." The next day Mohammed and Dawia went to the Hamadsha saints. Dawia dreamed there that Lalla 'A'isha came to her and took her by the hair and said. "You have come." "I said, 'Yes, I have come.' Lalla 'A'isha said, 'Come to me.' Then she dragged me by the hair to the spring. 'Now wash yourself,' she ordered. I washed, but the water was cold, very icy. When I washed, I ululated. Then I was awakened by someone [in the saint's tomb] who was possessed. Oh, I was sorry. I wanted to profit more from the dream and talk more to Lalla 'A'isha." After the dream, Dawia and Mohammed returned to Meknes and sponsored a Hamadsha ceremony. Dawia explained that they had been attacked because they had not invited the Hamadsha when they moved into their new house.[29]

Dawia considers herself to be possessed by two male jnun: Shaykh al-Kanun and Musawi, both of whom love the same colors, blue and yellow. Dawia often confuses the two jnun.[30] She always wears their favorite colors, burns their favorite incense, and adheres to either of their commands. "Ever since I first fell into trance *(hal)*, I loved these colors. When I wear them, all goes well in my body."

She has a rich sexual life with both her male jnun:

> There are times that 'A'isha's husband comes to me [in a dream] just like Mohammed and sits down at my feet. He sleeps there. He is dressed just like a Muslim—jallaba, slippers, and a turban. When he comes in a dream he is always dressed, never naked. He comes just like Mohammed. He asks if I want to sleep with him. I accept and sleep with him. Sometimes he comes to the house and spends a lot of time there. Other times I find myself somewhere else. I think it is his house. When he makes love to me, he takes off his clothes. He is a Muslim and exactly the color of Mohammed. He looks just like Mohammed but a little heavier. I see myself. I am dressed up beautifully, like a bride. When I sleep with him, I am naked . . . in my dreams we are not young. We are older. He is like a man who has returned from a long trip and sleeps with his wife . . . I have much pleasure and feel as though I have just been married. I am better satisfied with 'A'isha's husband than with a man; I am happy *(frahana)* afterward. Each time I am with him I see that I have on beautiful clothes.

Dawia explains that she is satisfied by 'A'isha's husband because he prepares her. "He caresses me and talks to me and laughs with me." Mohammed tends to be more perfunctory in his lovemaking. He does not remain inside her for long; he only kissed her on the genitals once after a long trip. Dawia does, however, derive some pleasure from Mohammed.

At times, Dawia says that 'A'isha's husband comes to her when 'A'isha goes to Mohammed. She and Mohammed have joked about this. "Sometimes Mohammed wakes up in the morning and tells me to get him some warm water [to cleanse himself]. I say, 'Why wash? You have not slept with me.' He says, 'Last night I slept with a woman. I must bathe.' I say, 'That's ridiculous. You wake up and wash without having made love to me.' Yes, I wash after I sleep with 'A'isha's husband. Mohammed laughs. He is amused by that." At other times, Dawia denies that she and Mohammed have complementary relations with their respective jinn partners. She notes that she dreams of 'A'isha whenever she suspects that Mohammed is unfaithful to her. She has had several anxiety dreams about his marrying another woman. "Mohammed was married to another woman. I was screaming. I was crazy *(hamqa)* in the dream. I saw him. He entered with his new wife, and I went outside and yelled, 'Let me leave. I will not stay.' I saw him sleeping with her." It is 'A'isha Qandisha who comforts her. "One night I saw 'A'isha. She said, 'Do not suspect Mohammed. He is not thinking of that. You, both of you, are followers of Sidi 'Ali. I will not let you get divorced. When you see Mohammed like that, fear nothing. It is his trance that makes him like that.' "

Mohammed and Dawia's articulation of their personal histories, including our central episode, are not altogether comparable. Mohammed's story was told to me in fragments over a period of nine months; Dawia's was told to my wife within a few weeks' time as a running narrative toward the end of our stay in Meknes. My wife had known Dawia, however, nearly as long as I had known Mohammed. She did not encourage as much free association as I did. Both of us had excellent rapport with Mohammed and his wife. They were our friends and the friends of our field assistant and his family.[31]

My relationship with Mohammed changed considerably with time. I attended my first "night" at the Hamadsha in March 1968 through his invitation. Mohammed was proud that he had introduced me to the world of the Hamadsha. He felt it his responsibility that I be told the truth about the brotherhood; he was somewhat concerned, if not jealous, about my interviews with other Hamadsha, especially those of whom he did not approve. Over the months, as I learned more about the brotherhood, Mohammed began to confide in me. He looked forward to our "talks" and even initiated them on his own accord. He was developing a dependence on me, which I did not want to encourage for fear that he would take my departure as yet another abandonment. This dependence was stimulated by practical help that we were able to extend to Mohammed and his family (Kramer, 1971).

Mohammed must have experienced a certain ambivalence toward me as well. Sometimes he would arrive for an interview distracted, if not withdrawn and suspicious. At other times he would talk to me about the most intimate aspects of his past—seldom his present—or about such potentially dangerous matters as his relationship with 'A'isha Qandisha and the other jnun. Perhaps in talking about them he was asserting his superiority or his independence of the *nasrani* (Christian) who was always asking him questions. "It is difficult to talk about her ['A'isha Qandisha] because she has told me not to say anything. It is possible that she will sit down on your notebook, and you will not see her." Mohammed's confidences seemed, however, to lack the depth, the inwardness, that I have come to expect in Westerners. As he revealed himself, 'A'isha became more and more threatening. "I was almost strangled by her." Mohammed always preferred to keep me aloof and distant, in order to confide in me. With the exception of asking me about circumcision once, he never questioned me about my life or beliefs.

Dawia's relationship to my wife was not one of dependence. She showed a genuine curiosity about my wife that Mohammed never did about me. She was pleased by my wife's attention and enjoyed her interviews even though she was puzzled by such detailed questions about the obvious and the trivial. These sessions were her equivalent to my interviews with her husband. Unlike Mohammed, who always emphasized differences, Dawia looked for similarities with my wife in their common womanhood. Theirs was a relationship of sharing. Dawia was confident. Neither she nor Mohammed ever tried to use us to influence the other.

Still, I think it would be a mistake to consider the different shapes of Mohammed and Dawia's stories solely in terms of their different interlocutors. The fragmented character of Mohammed's story and his digressions—which, however psychologically significant they may be, are not always to the point—reflect a fragmented identity. His articulation of his life experiences in terms of 'A'isha Qandisha and other jnun, and to a lesser extent in terms of the saints, enable him to express and structure his life in systemic terms external to himself. His inner life is immediately deflected outward onto the demonic stage. His identity is not anchored within but outside himself, in 'A'isha Qandisha. She becomes the principal element in the articulation of his personal history and, undoubtedly, in the interpretation of his present.

'A'isha Qandisha permits Mohammed the expression and even the acting out of desires which he, as a man, would find unacceptable. Thus conflicts are expressed in terms of male and female. Acceptable desires are articulated in terms of himself, or on occasion, in terms of a saint. Unacceptable desires are articulated in terms of 'A'isha Qandisha and sometimes of other women including his wife. 'A'isha Qandisha is, however, an ambiguous figure. She may appear as a beauty or a hag, as benevolent or malevolent, as a seductress or a strangler. "Sometimes she is red. Sometimes she is black." She is never white, a color Mohammed associates with goodness, piety, and prayer.[32] She always has the feet of a camel, even in her most beautiful manifestations, and she is always potentially dangerous, untrustworthy. She must be controlled, but to be controlled she must be obeyed. Control involves enslavement. Mohammed must be like a woman in order to be a man.[33] He is possessed of her, one with her, and is forced to slash his head. "I see her with the iron in front of me," he explained. "Then I want the halberd."

'A'isha Qandisha reflects Mohammed's experience of other women or, perhaps more accurately, his articulation of his experience of other women. His relationship to women is one of ambivalence. He both desires and fears them. The theme of castration runs through all his dealings with women. His mother, Dawia, was good to him and then abandoned him. He associates her disappearance to the war in which he lost a finger. As is the custom in the Gharb, he was led to the circumcision by a woman, perhaps even by his mother or stepmother. His reaction to the circumcision was one of rage: "I thought that had I been big, I would have killed him." He was betrayed. "I did not think it was going to happen. I thought I was the favorite son and was going to a feast." He was sure the barber had cut

off his penis. His stepmother, 'A'isha,[34] reported his disobedience to his father who beat him violently. (His only escape from
punishment was through illness.) She also made him do
woman's work. He did not have confidence in the Muslim prostitute, and the French one took his penis in her mouth. "I was
scared. I thought that she'd bite it off . . . I felt cornered. It was
like a second circumcision. I bit myself on the arm." His reaction to castration is to bite himself. To act as a man, he must
mutilate himself. His rage is directed toward himself. It is perhaps no accident that Dawia finds his lovemaking perfunctory.
Mohammed himself has told me that he does not like to remain
inside a woman for very long. He never complained, however,
of impotence.[35]

Mohammed's rage is not, however, always turned on himself.
He has a violent temper; he beats his wife and children. He
participated in the tantrum fights of his neighbors, who are
women. His aggression is, in the psychoanalytic sense, oral: He
bites off the nipple of his opponent in a fight; he deprives a cow
of her calf before intercourse and knocks her udders. 'A'isha
will not, however, tolerate Mohammed's anger. If she is not
obeyed, she will attack him, possess him. Illness, castration,
circumcision, and head-slashing—all of these, identified with
being a woman, are an escape from the burden of manhood. For
him the least acceptable desire is to escape manhood, to become
a woman. Possession by a she-demon and head-slashing during
the trance dance are compromises. Mohammed becomes a
woman in order to become a man, and he does so not by his
own volition but by the will of another, 'A'isha Qandisha, a
woman with distinctly phallic traits: camel's feet, long fingernails, maenad-like curls, pendulous breasts, and elongated
nipples.

Ultimately, the castrator is male. Like all fathers, Mohammed's was not present at his son's circumcision, allowed the
male barber to cut his son's penis, beat his son violently. Mohammed escapes in a dream from a jinn, whom he identifies
later with 'A'isha Qandisha (see Chapter 11). After losing several
animals in his care, he escapes through illness from his punishing father whom he remembers with little warmth, toward
whom he shows no manifest hostility, and with whom he cannot

identify. The saints too are distant in their sanctity and in their
ability to work miracles. They do not serve as models. It is,
however, their baraka that enables him to enter the very trance
in which he mutilates himself, in which he becomes one with
'A'isha Qandisha, and through which he finally becomes a man.

Dawia's life story, unlike Mohammed's fragmented history, is
a more or less consistent narrative designed to evoke a response
in her interlocutor. Dawia has a flair for the dramatic that she
displays in even the minor incidents of everyday life. She is a
storyteller. Despite the precariousness of her situation as a
woman in Morocco, she is more confident than her husband.
She talks on the "plane of reality." She has an edge on herself
and is able to admit ambivalence in herself and others. She does
not live in the constricted world of her husband; she does not
have the same vested interest in maintaining a symbolic superstructure. She accepts the demands of the jnun and her responsibility in meeting them. They are elements in her world with
which she must reckon. "Hadda died. It was my fault . . . He
who is in me was not satisfied with me. To avenge himself he
killed my daughter." Often she takes delight in her relationship
with the jnun. She has a sense of humor. Even 'A'isha Qandisha
is less menacing for her than for Mohammed. She offers Dawia
support.

Mohammed's narrative, deflected though it is onto the demonic stage, is centered on himself. Dawia's life is centered
on Mohammed. She is outer-directed. Her life begins with her
marriage. Until then her memories are vague and confused,
evoked only by questions; she was only twelve when she married. It is Mohammed's life, or perhaps more accurately, her life
as married to Mohammed, that provides the structure for
Dawia's experience. Her fate is Mohammed's; Mohammed's is
in the hands of 'A'isha Qandisha.

For Mohammed, the jnun serve to articulate desires which
are unacceptable to him, for Dawia they serve to regulate interpersonal relations. She is much more willing to accept desires
and other aspects of her being-in-the-world that may not measure up to her ideal self-image. (However ideal this image may
be, it is affected by her inferior status as a woman in Moroccan
society—a status that Mohammed accepts in his vision and ma-

nipulation of her.) The jnun serve either as compensations for deficient interpersonal relations or to mediate relations that may be on the verge of collapse. On the one hand, Dawia's sexual relations—her relations, perhaps, in general—with Shaykh al-Kanun and Musawi are more satisfying than her sexual relations with Mohammed. On the other hand, she is struck exactly when her marriage to Mohammed is about to dissolve.

The episode I have chosen to investigate is central to Dawia's personal history. (It does not play the same role for Mohammed. He ignores it, or tells it in terms of his wife.)[36] Dawia recasts her relationship to Mohammed in demonic terms. She learns to speak Mohammed's language. "The implicit problem of this [marital] conversation is how to match two individual definitions of reality," Berger and Kellner (1970:61) have written. "By the very logic of the relationship, a common overall definition must be arrived at—or the conversation will become impossible and, *ipso facto*, the relationship will be endangered." Until Khadija's birth Dawia looked down on the Hamadsha. "Look at the people! What do they do? They are stupid. They are crazy," she tells her sister. She is angry at Mohammed for slashing his head. She refuses to mount the mule—to speak his language. She is stung by the scorpion.

Mohammed refuses to accept responsibility for the death of his son. He tries to blame Dawia: she nursed Gueddar when she was already pregnant. (Dawia denies that she was pregnant. She did allow the woman in Meknes to give Gueddar the cookie and hold his hand—to take his baraka.) Mohammed cries. Crying, at least in trance, is "like hitting the head." He slashes his head more violently than ever before. He does not punish himself; it is 'A'isha who makes him slash his head. His relations with Dawia deteriorate. He smokes kif and frequents other women. He angers Dawia. He claims that he left a ball game to dance; Dawia claims that he left their meal. He complains about the problems of registering Gueddar's death and the compensation money they will lose. The burden is placed on Dawia: she must bear a son, a replacement for Gueddar.

Dawia gives birth to a girl. Mohammed is disappointed. He says nothing about it for seven days, but Dawia knows. "When I was pregnant with Khadija . . . I knew I should have a boy."

She is struck five days after Khadija's birth, putting out a fire in a brazier. This is no accident. Had Mohammed extinguished the fire, Gueddar would not have been scalded to death. She is in fact attacked by the Shaykh of the Brazier, the jinn responsible for Gueddar's death who looks just like Mohammed. (The Mohammed responsible for her son's death is cast out onto the demonic stage; she need not blame her husband.)[37] A few weeks later Mohammed complains about Khadija. "He did not exactly say it was my fault, but he suggested it," she says. "He bothered me a lot. 'I do not like this,' he screamed at me. He got very angry. It was true that he went to other women. It was true." Their marriage is about to collapse. Dawia is again struck by a jinn. She rearticulates her relationship with Mohammed in terms of the she-demon and her husband. "Mohammed no longer talked about the problem of Khadija. He was much gentler. He came to me and said, 'Ah, I am sorry that I screamed at you, that I bother you.' He feared the jnun, according to Dawia. "Mohammed was afraid of me. Ever since I threw the water on the fire, he thought that as they had attacked me, they would perhaps attack him."[38] She has learned to speak his language, but she has not forgotten her own—a point that Berger and Kellner ignore. "He knew that it was because of his yelling that I was sick." Dawia has a sophistication that Mohammed lacks.

Dawia has forced Mohammed to articulate their relationship in terms of 'A'isha Qandisha as herself. "If you show me a picture of 'A'isha at that moment, I would have said it was Dawia." Mohammed himself, undoubtedly ignorant of his wife's trance vision, makes the same equation. "Each night 'she' came to me. I sent someone to Moha. He stayed with Dawia for three days. Dawia dances to his air. I dreamed of 'her.' A night was necessary. I made two nights for 'her'." It is not sure who the final "her" is—Dawia or 'A'isha Qandisha and all the women she reflects.

'A'isha Qandisha, Shaykh al-Kanun, and the jnun generally have very different meanings for Mohammed and Dawia. They serve different articulatory functions in their apprehension of their personal histories. As elements in a common idiom, however, as collective representations subject to systemic constraints, more than the articulation of subjective life, these spirits enable the articulation and rearticulation of ongoing human relations, not simply by giving meaning to these events but by entering into them as third parties, as mediators, whose existence is reconfirmed for the believers whenever they take possession of a person. Whatever the truth of our central episode may have been, its articulation in terms of 'A'isha Qandisha and her husband enable both Dawia and Mohammed to preserve their marriage by casting onto the demonic stage the tensions and hostilities, the resentment and anger, and the acceptance and projection of guilt caused by the death of a favored son and the birth of an unwanted daugher. Thus Dawia and Mohammed are enabled to live together with greater warmth and more intimacy than I have observed in most Moroccan couples of their background.

8.
Dialogue

> And there stand those stupid languages, helpless as two bridges
> that go over the same river side by side but are separated from
> each other by an abyss. It is a mere bagatelle, an accident, and
> yet it separates.
>
> —Rainer Maria Rilke, *Letters*

Rainer Maria Rilke (1972) wrote these words to his wife, Clara, from Paris on September 2, 1902. He had been visiting Auguste Rodin and was describing the difficulties he had had talking to the sculptor. Rodin "asked and said many things, nothing important . . . The barrier of language is too great." He showed the sculptor his poems, and Rodin leafed through them. "The format surprised him, I think," Rilke noted.

Rilke's image of two bridges is striking. It describes many of the field situations in which the anthropologist finds himself. Rilke probably knew more French than most anthropologists know the language of the people they study. Rodin knew no German. "Bridges" and "bagatelles"—languages, separations, and on occasion (conventional) comings-together will be the subject of this chapter. I will be concerned with dialogue and its representations.

In the last few years there has been much talk about dialogue in anthropological circles. Some of it has a distinctly messianic tone. It heralds in a new paradigm. An anthropology sensitive to dialogue will provide a solution to whatever the current crisis is in anthropology. The talk, and the writing, are often confusing. "Dialogue" is bandied about with little concern for its meaning, its permissible metaphorical extensions, its dynamics, its ideology. Philosophical, linguistic, literary, and psychological approaches are conflated. Scant attention is given to levels of meaning. Dialogue, "dialogue," and " 'dialogue' " are confused.

The Ideology of Dialogue

A culturally and historically specific way of conceiving of certain verbal transactions, *dialogue*[1] has considerable rhetorical force that is exploited in anthropological discussion. For anthropologists "dialogue" seems at times to substitute for "participant observation." It evokes a sentimentality that is associated with the participational pole of anthropology's traditional oxymoronic badge of methodological uniqueness, and carries little of the anguish that centers on the observational pole—the anguish about the wrenching, the alienating, effect of observation. It suggests friendship, mutuality, authenticity—an egalitarian relationship. I am not questioning the possibility of egalitarian relationships of friendship, mutuality, and authenticity in the field. I note simply that dialogue, so understood, not only describes such relations but can create the illusion of such relations where they do not exist. I am not talking about bad faith here—that can of course occur—but about the possibility of blindness inherent in the (dialogical) situation in which the anthropologist finds himself. *Dialogue* then not only reveals but often enough conceals the power relations and the desires that lie behind the spoken word, and, in other contexts, the recorded and distributed word. Power and desire can contradict the amity that dialogue connotes.

Anthropologists often use "dialogue" so broadly as to include just about any verbal communication, even endopsychic ones. Dennis Tedlock (1983a), who is one of the principal advocates of a dialogical anthropology, understands dialogue, for example, simply as "a speaking alternatively" or "a speaking across." Determined to call attention to the dialogical grounding of all fieldwork, a grounding that is masked in conventional, analogical (from the Greek *ana-logos*, "talking above," "talking beyond," "talking later") ethnographies, Tedlock recognizes that anthropologists "do much more than engage in dialogues." They watch people hunt, gather, herd, hoe, shuck corn, and perform rituals. But, Tedlock asserts, the moment they talk about hunting, gathering, herding, hoeing, shucking corn, and performing rituals, something happens. They enter the realm of "human intersubjectivity" (Schutz's phrase), which Tedlock prefers to call "human interobjectivity." They enter into dialogue, into conversation.[2] "The anthropological dialogue creates a world, or an understanding of the difference between two worlds, that exists between persons who were indeterminately far apart, in all sorts of different ways, when they started out in their conversation" (Tedlock 1983a:323).

Like so many anthropologists, particularly in the United States, Tedlock exalts the anthropological field experience. The field experience, its representation and interpretation, the anthropologist himself become exceptional. The anthropologist's perceptions, to use the word in its broadest sense, can be neither fully appreciated nor evaluated by people who have not had a similar experience, and the anthropologist is deprived accordingly of any vantage point other than the one he "creates" for himself or arbitrarily adopts. He can "go with the experience" or take on a theoretical position. Anyone familiar with the discipline will immediately recognize the tensions and intellectual politics inherent in this situation. It certainly influences the field experience and its representations and interpretations. It is in fact difficult to see why an anthropological dialogue should be distinguished from any other when it is understood in Tedlock's terms. We are always "far apart," "in all sorts of different ways," when we start a conversation or a dialogue. Otherwise there would be no conversation, no dialogue, just a kind of phatic affirmation of a shared view.

Phenomenological Perspectives

Even in Tedlock's minimalist view of dialogue one discerns something more than a mere alternation of speakers. The dialogue "creates a world" or at least "an understanding of differences between two worlds," and it seems to bring people who were far apart closer together. There is here an implicit phenomenological orientation that stresses the constitution of a shared world (*Mitwelt*), a shared understanding, or a coming together.[3] Such a phenomenological-existential perspective is rather more explicit in other works that advocate a dialogical anthropology. Steven Webster (1982) argues, for example, that the "dialogue is the foundation of ethnographic authenticity rather than an impediment to proper understanding," and he proposes an epistemological stance in which both subjectification and objectification are seen as extrapolations from the ground of mutual understanding upon which any encounter must begin insofar as its participants recognize themselves as human beings.

Gerhard Bauer (1969:2) notes a strong ethical dimension in the dialogical orientation of phenomenology. The integrating function of conversation (*als 'Zwischen', als Horizont und dem einseln vorgebene Deutung der Welt*) is emphasized, and the differentiating function (*als Mittel der Kritik, der Abhebung, des Widerspruchs gegen die überkommenen Deutung*) is neglected.[4] The integrating function privileges—hypostatizes—a morally charged authentic relationship which transforms the partners in a conversation from a *you* to a *thou*. Romantic, ideologically powerful, resonating, the psychoanalyst might maintain, with a desire to regain the primal pre-Oedipal unity of mother and child, the emphasis on integration mystifies, certainly simplifies, the dynamics of dialogue. Agonism gives way to an often saccharine communion, and it is this communion that fits so nicely into the anthropologist's often patronizing idealization of his relationships—his friends—in the field. The other (and *pari passu* the anthropologist) ceases to be a *you*, as realistically he ought to be, in traditional ethnology at least, and becomes a *thou*. So strong is the desire for integration that an anthropologist like Kevin Dwyer (1982) sees in the very possibility of rupture the anthropologist's vulnerability. It is with some relief that we remember that in the *Laches* Plato took ironic pleasure in the break-up of a conversation devoted to the meaning of friendship!

Hans Georg Gadamer has given one of the fullest accounts of dialogue. His principal work, *Truth and Method*, reflects the ethical orientation and the romantic mode that Bauer notes. Like other phenomenologists, Gadamer discusses the nature of language but does not examine critically (or ironically, for that matter) his own use of language and the way his theory—his descriptions—reflect *that* language. As such, despite its claims to universality, his work has to be read as an expression of a culturally and historically specific ideology of language—one that many anthropologists (Steven Webster, for instance) find particularly compelling.

Language, the medium of conversation, is ultimately the medium for all understanding, Gadamer argues. Conversation is ideally a process through which two people come to understand each other.

> Thus it is characteristic of every true conversation that each opens himself to the other person, truly accepts his point of view as worthy of consideration and gets inside the other to such an extent that he understands not a particular individual, but what he says. The thing that has to be grasped is the objective rightness or otherwise of his opinion, so that they can agree with each other on the subject. Thus, one does not relate the other's opinion to him, but to one's own views. Where a person is concerned with the other as an individuality, e.g. in a therapeutic conversation or the examination of a man accused of a crime, this is not really a situation in which two people are trying to understand each other.   (1975:347)

For Gadamer there are three modes of understanding the other. In the first, we try to understand what is typical of the other's behavior in order to make predictions about him. We seek to understand human nature. This mode would correspond to the understanding sought by human biologists, students of national character, and role theorists. In the second mode, we understand the other as a person, but understanding is still in the form of self-relatedness. This is a dialectical—a reflective—relationship, but, if I understand Gadamer correctly, not an immediate one. "To every claim, there is a counter claim," he (1975:270) writes. The third mode is immediate, open, and authentic. Unlike the second, in which the claim to understand the other creates a distance, this third, open mode eliminates distance. The speakers are aware, though, of their own historical situation—their prejudices and pre-understandings—and are thus open to their interlocutors' questions and claims. "Openness to the other, then, includes the acknowledgement that I must accept some of the things that are against myself, even though there is no one else who asks this of me." This third understanding is, I believe, rare in anthropological research (precluded in part by the researcher's scientific intention and required observational stance). It is longed for by some anthropologists who feel that *something* is missing in their understanding of the people they study.[5]

For Gadamer, true conversation takes place on this third level of understanding, of the open but not boundless question. Conversation requires "that the partners to it do not talk at cross purposes," that they are "with" one another, and that they allow themselves "to be conducted by the object" of conversation (1975:330) and not to conduct the conversation (1975:345). In true conversation something new and independent of the participants emerges. Referring to the Platonic dialogue, but extending it further, Gadamer asserts: "What emerges in its truth is the logos, which is neither mine nor yours and hence so far transcends the subjective opinions of the partners to the dialogue that even the person leading the conversation is always ignorant" (1975:331; 489).

There is a difference for Gadamer between "conducting a conversation"—a fixed interview, for example—and "falling into conversation" out of which something new comes. (Free association and the open-ended interview would be compromises between the two.) In the one instance, I suggest, all we come up with is data, which can be arranged into a picture. In the second, we have understanding—"the creative fact; the fertile fact; the fact that suggests and engenders" that Virginia Woolf (1942) writes about in her study of biography. Such understanding can easily degenerate into mere knowledge of human beings. The "creative," "fertile" fact can easily become a mere datum. How do we preserve understanding—the fact that suggests and engenders? Or is such an understanding another romantic illusion?

A South African Example

Let me illustrate these three modes of understanding with South African examples, which reflect a romanticism prevalent in hermeneutical and anthropological circles to which I am not immune. I shall not use my own experience but that of a white South African whom I have called Peter Cooke (Crapanzano

1985:88–90;252–254). Peter was unusual. Unlike most South African whites, he tried from time to time to take a nonwhite perspective.

Everyone who visits white South Africa is immediately given bits of information about people of other races. They resemble the bits of knowledge with which one comes away from a museum of natural history or from having read an old fashioned manners-and-customs ethnography. "A Zulu will never greet you first. You must greet him. He is not being impolite. He is being polite in terms of his own tradition," a white will tell you. Or, "Blacks have to learn a job step by step. They think serially. They have no sense of the whole." Peter made such remarks, but, unlike other whites, he tried to understand the nonwhites in their own terms. He described a discussion over pay he had with one of his coloured farm workers, who told Peter he could not afford to buy his child a birthday present.

> I said, "Henry, that's terrible." We chatted a bit about the kids' birthdays, and then I asked him if he had bought any wine the previous weekend . . . He said he had. "And weekend before?" I asked. He said he had. And then I asked him if he would rather buy wine for himself or a birthday present for his kid. Silence. I explained to him that when you need something special, you have to save for it. "If I want to go on holiday, Henry," I said, "I have to save for it. I have to do without other things. If I want to buy a motor car, I've got to put away for it. It means sacrificing other things." You see he would never think of giving up his wine for his kid's birthday present. That just doesn't register being important. I made my point, but it was totally lost.   (Crapanzano 1985:252–253)

Peter added that his disillusionment with coloured workers came from trying to understand them according to his own standards. "I've got to keep pinching myself. Look, boy, they're not brought up the way you were. They don't think as you do. Don't get upset. Relate to them according to their own background."

We see a progression from the manners-and-customs mode of understanding in which the other is simply an object to be understood and predicted, to a reckoning with the other as a subject—in this case one not understood. Although Peter did not realize that his examples could mean nothing to poor Henry, who earned 15 dollars a week, never knew what a holiday was, and never dreamed of having a motor car, he did reckon, with whatever *méconnaissance,* with Henry as a subject. There was here, especially in Peter's comments, the beginning of a dialectical relation. Peter in his subjectivity was different from Henry in his subjectivity, whatever that was for Peter. Peter's understanding or lack of it corresponds to Gadamer's second mode.

On another occasion Peter described his friendship with a Xhosa boy when they were both adolescents. Peter was invited to the Xhosa's initiation. When I asked Peter if his relationship to the Xhosa changed after the initiation, he answered.

> As children we could play together, wrestle together, throw balls at each other; but then suddenly there comes a time when all that stops. [Peter grew silent, and then after a few saddened moments he said, without, I think, realizing the irony.] I remember once, after my friend had become a man, jogging down to his hut in the evening. I said I'd race him to a tree, as we had often done in the past, and he refused. "I am a man, and I must walk with dignity. I can jog but I can't run." He could no longer carry a knobkerrie around. He had to carry a staff.   (Crapanzano 1985:90)

There is here, I believe, a glimmering of Gadamer's third— immediate and open—mode of understanding. As all of this occurred in South Africa, a country riven by apartheid, the movement is through the absence of understanding.

There are many kinds of encounters in the field, and how we respond to them depends upon our own assumptions about the significance of the encounter, the meaning of language, and the nature of understanding. When Peter talked to me about how blacks think, I listened, took notes, and had my data. When he described his experience with Henry, I listened with fascination. And when Peter told me the story of his Xhosa's friend's refusal to run, the romantic part of me felt a certain authenticity in his words. I could respond to him with a sympathetic silence and then with a story of my own, if I recall correctly, which had to do with my own excitement and disappointment at an older friend's becoming a man. My experience of Peter's words seems to parallel Peter's experience of the exchanges he recounted. I suppose my account of my exchanges with Peter, as he re-counted his exchanges with Henry and his Xhosa friend, serves a similar function in my exchange with you, the reader.

The Dialogue as a Model for Interpretation

Understanding a text is, for Gadamer, like understanding a live conversation. A common language, which is more than "a tool for the purposes of understanding," has to "coincide with the very act of understanding and reaching an agreement." The meaning of a text cannot be "compared with an immovably and obstinately fixed point of view"; it emerges over time through a delicate conversation which, if it is to be authentic, demands of the interpreter that he take account of his prejudices and pre-understanding (1975:350).[6] The interpreter, unlike the conversationalist, however, has to give expression to his "conversational partner's"—the text's—meaning.

Romantically, incantatorally, conversation is more than a metaphor (stretched to the limit, I would say) for describing the work of interpreting a text. Gadamer, despite all his concern for history, seems never to be *critically* concerned with the effects of the recontextualizations that occur with the interpreter's expression or re-expression of the text's meaning: for him the hermeneutical conversation becomes a sort of memory, restoring "the original communication of meaning" (1975:331).[7]

Tedlock also invokes a dialogical model for interpretation or at least for the armchair sequelae of the field experience. The dialogue in the field does not stop, he maintains, when the anthropologist leaves the field. "Again the armchair dialogue is something we all do, listening, puzzling, questioning, and, as it were, talking back" (1983:324). Like Gadamer, Tedlock does not discuss the new status of the recordings he has made, the problems of their decontextualization and recontextualization—of their appropriation—in shadow dialogues (the thinking about the dialogue that occurs as one engages silently in dialogue with absent interlocutors). The partners in the primary dialogue become figures in this new dialogue that by-passes them.

To assume as Tedlock and others do that the interpreter can engage in a dialogue with his recordings, texts, and other materials is to err on three counts: (1) by taking a metaphorical relationship (the interpretation of a text is like a dialogue) nonmetaphorically; (2) by failing to recognize that the *dialogue* with which the interpreter is now dialoguing is no longer a dialogue but a "dialogue"—the theme of another dialogue; and (3) by granting the interpreter what has to be regarded as a superhuman ability to bracket off secondary dialogues and their language. Husserl's *epochè* fails inevitably because the transcendental reduction is carried through the language of description of his transcendentally reduced objects of consciousness (*noema*) and of the intentional consciousness themselves (*noesis*).

Spoken Genres

Dialogue comes from the Greek *dialogos*. *Dia* is a preposition that means "through," "between," "across," "by," and "of." It is akin to *dyo* and *di*, meaning "two." As a prefix in English *dia* suggests a "passing through" as in diathermy, "thoroughly" or "completely" as in diagnosis, a "going apart" as in dialysis, and "opposed in moment" as in diamagnetism. *Logos* comes from *legein*, "to speak." It may mean thought as well as speech— thought, as Onians (1951:76n9) points out, that is conceived materially as breath, spirit, *pneuma*. Hence etymologically a dialogue is a speech across, between, through two people. It is a passing through and a going apart. Dialogue has a transformational as well as an oppositional dimension—an agonistic one. It is a relationship of considerable tension.

The dialogue is opposed to the monograph. "Monograph" also comes from the Greek. *Monos* means "alone" and is perhaps akin to *manos*, "thin." As a prefix in English *mono* means "alone," "single," or "one." Graph, *graphe*, from *graphein* means a "representation by lines," a "drawing," a "painting," as well as "writing." *Graphein* was used, according to Onians (1951:417), to describe the tapestry or pattern embroidery of the *Moirai* (Fates) and even to mean fate. A monograph in the sense of writing is thus a single writing or a writing that stands alone—as a fatality, perhaps. It is pictorial—representational—without inherent tension.

Etymologically, at least, there is an immense difference between a dialogue, a speech passing between two who are in some way opposed, and a monograph, a writing, a text, that stands alone and is fated or embodies fate. The one is agonistic, live, dramatic; the other is pictorial, static, authoritative. Since Plato's *Phaedrus* at least, the two have been opposed to each other and have been defined accordingly.

The pitting of dialogue against monograph has probably led to an oversimplification of both. Certainly Tedlock's minimalist definition of dialogue is not adequate to the many modes of human communication, including the poetic. (Suffering in his last years from schizophrenia, Hölderlin seems to have lost the ability to take part in conversation, but he did not lose the ability to produce extraordinarily beautiful and "meaningful," if deicticless, poetry [Jakobson 1981].) Nor does Heidegger's (1971; 1967) rather more romantic definition do justice to these many modes: "Now, what does 'dialogue' mean? Apparently the speaking with each other about something. In the course of this, the speaking mediates the coming together."[8] There seems to be an awful lot of speaking that occurs that is not dialogical insofar as dialogue is conceived as a crossing, a reaching across, a sharing, if not of a common ground of understanding, then of a common communicative presumption, a "coming together," a fusion. Is the recitative a dialogue? Are people who "talk at each other" engaged in a dialogue? Is there dialogue in a nasty argument? In a verbal exchange between a master and a servant (between Peter and Henry)? In a seduction as opposed to lovemaking? Indeed, Rilke's two bridges separated by an abyss seems a more accurate model for many of the verbal exchanges even when the speakers speak the same language.

The point is that there are many genres of spoken as well as written communications with different implications, even within a single culture (Bakhtin 1986; Todorov 1984), and these genres can be distinguished not only through linguistic and stylistic analysis but more immediately, though not necessarily explicitly, by members of the culture themselves. As Alasdair Mac-

Intyre (1984:211) suggests, comprehension may well depend upon our ability to classify a particular conversation as "a drunken, rambling quarrel," "a serious intellectual disagreement," or "a comic, even farcical misconstrual of each other's motives."[9] MacIntyre is talking about a conversation overheard by a nonparticipant, but the same can be true for the participants, either retrospectively or in reflective moments of live conversation (Apel 1987). How often have we changed the course of a conversation when we realize that the person with whom we are talking has taken a different tack? We start out serious and end up joking; we start out joking and end up serious. There is tension in such genre allocations, as every writer knows. When Pierre begins to tell the dispirited, sardonic Andrei Bolkonsky about Freemasonry, the reader of *War and Peace* anxiously awaits Bolkonsky's response (as does Pierre himself). Will Bolkonsky dismiss Pierre's talk as the mere preaching of the newly converted? Will he accept it as an authentic discourse specifically addressed to him?

The failure to master the genres of social conversation is the outsider's weak point. Mikhail Bakhtin (1986:80) has observed that frequently a person who has an excellent command of speech in some areas, such as delivering a scholarly paper, is awkward in other conversational situations. The ability to master a repertoire of genres is not, in my view, fully coordinated with linguistic competence taken abstractly. I have known anthropologists who have mastered a language beautifully and yet remain cultural clods, and others who are conversationally graceful with little knowledge of a language.

The genres of oral discourse determine the course of any utterance. "We choose words according to their generic specifications," Bakhtin (1986:87) writes. Genres "correspond to typical situations of speech communication, and, consequently, also to particular contacts between the *meanings* of words and actual concrete reality under certain typical circumstances" (87). They are collective and demand completion—through the *responsive understanding* of the speaker's interlocutor (68).

The conventions of dialogue itself have varied in Western literary tradition, as has their presumed influence on nonliterary communication. We have, as Roger Deakins (1980) notes, "dia-

logue" and "familiar talk" in the sixteenth century; the "conference" and "meeting" in the seventeenth century; the eighteenth
century's "conversation"; the "colloquy" of the nineteenth; and
of course the "interview" of our own century. Such dialogue
genres may give the illusion of an open-ended conversation or
they may suggest a highly conventionalized closed communication, say, between diplomats or courtiers. They may serve as a
vehicle in which the author expresses his views through one
character—a sort of dialogically masked monologue—or they
may offer a range of current and competing views, without the
author's own position being explicitly given. Or they may even
suggest in some theater-of-the-absurd manner mere banter that
"never really goes anywhere."[10] Presumably these different
conventions have affected the way in which Westerners have
engaged with non-Westerners—a point that has not been given
sufficient attention by historians of anthropology and travel—
and it has certainly affected the way in which such engagements
have been reported and interpreted.

The genres of oral discourse are intimately related to these
literary genres and as Greg Urban (1986) has argued, to ritual
genres as well. Urban suggests that the ceremonial dialogues
characteristic of many Indian groups in South America not only
imitate ordinary conversation but provide a model for such conversation. More limited stylistically and pragmatically than ordinary conversation, the ceremonial dialogue becomes a sign vehicle for dialogue itself, directing attention, however, not only
to linguistic exchange but to social coordination and solidarity.
It could of course be argued that every dialogue, and not just
such privileged dialogue as the ceremonial or the literary,
serves as a model for itself. Such, presumably, would be Gregory Bateson's (1972:159–176) position: by participating in a dialogue the participant learns what a dialogue is and how to participate in it.[11] And, I should add, how to decontextualize it.

Negotiating Dialogical Conventions

Whatever effect indigenous dialogue models have on the dialogues the anthropologist witnesses and engages in, his own
models affect them and his understanding of them. The "negoti-

ations of reality" that take place in the field are not only concerned with what "reality" is, but, perhaps more significantly, with its expression (Crapanzano 1980). There is always a struggle between the anthropologist and the people he works with over the appropriate forms of discourse. Given the power relations in the field, the native often succumbs or appears to succumb to the ethnographer's insistent genre, the interview, where every "short" question demands a long, sincere, and relevant answer. Exotic, unexpected content can blind the ethnographer to the native's surrender to the ethnographer's form of expression, as the native understands it. All too often, when the effect of genre and convention are recognized, they are justified—or dismissed—on dubious methodological grounds. Mary Black's (1969) suggestion that the "white room" is ideal for collecting linguistic data for semantic analysis carries such methodological presumption to an absurdity that would vie, had she any humor, with Ionesco's.

We must not assume, however, that when a native appears to have acquiesced to the conventions of the interview, he has understood them as the anthropologist does and accepted them as the anthropologist desires. Faqir Mohammed, for example, a Moroccan farmer whom Kevin Dwyer (1982) interviewed over several months, seemed to have accepted the conventions of Dwyer's ethnographic interview, but this appears dubious after Dwyer (1982:219) asked him to reflect on their relationship and what they had been doing.[12]

> K.D. And what do you think that I think about·you? What might I say to myself about you?
> F.M. You're the one who understands that. Why, am I going to enter into your head?
> K.D. But you can't enter the sheikh's head, or Si Hasan's, yet you said something about what they might think of you.
> F.M. I don't know. That—I don't know about it. I don't know about that.
> K.D. All right.

Dwyer changed the subject. He notes that his question was too direct, producing "a somewhat uncomfortable moment," and that Mohammed "would not be drawn into an answer." Clearly, he found Dwyer's demand for self-reflection disturbing because it went against *his* "construction" of the interview, against his sense of propriety and etiquette, and presumably against his motivations (whatever they were) for participating in it.

Later in the same interview Dwyer (1982:225–226) asks Mohammed to explain what he thinks Dwyer is doing in the village.

F.M. My thoughts about that are what you've told me yourself, that's what I've put in my thoughts. What you write down is what you understand, and you try to understand a lot, so that you make the others understand, those whom you teach. That is as far as my thoughts go.

K.D. Well, I ask you a lot of things. To your mind, what is the most important subject that we talk about? You know, for some subjects you might say to yourself, "What is the sense of talking, for so long about such a thing?" Or, on the other hand, you might think, "Oh, that's really interesting."

F.M. As for me, I know that I'm not concerned with a single one of your questions. I know that these questions serve your purposes, not mine. I think about the questions, whether they are small questions or large ones, and I think about them because they serve your purposes, not mine.

K.D. Well, what do you like me to ask you about?

F.M. It doesn't matter to me, you could even ask me about snakes.

Negativism, snake symbolism, and propriety aside, it is clear that Mohammed's participation in Dwyer's interviews is not motivated by a fascination with the subjects Dwyer wants to talk about but by a desire to maintain a relationship that he values with Dwyer. Direct questions about the relationship threaten it by formulating and objectifying it. The relationship—the conversation, however extraordinary from a Moroccan's point of view—would lose the subtlety and flexibility that are so highly valued in Morocco.

Being in the Dialogue

The dialogues that Tedlock, Dwyer, and other proponents of a dialogical anthropology write about are primarily those in which the anthropologist is one of the participants. They do not, however, adequately consider the implications of this "position" on their understanding of dialogue. Although they acknowledge the role the anthropologist plays in the elicitation and formulation of his "objective" data, they do not recognize the peculiar authorial (if I may use the word in both a literal and metaphorical way) presumption in their participant-observational stance: a presumption that permits them to be both engaged in the field encounter (to the point even of determining its direction) and to be removed from it, rather like an otiose deity observing, recording, and interpreting its creation. The *real* problem, so often hidden in anthropological discussions of participant observation that focus on the participation, is how to extricate oneself from all the participation—how to observe, how to find an external vantage point, and how to recognize the legitimacy and the limitations of that vantage point. (The anthropologist in his objectivist mode can aspire to the otiose—and feel all the guilt that comes from such separation—but he is no deity and can never achieve that objectivity without the help of another, an authoritative interlocutor, whom in his presumption he often fails to acknowledge.)

Anthropologists often attempt to resolve the problems of extrication by clinging uncritically to some theoretical perspective that gives them an appropriate distance, or to some methodological strategy that is "independent" of their research encounter. Many folklorists and anthropologists (Darnell 1974; Barre 1969) interested in oral literature have succumbed to the illusion that with appropriate instruments they can obtain a near-perfect rendition of what transpired, and thereby either extricate themselves from the encounter or adequately appraise their role in it. We await impatiently the multiperspectival, gustato-tactico-olfactory holograph sensitive to body heat, heartbeat, brain waves, and sexual arousal, and the evolution of a being capable of comprehending all of its data from a universally acceptable vantage point, but until that day we have humbly to make do with our perceptual and interpretive limitations. We have to recognize that we are *inextricably* involved in our research encounters and that any attempt to extricate ourselves from them theoretically, methodologically, or technically will have to be justified by our research, and other, interests that are not totally independent of the encounters themselves, and not by fantasies of theoretical, methodological, and technical perfection, which keep us from acknowledging our own insufficiency. I hasten to add, lest I be misunderstood, that I do not deny the ability of theory, methodology, and technology to improve our perceptions and sharpen our interpretations. I wish simply to preserve a realistic view of that capacity.

Tedlock goes to great pains to show that the anthropologist cannot be eliminated from the ethnographic encounter. In "The Story of How a Story Was Made" (1983b), he describes several different ways in which his presence affected the narratives he heard. In one case Tedlock—his tape recorder, at any rate—forced an anticipation of the decontextualization that would occur in the playback, transcription, and publication of the tale he collected from the Zuni. It "dampened" the audience's response and prevented the performer from "entangling" members of the audience in the story (1983b:302). On another occasion, the absence of the tape recorder "bared the conversational ground not only between the performer and the audience but also between the performer and the fieldworker" (1983b:302).[13] This is how Tedlock saw it, though it may well be that the Zuni perceived a different attitude in Tedlock without his tape recorder, Tedlock and many other anthropologists who make use of the recording devices tend to symbolize the "split" between participant and observer in terms of the "fieldworker" and the "tape recorder." They do not appear to recognize this symbolism and its implications for their studies.

Despite all the concern anthropologists show for language, despite their recent interest in the writing of ethnography, they tend to regard their own language as transparent. They do not always appreciate the difference between themselves and their interlocutors in the immediate field situation and in various renditions and representations, including the endopsychic ones, that occur in retrospection and remembrance. Here they become characters in some secondary conversation or dialogue. Tedlock talking to the Zuni is no longer Tedlock but "Tedlock." This should be obvious, though it is not always so, when the anthropologist describes the field situation and his role in it. We succumb to what can be called an *autobiographical illusion* and ignore the literary strategies—the generic constraints and conventions—by which an author represents himself.[14]

It is of course less obvious that the anthropologist has become a character in a tape recording or a transcription of a tape recording, but despite the differences between recording an event and describing it, the recording, like the description, is not the event. It is a peculiarly evaluated, closed, repeatable rendition of the event that has been framed, even with the concurrence of its participants, in a way that bypasses it. It has become the theme of a second dialogue. The participants become characters in this second dialogue just as they do in the descriptions of the recorded event, and any characterization or evaluation will reflect their symbolic status. We see this clearly in Dwyer's preambles to his conversations with Faqir Mohammed and in his comments on specific exchanges. When Dwyer (1982:228) agrees, for example, with the comment that "There is talk women shouldn't hear"—Mohammed is explaining why he does not eat with his family—the author has to add a footnote: "I agreed with the Faqir here, although I certainly would not if the conversation were with someone from New York"! There is, I suppose, always something embarrassing about being quoted, for one both recognizes and does not recognize oneself.

Much has been written about the interview in methodological treatises that could be considered in literary terms as prescriptive of genre and convention as, say, the rules of prosody and unity were for French classical theater. We cannot of course know to what extent such rules are followed in the field. We do know, however, that they affect the way the data collected in the field (by whatever means) are reported. Indirectly, for example, data tend to be presented in a manner that does not focus on how they were specifically collected—on the role of the ethnographer in procuring them—creating thereby an objectivist, timeless aura that marks the data as data, the investigation as science. Directly, the effects of methodological prescription can be seen in the reports of such interviews. Granting even the accuracy of reportage (a possibility that can be contested, as I have suggested, on a number of grounds other than those of the reporter's sincerity and honesty), we find only truncated reports, if any, of what happened before and after the "interview," of how first contact was established, how the interview was explained, what trial runs were conducted, what comments were made afterward, what excerpting and editing rules were followed. A pseudo-formalism that betrays the lived field experience but meets the criteria of scientific investigation is thereby created. It is clear that such presentations of what occurred are determined not just by what transpired in the field but by the shadow dialogues of the ethnographer with his colleagues and theoretical positions.

Even in works as sensitive to the dynamics of the exchange as Dwyer's, the dialogues seem removed from their original context. Dwyer and Faqir Mohammed become cardboard figures in some minimalist drama that could be taking place almost anywhere were it not for its "Moroccan content" that serves deictically to place them in a highly stylized, ethnographic Morocco.[15] Is it this minimalism that renders the exchanges as "vulnerable" as Dwyer would have them? Although the exchanges are at times meta-discursive, that is, they become their own subject matter, more often they are concerned with external matters that are not explained or described in a way that gives even an inkling of the pragmatically creative dimension of the exchange. Those indexical locutions that do not refer immediately to the exchange itself, that are not shifters in Jakobson's (1963) sense, seem to reflect a flattened context (affirmed by an authoritative ethnographic introduction) that has none of the presumable "warmth," "character," and "texture" of the original exchanges. They leave the reader and the ethnographer with the feeling that something vital has been left out.[16]

"While ethnographies cast as encounters between two individuals may successfully dramatize the intersubjective give-and-take of fieldwork and introduce a counterpoint of authoritative voices," James Clifford (1988:43) writes (without explaining what he means by "successfully dramatize"), "they remain representations of dialogue." They may create the illusion of immediacy—a transparent repetition—and as such the ethnographies may, I suppose, be taken as fictions—but they are in fact subject to all sorts of representational constraints. The most notable of these I call radical pragmatic reduction and radical pragmatic reorientation. By *pragmatic reduction,* I mean the inevitable elimination of the continuously constituted context of the *original* utterance. By *pragmatic reorientation,* I refer to the inevitable recontextualization—the appropriation—of the dialogical utterance, any repeated utterance for that matter, that occurs with its representation and participation in secondary dialogues. Pragmatic reduction leads to the flattening I mentioned earlier, and pragmatic reorientation vivifies the secondary dialogues that appear at times to betray (for the ethnographer at least) the lived field encounter. We should recognize, as Socrates would surely have recognized, that Plato's compromise— the written dialogue—is indeed written and subject to all of the uses and misuses of the written, the quoted, word.

Contextualization

Although Henry James had written several dialogical novels like *Confidence,* in which there is minimum contextualization of the characters' utterances (certainly when compared to such hypercontextualized novels as *The Golden Bowl*), he came to regard the dialogical novel as inadequate because it lacked a "medium" or context. We have to recognize that what constitutes a satisfactory context is in fact culture-specific. Traditional ethnographies—Tedlock would call them analogic—such as Radin's *The Winnebago Tribe* or Lienhardt's *Divinity and Experience*—present timeless pictures of the society they are describing. They piece together bits and pieces of socio-cultural material according to a model that is methodologically or theoretically rationalized in such a way as to deny its literary conventions and the constraints they impose. Society, culture, become containers in which certain rarely particularized events— abstract socio-cultural processes—are staged. There is minimal narrative (historical) movement, and any that occur is frequently framed as a case study that exemplifies the abstract processes and legitimates their frame. We might say, following Bakhtin (1981:84–258), that in such traditional ethnographies the spatial dimension of the chronotype (literally, time-space, the way time and space, the "world," are characteristically organized in a particular genre) dominates the temporal dimension, which is highly elaborated in narrative literature. "In the literary artistic chronotope, spatial and temporal indicators are fused into one carefully thought-out, concrete whole. Time, as it were, thickens, takes on flesh, becomes artistically visible; likewise space becomes charged and responsive to the movement of time, plot, and history. The intersection of axes and fusions of indicators characterizes the artistic chronotope" (Bakhtin 1981:84). The "camp," the "village," the "slum," the "market," the "hearth," and the "ritual precinct" are the principal chronotopes of traditional ethnography. Perhaps because their temporal dimension is minimally and abstractly elaborated, they tend to be lifeless.

In dialogical ethnographies, or in ethnographies that are sensitive to the dialogues that gave birth to them, the representation of context presents particular problems. As Jiri Veltrusky (1977:128) observed, dialogue unfolds in both time and space. "Every single unit of dialogue is situated at a unique point of intersection of the continuum of time and the continuum of space or, to put it differently, in a specific "here and now." *This here and now keeps changing,* just as in every discourse the present continuously turns into the past and the future into the present" (emphasis mine). The relationship between the dialogue and this "constantly changing here and now"—Veltrusky calls it *the extralinguistic situation of the dialogue*—is "intense and reciprocal." The situation affects "the way the dialogue unfolds" and the dialogue "throws new light on the situation and often modifies or even transforms it" (Veltrusky 1977:128). Not only is there no unchanging context but there is no single context. Quoting Mukarovsky (1977), Veltrusky argues that in contrast to the monologue's "single and uninterupted context"—a point I would contest—the dialogue has at a minimum the two interpenetrating contexts of its participants. Insofar as they are opposed to each other, their dialogue is characterized by "sharp semantic reversals" at the borderline between their individual speeches. (Think of the exchanges between Kevin Dwyer and Faqir Mohammed.) What unity occurs derives from the subject matter or theme (Mukarovsky 1977). In other words, the essentially agonistic dimension of the dialogue (articulated pragmatically through the constitution of competitive contexts including the personnel) is marked by a semantically understood theme whose pragmatic effect—to create unity or the illusion of unity—is concealed by its very semanticity. For a theme to be pragmatically effective its pragmatic capacity has to be concealed behind a semantic veil: this paradox is what makes the discussion of the theme so fraught with tension. It may also account for the banality of most discussions, wherein the conventional preserves the phatic function, the coming together of the exchange. And it may further account for the particular vulnerability that participants, anthropologists and others, experience in cross-cultural dialogues.[17]

The tensions between several contexts and their continual changes are reflected in Gadamer's discussion of the fusion of horizons. "Every encounter with tradition that takes place within historical consciousness," writes Gadamer (1975:273), involves the experience of the tension between text and present. "Historical consciousness is aware of its own otherness and hence distinguishes the horizon of tradition from its own. On the other hand, it is itself, as we are trying to show, only something laid over a continuing tradition, and hence it immediately recombines what it has distinguished in order, in the unity of the historical horizon that it thus acquires, to become again one with itself." Here, as so often with Gadamer and the other phenomenologists, conversational exchanges are reflected, refracted perhaps, in their theory—a theory which, despite its interest in language, does not recognize the effects of that language on itself. The result is a confusion of description and prescription. Gadamer's discussion, which points at once to the agonistic dimension of dialogue and to its dissolution in "tradition," exemplifies the unifying function of the theme in a process that can only be called mystifying. A pseudo-temporality—from awareness of the tensions between contexts to fusion—conceals the contemporaneity of the pragmatically constituted separation of contexts (horizon, vantage point) and the pragmatically constituted (though semantically veiled) union (fusion, coincidence) of the theme. Whatever reality and significance the theme may have in itself, it also serves an ideological, a mystifying function.

If the extralinguistic situation of the dialogue is constantly changing (whether fully or in part) how is it possible to describe that context in a way that does justice to it? (And insofar as the representation of dialogue and its context, however described, are themselves dialogical), how is it possible to describe its changing context of representation?) Clearly, we have to face the limitations of our descriptive capacity. However we depict the context, however acceptable our choice of contextual features, however sensitive to the dialogical movement of the here and now, our contextualizations will always clash with the reality we are depicting. If we participate in the dialogue, as most anthropologists do in the dialogues they represent, then the choice of context (whatever its claim to objectivity) will always favor the anthropologist's context. (Such a position is of course intolerable to the proponents of dialogical anthropology who have been conned by the egalitarian ideology, the "mutuality," of dialogue [Clifford 1988].) If we depict a dialogue we have witnessed but in which we have not participated, we create a "third" context even when we wish to appropriate the context of one of the speakers. We cannot ask the parties to the dialogue to describe the context because their particular retrospective contextualizations will serve pragmatic functions in their talk with us and will be modified accordingly, even with the best of wills. In narrative literature, particularly in third person accounts, all sorts of conventions for describing changing contexts have been developed: descriptions of the verbal exchange itself, of expressions and gestures, of the object of indexical locutions, of the unstated perceptions and thoughts of the characters, of "objective" features of the surroundings as they are highlighted. Such conventions usually imply some sort of omniscient or partially omniscient, certainly disengaged, narrator. They have not been accepted in sciences that so privilege the recorded word as to exclude the imaginative context that comprehension will necessitate.

Whatever their objective claims, contextualizations are never neutral. They always have an imperative function; they tell us how the exchange they "enclose" is to be read. They confirm, thereby, the theoretical underpinning of—the rationalizations for—such instruction. The circle—theory-instruction-context-theory—is never complete (except in the most reductive social descriptions). It is, up to a point, always responsive to the pragmatic struggle of the enclosed exchange. In the primary dialogue the anthropologist and his informants struggle to determine the context of the dialogue. In the secondary dialogue—the anthropologist's description of the context of the primary dialogue—he is responsive to both the primary struggle and the secondary one with outside authorities. Insofar as there is a tension between the primary dialogical contextualization and the secondary anthropological contextualization, the latter does not fully dominate—does not reduce the situation to a mere confirmation of its theoretical claims.[18] Such a tension can be disquieting and produce all sorts of (conservative) reactions, ranging from the denial of the tension to an overestimation of the worth of the theoretical legitimation of the contextual choice.

Appropriation

At one point in "Analogical Tradition and Dialogical Anthropology," Tedlock (1983a) recalls taking his Zuni friend Andrew Peynetsa to a Hopi Snake Dance at Walpi. As the two men were crossing the dangerous neck that joins Walpi with the rest of First Mesa, Andrew said:

> Straight down!
> Both sides!
> You jump one way, and
> I'll jump the other.

But in fact, Tedlock (1983:331) notes, the two of them walked straight ahead, "staying in earshot of each other." The image is striking, particularly following the "poetic" form in which Tedlock transcribes Andrew's words. But for whom is it powerful? And in what way? In Tedlock's essay, the image relates to his discussion of dialogue, giving it the desired ethno-romantic tone. Jumping off the neck is symbolic of those analogical ethnographies in which the anthropologist abandons the dialogical, and walking on "in earshot of each other" is symbolic of a dialogical approach that continues even after the anthropologist has left the field. But what does Tedlock's rendition of Andrew's words have to do with Andrew and the Zuni? What did Andrew's words mean? Readers unfamiliar with Zuni culture, with

Tedlock's relationship with Andrew, have no way of knowing what Andrew meant. Was he making a suggestion? Was he making a joke? Was he reciting a poem? Was he expressing anxiety about attending a Snake Dance? Was he saying something about the dialogical space in which he and Tedlock found themselves? Was he referring to some previous conversation, perhaps even about dialogue, that he had with Tedlock? Despite Tedlock's concern for the contexts of the narratives he collects, he decontextualizes and recontextualizes—appropriates—Andrew's words in a way that gives them aesthetic significance in a dialogue that has little to do, one surmises, with their original occurrence. And now of course they are part of another dialogue, between my readers and me, including perhaps Tedlock, but probably not Andrew Peynetsa.

To argue that the reproduction of the field dialogue gives an independent voice to the participants to the dialogue—the native and the ethnographer—is to deny the ethnographer's power (Clifford 1988; Tylor 1981; Crapanzano 1980). It is the ethnographer who appropriates the word both through representation and contextualization, and, as any gossip knows, he who has the word has the power of the word. Such is the tyranny of quotation. Writing has drastically extended the range of quotation and the power inherent in the word's appropriation. Subject of course to political and economic considerations, which should not be so exaggerated as to remove responsibility from the ethnographer, he as author has final control over the word. It is he who decides to select, to edit, to publish, to provide the "appropriate" context and theoretical orientation. So much is obvious.

But what does it mean to say the ethnographer has control over the word? We must not grant him an irrealistic omnipotence (however strongly we are ruled by the nineteenth century's convention of the omniscient narrator that is characteristic, implicitly at least, of much ethnography). Like the people he talks to, the ethnographer engages in a verbal transaction which, whatever his power, he cannot control completely. Indeed, Gadamer (1975:343) would argue that any participant's control over a verbal exchange precludes its being an authentic conversation, for a conversation has a spirit of its own that escapes the will of its participants. We do not have to invoke conversational spirits and risk their reification to recognize that conversation, dialogue, and many other verbal exchanges (perhaps all exchanges, including the set questionnaire) are independent of their participants' control if only because the participants have no external vantage point from which to control these exchanges. (I am of course excluding consideration of the aleatory in such encounters.) The participants to the encounter (except perhaps when they are swept by its flow) are certainly able to disengage themselves from it and evaluate it. Such disengagements and evaluations are attested both experientially and through the presence of shifters and other reflective and evaluative locutions in the exchange itself. But such disengagements, as I have suggested, are never complete. There can be no fixed vantage point. Rather the process of disengagement depends upon the participation over time in shadow dialogues so authoritative for the participants as to sustain the illusion that they have a fixed, timeless, "objective" vantage point. The ethnographer's—anyone's—participation in these shadow dialogues, with a colleague, an important theoretical position, or a symbolically significant person provides him with a position external to the immediate exchange, though it is never fixed or timeless, that enables him to reproduce the exchange and offer an interpretation of it. I hasten to add that the other participants to the dialogue are also engaged in shadow dialogues that afford them external vantage points and enable them to reproduce and interpret the dialogue when they choose.

The recognition of such shadow dialogues is always disturbing in a conversation. It is as though a third party were observing and evaluating what one said. We become aware of them when our interlocutor uses, for example, a stylistic register that appears inappropriate. He may be distracted; he may appear to be addressing someone else; he makes "asides"; he speaks automatically; he "edits" what he has to say according to standards that have nothing to do with the occasion as we understand it and assume he does too. Revealing the existence of such shadow dialogues or at least their possibility is not without its effect. It can intimate an invisible presence. Think, for example, of the hushed tones, as though someone were listening, in a church, a cemetery, or a place that spirits are thought to frequent. It can suggest a special relationship one's interlocutor has with supernatural powers. I sometimes felt that my conversations with Moroccan Arabs who were said to be demonically possessed were mediated by the demon. They seemed to be addressing the demon or at least articulating what they had to say in terms that would be approved by the demon (Crapanzano 1980). This other audience can also give an aura of power to one's interlocutor. Think of the eloquent professor of philosophy who in his introductory lectures appears to be addressing the great minds of history, as he lectures his students.

Often we come to embody the secondary interlocutor and suffer a sort of cognitive vertigo. We don't know who we really are: our conventional selves or whoever it is we embody for our interlocutor. It is an old shaman's trick and one that Hamlet himself uses as he attempts to discover the truth about his father's death (see Chapter 13). Most often, however, we converse with others in such a way as to conceal our shadow evaluative dialogues from them.

Thus far I have used *shadow dialogue* loosely to refer to those dialogues that one partner to the primary dialogue has with an interlocutor, real or imaginary, who is not present at the primary dialogue. Such dialogues are "silent," "mental," "quasi-articulate," "beneath consciousness" though capable, at least in part, of becoming conscious. They are analogous to thought when it is conceived as a conversation (Vygotsky 1962). We have in fact to distinguish between at least two types of shadow dialogue. The first occurs during the primary dialogue; the second, interpretive one, takes place after the fact.

In the first type, the absent interlocutor gives at least the illusion of a more or less stable, external vantage point to the primary dialogue and permits thereby those reflective moments, self-conscious or not, that are marked by shifters, hedges, and other meta-discursive locutions ("as we were talking off the record," "as it were," "by that I suppose you mean," "figuratively speaking," "so-to-speak"). The absent interlocutor is a symbolically complex "figure" who is never so fixed, defined, and immutable (except perhaps for the paranoid, the obsessive) as the "real" interlocutors in primary discourse. Reflection radically recontextualizes the dialogue. It places it and its participants in quotation marks. The primary dialogue becomes the theme of the shadow dialogue; its participants become its characters. They—the dialogue and its characters—are appropriated. Given the pressures of the ongoing conversation, such an appropriation is transitory but not without its effect on the conversation.

In the second type of shadow dialogue—the interpretive dialogue—the interpreter engages with the primary dialogue dialogically. The dialogue, now in quotation marks, is appropriated and oriented toward an interlocutor who is wholly external to the primary dialogue and who provides *the* interpretive vantage point. (The instability of this secondary interlocutor causes the "shiftings" of perspective that occur in even the most rigorous interpretations.) This shadow dialogue seems to have escaped the critical attention of Gadamer and other proponents of a dialogical approach to interpretation. To be sure, insofar as Gadamer recognizes community, tradition, pre-understandings, and prejudices, he can account for some of the pressures produced by a significant, empowered interlocutor in the shadow dialogues, but "community," "tradition," "pre-understanding" and "prejudices" are too monolithic, too stable to provide a subtle enough basis for understanding the complex plays of power and desire in the production and reproduction, the representation and interpretation of dialogues. We have to remember that whatever the resistance of those with whom we converse, they are always a little our creation as we are a little their creation. That empirical fact may mark the limit of our empiricism.

· III ·

THE EXPERIENCED SELF

9.
Symbols and Symbolizing

In his "Remarques sur le symbolisme religieux," Mircea Eliade (1962) observes that the world "speaks" through symbols. The symbol, more accurately the religious symbol,[1] reveals something deeper and more fundamental than ordinary reality. It enables man to objectify his subjective experience and to recognize within its particularity a universality. It always points away from the immediate to another plane of reality that Eliade identifies as the sacred. Its function remains invariable: "to transform an object or an act into something other than that object or act as it appears from the perspective of profane experience" (Eliade 1975:374). There is in Eliade's thought a *rupture* between the contingent and the transcendent dimensions of the symbol: the symbol out of context and history *in that other, that mythic time and space*. The religious symbol, if not itself a hierophany, points to a manifestation of the sacred and can, at least for Eliade's putative archaic man, become one with it.

In Eliade's theory of symbolism, reference is understood in terms of a split between the vehicle of reference and the object of reference, in other words, between the signifying chain and the chain of signification. Restated in these terms, Eliade's symbol-as-vehicle, as a signifier, is identified with the immediate, the particular, the profane, with history. That which is symbolized, the signified, is identified with the transcendent, the universal, the sacred, with mythic time. The symbolized, like Plato's idea, has both an ontological and an epistemological priority over the vehicle of symbolization, over mundane reality. But the symbol is no mere copy of the symbolized—and here Eliade parts company with Plato (or at least certain readings of Plato) and joins with Plotinus, the Gnostics, and, for that matter, the nineteenth-century Symbolist poets: the symbol can become one with the symbolized. The profane vehicle of the symbol can coalesce with its sacred tenor to form a single hierophanous unity. The rupture between the symbol and the symbolized can be overcome by certain "participations," certain rituals to which modern man, that is, fallen man, is no longer or rarely susceptible, but to which archaic man, Eliade's (1975:763) version of prelapsarian man, was susceptible.

Eliade's emphasis on the symbol's relationship to a transcendent referent or "reality" *in illo tempore,* enables him to ignore the process by which a symbol becomes a symbol and is maintained as such. His approach is neither diacritical (as in structuralist linguistics) nor rigorously context-bound (as in certain hermeneutical studies). It is comparative in the philological sense of the word and rests ultimately on a naive phenomenology of the symbol. The meanings of a symbol, such as the Cosmic Tree in its various occurrences, are compared to uncover the symbol's ultimate structure. The several meanings of the Cosmic Tree as an *imago mundi,* as an *axis mundi* uniting heaven, earth, and the underworld, and as a principle of regeneration are rendered possible because the Cosmic Tree finally symbolizes "the mystery of the world in perpetual regeneration" (Eliade 1962:291). Eliade's aim is not to reduce any one symbolic expression to another but to discover the process or the structure—his language is loose—by which different meanings are borne by the "same" symbol. His approach is integrationist.

We must ask, however, what are the results of such comparisons? Why regard all occurrences of a symbol as forming a single solidarity? Why consider, for example, the Cosmic Tree in Indonesia today as, at some level, the same as the Cosmic Tree in ancient Mesopotamia? Do we not risk producing a new symbolikon, a meta-mythology that is legitimated through "scholarship"? What are the implications of such a symbolikon? What, if anything, does it conceal? The problem Eliade confronts is, at least implicitly, Platonic. How can we account for unity in diversity—a unity of meaning in a diversity of contexts? And as with Plato, so with Eliade and his archaic man, a transcendent reality is postulated and hypostatized.

My aim is not to criticize Eliade despite the many problems in his conceptualization of the symbol. Here, I should like to consider his thought as a precipitate of a particular approach to the symbol, to language more generally, and to the text. This way of thinking is deeply embedded in Western thought and restrained by those linguistically facilitated epistemological configurations that Foucault (1966) calls epistemes. Focused on the symbol, this approach risks reifying not only the symbol but, as in Plato and Eliade, the symbolized. It gives priority to the givenness of the symbol, the symbol *an sich*, its facticity, its permanence, its solidarity in multiple contexts rather than to the context-bound creation and re-creation, the continuous creation, of the symbol and, for that matter, the symbolized.

Does scholarship such as Eliade's, by declaring the permanence of symbolic meaning and efficacy, render the (profane) context of the symbol insignificant? Is such scholarship a compliment to ritual? Does not "ritual," by creating the illusion of a timeless context, create the illusion of a permanence of symbolic meaning and efficacy? (The quotation marks around "ritual" acknowledge it as a category of the very thought that is in question.) Has scholarship replaced or replicated mythology in the collusive conjunction of myth and ritual? We must remember the role of exegesis in even the most primitive ritual and myth. We must recognize the ease with which exegetic space can be occupied by outside scholarship and the risks of such an occupation.

Exegesis is the (illusory) fulfillment of a desire for completion. It is an inherent dimension of all referentially understood symbolic activity; for the symbol, as it has been understood in the West, is marked by a lack: it is mutilated—rent asunder. It refers always to that which is other than itself. In this respect Eliade's religious symbols are no different from ordinary, profane symbols. The symbol's link to its referent, at least since Plato's *Cratylus*, has always appeared tenuous. We have created various epistemological mysticisms to render the link "natural," "essential," somehow "adequate" even in its arbitrariness. We have declared it reflective: the symbols reflect empirical reality or, as in Eliade and Plato, transcendent reality. We have claimed an isomorphism between the structure of language in which symbols obtain their meaning and the structure of reality. We have imagined transparent symbols affording direct access to the symbolized just as religious icons have been said to transport the faithful beholder directly to the holy figures depicted on them. We have created special categories of symbols—Eliade's religious symbols, Jung's archetypes, the symbols of poetry— and argued that these symbols have a different (power of) linkage to the symbolized than do ordinary symbols. Through ritual, scholarship, and special incantatorial readings we have surrounded such symbols with a special aura. We are not content to acknowledge the arbitrariness of symbols except as "an analytic ploy" that has an important utilitarian function, though it is phenomenologically inaccurate. When we do accept squarely the arbitrariness of symbols, we tend to bracket off our acceptance and deny the metaphysical and the existential implications of such a position. We are doing science!

To what extent is our understanding of language a reflection of our experience of ourselves and our world? To what extent does our understanding of language provide the model for articulating our human condition? For creating our condition? These questions repeat the very questions we ask about the link between the symbol and the symbolized. To what extent do our exegetical activities reflect the great liturgical drama of man's salvation? (We should pay homage to the countless people who died because they questioned in one way or another the linkage between bread and wine and Him-who-came-to-save-mankind.) We must appreciate the extent to which our exegetical discoveries are structurally implicated in the play of ritual and myth. Is there not something magical about them?

Our exegeses, in turn, discover—produce—a new set of symbols operating in a "new" context which the symbols themselves mark. Nietzsche (1965) asked:

> What is truth then? A mobile army of metaphors, metonyms, and anthropomorphisms—in short, a sum of human relations— which have been enhanced, transposed, and embellished poetically and rhetorically, and which after long use seem firm, canonical, and obligatory to a people: truths are illusions about which one has forgotten that this is what they are: metaphors which are worn out and without sensuous power, coins that have lost their image and now come into view, no longer as coins, but as metal.
>
> To be truthful means using the customary metaphors—in

moral terms: the obligation to lie according to a fixed convention, to lie herdlike in a style obligatory to all.

Perhaps we should see anthropology as a moment, blinded by
its own claim to facticity, to data, to the symbol, in the questioning that began with Socrates, continued with Kant, reached
nihilistic limits with Nietzsche, and has been systematically distorted by followers of Wittgenstein, the later Wittgenstein, who
assume that meaning is use and fail at the same time to alter
their own discourse.

But let us proceed more cautiously. Let us look at a specific
symbol—one which would hardly qualify as a religious symbol
in Eliade's understanding but which exhibits perhaps too literally the entailments of the rupture, the mutilation, the lack to
which I have referred. Let us look at the symbolism of the rat
and the rat punishment in one of Freud's most famous case
histories, "Notes on a Case of Obsessional Neurosis."

> "I think I will begin to-day with the experience which was
> the immediate occasion of my coming to you. It was in August,
> during the manoeuvres at ——. I had been suffering before,
> and tormenting myself with all kinds of obsessional thoughts,
> but they had quickly passed off during the manoeuvres. I was
> keen to show the regular officers that people like me had not
> only learnt a good deal but could stand a good deal too. One
> day we started from—on a short march. During the halt I
> lost my pince-nez, and, although I could easily have found
> them, I did not want to delay the start, so I gave them up. But
> I wired to my opticians in Vienna to send me another pair by
> the next post. During the same halt I sat between two officers,
> one of whom, a captain with a Czech name, was to be of no
> small importance to me. I had a kind of dread of him, *for he
> was obviously fond of cruelty.* I do not say he was a bad man,
> but at the officers' mess he had repeatedly defended the intro-
> duction of corporal punishment, so that I had been obliged to
> disagree with him very sharply. Well, during this halt we got
> into conversation, and the captain told me he had read of a
> specially horrible punishment used in the East. . . ."

Here the patient broke off, got up from the sofa, and begged
me to spare him the recital of the details. I assured him that I
myself had no taste whatever for cruelty, and certainly had no

desire to torment him, but that naturally I could not grant him
something which was beyond my power. He might just as well
have asked me to give him the moon. The overcoming of re-
sistances was the law of the treatment, and on no consideration
could it be dispensed with. (I had explained the idea of "resistance" to him at the beginning of the hour, when he told me
there was much in himself he would have to overcome if he
was to relate this experience of his.) I went on to say that I
would do all I could, nevertheless, to guess the full meaning
of any hints he gave me. Was he perhaps thinking of im-
palement?

"No, not that . . . the criminal was tied up . . ."—he expressed himself so indistinctly that I could not immediately
guess in what position—". . . a pot was turned upside down
on his buttocks . . . some *rats* were put into it . . . and they
. . ." he had got up, and was showing every sign of horror and
resistance—*"bored their way in . . ."* Into his anus, I helped
him out. (Freud 1955:165–166).

Freud goes on to say that as the patient was telling this story,
his face took on "a very strange, composite expression" (*sonder-
bar zusammengesetzten Gesichtsausdrück*). Freud could only
"interpret it as one of horror at a pleasure of his own of which
he himself was unaware" (*den ich nur als Grausen vor seiner
ihn selbst unbekannten Lust auflösen kann*). The patient then
admitted that as the story was being told he had the idea that the
punishment was happening (meted out by an unknown agent) to
someone very dear to him—a lady he admired greatly. Then,
after explaining that these ideas were entirely foreign and re-
pugnant to him, he admitted that a second idea had also flashed
through his mind at the time: namely, that the punishment was
being applied to his father.

On the basis of the patient's associations, Freud determined
that the rat symbolized the penis, money, syphilis, and children
(see also Freud 1955b). The punishment represented both the
patient's desire to punish his father and his own fear of punishment and could be related to the Oedipal triangle—to castration
and its anxiety. Taken as such, the rat and the rat punishment
add nothing new to what the psychoanalyst has told us about
the human psyche. (I am not questioning therapeutic efficacy

here.) The specific symbols the patient employs are merely individual variants of universal symbols: symbolic figures in a universal plot. Exegesis confirms their position, authenticates them, and permits their determination, making them "firm, canonical, and obligatory."

This approach to the symbol masks the creative process by which the symbol was constituted. It led Freud, certainly at the beginning of his psychoanalytic career, away from considering the relationship—the transference and countertransference—between the patient and himself. Freud did acknowledge Rat Man's transference—his hostility toward him as a father figure—in determining the meaning of the symbol, but did not consider the anger and the hostility as constituting the symbol.)

The Freudian hermeneutic plays here a role that is not dissimilar to the grounding role that Western scholars have often given to the myth. "The principal function of myth," "Eliade (1975:345) writes, is "to fix exemplary models of all rites and all meaningful human actions." The myth is "archetypical," "paradigmatic," "exemplary." Viewed as *a special kind of text*, it is given the essential characteristics of the text (as it is understood in the West). (See Chapter 5; Barthes 1977.) Myths have traditionally been characterized as static, fixed in their own internal time, and subject to repetition in a multitude of contexts which they help to determine. (Repetition, Eliade remarks, abolishes profane time and history and projects man into that other time which has nothing to do with duration properly speaking, but which constitutes an eternal present.) Myths are subject to distortion, corruption, and bowdlerization—to falling away from some sort of perfect version.[2] Eliade himself refers to their "degradation." (There is an implicit morality in all these metaphors!) Myths are not only exemplary models for different social situations but rhetorical figures as well. The characteristics of myth, so conceived, are not dissimilar to those of the symbol. Both are determined, reified, and isolated, *firm, canonical*, and *obligatory*.

But suppose we look at the rat and the rat punishment not as significant givens in some sort of universal plot but as the creation, determined, reified, and isolated, to be sure, by Freud and his patient, of the particular transaction in which they occurred. Here we see that the patient who becomes known in the annals of psychoanalysis as Rat Man sets Freud up.[3] He begins his session by telling Freud that he is going to recount the experience that was "the direct occasion" of his coming to see Freud. He states that this experience involved a man, the Captain with a Czech name, who "was of no small importance" to him. He demands Freud's insistence, spikes his curiosity, and successfully implicates him in the creation of the symbol. It is Freud who suggests later in the Notes the associations of rat to *Spielratte,* "gambler," used for Rat Man's father; *Raten,* "installments," a reference to paying back the father's and the son's debts; and *heiraten,* "to marry," a dominant concern for Rat Man. It is of course Freud who gets the last word in the exchange quoted above: "into the anus, I helped him out." So strong is Rat Man's power over Freud, so eloquent his symbols, that the rat and the rat punishment become central to their mutual articulation of Rat Man's biography. They also become the principal figures in Freud's case history.

The transaction is not so different from those that occur in the field or in the interpretation of elliptical documents. What anthropologist has not on occasion filled in for his informant? The rat and the rat punishment permit a complicity between Freud and his patient and ultimately between Freud and his readers. Both Freud and his patient took the reality that was negotiated between them as belonging to one of them alone. The therapeutic relationship itself supported its attribution—to the patient, *bien entendu.*

How can we say that Rat Man's case history really belonged to him? Perhaps he had a certain interest in possessing it. Wolf Man, another of Freud's patients, apparently had such an interest (Gardiner 1971). It is also possible that Rat Man accepted it as Freud's. The unconscious, Lacan (1966) tells us, is the discourse of the other.

By extension, can we say that the culture or the religion that the anthropologist and the historian of religion attribute to the other is indeed the other's? If we were to take Lacan seriously—and perhaps we ought to—we might have to ask: is the culture, the religion, the discourse of the exotic our own unconscious in textual form? (An uncanny similarity characterizes Eliade's description of mythico-religious time and space and Freud's, and especially Jung's, description of the unconscious.) Stated less dramatically, such a position has been held by those who recognize the symbolic function of the anthropologist's and the historian's other. We would have to consider the creation of *culture* and not just "work" on it—interpret it and analyze it.

In his *Discours de Rome*, Lacan (1966; Wilden 1968) refers to Mallarmé's comparison "of the common use of language (*langage*) to the exchange of a coin whose obverse and reverse no longer bear any but worn effigies, and which people pass from hand to hand in 'silence'."[4] "This metaphor is sufficient," Lacan (1966:251) remarks, "to remind us that the Word, even when almost completely worn out, retains its value as a *tessera*." A *tessera* is a token of recognition, a password, literally two halves of a broken piece of pottery that were fitted together by the initiates of the early mystery religions. The Greek word for *tessera*, Anthony Wilden (1968:101) reminds us, was *sumbulon*— symbol. What did the *tessera* symbolize? Anything more than recognition? And the rat in the exchange between Freud and his patient, and between Freud and his readers? Do the symbols anthropologists discover symbolize anything more than recognition?

We are of course unwilling to limit our symbols, our data, our documents, to mere tokens of recognition and exchange. Mallarmé himself could never abandon completely the worn out image of his coins. Our symbols, their meaning (and here I condense drastically) are more than the products of usage. (Usage can always be reduced to an exchange of one sort or another.) Usage cannot provide for continuity through time and context. It cannot account for unity in diversity. We remain discontent with theoretical ploys that attempt to account for a unity of meaning by declaring naively a unity between the symbol and the symbolized or by arguing that symbols obtain their meaning from their relations to other symbols in a timeless structure. Neither usage nor these ploys can explain the "power" of certain symbols. Rat Man's eloquence would surely have lost effect had he substituted an Easter bunny for the rat! We insist on the effigies, however worn, on the coins we exchange. We distinguish special categories of symbols: religious symbols, sacred symbols, symbols of myth and ritual, those of the unconscious, archetypes, epiphanies, and hierophanies. We privilege them. We envisage other times and places, other cultures, in which the effigies are still fresh, pristine, and pure. We postulate others, like Eliade's archaic man, who are able to respond immediately to the effigies and their power. We look to our rituals, our therapies, our scholarship, and our readings for a renewal of symbolic understanding and potency. And we recognize, however reluctantly and with a certain feeling of entrapment, a familiar story in our epistemology and in our attempt at renewal: the story of man's Fall from Paradise and his impotent striving for salvation. "The nostalgia for Paradise is discovered in modern man's most banal acts," Eliade (1975:363) writes. "The *absolute* cannot be extirpated; it is only susceptible to degradation. And archaic spirituality survives in its fashion, not as an act, not as a possibility for real accomplishment for man, but as a creative nostalgia for autonomous values" (my translation).

"A whole mythology," Wittgenstein (1971:35) remarked, "is deposited in our language." Solidified in textual form in art, science, and in a social mystique, it offers a certain solace. For to give priority to the continuous creation of the symbol and its efficacy is to give recognition to the contingency of the symbol and its efficacy, and to the contingency and artifice of the symbolically constituted world that man has built for himself as a nest.

10.
Glossing Emotions

Do you love me?
Please don't ask me that.
Why?
You know. I've never been able to say that, not even when I
was a kid.
What's so terrible about saying, "I love you"?
Nothing, I suppose. I just can't say it. Why should I anyway?
They're just words. They have nothing to do with the way I
feel. You know that.
Now you're hurt.
No, I'm not. It's that you can't really talk about feelings. You
just know them.
*Ah, I get it. You're laying it on me now. I'm not sensitive
enough to know what you're feeling. I need a crutch. Words!*
Now I've hurt you. I didn't . . .
No you haven't. I'm used to your games.
I have made you angry.
No you haven't. I'm not angry. I wouldn't give you the credit.
Yes, I have.
You're right. I am angry.
So am I. I'm really mad.

I have not indicated the sex of the two speakers in this imaginary, but no doubt familiar dialogue. I am certain that you, as
speakers of American English, have identified the first speaker
(italics) as a woman and the second as a man. You probably have
a "reasonable" idea of who the speakers are—their class, age,
educational background, their income perhaps—and where the
conversation is taking place. We know, for example, that American middle-class wives like their husbands to tell them that
they love them and that American husbands find it difficult,
impossible even, to say, "I love you." Husbands make all sorts
of excuses, often of a meta-linguistic nature, declaring, like the

poet, the insufficiency of words. They seem willing at times, as in my imaginary dialogue, to sacrifice a presumably romantic mood and all of its possibilities for their meta-linguistic principles. Of course a husband's meta-linguistic principles can also protect him from all of those romantic possibilities. Frequently, the principles are supported, implicitly at least, by some background story—some traumatic event, some disillusionment or betrayal—that accounts for his linguistic paralysis. Such background stories, revealed in those confessional moments so characteristic of American middle-class courting, do help create a bond of intimacy, of confidence, between the lovers and thus figure mnemonically, as it were, in their future relationship. They add a rhetorical poignancy to such exchanges as those between our first and second speakers. Men do not hesitate, however, to sacrifice these same principles when it comes to declaring their anger. (Some women do hesitate to declare their anger but rarely, if ever, for meta-linguistic principles.)[1] Although love and anger have both been called emotions— certainly both men and women of the speakers' milieu would call them emotions—there seems to be no equivalency other than a grammatical one between the sentences "I love you" and "I am angry at you."[2] There is an economy here, not of emotions or even the expression of emotions, but of the glossing of emotions. It is important to distinguish carefully between emotions, the expression of emotions, and the glossing of emotions. The failure to do so has led, I believe, to considerable confusion in the discussion of emotions in anthropology and psychology.[3]

Here I shall be concerned primarily with glossing emotions, secondarily with the expression of emotions, and not at all with the emotions themselves. I am interested in the rhetorical use of words and other communicative forms that are said to denote emotions and not in the (internal) state of affairs of those who give expression to or gloss the emotions they are experiencing—anger, love, sadness, or elation.[4] I do not deny the existence of such states and I believe I know what someone experiences when he declares himself angry, in love, sad, or elated. Such experiences are simply irrelevant to the rhetorical level I am pursuing here, but *that* they are "known" to occur, I hasten to add, is not irrelevant. The nonverbal expression of emotions, through gesture, intonation, demeanor, or pallor is relevant inso-far as it marks the occurrence of emotions and offers an occasion for glossing them, and thereby affects the exchange in which it occurs.

Put simply, I am questioning at an analytic level the locus of emotions as being in some inherent way in the individual. Emotions in our society are considered (if I may be a native informant) to be "natural" and as such "involuntary," "autono-mous," "physiological"—consider such expressions as "the physiology of love"—in essence beyond complete conscious control. Think of our elaborate literature on love—on the chem-istry(!) of love—as arising spontaneously and condemning, as it were, the smitten to involuntary behaviors that under other circumstances might well be morally and aesthetically distaste-ful. Think of the equation of love qua emotion with love qua sexual intercourse. And think of the vast literature devoted to controlling undesirable emotions, of the institutions that prom-ise such control—of charm schools, for example, of psychothera-pies that cannot rid themselves of their medical model, their bodily concern, and their physiological imagery despite all the arguments of their Cartesian practitioners. Declared natural, lodged inherently in the individual, and deemed outside his complete control, emotions conform to, indeed confirm, our non-transactional, essentialistic notions of self and person. They at-test to the self's independence, uniqueness, individuality, facticity—its personality and character—and its duration. Of course emotions are stimulated by intra- and extra-corporeal stimuli, including the relations which the self has with other selves, but the self's emotional response is entirely its own, rising out of the deepest recesses of its being.[5] As such, emo-tions can determine the relations that ensue, as we might expect the two speakers' "anger" to determine the course of their rela-tionship.

Emotions have, I suggest, a transactional basis that is masked by our notions of the self and our psychology of emotion. They arise out of real, remembered, or fantasized relations, and they—their glossable or glossed expression—play an active role in determining these relations.[6] They have to be understood in terms of their pragmatic function within any real, fancied, or

remembered exchange. They help *call the context*.[7] Certainly,
as any dramatist knows, the sudden expression of anger, indig-
nation, elation, fear, or sadness can—and does—change the context in which it occurs. Through self-attribution, however, or
through the attribution of an "emotion" to another participant
in the exchange in which it occurs, its transactional basis is
denied. This denial has moral consequences. (It produces
strains in the individual and in those in a position to evaluate
his or her moral worth, as all the discussion about the appropri-
ateness of emotional response or of the sincerity of the expression of emotions attests.) There is a sense in which we are all
engaged in the game of who has got the emotion; for, as we all
know, having the emotion has its advantages. Of course, when
we play the game, we forget to ask whether we are playing with
emotions or "emotions."

Is there something about glosses of emotion, in English at
least, that facilitates the confusion of emotion and "emotion"? I
believe there is. I have no idea how universal the confusion is,
though given the fact that it is determined, as I hope to show,
by the way such glosses are meta-pragmatically regimented, that
is, by the way they mark their own reading, it seems likely that
it would vary from one linguistic community to another. From
the point of view of our dominant linguistic ideology, words and
propositions that gloss emotions derive their rhetorical force
from their putative referentiality. They are thought to refer to,
denote, describe, and signify a particular state of affairs: the
emotion being experienced. It is the existence of this state of
affairs, this emotion, their truth value, as it were, that gives such
words their rhetorical power. Thus saying "I love you" or "I am
angry at you" is thought to refer to those particular perturbations
of the soul that we call "anger" and "love." Such utterances are
said to be true or false and if deemed true (and in a different
way, if deemed false) they have considerable (moral) weight in
the exchanges in which they occur. Their referent, reified, I
believe, in one fashion or another, has to be reckoned with in
accordance with the prevalent psychology of emotion and its
moral entailments.

Studies of emotion, for example those in cognitive anthropology that attempt to lay out the "psychology" of emotion of a particular group through the analysis of their vocabulary ("their words for" emotion, even when such words are contextually sensitive), seem to replicate a certain socio-linguistic process that is characteristic of our own speech community. We tend to "translate" pragmatic, that is, context-dependent, features of an utterance or, more accurately, of a conversation into context-independent "entities" that can be ascribed, essentially, to any one of the participants in the encounter, or indeed abstracted from any encounter and any particular individual, and described and discussed scientifically. Witness the rich phenomenological descriptions of emotions that characterize so much of our philosophy and psychology and so much more of our literature. They reinforce *our* psychologies of emotion and *our* notions of the self as a bearer of emotion by universalizing the semanticity—the context-independence—of such emotion words. They function very much like the phenomenological descriptions of emotion by providing a set of compelling background propositions about, and images of, *emotions*. They strengthen the referentially derived rhetorical force of our emotion words and propositions by granting them a special status. But if we take, heuristically, the position that there may well be different ways of conceptualizing the self, its relationship to other selves, to social interaction generally, and to those experiences, whatever their (final) locus, that *we* call emotion, it then becomes clear that a description, if not a theory, of emotions, generated from lexemes and understood semantistically as referring to discrete and context-independent entities, cannot do justice to other ways of conceptualizing emotions.[8] We have in fact to look at the pragmatic and meta-pragmatic dimensions of those exchanges in which locutions about emotion—the expressions and glosses of emotion—occur.

Let me illustrate this in a very tentative manner by returning to the question I posed earlier: Is there something about our glosses of emotion that facilitates the confusion between emotion and "emotion"? There are important differences between the propositions "I love you" and "I am angry at you" and "he loves you" and "he is angry at you," as those familiar with the literature on performatives will readily recognize. The difference can be illuminated in two different but coordinate ways, which I shall call the indexical and the performative.[9]

To begin with the performative way: I do not claim that such utterances as "I love you" or "I am angry at you" are explicit performatives. They certainly do not meet all of either Austin's (1970) or Searle's (1985) criteria, but they do have considerable illocutionary force (Searle 1983). They do bring about through their very utterance a change in the context of that utterance (that is, they are not simply descriptive of it), and this change has to be acknowledged (even if through denial) by all those who participate in the encounter in which the utterance was made. The interesting question is not whether a change was brought about through the utterance but exactly what the nature of that change is. This seems to be a matter of negotiation, and it is this negotiation that gives spice to a conversation in which people say such things as "I love you" and "I am angry at you." What is being negotiated, to use the jargon of the performative philosophers, is the covert prefix behind the utterance. When a speaker says "I love you," for example, he can be taken to be saying—more accurately to be doing—many things. Think of the various possible implications of the following covert prefixes that I have taken at random from Austin's (1970) list of performatives: I reckon, proclaim, declare, believe, accept, report, promise, deny, warn (you), recognize, or concede that I love you; that I am angry at you. We can easily see how important such negotiations are, and we can imagine all of the advantages and disadvantages that come with preserving the prefixes' cover. We can see how their covertness determines future conversational moves in all sorts of intriguing ways. Not only does the consequential negotiation allow the speakers to constitute themselves, their relationship and their values, but it also allows those playful maneuvers that create suspense, permit seductions, and render conversation entertaining. For our purposes, the important point is to recognize that the choice of a covert prefix is determined not just by the "grammar" of the sentence but by pragmatic considerations that are understood metapragmatically, usually metaphorically, in nonlinguistic terms reflective of broader ideological and axiological presuppositions.

In the case in point, they are understood in terms of a prevailing psychology of emotions and its entailing morality and etiquette.

First person propositions such as "I love you" or "I am angry at you" have, when uttered, an illocutionary force that is normally absent from third person propositions, uttered or not, such as "he loves you" or "he is angry at you." Their very utterance is taken as a manifestation, a symptom, of the condition—the emotion—they are said to be describing, in a way which is simply not true of the third person propositions. It is as though their referentiality looped over onto itself and became at once its own object and yet, through some sort of topological contortion, other than itself. Were we not appalled by the idea of creating yet another linguistic category, we would call such locutions "symptomatizers." In this respect these first person utterances are, on an ideological level, equivalent to nonverbal, "involuntary," "autonomous" expressions of emotion. It is as though their presumed referentiality—in Peirce's (1974) terms, their symbolicity, their semanticity[10] slips into a sort of symptomatology—into, again in Peirce's terms, an immediate indexicality.

This slippage from symbolic reference to sheer indexicality has certain curious implications. For one, it facilitates the confusion between emotion and "emotion"; that is, between the expression of emotion and the glossing of emotion. Second, it reinforces the referentially derived rhetorical capacity of such utterances and may well promote their illocutionary force. And third, it raises a puzzling set of questions about truth and sincerity in such utterances. Insofar as these utterances are taken symbolically as describing a state of affairs, their truth value may be questioned. Am I truly describing the perturbations of my soul when I say I love you or I am angry at you? Am I being sincere? But if these utterances are taken as indices or symptoms of such perturbations, then their truth and sincerity cannot be questioned, for they point to those perturbations as unquestionably, as nonarbitrarily, as smoke points to fire.

It would seem that the coincidence of the symbolic and the indexical dimensions of such utterances motivates much of the discussion about their truthfulness, their sincerity. Can I say "I love you" or "I am angry at you" without being truthful?

Insincerely? Can I be mistaken when I say "I love you" or "I am angry at you"? Does an actor have to feel love or anger when he says on stage, "I love you" or "I am angry at you"? Certainly contemporary theories of acting reflect the ambiguities this coincidence of the symbolic and the indexical produces.

We have invented many ways of covering the problems that arise from this coincidence of linguistic functions. One is to argue, negotiate, and attempt to determine exactly what I meant when I said "I love you" or "I am angry at you"; that is, in terms of the theory of performatives, to determine exactly what the covert prefix was. ("What precisely did you mean when you said you love me?" "I suppose I meant that I could easily love you were we really to get to know each other" [a prediction]; or, "I meant that I would love you no matter what happened" [a promise]; or, "I really meant it" [an assertion].) Such strategies stress the symbolic dimension of the utterance. Often they are elaborated in retrospective accounts of what transpired when the confession(!) of love or anger was made. A second way of covering the problems arising from the coincidence of linguistic functions is to postulate a state of mind, the "unconscious" for example, that permits one to mean other than what one meant. And a third is to elaborate a theory of fictional representation, of mimicry.

One interesting consequence of the confusion of emotion and "emotion" is, to speak figuratively, the domination of verbal expressions, the gloss properly speaking, over other modes of emotional expression. Coordinated with a prevalent notion of emotional unity—when one is angry, one is angry; when one is in love, one is in love—these other modes of emotional expression are seen, frequently, as ancillary, as suprasegmentals. But as Judith Irvine (1982) has noted, there is no necessary correlation between the various registers in which emotions are expressed. Certainly there is no necessary relationship between the expression of emotion and its gloss.[11] It is possible to say, as the first speaker did in our imaginary dialogue that she—I make a reluctant stereotypic gender attribution—was not angry when we have reason to believe that she was indeed angry (as she herself eventually had to admit). And it is also possible that although the second speaker could not say "I love you," he was still expressing his adoration.

The disjunction between the expression of emotion and its gloss as well as the disjunction between different registers in which emotions are expressed can lead to all sorts of double-binding situations.[12] That doublebinding is necessarily pathogenic is, in my view, questionable. Certainly even the most superficial study of classical rhetoric reveals that disjunction is one of its most powerful devices. Consider the following figures taken from Lanhams's *Handlist* (1968): antiphrasis (a dwarf for a giant), apophonema (a sententia put in antithetical form), contrarium (one of the two opposite statements used to prove the other), dialysis (arguing from a series of disjunctive propositions), dilemma, enigma, litotes, oxymoron, paradox, syncrisis (an expanded paradox), and of course, in its way, irony.[13] And there are many more.

It is important to stress that the disjunction between the expression of emotion and its glossing (in a nonindexical sense) has considerable rhetorical force. It figures mightily in the negotiations that occur in any exchange. To express anger and to deny that one is angry at one and the same time, to express love and to assert that one is incapable of declaring love, to look happy and to say one is sad, to tremble with fear and claim there is nothing to fear—these disjunctions do call contexts, do constitute the parties to the encounter in which such double messages are transmitted, do permit explicit and implicit characterizations of personality, moral worth, and the like, and do facilitate the play that keeps so much conversation going. Less dramatically perhaps, conjunctive expressions of emotion and their gloss also have rhetorical force. Suppose, for example, the second speaker had been expressing love, even angry love, all through our imaginary dialogue and suppose having said, "So am I. I'm really mad," he suddenly added, "I do love you, you know." I leave the sequel to your imagination and only caution you to remember that at my level of argument the emotion the speaker was *really* experiencing is totally irrelevant.

However you envision the sequel, it should be clear that any theory of emotion has to recognize the meta-pragmatically regimented pragmatic plays that the expression and the gloss of emotions have. That these differ from one culture to another appears likely, particularly because the meta-pragmatic interpretation of such plays is often metaphorically expressed in non-linguistic terms, in folk psychological terms, for example. Such nonlinguistic terms provide the vehicles for metaphorical understanding. Are they—the folk psychologies, for example—in fact refractions of the very linguistic processes they come to describe?

11.
Saints, *Jnun*, and Dreams

My concern here is with psychological idiom, its articulation, and its effect on the subjective life of the individual. My argument is necessarily hypothetical.[1] Human beings as members of a society share an idiom by which they structure and evaluate their reality, including themselves, insofar as the experience of reality can be distinguished from the reality itself, their experience of reality. Although this idiom is necessarily expressed through language, it is more than language. Within it are sedimented traditional symbols and values which form the basis for schemata by which reality is interpreted. Not only does the idiom enable the articulation of an explicit psychology, it also renders possible the articulation of subjective experience. By "explicit psychology" I mean all commonly recognized assumptions about the human "psyche." These would include theories of personality, character formation, motivation, cognition, and perception.

This explicit psychology should not be confused with implicit psychology, that is, the generally unarticulated assumptions about the "human psyche" that are grounded in the idiom itself. Although the explicit psychology can provide the vocabulary for self-articulation, it is but one type of discourse from which the implicit psychology can be rendered explicit. Other types include the reports of what we would call "psychic reality," "consciousness," or "subjective experience." They must not be equated with introspective reportage, however, for it is possible that much of what we, given our implicit psychology, articulate as "within" is in other cultures articulated as "without" (Lienhardt 1967:147–170; Doutté 1909:224–245; see also Chapter 7). Elements or figures believed to be external to the individual, such as demons, angels, and saints, can serve to symbolize certain "psychological dispositions," and the relationship that obtains between these elements may be symbolic of certain "psychic structures" or "psychological processes" (Crapanzano 1971). These "symbolic-interpretive" elements (Crapanzano 1973a:5–6) may even create the dispositions, much as the telling of a dream creates the dream (Pfander 1967:10–11). In any case, the idiom determines the articulation of "psychic reality," upon which psychological, and psychoanalytic investigations are based.[2]

I will illustrate my argument with dream and life-history material which I collected from Moroccan Arabs of the shantytowns of Meknes.[3] I do not claim that my findings can be generalized to even the Arab population of Morocco, let alone to that of North Africa or the Middle East.[4] Nor do I propose to treat the entire psychology of the Moroccans of this milieu but simply to consider some of the consequences of the particular idiom by which they articulate certain "psychological" experiences.

Most of my informants were illiterate fellahin who had moved to Meknes in search of work from the plains of northern Morocco. Like other Moroccans, they believe in saints and demons (*jnun*). Saints (*siyyid, salih,* or *wali*) are intermediaries to Allah that can confer the blessing, *baraka,* on those who venerate them. They may have been descendants of the Prophet, founders and sheikhs of religious brotherhoods, political heroes, pious scholars, holy fools, or "simply vivid individuals who had tried to make something happen" (Geertz 1968:8; Dermenghem 1954:1–25). The object of their cult is the saint's tomb—usually a squat white building with a domed roof—that pilgrims visit to obtain some favor such as a male child, a cure for devil-possession, a favorable verdict in court, or simply the saint's blessing. The saint is popularly believed to be alive in his tomb and may appear to pilgrims in a dream or vision. Sacred springs and grottos, trees, stones, and animals believed to contain baraka, and spots to which the jnun are said to gravitate are often found near the tomb (Basset 1929). Some Moroccans feel especially supported (*msannad*) by a particular saint whom they regard as a sort of guardian. Often this relationship was established when their parents took them to the saint's tomb for their first haircut or asked one of the descendants of the saint to bless them. Sometimes, however, the relationship is not established until later in life, as are the relations with the jnun, which are defined by various curers and magicians and through the exorcistic rituals of the Hamadsha and other popular religious brotherhoods. Both saint and demon help articulate the Moroccan's self-understanding and experience of reality.[5]

Dream Theory

The Moroccans with whom I worked value their dreams highly as portents of the future. They have not, however, elaborated a particularly consistent dream theory nor have they developed dream rituals as complex as those of the Iroquois (Wallace 1958) or the Senmoi of Malaya (Stewart 1969). The dream is generally believed to result from the wandering of the soul (*ruh*) during sleep.[6] "When a man sleeps, his soul leaves his body and walks around. No one sleeps with his soul." Daydreams, too, result when the soul leaves the body but stays close to it. The dream is what the soul witnesses; it is remembered by the *'aqel* or mind. The dream gives access to a reality which, however different it may appear to be from ordinary waking reality, is as real. "The Moors," Westermarck (1926, vol. 2:46ff.) has written, "do not draw the same distinction as we do between that which a person experiences while awake and that which he dreams . . . and they maintain that what they hear or see in their dreams is a reality and not an illusion." We must not conclude from this that Moroccans confuse dream experiences with the experiences of waking life. Rather, they evaluate the ontological status of the two experiences differently from the way Westerners do. For them, as for the dream scholar of the classical Islamic era, the cognitive power of the dream has never presented an epistemological problem (von Grunebaum 1966).

The Moroccans do acknowledge the existence of false dreams, which, they say, are caused by the devil, Shitan.[7] They are not, however, particularly concerned with the criteria (within the dream itself) by which false dreams are distinguished from true ones. That is a matter for oneiromancers and other dream specialists. The Moroccan is far more concerned with the condition of the dreamer himself in determining the truth or falsehood—and the goodness or badness—of a dream. A good, pious man is less likely to have false and bad dreams than a man who does not follow the teachings of the Prophet. The same is true of a clean man.

If dreams are affected by the condition of the dreamer, it follows that the dreamer, insofar as he can affect his condition, can influence his dreams. Unlike the Westerner, who accepts his dreams passively, the Moroccan will actively seek to influence his dreams. He will refrain from sexual intercourse, he will sleep on his right side, not on his left side, in order to have good dreams. Before sleeping he will say the *shahada*, or profession of faith, other verses of the Koran, or sacred formulae and prayers he happens to know. One man gave me the following amusing example. "If you see a pretty girl during the day and retain her image and say the shahada before going to bed, then you will dream of her as pretty. If you don't say the shahada, then it will be different. You will dream that you see her in the river, in the mud, or in a puddle." That is, you will see her as a jinn, for the jnun are said to live in rivers and to gravitate to damp, muddy places. Usually such recitations, known in the Moroccan dialect as *stikhara*, are reserved for more serious occasions.[8]

Stikhara also refers to the very important practice of visiting a saint's tomb, or some other sacred place, in order to have a dream. If a man is troubled by bad dreams, he may consult a *fqih*, the traditional teacher who will give him special prayers to recite and perhaps an amulet to ward off the dream. Bad dreams are said to be caused by the jnun, and the same apotropaic principles are applied to their control as are applied to the control of any other interference from the jnun. Bad dreams are often told to rocks to neutralize their effect on the dreamer and on anyone else to whom the dream is repeated, for it is believed that in telling a dream you can convey its influence.[9] A strong affective bond may be created by telling someone that you have dreamed of him. Often a host will tell an unexpected visitor, a stranger even, that he dreamed of his visit.[10]

That dreams are valued by Moroccans mainly as an indication of the future needs elaboration. Dreams may be related to the future in two principal ways. First, they may simply foretell the future. The meaning of such prognostic dreams may be transparent, as, for example, when a man dreams that a friend makes a trip and the friend in fact leaves town. The meaning may at times be the opposite of that which was dreamed: tears may be a sign of happiness. Or the meaning may be symbolic. "If you dream that you are riding on a female burro, then you will have a lot of (marriage) problems." "If you dream you are riding on a mule, then you will marry and divorce." "If you dream you are riding on a camel, then you will never have any problems." Such symbolic equations are in current use throughout Morocco; they are by no means consistent. Westermarck (1926, vol. 2:48–54) lists several pages of them, many of which I have heard in Meknes. Second, the dreams may relate to the future by indicating an action to be taken. If you dream of a good place, I have been told, then you must visit it.

> Ali felt depressed. He remembered seeing the grill work of a *zawiya* [the lodge of a religious brotherhood] in a dream. He spent the day visiting all of the lodges of Meknes in search of the one with the grill work. When he finally found the lodge in question—he claimed he had never been in it before—he prayed there for several hours and felt much better when he left. He explained that it was the baraka of the founding saint that had cured him of his depression. The saint had indicated in the dream the necessary remedy.

Dreams can be indicative of an action that is to be taken not by the dreamer but by someone the dreamer knows.

> When Fatna was pregnant, a neighbor who was a midwife, dreamed that Fatna was washing a sheepskin rug in the fountain. The hair of the sheepskin had been shaved off, and the rug was smooth. The neighbor instructed Fatna to have her child's hair shaved at the tomb of Sidi 'Ali ben Hamdush. When Fatna's baby girl was born she took her to the saint's tomb to have her head shaved" (see Crapanzano 1973a).

Certain diviners specialize in dreaming of actions to be taken by those who consult them:

> Moha, who is said to be married to 'A'isha Qandisha, lives near a river and is consulted by the sick. Men bring him a thread from their turbans; women a thread from their scarves. He places the thread under his right cheek before going to

bed and dreams of 'A'isha who tells him what is wrong with
the patient and what cure to follow.

Pilgrims usually look to their incubation dreams not simply to
learn what will happen but what they ought to do. The line
between dreams of prognosis and dreams indicating action cannot be drawn too strictly. Prognostic dreams of course influence
the acts of the dreamer, and dreams indicative of action influence the dreamer's future.

The distinction between these two types of dreams is reflected in an ambiguity in the Moroccan's dream lore. If asked
what happens when someone dreams, the Morrocan will explain, as I have said, that dreams result from the wandering of
the soul. The soul witnesses *real* events that occur elsewhere
in space and time. The dreams may be about creatures of the
phenomenal world or of the world of saints and jnun. (A very
frequent dream in Moroccan folklore, reminiscent of the shamanistic dreams of Siberia, is of a voyage to the jnun at the
bottom of a river [Eliade 1972].) The dream-events are thought
to be related, most often symbolically, to the dreamer's future.
This relationship, that is, the meaning of the dream for the
dreamer, must be disclosed through interpretation.

A special class of dreams, however, is not, to my knowledge,
linguistically distinguished from ordinary dreams: these
dreams—I will call them visitational dreams—involve the appearance of saints, jnun, and other spiritual beings. Often the
spirit resembles someone the dreamer knows but with a different name—the name of the jinn or saint. Visitational dreams
must not be confused with bad dreams, which are said to be
caused by the jnun but in which the jnun do not appear, nor
must they be confused with false dreams, which are caused by
Shitan but in which he does not appear. In describing visitational dreams, the Hamadsha and other Moroccans do not emphasize the wandering of the soul but the fact that the saint or
jinn has come to them.

Through the analysis of visitational dreams I hope to demonstrate how the implicit folk psychology affects the articulation
of experience, if not the experience itself. Visitational dreams
have three primary functions. (1) They articulate, often symboli-

cally, a conflict that may not be acceptable or even known to the dreamer. (2) They often serve to resolve a conflict either by sanctioning a particular desire which may not be acceptable to the dreamer but which he has to accept as a command from a being external to him, or by symbolizing the conflict in such a manner as to make therapeutic intervention possible. (3) They provide a primary orientation point for the articulation of the subjective apprehension of the dreamer's biographical experience (Berger and Luckmann 1967:97). The cases presented are ordered in terms of progressive dislocation of the symbolic-interpretive elements from the real-life context.[11]

Visitational Dreams and the Resolution of Conflict

Frequently visitational dreams serve to resolve conflicts that may not be clearly articulated by the dreamer. In such dreams a saint, often but not necessarily the saint by whom the dreamer is supported, reveals a path the dreamer must follow. If the dreamer does not follow this path, it is said that he will suffer illness or some other dire consequence. Such visitational dreams may sanction a decision that goes counter to the expressed or socially expected desire of the dreamer. Responsibility for such a decision is shifted from the individual to the saint, who is external to him and whose authority cannot be challenged.

The role of visitational dreams in the resolution of conflict is illustrated in the following case.[12] When Moulay Abedsalem, a saddlemaker and pallbearer by trade, was in his late twenties, he was sent to Meknes from his hometown of Marrakech. He explained that in those days, about fifty years ago, there was a shortage of pallbearers in Meknes. The pasha of Meknes asked the pasha of Marrakech to send him reinforcements. The pasha of Marrakech called in his pallbearers; lots were drawn, and Moulay Abedsalem was among the four chosen. He was very unhappy. Marrakech was his home; his family and friends lived there; his property and business were there; his wife, then six months pregnant, wanted to remain near her mother. (She joined him several months after her child was born.) When Moulay Abedsalem arrived in Meknes, he was given a house and a shop where he could ply his trade. His business was successful; he introduced himself to the local Hamadsha and soon had a number of friends in the city. Still, he missed Marrakech. He claims that he was not allowed to leave Meknes, but this seems unlikely. The other pallbearers had trained replacements and had returned home. After three years, however, Moulay Abedsalem finally decided to move back to his hometown and even purchased bus tickets. The night before he and his family were to leave, both Moulay Abedsalem and his wife had dreams. I quote Moulay Abedsalem:[13]

> When I came to Meknes, I was so sad. I wanted to leave. I told my wife I wanted to leave. She packed everything. Then we went to sleep and had the same dream. It was very hot. I dreamed that I was in front of Sheikh al-Kamal [The Perfect Sheikh, Sidi M'hamed ben 'Isa, the patron saint of Meknes and the founder of the famed 'Isawa brotherhood]. There the two walls [that led up to the sanctuary] were even bigger than they are now. There was a place there that was very well swept. It was washed. There was a pole in the center. "This place is clean; there is a pole; if the people [the 'Isawa] dance, I'll stay and watch," I thought. "Perhaps someone will bring a horse and attach it to the pole. Then I'll leave." I sat down and suddenly saw someone come out of the window next to the door to [the sanctuary of] Sheikh al-Kamal. The man was tall; he was in a white chemise; he had a hammer in his hand. He came up to the pole and looked at me. "Are you not ashamed to want to leave," he asked. He hammered the pole all the way into the ground. When the pole was hammered in, he said, "You can stay or leave." The man disappeared. My wife dreamed that she had seen a woman, an 'Isawiyya, dancing. The woman told her, "Welcome. Rest assured, you will not leave." In the morning my wife waited for me to leave, but I couldn't even get up until after the sun rose. The bus had already left. Then I told my wife to unpack everything.

Moulay Abedsalem remained in Meknes for the next fifty years. He told me the dream after I had asked him if he had ever chewed his fingernails.[14] He answered, "I used to chew my nails, and my father beat me hard when he caught me," and he continued with the story quoted above. The following associations were elicited.

◆

[*Who was the man?*] Sheikh al-Kamal. There are many people who have seen him leave by that window. His face was white, and he was tall. He did not have on a belt. When I saw him coming, I thought that he had cleaned the place. I was afraid. If he tells me to leave, I'll leave. If he tells me to stay, I'll stay. It's clean.

[*Does the place remind you of somewhere?*] No, never until the dream. It was very clean. Now it is not as clean as it had been. I was very hot and left and found the place [Presumably referring to the dream]. My wife didn't ask why we didn't leave until after we had breakfast. I told her the dream. That was the reason why I didn't want to leave. Then my wife told me her dream.

[*What does the pole remind you of?*] The pole means that the "pole" is planted here by Sheikh al-Kamal. Even now when I go to Marrakech and stay for two months, I get nervous and want to come back here.

[Have you ever seen other poles like it?] No.

[Why did the man hammer the pole into the earth?] He knew I wanted to leave. God and Sheikh al-Kamal did this to tell me that I should not leave. I dreamed this, and then if I had left, the bus would have had an accident or a car would have hit me. God shows us things that are true in dreams.

I asked Moulay Abedsalem to tell me whatever else occurred to him. He described how he was so terrified by the war in the Rif—he had taken part in it as a young man—that he dreamed about it all the time. Finally, after he had gone to a local saint, he stopped dreaming about the war. I then asked him if he had ever had a fight with his father. He reported that he had once had such a bad fight that he had run away. Once he threatened to leave in a fight with his mother.

It seems clear that Moulay Abedsalem could not admit his ambivalence about leaving Meknes. On the one hand, it was expected that he, an eldest son, should want to return home to Marrakech and his family. His father was old, and his brothers were already vying for the family property. Moreover, his wife was unhappy in Meknes and wanted to return to Marrakech. On the other hand, Moulay Abedsalem was well established in Meknes. He was "on his own," away from a father who, even by Moroccan standards, was a tyrant. (Moulay Abedsalem in fact had spent much of his early life running away from Marrakech.) The figure of the saint served to counter familial demands, especially those of his father. Moulay Abedsalem was frightened by the saint, who wore no belt and carried a hammer. He would have left if a horse had been attached to the pole, but the saint hammered the pole all the way into the earth and then gave him a choice. (His wife, at least as Moulay Abedsalem reported it, was given no choice.) The saint, even more powerful and holy (white equals holy) than this father, had fixed him there in a clean place. He had to follow the saint's command. He was not responsible for his decision. The saint freed him from dreams of war.

Visitational Dreams and Symbolic Conflict Resolution

In Moulay Abedsalem's case the conflict—to stay or to leave Meknes—was articulated by Moulay Abedsalem himself, although he could not admit his ambivalence and identify all the factors that entered into his decision. Often, however, the dreamer is incapable of articulating the conflict in terms of his real-life situation. The dream serves to articulate the conflict symbolically and to resolve it symbolically. The figures of saint and jinn—more frequently jinniyya—symbolize the two sides of the conflict; it is formulated in terms of beings external to the dreamer who are elements in a socially shared belief system and who are more or less subject to the logic of that belief system. In this perspective, the elements symbolic of the conflict are collective rather than individual representations. Casting the conflict into a dream world of saints and jnun opens the way for its resolution on the level of collective, and not individual, symbolic action—that is, in terms of the rituals of the Hamadsha and other similar brotherhoods.

The case of Mohammed illustrates how conflict is articulated and resolved through saints and jnun.[15] Mohammed is a Hamdushi who often slashes his head during trance. He claims to see the jnun and to have sexual relations with a female jinn who visits him at night. He is given to depression, and his anxiety reactions are often somatized. Projective material reveals a strong fear of femininity. When I asked him, on our second meeting, how he had become a Hamdushi, he answered:

When I was eleven or twelve years old,[16] I was a shepherd. One day I saw my flock nearing the river. Two he-goats fell in. I went to the river to get them out, and after I had saved them, I climbed out of the river and fell down unconscious. The invisibles [the jnun] are often found in rivers. I was sick for a month. I was fainting all the time. I could not tell night from day. One night I dreamed that two men came to my place. One was in a *darbala* [a tattered outer garment] and the other in clean clothes. I was with several children at the river's edge as the two men approached. There were four or five children. When the men came up to me, the man in the darbala wanted to stab me with a knife. The man in the clean clothes wanted to excuse me. The man in the clean clothes—his name was Bushta—and the man in the darbala began to fight, and I ran away. When I awoke the next morning, I saw that I was a man and was no longer sick. A few days later a neighbor invited the Hamadsha. I heard the music and danced with them and was then completely cured.

Mohammed did not know the name of the man in the darbala. Bushta was the saint Moulay Bushta. "When I was eight years old, Mohammed explained, "I had saved 25 centimes and wanted to buy something, but a friend of my father's took me to Moulay Bushta and I gave my money to the saint. I think that it was he who saved me." Five months later Mohammed spontaneously recounted the story in more detail:

Two goats began to fight, and one knocked the other into the river. The second jumped in on him. I pulled the first out, and when I started to pull the second out, I fell in too. I climbed out, and then the sickness began. I fell asleep, and the goats got lost. At home they thought I had been killed when they saw a few of the goats return alone. They asked the shepherds were I was. They said I was last seen at the river. There they found me unconscious. They lost five sheep. I was sick for a month. I dreamed that night that someone had come and was dressed in a darbala. He had a beautiful knife in his hand. I saw that I had fallen in the river with three boys. We were swimming in the river. The man in the darbala chased us. Everyone escaped but me. Then a second man came along and asked the man in the darbala what he was doing with the child. The man in the darbala answered that he was going to kill him. The second man had a pebble in his hand. "If you kill the boy," he said "I will hit you with this pebble." As the two men were fighting, I sneaked off. In the morning I felt better. I wanted to eat some grapes, but there were none. A month later, they brought me some grapes and the moment I ate them I could walk with a stick. The Hamadsha came to someone's house, and my head told me to make the trance-dance. I made it and got better.

The following associations were elicited.

[*What does the dream mean?*] I know the man with the dar-bala lived in the river. [In other words, he was a jinn.] The moment I made the trance-dance with the Hamadsha I was better. Since then I made the trance-dance and hit my head with the axe. And when my father watches me making the dance, he says, "My son will die." Thus the soldier who was sick got better. [Mohammed is referring to a soldier who was struck by 'A'isha Qandisha as he was entering his bride's room on his wedding night.] He spent the night with his wife and got strong. He now invites the Hamadsha.

Mohammed suddenly stopped. He was very nervous. A few days later I asked him a few more questions about the dream.

[*What do you think the pebble meant?*] The man with the darbala had a knife, the other a stone. He wanted to beat the other with a stone. I was with my friends bathing. The man with the darbala came, and the others ran off. I was caught. My friends were fast like birds. I couldn't walk.
[*Why couldn't you walk?*] Well, I walked but I wasn't like my friends. I walked. I ran full speed, but I couldn't go far. I have remembered that dream since I was twelve. From time to time I dream that I am in a river. Sometimes it is filled with water, and sometimes it is not. [He becomes silent.]
[*Even now, you dream of the river?*] I dreamed of the river twice. Once I dreamed I was crossing the river. Half the river was dry; half the river was water. From time to time the water reached my waist. That was all. Sometimes I dream I make the trance-dance. There was a river. I passed the bed of the river and came to a little bed of water. "That's nothing," I thought. I entered and found myself in the center of a big river.

[*What do you think it all means?*] [Shifts around a lot.] I think it was 'A'isha who dragged me there and made all of this.

It seems likely that Mohammed's sudden illness was a somatized reaction to the complex of emotions he experienced when the goats fell into the river.[17] It is probable that one of the primary emotions was fear—fear, at one level, of punishment for losing the livestock. Mohammed denies that he would have been punished had he not become ill; however, he was often beaten by his father for not taking adequate care of the herd. (It was only in the second version, by the way, that Mohammed was able to admit that five sheep were lost.) Illness provides an escape from punishment. It forces the transformation of the punishing father into the sympathetic, concerned, and protective father. Bushta, the saint, fights the jinn, the man in the darbala. "My friends were fast like birds. I couldn't walk." Even this is difficult for Mohammed to admit. "Well, I walked but I wasn't like my friends. I walked, I ran full speed, but I couldn't go far." Illness itself is not a satisfactory solution. It is associated with a loss of manhood. Mohammed sneaks off as the saint and the jinn fight. He is not able to resist the man with the darbala, but the saint is able to resist with just a pebble. (He wakes with the desire for grapes—are they the symbolic equivalent to pebbles?—and is not cured until he has been given them.[18]) "When I awoke the next morning, I saw that I was a man and was no longer sick." The soldier who was struck by 'A'isha Qandisha could not meet the test of manhood on his wedding night. Recovery comes only when Mohammed performs the trance-dance. "The moment I made the trance-dance with the Hamadsha, I was better." Like illness, the trance-dance affects the father. "And when my father watches me making the dance, he says, 'My son will die'." The dance is also associated with femininity. Mohammed holds 'A'isha Qandisha responsible for his head-slashing. The man in the darbala is associated with 'A'isha. It is she who prevents him from crossing the river (into manhood). The Hamadsha cures involve the symbolic transformation of man into woman in order for him to become man once again (1973a:219–229).

Visitational Dreams without Conflict Resolution

In Mohammed's dream conflict was both symbolically articulated and resolved in terms of saint and jinn. The dream seems to have prepared the way for the Hamadsha cure in his case, as in several other cases I recorded.

> Hamid had been totally paralyzed so he claims for over a year.[19] He was struck by 'A'isha Qandisha as he was working in the fields, but he does not know why. He may have bumped into her. He lived alone with his mother and could not make the pilgrimage to Sidi 'Ali. Although his mother had called in the Hamadsha, he did not respond to their cure. Finally he was taken to Sidi 'Ali. He spent three nights there, and on the third night, he had the following dream. "Sidi 'Ali came up to me and asked me why I was still there. I told him I was sick. He gave me a massage. Then I woke up and was a little afraid." Hamid was able to walk a little and was "completely" cured after dancing the trance-dance. He must now dance whenever he hears his special air. After telling me the dream, he added that on the night that he was struck he dreamed of 'A'isha Qandisha. "I saw 'A'isha Qandisha. She told me that she had paralyzed me. I asked why. She said: 'Just because.' She said that I must be on her side or I would never be cured. 'When you are willing to make the trance-dance to Sidi 'Ali, then I will free you,' she said."

There are dreams, however that articulate a conflict but do not resolve it, not even symbolically. They do not pave the way for a ritual cure.

Tuhami was a balding, black man in his middle forties.[20] He was a bachelor who wanted desperately to marry but could not. "Each time I want to marry I can't. If I ask a girl, she'll say, 'I want someone more civilized.' If I ask an older woman, she says she wants a civil servant. They say I have a bald head, but they don't know what is in my head. I'm always in misery, and it will continue." It was said—and after many interviews Tuhami himself admitted it—that he was married to 'A'isha Qandisha. She prevented him, he said, from having sexual intercourse with women; he was in fact impotent. (Tuhami admitted this six months after our first meeting.) Most Moroccan men did not find him threatening and even allowed him to visit their womenfolk,

who listened with fascination to his lore. Tuhami, a born storyteller, had what used to be called an over-active imagination.
He was not always careful to distinguish among dreams, visionary and hallucinatory experiences, fantasies, and reality. He
dreamed nightly about saints and female jnun and obsessively
followed "instructions" he received from saints in his dreams.
Most of these involved visiting saints' tombs. He had an imaginary (jinn) companion with whom he had long conversations in
the privacy of his little hovel. He had had fugues—I even met
him in a fugue state once—and was given to extreme depression. He was never able to perform the trance-dance of any
brotherhood, from which he might expect a cure.

When Tuhami was in his late teens or early twenties, he fell
ill and was hospitalized, he claimed, for over a year. He was
extremely weak, feverish, and frequently became unconscious.[21] The following exchange illustrates Tuhami's inability
to articulate, even symbolically, conflict in such a manner as to
afford himself the possibility of its resolution.[22] There was a lack
of focus in his articulation of an incident of central importance
to him. Dreams and reality were translated into one another. All
experience was ultimately anchored in (his marriage to) 'A'isha
Qandisha.

[*How did you become sick?*] I was working one night in the
factory, pushing a dolly. Suddenly someone called to me. I
turned around, and a man threw a rock and hit me between
the shoulders. From that time on, my knees and head hurt. I
went to Sheikh al-Kamal, but it did not help me. Then I went
to the hospital. Even now my left knee still hurts me.

[*Who was the man?*] He was invisible. I did not see his face
when he threw the stone. When I was sick, I dreamed of a
woman. She was a little black. She was dressed in blue, white,
red, and yellow. After I dreamed of this woman, I went to see
Moulay Mohammed [a very old sherif who interprets dreams,
diagnoses illnesses, and prescribes amulets]. Moulay Mohammed told me what the dream meant and told me to visit . . .
[Tuhami lists the names of twenty saints. He seems to have
lost track of what he was talking about.]

[*What was the dream?*] The woman told me to dress like
her. [Tuhami does not in fact dress in a feminine fashion.] She
told me to do what she does and do everything she says. I did

not know who the woman was until I went to Sidi 'Ali . . . In
the morning I went to the place where the dream took place.
If I dream of a river or a saint, I always go there. I dreamed
that I was at Sidi 'Ali's and so I went to Sidi 'Ali. I went to
Lalla 'A'isha's place [a grotto where 'A'isha Qandisha is said
to live]. I took some candles with me and slept there. I
dreamed of Lalla 'A'isha. She told me that [Tuhami interrupts
himself]. The day I dreamed of the black woman I went to
Moulay Mohammed. He wrote down something [an amulet]
for me to wear around my neck. Then he fell sick for six
months. I wanted to hang it around my neck, but I was told—
Lalla 'A'isha told me not to wear it. I used to go to Sidi 'Ali
every week. I visited all the saints. And I felt better afterwards.
[Tuhami tells how he visited saint after saint before being
hospitalized. Upon my prompting he describes his symptoms.]
Every night I was in the hospital I dreamed of Lalla 'A'isha.
She tole me to leave the hospital. I dreamed that I was fighting
with people, and that this woman [Lalla 'A'isha] was always
at my side, and so I always won my battles.

[*What did she tell you?*] She told me a lot, but I can't say.

[*Who were the people?*] It was those other people [the jnun].
I was always fighting with them. They were with horns and
without horns. They had slippers, and they did not have slippers. They had hair, and they did not have hair. All of them
were men. The women were always on my side. [Tuhami describes his treatment in the hospital.] They gave me a room
all to myself. They did not lock it. I left in the night. I didn't
say anything. My nurse did not know. My knees did not hurt
me. I went to Sheikh al-Kamal and spent the night there. Lalla
'A'isha visited me that night and told me not to go back to the
hospital.

Tuhami felt much better the next day and returned to the factory
and worked for a week before having a dream of a saint whom
he immediately visited. This began a series of dreams about
saints and consequent pilgrimages to their tombs which lasted
for the better part of six months. Tuhami still visits saints' tombs
whenever he dreams of them.

Although Tuhami does not tell us much about his dreams, it
is clear that he holds the figures who appear to him responsible
for his condition. Once again conflict is expressed in terms of
male saints and female jnun, and, as in Mohammed's case, the

initial attack by a male jinn is immediately associated with 'A'isha Qandisha. Tuhami is victimized by 'A'isha, but he is protected by her as well. His motivation seems to be articulated in terms of her wishes and her commands. In one of our meetings he explained how he had first encountered the she-demon. The experience is formulated in standard, folkloristic terms.

On my way home from work one night, I met a woman. She greeted me. She asked me if she could spend the night with me. I asked if she were alone. "I'm not from around here," she said. "I'm from a place a little way off." I agreed. She came in and said she liked my room. She told me that I would marry soon. I prepared a stew. We ate and drank tea. My heart was not afraid. I looked at her. She was really a woman. When it was time to go to bed, I said, "You are my guest. I'll sleep on the ground." She answered, "I want to sleep with you." I said that it was better to sleep apart. She answered, "You don't want to admit that you want to sleep with me, but you do." I slept next to her and made love to her. Then she said: "I like to be with you. I see you always."

Tuhami was puzzled by her last remark. When she returned a month later, he was suspicious and did not sleep with her. Two years later she visited him again.

She was very flirtatious and was dressed in new clothes. I bought milk to prepare coffee. She came shortly after I finished work. She entered my room and sat down. I was kindling the fire when she entered. She came in with her slippers on. [Moroccans always remove their slippers before entering a room.] I looked at her feet. She kept looking at me. She suspected I saw something. "Why are you looking at my feet?," she asked. "You have pretty thighs," I answered. "That's why I'm looking." "Now you know," she said. [Presumably Tuhami noticed that she had camel's feet.] She took off her slippers, her scarf, her jallaba. "Why didn't you show yourself the first time?" I asked. "You have tricked me. Now that I know who you are I am finished. I don't want to talk to you again." "If you want to marry, I'll choose the woman," she said. "She will be *my* choice. It is I who command. If you don't want to accept, you will remain a bachelor for the rest of your life." That is where we left it. She never came back.

Tuhami seemed very detached from his story. If anything, he was caught up in making it suspenseful. It was only when I asked him how he felt when he saw the woman's feet that he showed any emotion. "My head spun. My head was swollen. My mind told me to put a knife in the woman. But I did not have a steel knife, or I would have killed her. I would have put the knife in the ground, and then it would have been *I* who commanded. It is the steel knife that commands." The conflict is one of domination, associated with being a man, and submission, associated with being a woman. Tuhami is doubly submissive insofar as he is dominated by a female demon. She is both the one that dominates and the part of him which is dominated. His feelings of submissiveness, of femininity, are expressed in terms of 'A'isha Qandisha. She is responsible for his inability to marry, for his impotence. He himself is not responsible.

Given Tuhami's obsessive production of dreams and fantasies, given his marked propensity to confuse time sequences, and given the cultural proscription against talking about a "marriage" with 'A'isha Qandisha, it is difficult to discover how saints and jnun are related to his concrete, biographical experience. They do not provide him with a means of articulating symbolically conflicts and other facts of life, most notably his impotence, which he is not normally able to express on a more realistic plane. They do not appear to offer him more than partial resolutions. Unlike Mohammed, Tuhami has not recast his conflicts in terms of collective representations that permit symbolic resolution. Incapable of either relating dream and fantasy to real biography or of permitting them to become symbolic orientation points for the articulation of his biographical experience, he is compelled to translate dream into dream—and even dream into reality and reality into dream—and to cling to his "marriage" to 'A'isha Qandisha as the one constant in his life experience.

Saints, Jnun, and Primary Biographical Orientation Points

In the cases we have considered, we have seen that saints and jnun, most often appearing in dreams, serve as primary orientation points for what Berger and Luckmann call the "subjective apprehension of biographical experience." Saints and jnun serve, in other words, as symbolic-interpretive elements in the articulation of experiences that are central to the individual's personal history. In my three principal cases we perceive the effect of a progressive dislocation of these symbolic-interpretive elements from their real-life contexts. In Moulay Abedsalem's case, the appearance of a saint affected a decision that may not have been fully acceptable to him and may have even run counter to what was socially expected of him. Responsibility was shifted to an external being, and insofar as that being was recognized as a saint, the event was given religious sanction. The articulation of conflict in Mohammed's case provided the possibility for symbolic resolution in both dream and ritual. (Repetition is perhaps the more appropriate term.) In the dream, Mohammed is only capable of running away; in the ritual, he becomes as woman in order to become man again. The ritual does not, however, permanently resolve the conflict. Mohammed must perform the trance-dance again and again. This suggests that through recasting the conflict in terms of collective representations, the ritual serves to structure what would otherwise be an obsessional replay of an essentially irresolvable conflict. It suggests further the rather gloomy proposition that symbolic articulation and resolution of conflict can never lead to real cure. In Tuhami's case conflict is formulated symbolically but there appears to be no possibility of symbolic resolution in dream or ritual. Tuhami is incapable of participating in the trance-dance and structuring in this way his obsessive response to conflict. Dreams, fantasies, and pilgrimages remain obsessive. What structure there is lies in compulsive ideation: his marriage to 'A'isha Qandisha.

The extent to which such compulsive ideation can articulate the entire range of life experience is illustrated in the following abbreviated case.

> Driss, a man in his middle fifties, is a Hamdushi who is known for the violence with which he slashes his head. He considers himself to be 'A'isha's slave and is generally thought to be possessed by the she-demon. There is in fact some evidence of epilepsy or brain damage. Driss had been a Miliani, a member of a religious brotherhood whose adepts play with fire,

until he was attacked by 'A'isha Qandisha, "When 'A'isha came, playing with fire was finished. I was sleeping. 'A'isha grabbed me by the neck and threw me to the ground. This happened three times. When I changed over to the Hamadsha I got better, 'A'isha told me: 'Either you work for me, or I'll have your neck.' 'God is my witness,' I cried with all my might [to prevent his victimization by the she-demon]. But there was nothing to be done. I was sick the next day. My whole body was sick. I could not walk. My wife brought me this black chemise and this red turban, and I got better. [Driss always wears 'A'isha's colors.] This dream occurred three nights in a row. She asked me to work for her for the rest of my life. I will always work for 'A'isha Qandisha."

In all my interviews with Driss, he repeated the story. Whenever I asked him why he had done or was going to do something, he answered that it was because of 'A'isha. Once he dreamed of two women, one in white and one in black. I asked him who they were. "Lalla 'A'isha was in white. I do not know who the woman in black was. I think it was 'A'isha too. She just changed. She is always changing. She changes into a cow, a cat, a dog. [Driss points to his dog.] She keeps changing." I asked him if the woman in black reminded him of someone. "No, no one. I know it was 'A'isha. I know I am inhabited by her alone. I was always inhabited by her." I asked Driss if he was already married to his present wife when he dreamed of 'A'isha. "Yes, she performs the trance-dance. There are 'kings' in her body. I see her, 'A'isha, during the trance-dance and at other times too. If I walk alone at night, I see her in front of me like I see that house. I am always alongside her."

'A'isha has become the one significant element in Driss's formulation of his life experience.

Insofar as the individual's experience is articulated in terms of external saints and jnun, the locus of selfhood appears to be differently oriented and the dimensions of individuality appear to be differently determined for the Moroccan of the Hamadsha's background than for the Westerner. When responsibility for action is attributed to saints and jnun, the locus of responsibility lies outside the individual. His actions and dispositions are subject to outside "forces" which are largely but by no means completely beyond his control. The drama of individual experience is played out on a collective stage. Such formulations afford the Moroccan a means of mitigating the horror of private fantasies and visions—hallucinations—and individual compulsions and obsessions that haunt the Westerner trapped within an ideology, an idiom, of extreme individualism. Or they may be nothing more than another collectively sanctioned and ritually reinforced subterfuge to mask man's essential loneliness.

12.
Rite of Return

> How does one create a memory for the human animal? How
> does one go to impress anything on the partly dull, partly
> flighty human intelligence—that incarnation of forgetful-
> ness—so as to make it stick?
>
> —Nietzsche, *The Genealogy of Morals*

The primitive world, like the worlds of the child and the psychotic, offers a convenient space for projection. The line between folk anthropology and myth is hard to draw. The man-in-
the-street with virtually no experience of the primitive will
often discourse at great length about primitive customs. Even
the serious ethnographies of the past, certainly past ethnological
speculation, frequently impress later anthropologists rather
more as myth than science; the vulgarized claims of such ethnographies and ethnologies are retained, symptomatically, in
the popular imagination. They often appear as antithetical constructs, antiworlds really, which serve, as Lévi-Strauss (1963)
and Michel Foucault (1965) maintain, a definitional function.
This is of course most evident in nineteenth-century tracts on
primitive sexual promiscuity (Bachofen 1967), marriage by ab-
duction and female infanticide (McLennan 1865), incest (Morgan 1877; Tylor 1958), the priority of matriarchy (Bachofen
1967) or patriarchy (Maine 1861), and the absence even of religion among savages (Lubbock 1870). It is evident, too, in the
writings of later anthropologists and will undoubtedly be observed by future scholars looking back at contemporary anthropology. If the fears and anxieties, the desires and longings, the
needs for identity and definition of an age are not given direct
expression in more scientific anthropological works, they do,
nevertheless, influence the concerns, evaluations, and theoretical foci of such works. They determine, too, at least in part, the
biases of these works.

◆

I suggest that the description of a certain class of rituals as rites of transition, *rites de passage,* may reflect less the reality of the ritual than the culture of the anthropologist. My point is that the emphasis on transition may be a (culturally if not psychologically induced) distortion of the ritual process: an oversimplification. I do not mean to deny the existence of the classical *rite de passage;* such rites undoubtedly exist. I mean simply to suggest that some rituals, traditionally described as rites of passage, do not involve passage or give only the illusion of passage. These rites shall be called rites of return, *rites de retour.* In the second half of this paper I shall examine one such rite, the rite of circumcision among the Moroccan Arabs living near Meknes.

Arnold van Gennep (1960) first described the *rite de passage* in 1908: "the life of the individual in any society is a series of passages from one age to another and from one occupation to another." Progression from one occupational group to another is marked by special acts which, among the "semi-civilized," are enveloped in sacred ceremonies.

> Transition from group to group and from one social situation to the next are looked on as implicit in the very fact of existence, so that a man's life comes to be made up of a succession of stages with similar ends and beginnings: birth, social puberty, marriage, fatherhood, advancement to a higher class, occupational specialization and death. *For every one of these events there are ceremonies whose essential purpose is to enable the individual to pass from one defined position to another which is equally well-defined.*   (1960:3, italics mine)

All these ceremonies, van Gennep argues, exhibit a pattern (*schema*) of three essential phases which vary in importance in different transitional contexts: separation (*séparation*), transition (*marge*), and incorporation (*agrégation*). The rite of circumcision is for van Gennep a rite of separation.

Despite van Gennep's assertion that the "essential purpose" of the rite of passage "is to enable the individual to pass from one defined position to another which is equally well-defined," he himself is not particularly clear about the nature of these "positions" (see Gluckman 1962:1–52). He refers to occupational groups, age grades, membership in societies, brother-hoods, religious and tribal groups; he refers to such celestially determined units as months, seasons, and years. He lacks the conceptual apparatus of status and role that later scholars have (not without the danger of oversimplification) attached to his theories. Van Gennep's failure to define "position" adequately has, I believe, impeded an appreciation of the intricacy of the ritual process.[1] Moreover, his failure to consider ritual, however arbitrarily, from the experiential vantage point of any one of its participants has led him to simplify the ritual experience itself.[2] Here I will look at the rite of circumcision from the point of view of a single participant, the boy who undergoes the operation. My decision is arbitrary but I hope it is of heuristic value. In no way is it a denial of the significance of the rite for other participants.[3]

In their desire for analytic purity, if not in their fright before the "subjective" vantage point of experience, many scholars have succumbed to what can be called the ritual illusion. It is the assumption that the ritual does what it is said to do. That a boy is treated as a man, for example, that he is declared to be a man *in a particular ritual context* does not necessarily extend to his treatment and conceptualization in other contexts. He may well be treated as a man, a boy, or an infant—or as all three in different contexts. (These different contexts would include everyday life, other rituals, and stories about the boy himself or myths and legends in which he is tacitly identified with one of the characters.) It is important to assume neither continuity nor discontinuity of treatment and conceptualization from one context to another. Ritual exegesis and the exegetical method in ritual analysis frequently (if not inevitably) promote the illusion of continuity and mask both discontinuities and dissonant experiences.

A striking example of how an analytic strategy can produce a blindness to possible discontinuities in the ritual process and dissonances in the ritual experience is van Gennep's (1960) distinction between physiological and social puberty, a distinction which has provided the rationale for purely sociological analyses of ritual. Van Gennep (1960:68) notes quite simply that since the time of so-called puberty rites rarely coincides with the physical puberty of the initiate, "it is appropriate to distinguish between *physical puberty* and *social puberty*, just as we distinguish between *physical kinship* (consanguinity) and *social kinship*, between *physical maturity* and *social maturity* (majority)." With regard to circumcision, he notes:

> Variations in the age at which circumcision is practiced should themselves show that this is an act of social and not physiological significance. Among many peoples the operation is performed at fairly great intervals—for instance, every two, three, four or five years—so that children of different degrees of sexual development are circumcised at the same time. Moreover, within a single region inhabited by populations of the same somatic type (race), remarkable variations will be found. (1960:70)

As evidence, van Gennep quotes Doutté's finding on the age of circumcision in Morocco: from seven to eight days after birth to twelve or thirteen years among the Dukalla, from two to five years among the Rahuna, from two to ten in Fez, at eight in Tangiers, from five to ten among the Djabala, and from two to four around Mogador. Circumcision is then according to van Gennep (1960:72) a rite of social, not physiological significance. It is a rite of separation that removes the mutilated individual "from the common mass of humanity" and permanently incorporates him in a "defined group" since the operation leaves "ineradicable traces."

By isolating the physiological from the social, van Gennep precludes consideration of the significance of their frequent disjunction. He oversimplifies the ritual process and fails to appreciate the complexity of the ritual experience. It is important to note that *both* the physiological and the social are cultural categories.[4] Van Gennep frequently confuses an emic or in-cultural definition of group membership with an etic or extra-cultural definition of physiological puberty. From an experiential point of view, it is necessary to maintain an emic approach to group membership, identity, role, and status as well as physical maturity.

Even among scholars who have accepted the experiential or phenomenological vantage point there is a marked tendency to succumb to the ritual illusion. Peter Berger and Thomas Luckmann note in *The Social Construction of Reality* (1967:99) that the socially constructed symbolic universe "makes possible the ordering of different phases of biography."

> In primitive societies the rites of passage represent this nomic function in pristine form. The periodization of biography is symbolized at each stage with the totality of human meanings. To be a child, to be an adolescent, to be an adult, and so forth—each of these biographical phases is legitimated as a mode of being in the symbolic universe (most often, as a particular mode of relating to the worlds of the gods.) *We need not belabor the obvious point that such symbolization is conducive to feeling of security and belonging.* (italics mine)

Berger and Luckmann (1967:99–100) go on to suggest that a modern psychological theory of personality development can fulfill the same nomic function.

> In both cases, the individual passing from one biographical phase to another can view himself as repeating a sequence that is given in the "nature of things" or his own "nature." *That is, he can reassure himself that he is living "correctly."* The "correctness" of his life program is thus legitimated on the highest level of generality. As the individual looks back upon his past, his biography is intelligible to him in these terms. As he projects himself into the future, he may conceive of his biography as unfolding within a universe whose ultimate coordinates are known. (italics mine)

Berger and Luckmann are correct in pointing to the nomic function that the rite of passage plays in the "periodization" of biography. But by failing to take into account a possible disjunction between the ritually periodized biography of the individual and his *everyday* experience of himself, and his personal history with all its contingencies, particularities, and deviations, Berger and Luckmann render personal history a stereotype, the individual a cipher, and time *angstlos.*

Indeed, one of the effects of the disjunction between these two orders, here ritualized biography and mundane personal history, is an anxiety which must not be considered only in terms of pathology (Fromm-Reichmann 1955). Berger and Luckmann's "obvious point" that the ritual periodization of biography is "conducive to feelings of security and belonging" may not be so obvious after all. The ritual may give the individual no assurance whatsoever that he is living "correctly." As every therapist knows, it is the disjunction between a "normal" if not an *ideal* biography and one's own personal history that produces anxiety, guilt, and symptomatology. Civilization, as Freud (1930) has pointed out, imposes cruel sacrifice on man, on his sexuality and aggressivity. One sacrifice is dramatically enacted in the Moroccan circumcision ritual that I will describe. We may understand it in Oedipal terms as the birth of conscience, the repression of desire, and the creation of profound feelings of inadequacy, inferiority, and worthlessness that demand compensation. To the Moroccan, the rite will be understood with little elaboration as a necessary prerequisite for both spiritual and sexual manhood.

The theories which have been put forth to explain the very widespread practice of circumcision (Jensen 1933) are, as Ashley-Montagu (1946) remarked, "as numerous as the leaves in the Vallombrosa." Bryk (1934) notes that the explanations for circumcision "furnish a splendid example of the versatility of human extravagant imagination, and are, at the same time, a document of the ambivalent validity of casuistic argumentation." Weston LaBarre (1964) remarks too on the ingenuity used to "explain" circumcision in conceptually comfortable terms. The Australian initiation rites which include circumcision and subincision have served as a prototype for much of the speculation on the "meaning" of circumcision (Bettelheim 1955; Radin 1957; Roheim 1942, 1945, 1972).

Early anthropological theories tended to be universal and rationalist. Briffault (1927) suggested that circumcision is an attempt on the part of the male to imitate female genital defloration; Westermarck (1926) saw it as a means of making the boy capable of procreation and marriage; Crawley (1927) regarded it as both means of preventing the retention of magically dangerous secretions and as sacrifice of part that guaranteed thereby the well-being of the whole; Meiners, Boettiger, and Vatke among others (Bryk 1934) explained circumcision as a substitute for human sacrifice and castration. Frazer (1922) understood it in terms of reincarnation. Circumcision has been explained too in terms of increased or decreased sensuality, the prevention of onanism and pederasty, ritual cleanliness, endurance tests, and increased fertility (Bryk 1934; Gray 1911). Van Gennep (1960) regarded it as a mark of group membership. In 1829 van Autenreith (quoted in Bryk 1934) proposed an absurd extreme of this view by deriving circumcision from the barbarian warriors' custom of bringing back the genitals of fallen enemies. To avoid suspicion that these phallic trophies were plundered from their own dead, the warriors adopted the custom of circumcision. Numerous medical and hygienic reasons—the prevention of paraphimosis, phimosis, *calculi praeputiales*, cancer, gonorrhoea, and syphilis—have also been offered, usually without regard to native medical beliefs (Bryk 1934).

Aside from the more universalistic (statistical explanations for circumcision such as Whiting's (1964) attempt to correlate it with rainy tropics, kwashiorkor, and patrilineal polygyny(!), most recent anthropological investigations have focused on the practice within a specific socio-cultural context. Circumcision is usually viewed as an important segment of an initiation ceremony. (As Radin [1957] pointed out, such initiations have the puberty rite as their prototype.) Raymond Firth (1963:429) writes, typically, with regard to the Tikopian practice of superincision (a longitudinal slitting of the upper surface of the anterior portion of the prepuce): "The ceremonies of initiation cannot then be explained as the outcome of the particular operation of superincision; this must be explained in terms of the ritual as a whole from which it derives its justification." Superincision for the Tikopian, Firth argues, "confers the appropriate material token of distinction upon the individual who has been the subject of the qualifying ritual." It characterizes the boy as sexually mature. (Here I should note that like circumcision in Morocco the operation is often precocious.) The initiation ritual itself shapes the boy's relation to other persons in the community and thus helps "to fit him for future life." Not only does Firth ignore the possible consequences of the disjunction between social and physical puberty but he tends to look at contradictory elements within the ritual context itself as ultimately integrative.

In his detailed analysis of Mukanda, the circumcision rite of the matrilineal Ndembu of Zambia, Victor Turner (1967; 1962)

does recognize the complex, polysemic, sometimes contradictory, certainly bipolar referentiality of ritual symbols. Circumcision is the central episode in the Ndembu's seemingly
classical rite of passage in which the boy is made a man. This
rite, Turner stresses, not only changes the status of the initiate
but serves to reconfirm or realign social relations. One of the
most important of these is the parent-child relationship, which
Turner (1967:265) understands in its broader socio-symbolic dimension. "From being 'unclean' children, partially effeminized
by constant contact with their mothers and other women, boys
are converted by the mystical efficacy of the ritual into purified
members of a male moral community, able to begin to take part
in the jural, political and ritual affairs of Ndembu society." This
change not only affects the relationship between sons and parents but also the "extrafamilial links of matrilineal descent and
patrilateral affiliation."

> The separation of men and women in Mukanda is not only a
> ritualized expression, indeed an exaggeration, of the physical
> and psychological differences between men and women, but it
> also utilizes the idiom of sexuality to represent the difference
> between opposed modes of ordering social relations, which in
> Ndembu culture have become associated with descent
> through parents of opposite sex. The mother-son and father-
> son relationship have, in Mukanda, become symbols of wider,
> more complex relationships. (Turner 1967:266)

Turner recognizes but does not explain the *force* of the sexual
idiom. He (1967:37) notes that ritual symbols are a "compromise
between the need for social control, and certain innate and universal human drives whose complete gratification would result
in the breakdown of such control." Contrary goals are represented by the same form. Thus, Mukanda explicitly seeks to
bring life to boys as men and implicitly (unconsciously) enables
older men to "go as near as they dare to castrating or killing the
boys." Turner does not, however, explore the effect of such
disjunctions both within the ritual order and between the ritual
order and everyday life. By seeking to distinguish all too completely between the sociological and the psychological, both

Turner and Firth fail to recognize that the ritual disjunctions produce, *inter alia,* a unique frame for the (psychological) experience of time.

Psychoanalytic theories of circumcision have also ignored the role that the operation has on the individual's experience of time. They have tended to be speculative and have ignored the effect of the operation on personality. Freud (1912, 1933, 1939; see also Kitahara 1976) regarded circumcision as a symbolic substitute for the actual castration practiced by the jealous father of the primal horde on his sons. Theodor Reik (1946) too considered circumcision as a castration equivalent that effectively supports the prohibition against incest. For the father, the puberty rite of which circumcision is an important component "represents a number of hostile and homosexual acts, which in this form correspond to the paternal ambivalence toward the youth." They transform the youth's "unconscious impulses of hostility against his father into friendly ones." "We recognized in all these rites the strong tendency to detach the youths from their mothers, to chain them more firmly to the community of men, and to seal more closely the union between father and son which has been loosened by the youths' unconscious strivings toward incest" (Reik 1946:145). Roheim (1942) also argues that puberty rites are based on the primal separation of the child from the mother. He follows Freud in viewing object loss as the contributing cause of all anxiety. Rites of transition are repetitions of the separation carried out on the body of the person who undergoes the rite. Separation from the mother is represented as separation of part of the body from the whole. Such separation is compensated for by a symbolic omnipotent penis (for example the bull roarer) and by a father-son unity.

Nunberg (1965; see also Orgel 1956) accepts the view that circumcision is a symbolic substitute for castration; he regards the foreskin as a symbolic residue of femininity—an identification that occurs in a number of mythologies including the Ndembu (Turner 1967) and the Dogon (Griaule 1970). Khan in his 1965 study of a foreskin-fetishist notes too that the uncircumcised penis is an "ideal bisexual object." Daly (1960:220; see also Schlossman 1966) suggests that the original function of circumcision and clitoridectomy was "to modify the psycho-bisexuality which had resulted from the traumatic frustration of the hetero-sexual impulses in the original repression of incest. It represented a second wave of repression by means of which boys re-identified themselves with women."

Bettelheim (1955) argues that an adequate explanation of initiation will have to take into account the consequences of pre-Oedipal emotional experiences, including those resulting from the infant's close attachment to the mother. He suggests that one sex envies the sexual organs and functions of the other. Male initiation rites may result then from "the desire to alleviate fear and envy of the mother and of women in general, and to reassert the relative power and importance of men as compared to women" (83). They may assert that men too can bear children. Genital mutilation, particularly subincision, may be an attempt to imitate female genital and sexual functioning.

Ozturk (1973) notes that the psychoanalytic studies of circumcision have been rather more concerned with the psychological origin of the practice than with its significance for the individual. He suggests that ultimately circumcision may have "acquired complete or relative autonomy from (its) original functions." The various forms, ages, and social meanings of circumcision suggest that no one theory is applicable to all ritual circumcision. Ozturk's own research in Turkey, where the circumcision rite is not dissimilar to that in Morocco, reveals two conflicting effects of the operation. One is the fear of castration during and shortly after the operation; the other is "the provision of status, prestige, gifts, entertainment, and above all a sense of masculinity." Circumcision, Ozturk argues, "becomes an important ego need in the development of self-concept and identity." He notes that there is no passage from childhood to adulthood in the Turkish circumcision rite but probably passage from "an ambiguous sexual concept of self to a more clear-cut sexual concept of self." Ozturk's argument is well-taken as far as it goes, but it does not address itself to the question of why the excision of the foreskin should become an "important ego need." Cansever (1965), also in a study of circumcision in Turkey, notes that the operation is perceived by the child as an aggressive attack on his body; he feels inadequate, helpless, and functionally less efficient. His main reaction to the operation is one of defensive withdrawal accompanied by aggressive desires. In a rather noncommitted fashion, Cansever (1965:329) suggests "that after the initial experience of defensive withdrawal disappears, during which time the ego will gain its strength over the instinctual drives and outside threats, it will integrate and synthesize the trauma and the resulting feelings from it into the structure of the personality." The question must still be asked: what are the effects of this painful operation on the structure of personality?

Although there is no specific Koranic authority, circumcision is obligatory and widespread for all Muslims.[5] It is of pre-Islamic origin (Patai 1969), and Mohammed seems to have accepted it without question. The several schools of Muslim jurisprudence differ as to its status. The Maliki, the dominant school in North Africa, regards it as commendable (*sunna*) but not indispensable (*wajub*). Muslim scholars justify its practice as being part of the religion of Muhammed or of the natural primitive religion (*fitra*), into which man is born (Levy 1962). In Morocco circumcision was considered an inviolable tradition based on Koranic authority. It was the mark not only of a Muslim but of a Maghrebi, for Jews too were circumcised.[6] Circumcision served to differentiate the Moroccan from the Christian, the European.

Unlike female excision, which is usually veiled in secrecy and mystery, circumcision throughout the Middle East and North Africa is "always a public, joyous, and festive occasion" (Patai 1969). It is the first ceremony to follow the name-day celebration, which occurs seven days after a child's birth, and the celebration of the first haircut, which takes place at an indeterminate age in the child's first year or two of life. Like the first haircut, circumcision is frequently performed in a saint's sanctuary and is accompanied by the sacrifice of a sheep or goat (von Grunebaum 1951). The age at which the operation is performed varies throughout the area. Although it is performed at fourteen, or later, on the island of Soqotra and in some parts of Libya and Egypt, it usually takes place between the ages of three and seven (Patai 1969). There is, in fact, considerable variation even within a single family. Recently, with modernization, there has been a tendency to perform the operation within

a few months of birth. In Meknes and its environs, I was told
that it was better to circumcise a boy as early as possible, for
then the operation would be less painful. Still, most of the men
with whom I worked were circumcised between the ages of
three and six, one as late as twelve.[7] Often a family would wait
until two or more brothers could be circumcised, or until the
occasion of a marriage.

As Patai (1969) has noted, there is frequently a connection
between circumcision and marriage. This is reflected in one of
the words for circumcision, *khtana* in Moroccan Arabic, which
is derived from the same Semitic root as the Hebrew for bridegroom, *hatan,* and for marriage, *hatanah* (Patai 1969). In some
areas of Morocco the boy about to be circumcised is called a
bridegroom and the circumcision itself the boy's first marriage
(Westermarck 1926). (I have heard these terms used in Meknes
in a joking fashion.) In some Arabian tribes a boy's circumcision
is performed in the presence of his betrothed. Here the operation involves the removal of the skin on the entire penis and
surrounding sections of the belly and inner thighs. The boy
must stand upright, shout with joy, and brandish a dagger. His
betrothed sits in front of him ululating and beating a drum.
Should he utter a cry of pain, she has the right to refuse him
(Henniger quoted in Patai 1969).[8] Among the 'Ababda of the
Eastern Desert of Egypt, circumcision immediately precedes
marriage; the hut in which the operation is performed is later
used by the bride and groom as their residence. Both marriage
and circumcision are called *'irs,* literally wedding (Murray
quoted in Patai 1969). In Morocco the co-occurrence of a circumcision and marriage was not uncommon; it was never the groom,
however, who was circumcised but a boy in his or his betrothed's family (see Lane 1963). The justification given was
always economic. Most circumcisions and marriages took place
after the summer harvest "when there was money."

Among the Moroccan Arabs with whom I worked, circumcision is an unquestioned given in the life of a man. It is said to
make a boy a man and is justified on religious, hygienic, and
sexual grounds. The sexual and, to a lesser extent, the hygienic
are, in my observation, more important than the religious to the
individual. Circumcision is considered a necessary prerequi-

site—a cleansing—for entering the mosque and for praying. In fact, one of the words for circumcision in Moroccan Arabic is *thara* which means, literally, a cleansing, an ablution. Both entering a mosque and reciting prayers, I should note, are male prerogatives.[9] An uncircumcised penis is said to be particularly vulnerable to infection from chafing, sweating, and sexual intercourse. Men frequently remember getting sand painfully lodged in their foreskins before they were circumcised; they did not remember, however, that it was usually their mothers who cleaned it out. The uncircumcised are thought to be particularly vulnerable to *l-berd* (gonorrhea) and other venereal diseases. Indeed, women who have slept with uncircumcised men are said to spread *l-berd*. Circumcision is thought to make the man more potent and sexual intercourse more pleasurable.[10] One of my frankest informants wondered whether the uncircumcised derived any pleasure from sexual intercourse.

Although there is considerable variation in ritual detail, the circumcision rite is surprisingly uniform throughout Morocco and bears a striking resemblance to the rite elsewhere in North Africa and the Middle East (see Westermarck 1926 for variations). I will restrict my discussion here to the rite as practiced by various Arab groups (Zerhana, Shrarda, and others) who live in the countryside near Meknes (see Talha 1965).[11]

The circumcision rite is a festive occasion—an important and expensive ceremony to which considerable prestige is attached. It is also a very tense affair, marked within the boy's family by a particularly heavy sense of obligation. The rite *must* be carried out correctly. It provides an arena (not as structured as that, for example, of the Ndembu), in which everyday social relations of envy and animosity as well as considerateness, friendship, and loyalty are sublated in ceremonial form and etiquette.

The tension between everyday and ritual relations can be near explosive. I remember attending a circumcision in a small hamlet on a large government farm where the men worked on a daily basis according to the whims of a rather corrupt farm manager. With more workers than jobs, there was obviously considerable strain among the men of the hamlet—strain that under normal circumstances was controlled by avoidance. During the circumcision ceremony avoidance was impossible; the entire hamlet was invited and with the exception of one man, a professed enemy of the sponsor, everybody came. At one point in the ceremony, well over twenty tense minutes were spent in deciding which guest would have the honor of preparing tea.[12] Exceptional attention was paid to the amount of tea each guest was served. Conversation was virtually precluded by the blasting of a transistor radio.

The ceremony places the sponsor,[13] usually the boy's family, under considerable financial strain. Poorer families will often wait several (anxious) years before they can afford to sponsor it correctly. I write "anxious" here because fathers "know" that the longer they wait the more painful the circumcision will be for their sons. It can be said that in certain cases the son is sacrificed for the prestige of his father. Of course, the son shares this prestige.

The circumcision ceremony begins the day before the actual performance. That evening, after a festive meal for which a sheep or goat has been slaughtered (*dbeh*), if the family can afford it, an older woman paints the boy's hands and feet with henna—like a girl's. The application of henna takes place in the women's quarters in the exclusive presence of women who cluster tightly around the boy. Henna, which is deemed to have all sorts of curative and protective properties, is said to give the boy *baraka*, or blessing. The boy who is considered unusually vulnerable to the evil eye and to demonic attack at this time is also given a protective amulet to wear. Most often this is a string of beads, animal bones, and other miscellaneous objects, including a small pouch containing alum and harmal. (The latter are especially regarded for their apotropaic properties.) The amulet is worn on the boy's right ankle for seven days after the operation. The boy, or more accurately his mother, receives presents after the henna has been applied. There is dancing if the musicians arrive in the evening.

The following morning the boy is dressed in new clothes, usually a white chemise, occasionally a green one covered with a diaphanous white one, and a burnous. An embroidered bag which contains amulets is hung from his left shoulder. His head may be ritually shaved at this time in the presence of the male guests who give him gifts (*grama*). The donors are publicly praised by the village bard (*berrah*) who stands next to the boy. The head shaving (*hsana*) is not obligatory.

The boy is then hoisted onto a horse or mule; his head is hidden in the hood of his burnous to protect him from the evil eye; and he is paraded through the village by his father to the local mosque or saint's sanctuary. *Ghiyyata,* or oboe-players, who in the smaller villages and hamlets are strangers, lead the parade, playing the whining circumcision music. Men, women, and children follow behind the boy. After the mosque or sanctuary has been circumambulated three times, the boy's father carries him in to have a few prayers said for him. He is not allowed to touch the ground at this time. Unless the circumcision is to take place in the sanctuary—and I have not seen such a ceremony—the boy is led back to his house where the circumcision will take place. The boy's mother does not accompany her son on the parade. His father disappears as soon as the boy is home; for, as one Moroccan man put it, "what father can bear to see his son submitted to such pain?"

In the poorer, more forlorn villages the parade is a rather shabby affair. The mosque may be circumambulated only once or the parade may be stopped altogether if "it is too hot." There is usually a clutch of people immediately behind the boy and then a chain of stragglers. A prostitute (*shikha*) who usually accompanies the itinerant musicians from one village circumcision to another is very much in evidence. Village boys are excited by the parade, but I have noticed that those who have been circumcised within a year or two withdraw when the parade returns to the boy's house. They look frightened or emotionally drained. Unmarried girls are unveiled and wear their hair down on this occasion.

The circumcision itself is performed by a barber shortly after the boy has returned from the mosque or sanctuary. In small villages the barber, like the musicians and the prostitute, is a stranger, who in the month following the harvest rushes busily from village to village performing as many as a dozen circumcisions in a day. They seemed to me to be cold, efficient, and peremptory; they dictated the schedule of events, offered minimal advice, showed little or no sympathy to the boys they circumcised, and barely accepted the hospitality of their hosts. Although a boy is supposed to respect the barber who circumcised him, most younger circumcised boys disappeared when they saw him arrive.

The boy is carried by his mother to the room where the operation is to take place. A crowd of women, including the prostitute, gather in front of the house with the men behind them. The mother—or some other female relative or a midwife—stands in front of the door. Her left foot is in a bowl of water which contains a piece of iron; in her left hand she holds a mirror into which she stares; in her right hand she holds a white flag. The iron is said to draw the pain from the scissors, ultimately from the wound, to the bowl where it is cooled down by the water. The mother stares into the mirror to prevent herself—and the boy—from crying; the flag represents the flag of Ali, of Islam.[14] Mother and son are for the moment symbolically equated.

The operation itself is a simple affair. The boy is held by an older man, preferably but not necessarily his paternal uncle, and is told to look up at a tiny bird.[15] The barber pulls the foreskin up, slips some sheep's dung in between the foreskin and the glans, and with a single cut of a scissors snips off the foreskin. The dung is said to protect the glans from nicking. The penis is then plunged into a broken egg to which a little rabbit dung and henna have been added. This is said to cool the wound down and aid in healing.

As soon as the foreskin is clipped, a signal is given to the musicians who are waiting with the villagers in front of the house. They begin to play the circumcision music; women begin to dance. The boy is swaddled like an infant in a cloth (*izar*); heat is said to hasten healing. He is placed on his mother's naked back—or the back of another woman—in such a way that his bleeding penis presses against her.[16] His mother dances along with other women until he stops crying. Then he is put to bed. In some ceremonies at this time women give him candies and other tidbits. He is fed a hard-boiled egg and gravy when he wakes up, to give him strength. His mother cares for the wound until it has healed; she sprinkles it with powdered henna. His father returns after the boy is asleep.

The dancing continues after the boy has been put to sleep.

The prostitute who performs a belly dance is the center of attention. She is watched salaciously by the men and critically by the women. The circumcision rite affords one of the few occasions when both men and women can watch such dancing together. When the dance ends the prostitute eats with the men. (If the family is rich enough, a goat or sheep is slaughtered in the morning before the parade.) Conversation tends to be erotic.[17] When the meal is over, the prostitute makes love to any man in the village who can afford to pay her. She leaves with the musicians.

Many Moroccan men with whom I talked remember their circumcision vividly. It is often said that a circumcision should not be performed before a boy is old enough to remember it. It is in fact a subject of great anxiety. Moroccan men joke about it, especially in the baths. (Baths are considered to be a place of sexual temptation; they are said to be haunted by demons.) They talk about mutilations, jagged foreskins, and amputated penises. They show no particular pride in the operation. It is just carried out. An explanation is rarely offered to the boy either before or after the operation. He must simply submit without questioning, as he must submit to so much in a world that often seems needlessly arbitrary to the Westerner.

This attitude of unquestioned submission is aptly illustrated in the following retrospective account of the ceremony by a musician (rather a Lothario) in his middle twenties who often played at circumcisions and weddings. He laughed nervously throughout this recitation. He did not remember exactly when the operation took place.

> I was little. The barber came, and I came into the room. My paternal uncle was in the room. I did not know what was going to happen. I had been playing outside. First they circumcised my brother who left crying. I asked what had happened, but they said nothing had happened. Then they brought me into the room, telling me I was going to see some birds. I saw scissors next to me. My uncle held me. The barber touched my penis, and I was told to look up at the birds. Then I heard a drrb. The moment he touched my penis, my tongue rolled to the back of my mouth. And the blood that flowed tickled me. They put medicine on it, and I fell asleep. My friends

watched me crying. I had a chemise on so that it would touch my penis. I did not wear pants. The worst was when I had to pee. It burned terribly. Slowly I began to go out, but I couldn't play with the other boys because I was afraid I would fall. I got better before my brother. Perhaps the barber nicked his glans . . . My mother was not allowed to watch. She was at the door. Our custom is that when a boy is circumcised, his mother puts him on her back after she has removed the clothes from her back. The boy is against her naked back. The penis touches the mother's skin, and the blood flows down her back. The mother walks around and even dances a little. When the child is tired, she brings him to the room to sleep. . . . [How did you feel when your mother carried you?] I remember my penis touching my mother's skin. I wanted to jump in the air. It stung even more on my mother's flesh. I cried a lot . . . [Where was your father?] No, I didn't see my father until I woke up. I was afraid of him. Even when my penis hurt, I didn't cry in front of him. My father told me not to cry, and he promised me all kinds of gifts. My mother put powder on my penis each day, and it stung for hours.

The operation is described matter-of-factly. The musician does not view the operation as a betrayal, as some Moroccan men did (see Chapter 7). It is described out of ritual context; his emphasis on the unexpected is not unusual. He is particularly conscious of how he appears in front of his father and friends; he compares his reaction to that of his brother. In Morocco there is considerable hostility between brothers and little overt hostility toward the father. Above all, the musician remembers the pain of his penis pressed against his mother's back.

The "movement" of the rite is circular. Symbolically—and in fact—the boy is led from the woman's world back to the woman's world. The circumcision rite itself is a period of liminality in which male and female elements are interrelated in a complex dialectic. The boy's (the bride's) hand and feet are hennaed like a woman's—by women in an intensely feminine atmosphere. His hair may be shaved. (I should note too that unmarried girls, presumably virgins, are permitted at this time to wear *their* hair down in public—a highly eroticized sign of immodesty permitted only at circumcisions and marriages. There is perhaps an element of role reversal here.) The boy is then declared a man—symbolized by the parade through town on horseback, his entrance into the mosque where women are not permitted, and the attention of his father and other men in the village. In this "manly" condition he is, however, vulnerable to the evil eye and to demonic attack. He is protected by amulets; he hides his head in a hood; he must be carried. He is treated like an infant.

The boy is then returned from the public world of men back to the private world of female domesticity. He is led by his mother—his father disappears—into a room where he will be circumcised; "one" with him, she will symbolically bear his pain and give him strength. She will lead him into the room where he will be declared a man through an act that is unmanning. (I need not invoke Freud, Reik, or Bettelheim here; the anxiety aroused by circumcision is great. Several of my informants claimed that they thought their penises had been cut off and dared not to look down for days.) The boy is then placed on his mother's back—the Oedipal implications are, to the Westerner, self-evident—in a manner that is at once intimate and painful. He is, of course, swaddled as a baby. He is in the presence, too, of a prostitute who dances erotically—a stranger whom he cannot know. He is carried to the women's quarters and cared for by his mother. The men of the village, in a gesture that reaffirms *their* manhood—and differentiates them from the boy—have license to sleep with the prostitute. It is my impression that following the circumcision the boy is treated much as he was treated before the ritual interlude. He appears to suffer great anxiety when other circumcisions take place and when, in jest or as a disciplinary measure, he is threatened with a circumcision, sometimes called a second marriage.

The circumcision rite is disjunctive. It declares passage where there is in both ritual and everyday life no passage whatsoever—only the *mark* of passage, the mutilation that is itself an absence, a negation. It is a precocious rite. The boy is declared a man before he is (emically as well as etically) physically a man—or is treated as a man. It removes him temporarily from the private world of women and children, from hearth and harem, to the public world of men, prowess and religion. It announces a transition yet to come—the passage into manhood—and provides him with an essential but insufficient prerequisite for that transition. It gives him, if I may speak figuratively, a preview of manhood that is, however, dramatically arrested. He is in his "manhood" deprived of his manhood. He is triumphantly carried back from the mosque to his mother, who will not have him until he has been mutilated and then only as an infant. He is cruelly punished in the symbolic fulfillment of his *putative* desire: his penis, now mutilated, is pressed against his mother's sweating back. His separation—the root of all anxiety in the Freudian schema—is both declared and undeclared. He is ritually separated from his mother—only to be reunited with her in everyday life not as the man he has been ritually declared but as the infant he has been ritually undeclared. He suffers, one would surmise, an indelible sense of inadequacy and inferiority, particularly with respect to men, and an intense fear of women. These feelings of inadequacy, inferiority, and fear are reflected, presumably, in the Moroccan man's image of himself, of women, and in the relations between the two sexes. It is perhaps no accident that the most virulent and capricious demons (*jnun*) in Morocco are female.

To look upon the Moroccan rite of circumcision as simply a ritualized punishment of incestuous desires, a disambiguation of the boy's primordial bisexuality or ritualized conversion of the infant's separation anxiety into castration anxiety, all determinant of Moroccan personality and culture, is to lose sight of the complexity of the ritual process. The rite, as I have said, is essentially *disjunctive:* a series of contradictory messages that remain unresolved, at least in the ritual immediate. What resolution, if any, comes with time—the ritually unmarked time of physical maturation which culminates in an almost obsessive concern for frequency of sexual performance and in the ritually marked transition into marriage.[18] (Not only is there a frequent symbolic and even temporal association of marriage and circumcision, but the Moroccan marriage ceremony itself is in many respects a symbolic undoing of circumcision [for details see Westermarck 1914].) Resolution may come, too, with fatherhood and perhaps even with the son's circumcision. But here we must be careful. The father is not simply doing unto his son what was done unto him, as some theorists have rather too crudely suggested. The father is also vicariously reliving, anxiously remembering and repeating his own circumcision: he too is submitting now as he did then to the manifest message of the rite, to custom and tradition, ultimately to the will of God. Resolution may also come in the curing trance-dances of the Hamadsha, Jilala, and Isawa (Crapanzano 1973a; Brunel 1926) which are so often accompanied by acts of self-mutilation. As I have suggested specifically regarding the Hamadsha, these rituals need not be conceived as affording resolution but, in a manner similar to myth, as offering the illusion of resolution.

The Moroccan circumcision rite renders the timeless repetition of separation anxiety into an event within time, to be remembered. It is the time of desire that has succumbed to symbolic substitutions, to culture and history. It is a time that rests cruelly upon mutilation and pain—the great sacrifice that Freud claims civilization requires. It is ritualized, discontinuous time. Rural Moroccans, Dale Eikelman (1977) has noted for the Bni Battu, "conceive events temporally in terms of sequences of irregular, island-like concrete experiences." These events serve as symbolic orientation points for the articulation of personal history, ultimately of self. They rest—and this is the message that *I* see in the Moroccan circumcision ceremony—not on conjunction but on disjunction. It is for this reason perhaps that Moroccans say that circumcision should take place as early as possible to be as painless as possible, but not so early as to be forgotten. "Whenever man has thought it necessary to create a memory for himself," Nietzsche observed in *The Genealogy of Morals,* "his effort has been attended with torture, blood, sacrifice." It is this pain that grounds the individual in civilization and history. It may give him biographical and personal security, as Berger and Luckmann (1967) suggest, but only if the disjunction, ultimately the separation, are too painful to be acknowledged. What was desired can no longer be desired; what is desired must be seen as real, not symbolic. The illusion of ritual must be denied; the ritual illusion must be taken as real—not only by the ritual participant but by the stranger to the ritual too, the anthropologist or the psychoanalyst, who understandably finds the impossibility of resolution intolerable. Transition, if only from a state of being uncircumcised to a state of being circumcised, must be witnessed—even where there is no transition, only repetition and return.

· IV ·

THE SUBMERGED SELF

13.
Maimed Rites and Wild and Whirling Words

> Seems, madam? Nay, it is. I know not "seems."
> 'Tis not alone my inky cloak, good mother,
> Nor customary suits of solemn black,
> Nor windy suspiration of forc'd breath,
> No, nor the fruitful river in the eye,
> Nor the dejected havior of the visage,
> Together with all forms, moods, shapes of grief,
> That can denote me truly. These indeed seem,
> For they are actions a man might play;
> But I have that within which passes show,
> These but the trappings and suits of woe.
>
> —Hamlet, I,ii,76–86

With these bitter words Hamlet answers his mother's request that he cast off his "nighted colour" and let his eye "look like a friend on Denmark." By "Denmark" Gertrude means her new husband, Claudius, Hamlet's uncle and usurper of the throne, who "popp'd in between th' election and [Hamlet's] hopes"—a point Goethe (1973) stressed and contemporary critics have more or less ignored—regicide, as we learn, and fratricide, as well as the kingdom of Denmark whose sickly state is marked by Hamlet's "inky cloak."

Hamlet's reflection on appearance, denotation, play, and hypocrisy is in response to his mother's "common" wisdom: "all that lives must die, passing through nature to eternity." But Hamlet is also responding to the state of Denmark, where, as Phyllis Gorfain (1986:220) notes, the King's actions have undermined "the fiction that social conventions are natural law," that "all rules are just rulings."[1] In the court at least, costume, "suspirations," tears, demeanor, external appearances, and even the shape of grief have become a form of (serious) play.[2] Ordinary language and custom, which are normally taken literally or in a conventionally symbolic fashion, become "figures" whose literal or conventionally symbolic referent is sacrificed for pragmatic effect.[3]

Here I will attempt to examine the epistemic foundations of Hamlet's world much as an anthropologist examines the episteme of the people he studies. I recognize that this world is a *represented world* subject to the constraints of representation and that the representation itself is, like all theatrical representations, complex, falling, as it were, between performance and text. The tension between performance and text has posed all sorts of problems for those who have tried to develop a theory of theater from either a purely textual or a purely performative point of view. For those who have attempted to reckon with both the performative and textual dimensions of a theatrical representation, "text" and "performance" and their examples are often simply rhetorical. Conditions of representation certainly affect the way a particular world, the world of Elsinore, is represented. Weiman (1985:278) argues, for example, that just as Shakespeare's plays "represent the triumphs and defeats of authority," so are "the divisions and suspensions of authority" written into their mode of representation. That the conditions of representation, rhetoric, and theatricality are refracted in representations is perhaps a truism in this deconstructivist age; that this refraction permits a *glissement* from representing to representation does present particular expository and analytic problems, especially for those critics (Weiman is an exception) who deny the possibility of meta-commentary and hence of an authoritative, controlling vantage point. Their denial of a text-transcendent position masks their control over their "text-imbricated" commentaries.

I will not take up these matters, however, just as I will not consider the effects on *Hamlet* of Shakespeare's own world. What interests me here is the way in which the linguistic episteme of *Hamlet*, however generated, constrains the action (and the words) of the play. I believe that this kind of analysis has to precede any psychological or sociological interpretation of the play. Given the universalist claims of the psychologies and sociologies usually appealed to in the psychological and sociological studies of *Hamlet* and other of Shakespeare's plays, internal epistemic constraints tend to be ignored. The world of Hamlet is universalized or the psychological mechanisms (less often the sociological ones) are held accountable for the representational constraints.

I will be concerned primarily with how the King's "unnatural acts" send Elsinore, perhaps all of Denmark, into a semantic— an evidential—crisis. There is, there can be, no certainty, for when the King breaches the moral and ritual order of society, he can no longer serve as a symbolic, indeed as an empowered, guarantor of meaning, however much of an artifice that meaning may be. Under such circumstances, there is no way for anyone at Elsinore to evaluate (the truth of) any utterance, any symbolic or potentially symbolic act. In technical terms, there is a collapse of the meta-pragmatic regimentation of meaning—the pragmatic determination of semantico-referential meaning to both code and context—upon which any socially adequate hermeneutics rests. This is particularly true in court society, and other similar societies, where, for political survival, words and acts have conventionally concealed meanings, which, though known, cannot normally be acknowledged. With the loss of pragmatic constraints on meaning, meaning, contextual relevance really, is determined, if at all, through the ruthless struggle of differentially empowered desires. This struggle is represented in many of Shakespeare's plays, most notably *Macbeth*, but in *Hamlet* the consequences of moral and ritual breaches on language are most fully displayed. Neither the King nor Hamlet nor, for that matter, the other courtiers, can be certain of the meaning of any utterance or act. The King's power seems insufficient (for his position is precarious) to dictate meaning and relevance. He is a victim of his own meaning-destroying act. Like Hamlet he has to proceed in devious ways to determine contextual relevance, but, as King, he does not have Hamlet's possibility. He cannot play the fool, the madman, the shaman (in terms of which I describe some of Hamlet's antics), or the stage manager. He has to make use, at times crudely, of others—of Polonius, of Rosencrantz and Guildenstern, of Gertrude, and, most tragically, of Ophelia. Despite his play, Hamlet remains a victim of the crisis at Elsinore. He has no more sure

◆

footing than the King, and it is in these terms that his delay as well as his impetuosity have to be understood. We have, I should add, to be careful not to attribute defined intentions to any of the characters, for in such semantic crises intention itself becomes problematic.[4] The court at Elsinore is in one of those no-win-no-exit situations that occur so often in history and that we prefer to ignore. It can only self-destruct. A narrator alone is left, and the inevitable conventionality of his tale will betray its subject matter.

In his *The Arte of English Poesie*, written in 1589, George Puttenham [1936:154], suggests that dissembling or disguise is an essential feature of all figurative language and a source of its poetic effect. He also notes a danger. "As figures be the instruments of ornament in euery language, so be they also in a sorte abuses or rather trespasses in speach, because they passe the ordinary limits of common vtterance, and be occupied of purpose to deceiue the eare and also the minde, drawing it from plainnesse and simplicitie to a certaine doublenesse, whereby our talke is the more guilefull & abusing." The danger is particularly great where, as in Hamlet's Denmark, it is no longer possible to determine how discourse is to be framed.[5] Hamlet's world is, as Maynard Mack (1952) noted, mysterious and filled with riddles, preeminently in the interrogative mood. Words become arbitrary signs that are to be read according to the whims of desire or the dictates of power. They become false indices of identity and allegiance, indeed, of false identity and dubious allegiance. Insofar as he can, as a participant in such a semantically destabilized world, Hamlet recognizes that words, his included, have become empty markers of a world that ought perhaps to be and may have been before the death of his father but is no more. Truth can no longer be found in words and evidence in appearance—at least not consistently, not by traditional criteria. Like the old King's ghost who may yet be the devil "in fair and warlike form," appearances loosened from reality, words from things, become uncertain portents, "harbingers preceding still the fates and prologue to the omen coming on" (I,i,125–126). They may bode, as they did in Rome before Caesar's death, "some strange eruption in our state" (I,i,72).

The analogy with Caesar's death is appropriate. In Rome an

Emperor is murdered. In Denmark the King has been slain, and his successor is the very man who slew him. The murder of a king is more than the murder of a man. A king is, as Claudius (IV,v,123) says, hedged with divinity. In medieval political theology, a king was thought to have two bodies—a physical body and a body politic—(Kantorowicz 1957), and we find traces of this belief in Shakespeare. Despite their flattery and hypocrisy, Rosencrantz and Guildenstern express this political theology when Claudius tells them he can no longer endure the hazard that "doth hourly grow out of [Hamlet's] brow" (III,iii,5–7) (MacLaughlan 1979; Alexander 1971:84–85). Guildenstern stresses practically the Danes' dependency on the King (III,iii,8–10). Rosencrantz refers to the symbolic dimension of kingship. If an ordinary individual is bound to keep himself from "noyance" with all his strength and "armour of the mind," then all the more must a king, "upon whose weal depends and rests the lives of many."

> The cess of majesty
> Dies not alone, but like a gulf doth draw
> What's near it with it. Or it is a massy wheel
> Fix'd on the summit of the highest mount,
> To whose huge spokes ten thousand lesser things
> Are mortis'd and adjoin'd, which when it fails,
> Each small annexment, petty consequence,
> Attends the boist'rous ruin. Never alone
> Did the King sigh, but with a general groan.
>
> (III,iii,15–23)

The King is a keystone to the political and the symbolic order. His death causes "a general groan," and his successor has to end that groan if he is to become the "massy wheel" to whose spokes "ten thousand lesser things are mortis'd and adjoin'd." What happens when that successor is himself the regicide? Then the groaning will not end, for the new King is an illegitimate ruler, a usurper, a murderer whose violations of the political, the moral, and the ritual order preclude his guaranty of meaning. He can only signify arbitrarily, illegitimately, the king(ship). He is, so to speak, a king with only one body. Claudius needs desperately to preserve the secret of regicide if he is to retain authority and maintain order in Denmark, but his secrecy is in vain. For, as Hamlet says, "murder, though it have no tongue, will speak with most miraculous organ" (II,ii,589–590).

The ghost may portend a "strange eruption," but he is in fact the issue, and the enunciator, of an eruption that has already occurred, the moral and ritual violation, which has produced the "seemingness" of appearance, the semantic vertigo, Denmark's evidential crisis. Hamlet describes the effects of the King's murder to Gertrude in the famous closet scene.

> Such an act
> That blurs the grace and blush of modesty,
> Calls virtue hypocrite, takes off the rose
> From the fair forehead of an innocent love
> And sets a blister there, makes marriage vows
> As false as dicers' oaths—O, such a deed
> As from the body of contraction plucks
> The very soul, and sweet religion makes
> A rhapsody of words.   (III,iv,40–48)

This "rhapsody of words," this crisis in evidence, occurs when the bond of signification between word and thing, sign and reality, signifier and signified (I am using the words loosely) is no longer *experienced* as natural but as arbitrary. As Pierre Bourdieu (1977:164) notes, every established order—and I would include here that of signification—tends to produce "the naturalization of its own arbitrariness."[6] Legitimacy rests, at least in traditional societies, on the refusal to recognize its own artifice or on assuming the naturalness or inevitability of that artifice.

Claudius' murder of the King does not challenge the fundamental order of society; it does not permit the development of a special discourse that would give systematic expression to the extraordinary experiences produced by such a challenge. Indeed, it precludes the development of such a language. Hamlet is left with only a sense of the world's artifice. He "seems master of all styles but has no distinctive utterance of his own" (Foakes 1956). He cannot become the charismatic leader with a special language who often arises in traditional societies in structural crisis (Weber 1968). He cannot even obey his dead father's command. He is left seeking an adequate language, a meta-pragmatic language really, a vantage point for understanding, evidence to justify action. But insofar as the regicide has undermined the "naturalization" of meaning, he, like the rest of the court (though they may not know it) is left with a "rhapsody of words" composed by the whims, the perverted desires, the power plays of the speaking subject.[7]

Without entering into the intricate ways in which language relates to—and changes in accordance with—social and cultural institutions, I should like to suggest that how language is understood ideologically, how it is said to be experienced conventionally, does "depend" upon what Hegel would call its world-condition. In other words, language—understood broadly enough to include its own particular (ideological) self-understanding—both facilitates and responds to the moral state of society. During periods of crisis, radical disturbances in the social and cultural order, revolutions, rapid technological change, and unanticipated invasions by conquerors with different social and cultural orientations, result in a breakdown in the way in which language itself is understood—in its accepted meta-pragmatic regimentation. This breakdown can also occur, as in the court at Elsinore, when there has been a heinous violation of what is considered to be the moral, political, or ritual order by those in or aspiring to power, like Claudius, so that society becomes "an unweeded garden." Through maimed rites words can become wild and whirling. In Saussurian terms, the bond of signification is no longer experienced as "natural," as socially fated, and even the appreciation of its arbitrariness, its conventionality (when such appreciation occurs), is no longer sanctioned by the community of speakers. The cards, to use Saussure's expression, are no longer stacked; the speaker is no longer certain that he and his interlocutor are restrained by his linguistic heritage. The sign is sundered; the signifier is cleft from the signified; the word from the thing.

Denmark, we are told repeatedly, is in a rank, sickly, and rotten state (Spurgeon 1935). Francisco, the sentinel, announces that he is "sick at heart" at the very beginning of the play, and his relief Barnardo does not even bother to ask why. Elsinore is in "post-haste" preparation for war. As we noted, Horatio likens the appearance of the ghost to those portents that appeared in Rome "a little ere the mightiest Julius fell" (I,i,117).

Hamlet refers to the drunkenness of the Dane (I,iv,17–22) and to the King's nightly "rouse" (I,iv,8–11). The country is at once in a state of mourning for the dead King and of celebration for the new King's marriage. The ambivalence that Claudius expresses through relentless oxymorons in his first speech must not be seen only in terms of his ambiguous position, his callousness, his guilt but also as a calculated articulation of what the Danes, those at the court at least, must be experiencing.[8] He has taken to wife Gertrude

> as 'twere with a defeated joy,
> With an auspicious and a dropping eye,
> With mirth in funeral and with dirge in marriage
> In equal scale weighing delight and dole.   (I,ii,10–13)

Even the Norwegian Fortinbras, so Claudius tells us in this same speech, thinks Denmark "to be disjoint and out of frame" (I,ii,20).

Hamlet's view of Denmark is of course intensely, indulgently subjective. Even before he meets the ghost, responding to his father's death and his mother's all too quick and incestuous marriage, he finds the "uses of this world" "weary, flat, and unprofitable."[9] And after learning of his father's murder, he describes, not without rhetorical ploy and melancholy play, but with insight all the same, his debilitating worldweariness to Rosencrantz and Guildenstern.

> I have of late, but wherefore I know not, lost all my mirth, forgone all custom of exercises; and indeed it goes so heavily with my disposition that this goodly frame the earth seems to me a sterile promontory, this most excellent canopy the air, look you, this brave o'erchanging firmament, this majestical roof fretted with golden fire, why, it appeareth nothing to me but a foul and pestilent congregation of vapours. (II,ii,295–302)

Paradoxically, Hamlet uses inordinately strong imagery—"a foul and pestilent congregation of vapours"—to describe his flat and weary experience of the world. It is as if he were trying to intensify his experience through a figurative language, which no longer has the power to do.

The ghost also uses exceptionally strong language in his description of his present condition ("I could a tale unfold whose lightest word / Would harrow up thy soul, freeze thy young blood" [I,v,15–20]), of Claudius ("Ay, that incestuous, that adulterate beast" [I,v,42]) and of the effect of the poison ("And a most instant tetter bark'd about, / Most lazar-like, with vile and loathsome crust" [I,v,71–73]). Is Hamlet imitating his father? Is he attempting to obtain his father's strength through the imitation of his father's strong, figurative language?

The ghost stresses ritual violation. He has been deprived not only of life, crown, and queen but also of the Eucharist ("unhousel'd"), of the time to prepare for death ("disappointment"), and of extreme unction ("unanel'd).

> Thus was I, sleeping, by a brother's hand
> Of life, of crown, of queen at once dispatch'd,
> Cut off even in the blossoms of my sin,
> Unhousel'd, disappointed, unanel'd,
> No reck'ning made, but sent to my account
> With all my imperfections on my head.   (I,v,74–79)

He puts Hamlet under a (ritual) obligation, expressed in highly erotic language, to revenge his murder ("Let not the royal bed of Denmark be a couch for luxury and damned incest." [Iv,82–83]), but he also places Hamlet under a double-binding interdiction that prevents him from responding fully to the ghost's eroticized depiction, his condemnation, of his "most seeming-virtuous queen" (I,v,46).[10] Hamlet must neither offend nor condemn his mother (I,v,84–86).

Hamlet's reaction to the ghost's revelation—"to put an antic disposition on" (I,v,180)—has puzzled commentators and given rise to all sorts of psychological explanations which, however perceptive, slight the stunning blow the ghost's pronouncement gives to Hamlet's (semantical) world. Hamlet's decision to bear himself in a grotesque manner is framed by parallel episodes (I,v,148–169; I,v,176–189) that suggest a loss of faith in language. Hamlet insists in a "strange and odd" manner that his friends, Marcellus and Horatio, swear first on his sword, indeed twice, that they will tell neither what they saw that night nor what they know of Hamlet—of the man behind the antic disposition.[11] ("Antic," Harold Jenkins [1982] tells us, was used for an actor with a false head or grotesque mask.) By affecting madness, Hamlet will conceal his "true" self. He will participate in the *seeming* world of the court; he will parody that world, calling attention to its sham; and he will try to see through all of the double talk.

Court speech, that speech of heightened innuendo and subtle message where words mean precisely what they do not mean, requires, like metaphor, a literalist view of language, in law at least, that protects the courtier, when challenged, from the import of his words. The courtier's problem is to let it be known that behind his words literally taken is another meaning, without putting himself in a position in which he can be held responsible for that hidden meaning. He has, as Polonius says, "by indirections [to] find directions out." His interlocutor faces another problem. He has to determine what that meaning is without becoming collusive. There are dangers to such indirections. Francis Bacon (1937:19), certainly a man in a position to appreciate the dangers of indirection, lists three of them. Simulation and dissimulation can reveal fear in those who practice them; they puzzle and perplex those who might otherwise cooperate and "make a man walk almost alone to his own ends"; and they deprive one of trust and belief.

The courtier, even a fop like Osric, plays a perilous game. His words are never mere "noise" even at Elsinore, as Calderwood (1983:73–79) suggests, because the uncertainty they produce precludes their ever being taken as such. Even when their semantic meaning, at whatever figurative level, is no longer certain, there can still be the illusion that the context they call can be read; that they have, in other words, a determinable pragmatic significance. When Polonius listens to Hamlet's "mad" banter, he ignores its semantic meaning and attends to what it reveals, pragmatically, of Hamlet's state of mind.[12] Hamlet's calling him a "fishmonger" or punning on "conception" is an index of Hamlet's love for Ophelia. Were Polonius to have considered seriously the meaning of Hamlet's words he would have been insulted and worried about his daughter's purity.

Life at court is a serious, melancholy game, La Bruyère (1965:217, par. 63) remarks a little less than a century after Shakespeare wrote *Hamlet*. "There is a country where pleasures are visible but false and sorrows hidden but real. Who would believe that the enthusiasm for plays, the shouts and applause for Molière's and d'Arlequin's theater, meals, the hunt, ballet, and carrousels could cover up such anxiety, care, and varied interests, such fears and hopes, such lively passions and serious affairs?" Like the hand of a clock whose mechanism remains hidden, the courtier risks returning to the position from which he started (La Bruyère 1963: 217–218, par. 65). The very faults which lead to his success may lead to his downfall (La Bruyère 1963: 209, par. 34). There is, if not the actual understanding of heightened innuendo and subtle message, then the dread knowledge of its existence, the certainty of dissimilitude, and the fear of high-stake intrigue that is hidden behind the word literally taken.

It is in this world that the fool and the madman become prominent. According to Empson (1964), they formed a "semantic complex" in Elizabethan England. The fool and the madman have considerable power and they are protected by their roles, for their words can always be dismissed as those of a fool or a madman (Gorfain 1986:222–223). Through their clowning and word play they can discover and expose truths that lay hidden behind words falsely given. They can break those failures of communication, those glitches, entrapments really, that occur when all the partners in a conversation are forced, for whatever reasons, to adhere to a literalist "understanding" even though they know the words have another more important meaning. And of course they know that all their conversational partners know that they know it.

Like the avenger whose revenge produces more avengers, the fool and the madman produce what Empson (1964:108) calls a mutuality and I would call a complicity: "I call you a fool of one sort speaking as myself a fool of another sort." This mutuality, this complicity, as theorists of revenge and blood feuding have shown, is asymmetrical and fraught with tension. He who triggers off a round in the chain of revenge or fool-playing is at once powerful and vulnerable. In attacking he lays himself open to attack. Empson (1964:109) suggests that the "apparently far-fetched connection" between the fool and the revenger leads to the weight put onto Hamlet's fooling, itself "an obscure threat of revenge," but unfortunately Empson does not elaborate. Certainly Hamlet puts himself in danger through his antics; his stakes are higher than those of the fool, and he does not have the protection that the fool qua fool or the madman qua madman has. He can only be fool-like or mad-like. The King cannot play the fool; he has to anticipate Hamlet's revenge—to do away with him.

But at Elsinore there can be no surety of meaning at either a literalist or a court-figurative level,[13] and the fool, or those who play at being a fool, are no longer able to determine and expose meaning as they would normally have done. They risk becoming madmen. Hamlet is caught between the fool and the madman, and his words to Horatio and Marcellus about his assumption of an antic disposition have perhaps to be read less actively, in terms of intention, than passively, in terms of prediction.

> How strange or odd some'er I bear myself—
> As I perchance hereafter shall think meet
> To put an antic disposition on—   (I,v,178–180)

Note the peculiarly passive tonality of "I shall think meet," modified as it is by "perchance."

Hamlet can only proceed through indirection, antic disposition, punning, and dramatic evocation. He has to play, as best he can, with the context—with language itself—in the hope that the "real" context will manifest itself forcefully, thereby restoring the possibility of meaning and interpretation.[14] Hamlet plays with words before meeting the ghost, and I certainly do not want to suggest that his word games result only from the moral and ritual violations of his society. What concerns me is how Hamlet's word games reflect the semantic condition of his society and how, and to what effect, he uses this condition and is used by it.

Hamlet's first three utterances (I,ii,65,67,73) are plays on words. To Claudius's address, "my cousin Hamlet, and my son," he retorts, "A little more than kin, and less than kind"; to Claudius's question, "How is it that clouds still hang on you," he answers, "Not so, my lord, I am too much in the son"; and to the Queen's banal "Thou know'st 'tis common: all that lives must die," he comments, with rhetorical resignation, one supposes, "Ay, madam, it is common." In all three instances, his word play serves both to call attention (almost cruelly in the case of his mother) to the conventionality—hypocrisy and banality—of his interlocutor's words and to disturb their seemingly complacent acceptance of such conventions.[15] He reminds them (and himself) of what their words conceal and calls their attention implicitly to the insufficiency of their conventional, or more accurately, their conventionalized and empty formulations.

Hamlet's antic disposition has an immediate and dramatic effect upon the court. Wittingly or unwittingly—we never know—Hamlet comes at once to disquiet the court and to symbolize the (pre-existing) disquiet of the court.[16] He is more than the fool, however, more than the madman, for through his antics he confuses the situation while attempting, pathetically at times, to take (verbal) command of it. He is, in this respect, like a shaman. One never knows for sure if the shaman is mad or acting in a maddening fashion at being mad-like. Through word play, extravagant gesture, and histrionic behavior, through sudden changes in mood and attitude, always unpredictable but never completely so, the shaman—like Hamlet—produces in those around him a cognitive vertigo and then takes command of the situation (Crapanzano 1973b). He becomes a sort of stage manager—the relevance of the metaphor should be apparent—and, unlike the fool or madman, he attempts to rearrange matters in his own fashion: to discover truths that are normally hidden and to act upon or in accordance with them.

But Hamlet poses a problem: he has neither the authority nor the power of the shaman. He cannot call a ceremonial context. He can act the fool but he is no fool. He can act the madman but can offer no surety of his madness. He can only play, in other words, with the framing of his paradoxical antics (Gorfain 1986). He becomes in his own right a subject of detection—a mystery. For Polonius and Ophelia, for Gertrude, for Rosencrantz and Guildenstern, the problem is why he acts as he does. For Claudius, of course, the problem is what, if anything, he

knows. Hamlet's antics turn everyone in court into a detective
(Mahood 1957:111), but insofar as he calls attention to the untrustworthiness of words, of gestures, of costumes and demeanor, of the seemingness of everything in Denmark's violated
court, he precludes, symbolically at least, the possibility of any
firm evidence.[17] What is extraordinary about *Hamlet* is that until
the very end, and even then, we hardly know what anyone really
knows or is willing to acknowledge.

We first learn of Hamlet's antics, his "lunacy," as Polonius
calls it, through an indirect representation. The description is
Ophelia's, and it is addressed to her father who has just told
Reynaldo how to use the "bait of falsehood" to learn about
Laertes' conduct in Paris. Ophelia is frightened by Hamlet's
"doublet all unbrac'd," his "stockings foul'd," his "knees knocking each other," his frenzied gaze, and his "sigh so piteous and
profound" (II,i,77–100). Polonius immediately decides Hamlet
is madly in love with his daughter. Ophelia fears it too. Repelled
by Ophelia, according to Polonius, Hamlet

> Fell into sadness, then into a fast
> Thence to a watch, thence into a weakness
> Thence to a lightness, and, by this declension,
> Into the madness wherein now he raves
> And all we mourn for.   (II,ii,147–151)

All the talk of Hamlet's madness builds up to Hamlet's actual
appearance. He plays the madman, but within his discourse
there is, as even Polonius recognizes, "method." (Charney
[1969] stresses Polonius' perception of the stylistic advantage
of madness: "How pregnant sometimes his replies are—a happiness that often madness hits on, which reason and sanity could
not so prosperously be delivered of" [II,2,209–211].) Polonius
makes a number of asides. They frame his exchanges with Hamlet, turning them into a sort of inner spectacle—to be viewed
not in their own terms but as a symptom of Hamlet's condition.
Hamlet plays on notions of honesty and slander; he puns; he
becomes a concrete hyper-literalist. When Polonius asks him
what he is reading—he enters reading a book—he answers:
"Words, words, words" (II,ii,92). He calls a "realistic" picture
of old men (of Polonius no doubt) in what he claims to have

been reading slanderous. His comment on the passage is contradictory: "all which, sir, though I most powerfully and potently believe, yet I hold it not honesty to have it thus set down" (II,ii,200–202). His double-, his treble-binding words put into question the notion of honesty—in court speech, in Polonius' spying discourse. Insofar as Polonius takes Hamlet's words as symptoms of his love madness, they do not unsettle him. As Polonius leaves, perhaps within his earshot, perhaps as an aside, Hamlet observes—his words are to the mark: "These tedious old fools" (II,ii,219).

Hamlet's words anticipate metalinguistically the scene that follows.[18] Rosencrantz and Guildenstern have been instructed by the King and Queen to find out what is troubling Hamlet (II,ii,17–18). Hamlet is now sober; he jests with the courtiers, in their manner, at times sardonically. He outwits them, ridicules them, tests the limits of their patience. He pushes them, parodied figures of ambition, to admit that ambition is "so airy and light a quality that it is but a shadow's" (II,ii,261–262), and then, with a sharp thrust, he concludes: "Then are our beggars bodies, and our monarchs and outstretched heroes the beggars' shadow." He forces them to assume an uncomfortable frankness, albeit calculated on their part: they admit they were sent by the King and Queen. With terrible cynicism he gives them their story—a description of his melancholy mood: "so shall my anticipation prevent your discovery, and your secrecy to the King and Queen moult no feather" (II,ii,293–295). Rosencrantz denies that he could ever have had such thoughts of Hamlet, and when Hamlet calls him up by asking why he laughed when Hamlet said "man delights not me," Rosencrantz retorts with a heavy-handed flourish: "To think, my lord if you delight not in man, what Lenten entertainment the players shall receive from you" (II,ii,314–315).

So are the players announced—illusionists who will through their illusions give reality to the ghost's words. Hamlet asks them to play *The Murder of Gonzago* and to "study a speech of some dozen or sixteen lines" that he will have inserted in the play. They will "play something like the murder of [his] father before [his] uncle," we learn in the soliloquy, "O what a rogue and peasant slave am I." Through the play Hamlet will "catch the conscience of the King" (II,ii,600–601).[19] He has heard that a play can so strike the guilty that they have to proclaim their malefactions (II,ii,585–588).

Impressed by the way in which a "fiction," a "dream of passion," a "conceit" can move an actor, Hamlet decries melodramatically his own "pigeon-liver'd" cowardice, his "lack of gall," his inability to respond to a real cause. The actor can respond to Hecuba with tears but Hamlet is incapable of responding to his father's murder, to the ghost's command. Like a whore he must unpack his "heart with words and fall a cursing like a very drab, a scullion (II,ii,578–583). Words substitute for action for Hamlet, and they have as little content as the flatterings of a whore. Hamlet identifies hypocrisy, hollow conventions, empty words, mere appearance, and seeming behavior with "painted" women, with whores, drabs, and scullions, with his mother, and the innocent Ophelia.[20]

In the meeting with Ophelia Polonius and the King have arranged to determine the cause of his madness, Hamlet rants at Ophelia as though she were Gertrude. (His fury is reminiscent of the ghost's [I,v,47–57].)

> I have heard of your paintings well enough. God hath given you one face and you make yourselves another. You jig and amble, and you lisp, you nick-name God's creatures, and make your wantonness your ignorance.   (III,i,144–148)

Has Hamlet caught sight of Polonius and the King watching? Ophelia is of course acting most uninnocently. She is caught in a bind. On the one hand, she has been told by her father to be "scanter" of her "maiden presence" and to set her "entreatments at a higher rate than to command to parley" (I,iii,120ff) and, on the other, she has been ordered to act as before, when she believed in Hamlet's love. She knows what Hamlet may not know, or at least does not at first know, that they are being watched, that their encounter is a spectacle, and that what transpires is to be read not in its own terms but as clues to the state of Hamlet's soul and its cause. Under such circumstances her words lose their perfume just as the remembrances Hamlet had given her lose their perfume. Ophelia's closing soliloquy, "O, what a noble mind is here o'erthrown!"

(III,i,152–163), sounds as stiff and mannered as it was bound to, removed from what she has just experienced. She has been subsumed by her father's and the King's intentions. Their complete insensitivity to her feelings as they discuss what they have witnessed has to be understood in terms not just of their callousness, their indifference to women, but also of the "irreality" their peculiar observational stance confers on the scene—an irreality to which Ophelia also responds.

The King smells danger and will ship Hamlet off to England; Polonius wants to try one last time to unfathom the prince. Let the Queen "be round"—plainspoken—with him while Polonius, always having faith in spying, places himself "in the ear of all their conference" (III,i,186–187). But before Polonius can unfathom the prince, Hamlet catches the conscience of the King. The play scene is prefaced by a meta-linguistic commentary. Hamlet tells the players to do on stage what he has not been able to do in real life: "Suit the action to the word, the word to the action, with this special observance, that you o'erstep not the modesty of nature" (III,ii,17–19).[21] He articulates a theory of drama, from Donatus, common in the Renaissance. The purpose of playing is "to hold as 'twere the mirror up to nature." There has to be, in other words, a mirroring verisimilitude in any successful representation. To transgress the modesty of nature may cause the "unskilful" to laugh but it will make "the judicious grieve." Hamlet could be talking about the language at court.[22]

Only when Hamlet asks Horatio to observe carefully the King's reaction to the play do we learn that he has told his friend about his father's murder. He speaks to the point, but as soon as the court enters he puts on his antic disposition again. He puns; he repudiates his words; he jokes with Polonius, who was "killed" in the role of Julius Caesar, and with Ophelia, obscenely. He falls back into melancholy. He is, in effect, setting up his audience by confusing them. It is the shaman's old trick—a prelude to his own commentary after the dumb show and during the play itself. It is, as such, a representation of the representation—the play within the play—that represents the ghost's verbal representation of how he was killed. (All of these representations occur within a representation, Shakespeare's tragedy, that is only tenuously grounded in historical—mythical—reality.) The layering of these representations parallels the layering of signification in court speech, but once the King has confirmed the "truth" of the representation, the multiple representations all affirm rather than mark that truth. The dumb show, the play, the ghost's tale all refer to the same "true" reality: Claudius' fratricidal regicide. They turn court life itself into a representation that masks its reality. Hamlet's unmasking produces the same effect that the unmasking of an actor on stage would produce. More than a half century before Shakespeare wrote *Hamlet,* Erasmus (1958:44) wrote, "If anyone seeing a player acting his part on stage should go about to strip him of his disguise and show him to the people in his true native form, would he not, think you, not only spoil the whole design of the play, but deserve himself to be pelted off with stones as a phantastical fool and one out of his wits." Though the King treats Hamlet as a "phantastical fool" he has also to "pelt him off with stones."

The acts that trigger the King's response are the poisoning in the ear and Hamlet's announcement that Gonzago, the poisoner, will soon marry the Queen.[23] It is Hamlet's orchestration, his setting up the scene and his commentaries, that force the King to react. Unassisted representation, as suggested by the King's coolly watching the dumb show before Hamlet makes any comment, does not have the same effect as assisted representation. Rhetorical manipulation and contextualization aid in the discovery of truth, but they preclude the confidence that comes from unasssisted representation. Hence there is still room for Hamlet's doubt, despite all the certainty he expresses as soon as the King leaves. "O good Horatio, I'll take the ghost's word for a thousand pound" (III,ii,280–281). There is still time for delay despite the passion for action ("Now could I drink hot blood" [III,ii,381–383]) he expresses melodramatically in the soliloquy with which the play scene ends.

For Claudius the poisoning is no "jest." He rises. He asks for light. He leaves with the court. He is "marvellous distempered." And later (III,iii,35–98) he is tortured less by guilt than by his inability to pray.

My words fly up, my thoughts remain below.
Words without thoughts never to heaven go.

(III,iii,97–98)

The Queen's spirit is also afflicted. Hamlet's behavior "hath struck her into amazement and admiration." She desires to speak to him. (She does not know, at least she has not yet been told by Hamlet, that Claudius is the murderer.) Hiding behind the arras in the Queen's closet, Polonius will make his last attempt to unfathom Hamlet.

Polonius's strategy fails abysmally. (It would probably have had little effect, for the King has already decided upon his nephew's death [III,iii,1ff].) Hamlet is frenzied. He murders Polonius. He tells the Queen that Claudius has murdered. The import of his words escape the Queen despite her claim that they enter her ears like daggers, that they turn her eyes into her very soul "and there [she] sees such black and grained spots as will not leave their tinct" (III,iv,95; 88–91). She promises not to tell the King what Hamlet has told her. We never know whether she keeps Hamlet's secret because she respects the vow she has made or because she has forgotten his confidence.

Hamlet plays on the Queen's use of "father" for his uncle. "Mother, you have my father much offended" (III,iv,9). She accuses him of an "idle tongue," and he her of a "wicked tongue." She calls him up: "Have you forgot me?" He answers:

No, by the rood, not so.
You are the Queen, your husband's brother's wife,
And, would it not so, you are my mother."

(III,iv,13–15)

Hamlet forces her to look into a mirror where she will see her innermost self—what lies behind her "painted" face, her courtly manners and her vacuous words. (Innerness is the "space" of truth for Hamlet.) Hamlet is brutal. The Queen calls for help. Polonius behind the arras reveals his presence. Hamlet cries out, "How now? A rat! Dead for a ducat, dead" (III,iv,22) and thrusts his rapier through the arras without actually knowing who is behind it. He asks if it is the King. He lifts the arras and discovers Polonius, dead. His mother says, "O what a rash and bloody deed is this!" He echoes her "bloody deed."

> A bloody deed. Almost as bad, good mother,
> As kill a king and marry with his brother. (III,iv,27–28)

Stunned, the Queen questions what he said, "As kill a king?" and Hamlet answers, "Ay, lady, it was my word." Note the shift to the word. He addresses the corpse ("Thou wretched, rash, intruding fool, farewell. / I took thee for thy better" [III,iv,31ff]) and he turns in fury on his mother. He will wring her heart.

The sequence is important. Like the play within the play, Hamlet's murder of Polonius reflects the disrupted signification at the Danish court. When Hamlet thrusts his rapier through the arras, he cries out "a rat," thinks he is killing the King, in fact kills Polonius.[24] The layering of signification parallels the layering of court speech where signs have two referents, a literal and a figurative one. Under normal circumstances Hamlet's cry of "rat" would have signified both a rat and the King, but at Elsinore, though signifying a rat and the King, its *real* referent turns out to be Polonius. The arras—that curtain that permits, perversely, the revelation of truth for whoever is behind it— bars the identity of that person from those in front of it.

The arras is, if I may indulge in a Lacanian figure, the bar that separates the signifier from its true (its unconscious!) signified. The Lacanian would probably argue that Polonius, like the King and the rat, is in fact a signifier of the father and that so terrible is the symbolic slaying of the father for Hamlet that he has immediately to deflect the real slaying of the father from even a symbol of the father—the King—onto his mother. "Almost as bad, good mother, as kill a king and marry with his brother." The syntax of the utterance is peculiar, for, though it modifies "bloody deed," it has no subject—no perpetrator. "Good mother" is a vocative and only by allusion, if at all, the subject. I should add that when Hamlet goes on to describe the effect of the deed (III,iv,40–51), he does not specify what it was again until later in the scene when he declares Claudius his father's murderer. It is only then that the ghost appears—can appear.

As soon as the King learns of Polonius' murder, he realizes he was meant to be the victim (IV,i,13). He has to dispatch

Hamlet as soon as possible, but first he must find Polonius' body, which Hamlet has hidden. He sends Rosencrantz and Guildenstern to search for it. Hamlet refuses to tell them where it is. He calls them a sponge which soaks up the King's favors and then can be wrung dry when the King needs what they have gleaned (IV,ii,11–20). (La Bruyère would have understood the metaphor, though he would have found it crude.) Hamlet plays cruelly with the King, obscenely with death. He tells the King that Polonius is at supper and then describes the court as a "convocation of politic worms" that are eating him. King and beggars are "variable service" for the maggots. (IV,iii,36–37)

Despite its black humor, which prefigures the graveyard scene, and despite the opportunity the scene gives Hamlet to torture the King, it seems unmotivated unless we consider the symbolic significance of Polonius' corpse. Polonius was the real, though not the intended, referent of Hamlet's cry, "a rat." By hiding the corpse Hamlet hides the real referent and leaves exposed the intended referent—the King. By seeking the corpse, the King seeks the real referent and thereby the justification for his dispatching Hamlet. He eliminates the intended referent, himself, by eliminating the person who makes the reference. But at another level, by hiding the real referent, Hamlet preserves precisely the confusion of court speech which he has come to use for his own purposes—for discovery and delay. By seeking the real referent the King seeks to end the distorted communication of the court. He will have *the* real referent. When Hamlet finally gives in and provides the location of the corpse, he does so obliquely by referring to odor: "But if indeed you find him not within this month, you shall nose him as you go up the stairs to the lobby" (IV,iii,35–37). Odor is in Peircean terms indexical. Unlike the symbol, it bears a nonarbitrary metonymous relationship to its referent. In his search for Polonius' corpse the King attempts what Hamlet accomplished through the play within the play. Having got the "real referent," the King returns to his dissimulating court speech. He tells Hamlet for his safety's sake to leave for England "with fiery quickness" (IV,iii,40ff). When Hamlet says "good," the King says ominously, "So it is, if thou knew'st our purposes." Hamlet, who may now understand the King's masked language, remarks, "I see a cherub that sees them" (IV,iii,50–51). Was Hamlet meant to hear the King's words? Was the King meant to hear Hamlet's? I would take them as overheard asides, each a verbal display to be understood not referentially but pragmatically as a symptom rather than a statement of knowledge. Despite the play within the play, despite the search for Polonius, the two undeclared enemies are still left to a pragmatic reading of each others utterances. Only when the King is left alone is he able to speak straightforwardly.

The pace of the play increases. "One woe doth tread upon another's heel, so fast they follow," the Queen observes (IV,vii,162–163). The action is no longer only at Elsinore. Hamlet leaves for England. He passes Fortinbras' army on its way to Poland to claim a bit of worthless land. He is given, thereby, another occasion to deride himself. He who has a real cause delays while Fortinbras is prepared to risk the death of twenty thousand men for "a fantasy and trick of fame"—a symbol (IV,iv,32–66). The ship that is to carry Hamlet to England, to his death, is attacked by pirates, we learn in a letter he sends to Horatio (IV,vii). He asks his friend to join him with as much speed as he would flee from death. "I have words to speak in thine ear will make thee dumb," he writes (IV,vii,22–23). His words, like poison, promise to be most effective. They remind us of his father's death, the dumb show, the play within the play, the King's guilty departure from it. In a second letter, with no explanation, he informs the King of his "sudden and more strange return" (IV,vii,42–46).[25] The King is stunned. With Laertes he devises the plot—the duel, the unbated and venomed rapier, the poisoned drink—that will be Hamlet's undoing and the undoing, and the redoing, of the court. Later Hamlet will tell Horatio how he "finger'd" the commission the King had given Rosencrantz and Guildenstern, discovered that it commanded England to behead him, forged a second letter asking England to put the bearers of the letter to death, and sealed it with his father's signet, which he happened to have in his pocket.

Hamlet's first planned act occurs on shipboard, away from the semantic chaos of Elsinore. Here, it is the word—the written word—that both triggers and facilitates the act. Hamlet does not doubt the contents of the King's letter, and he does not hesitate to compose, forge, and seal a second letter—with his father's signet, the royal authority he himself should have had. He proceeds by "indiscretions" and has even to overcome a prejudice against writing fairly (V,ii,33–36). He proudly recounts the contents of *his* letter to Horatio—not his exact words, however. Ironically, it is another letter, the letter he sends to the King, that will be his undoing.

These events, for the most part reported, punctuate those at Elsinore. Ophelia goes mad. She represents the innocence of understanding and is a victim of that innocence. She wishes to see the Queen, but the Queen will not see her. Her messenger says she is importunate. He describes her speech, preparing us for the scene that follows.

> She speaks much of her father, says she hears
> There's tricks i' th' world, and hems, and beats her
>   heart,
> Spurns enviously at straws, speaks things in doubt
> That carry but half sense. Her speech is nothing,
> Yet the unshaped use of it doth move
> The hearers to collection. They aim at it,
> And botch the words up fit to their own thoughts,
> Which, as her winks and nods and gestures yield them,
> Indeed would make one think there might be thought,
> Though nothing sure, yet much unhappily. (IV,v,4–13)

Ophelia (at least as the messenger describes her) sees—responds to—a reality, a truth, that is masked by convention: "There's tricks i' th' world." Her hemming, her beating her heart, her taking offense at trifles, her nonsense, her "unshaped use" of speech force her interlocutors to try to make sense of her words. They conjecture and project their own meanings of them ("botch the words up fit to their own thoughts"). Unlike the fool, unlike the shaman, unlike Hamlet, who is always in some control of his words, Ophelia has lost all control. Her words, her winks, nods, and gestures, become an unwitting, an exaggerated parody of the very words responsible for her condition.

The Queen finally agrees to see Ophelia. Opelia enters asking where "the beauteous Majesty of Denmark is." Does she refer to the former King, Hamlet's father, or to the present King? Does she refer to the kingdom itself? She is distracted. She sings piteously. How can you know your true love from another? she asks in song, and answers nonsensically, "by his cockle hat and staff and his sandal shoon" (IV,v,25–26), calling attention, thereby, to the problem of knowing. She sings of the dead— literally, one supposes, of her father (and by extension, of Hamlet's father) and figuratively, perhaps, of Hamlet himself. She sings of the perfunctory, faithless love of men in words that belie her innocence or mark her innocence (if she does not understand them). She refers obliquely to the violation of burial rites for her father—a violation that recalls that of the late King's burial and anticipates that of her own. "But I cannot choose but weep to think they would lay him i' th' cold ground," she says (IV,v,69–70). (Even the King admits the violation: "and we have done but greenly in hugger-mugger to inter him" [IV,v,83–84].) We learn later from Laertes that Polonius was buried obscurely with

> No trophy, sword, nor hatchment o'er his bones,
> No noble rite, nor formal ostentation.   (IV,vi,211–212)

The custom was to bury a knight with his helmet, sword, and coat-of-arms ("hatchment").

The King is moved by Ophelia. He understands her words only in terms of the death of her father, and not of Hamlet's betrayal or departure. He describes her as "divided from herself and her fair judgment" and, as such, seeing everyone as "pictures," that is, forms without souls, caricatures we would say, or as "beasts" (IV,v,84–85). Is he—one wonders—describing his own style of perception? He intertwines his pity for her with concerns about his own position. The people are confused about Polonius' death. Rumor is rife. Laertes has returned and, infected by "pestilent speeches of his father's death," will accuse even the King of it (IV,v,87–96).

The King's words are stunningly prophetic. A noise is heard. A messenger announces Laertes' arrival. Laertes is headstrong and bent on a coup. We realize for the first time how riotous the state of Denmark is. Tradition and custom have lost their hold on the word—on the maxims which uphold conduct (IV,v,104–105). The rabble act "as the world were now but to begin" (IV,v,103). They want Laertes to be king. Laertes forces his way in and demands revenge for the death of his father.

> To hell, allegiance! Vows to the blackest devil!
> Conscience and grace, to the profoundest pit.
> I dare damnation.   (IV,v,131–133)

Critics have compared Laertes to Hamlet. They see him as Hamlet's alter ego. Even Hamlet contrasts himself to Laertes. The Queen tries to hold Laertes back. With masterful calm and faith in his position ("There's such divinity doth hedge a king" [IV,v,123]), Claudius manages to pacify—virtually to infantilize—Laertes. ("Why now you speak like a good child and a true gentleman" [IV,v,148–149]). Ophelia enters, distracted, singing as before of death, never addressing her brother, describing the virtues of flowers and herbs—as though she were trying to rejoin, in this most "natural" idiom, symbol and referent, sign and reality.[26] The King pledges his kingdom, his life, to Laertes if Laertes finds him guilty of Polonius' death.

As disorder increases, the meaning of the word—of vows and promises—can only be guaranteed, if at all, by violent exaggeration, by violence itself. Hamlet made Horatio and Marcellus swear their oath of secrecy on his sword. His words to Horatio will make his friend dumb. The Queen refers to Hamlet's words as "daggers." The messenger who announces Laertes' rebellious arrival speaks of his being infected by "pestilent" speeches.

Ophelia dies in "fantastic garlands" of flowers—not the same (except for the daisy, a symbol of forsaken love) she described in front of the King and her brother, as she tried, I believe, to reunite symbolically the "natural" bond between word and thing, but flowers all the same. The Queen's description of her death is reminiscent of a chorus in ancient tragedy. Detached from her character, it is, as Evans (1952:95–96) remarked, "a necessary epitaph" that defines the emotional place of Ophelia in the tragedy. We are presented with a picture, independent, so to speak, complete in and of itself. Rimbaud (1954) stresses its timelessness. (*Voici plus de mille ans que la triste Ophélie /*

*Passe, fantôme blanc, sur le long fleuve noir; / Voici plus de
mille ans que sa douce folie / Murmure sa romance à la brise du
soir).* We do not know the Queen's vantage point. We—she—are
carried away by the narcissistic ritualism of Ophelia's act, its·
autonomy, its privacy. Despite its florid, pre-Raphaelite orna-
mentation, John Everett Millais has caught something of this
quality in his painting of Ophelia's death. It does not matter
whether her death was accidental, as the Queen's description
suggests, or suicidal, as her burial indicates.

> There is a willow grows askant the brook
> That shows his hoary leaves in the glassy stream.
> Therewith fantastic garlands did she make
> Of crow-flowers, nettles, daisies, and long purples,
> That liberal shepherds give a grosser name,
> But our cold maids do dead men's fingers call them.
> There on the pendent boughs her crownet weeds
> Clamb'ring to hang, an envious sliver broke,
> When down her weedy trophies and herself
> Fell in the weeping brook. Her clothes spread wide,
> And mermaid-like awhile they bore her up,
> When time she chanted snatches of old lauds,
> As one incapable of her own distress,
> Or like a creature native and indued
> Unto that element. But long it could not be
> Till that her garments, heavy with drink,
> Pull'd the poor wretch from her melodious lay
> To muddy death.   (IV,vii,165–182)

The Queen's description is centripetal. Images which, like
weeds and garlands woven of willow branches, suggest min-
gling and confusion, do themselves intermingle and confuse.
Symbol and reality are blended. Jenkins (1982:545) notes the
realism of the description: the willow leaning across the stream.
The willow is an emblem of sadness. It covers the place of
Ophelia's death. Its "hoary leaves" are reflected in the "glassy
stream," later called a "weeping brook." (Mirroring suggests a
coalescence of symbol and reality.) Flowers, rich in symbolism
and name, are woven into its boughs, one of which, described
as "envious" (that is, malicious) breaks, causing Ophelia and
her "weedy trophies" to fall into the stream. (Trophy, together

with "crownet," also suggest virginity and the memorial placed on a grave, reminding us of her father's obscure burial and prefiguring her own "maimed" funeral rites.) Buoyed by "clothes spread wide," oblivious to her surroundings and the danger of drowning, as though she were "indued" for living in water, she sings songs of praise. The involution is complete. Her clothes, heavy with water, pull her to "muddy death." The alliteration of "melodious" and "muddy"—as well as a possible play on "lay" meaning song and also "to bury"—suggest a merging of song and death, of discrimination, as in melody, and the absence of discrimination, as in mud.[27] (Derrida would refer to "differance" and its absence.) Without discrimination, without *differance*, with the merging of signifier and signified, sign and reality, there can only be an absence of consciousness—death.

Death may well be the only way to restore the "natural" bond of signification. In the following scene, a gravedigger and a clown mock the Christian burial that will be given Ophelia despite her suicide. They blaspheme death's hallow rites. Hamlet meditates on the transitoriness of life, the pretentiousness of the living, and the ultimate meaninglessness of the categories of human endeavor. He notes the recent confusion of these, here social, categories. "By the Lord, Horatio, this three years I have took note of it, the age is grown so picked that the toe of the peasant comes so near the heel of the courtier he galls his kibe" (V,i,134–138). Ophelia's funeral procession arrives. Hamlet, who does not know who is being buried, immediately discerns the "maimed rites" that betoken suicide. The priest explains to Laertes that Ophelia's obsequies "have been so far enlarg'd as we have warranty" (V,i,218–219). Indeed, had it not been for a "great command," presumably the King's, that "o'ersays the order" of burial, "she should in ground unsanctified been lodged." Discovering that it is Ophelia who is being buried and seeing Laertes in her grave embracing her, Hamlet jumps into the grave and struggles with Laertes. It is the most grotesque scene in *Hamlet* and marks a final, ritual desecration before the restorative slaughter with which the play ends.

Like the dumb show, the play within the play, and, in their fashion, the spying scenes set up by Polonius, the duel between Laertes and Hamlet is a spectacle. (We should note the parallel with these observed scenes, like Hamlet's and Ophelia's mad scenes, which also become spectacles, or more accurately spectacle-like, through meta-linguistic prologues.) The duel is also a game, with definite rules, that mimics, if you will, a high-stake reality, a fight-to-the-death, which is itself couched in ceremony and rule-bound. Hamlet's duel with Laertes mirrors the distorted communication at Elsinore.[28] It is a bit like the commission that Claudius sent to England, ostensibly a diplomatic commission for Hamlet, in fact a request for his death. For Laertes and the King, it is the mimicked reality, the fight-to-the-death, that is masked by the mimicking game. For Hamlet and the Queen, so we must believe, it is only a game—the mimicking—that relates symbolically to reality. The participants are caught in an asymmetrical understanding. Laertes plays for real; he is out to revenge his father's murder (and his sister's mad death). Hamlet plays for the sake of play, for honor and proof of prowess, for yet another confirmation of his manhood, his ability to revenge his father's death, or perhaps he wishes to delay, to slay the King symbolically, to risk his own death, even to die. Claudius has of course put Hamlet in the odd position of being his representative, for he wagers that Hamlet will win the duel. He wants Hamlet dead in order to save himself from Hamlet's knowledge, his revenge. Laertes does not know this nor does the King know that Horatio knows he has killed his brother. What the Queen knows we never know. She is the ultimate dupe. Those who know the real rules of the game cannot reveal them, in any case, to those who do not know. The stakes are too high. There can be no duel; there can be no fight. There is only a maimed duel, a maimed fight, that parallels the maimed rites that were the inevitable consequence of Claudius' murder of the old king.

After his "tow'ring rage" at Ophelia's grave, Hamlet comes to himself with an abrupt self-mastery that strains our credulity. He tells Horatio how he arranged for the death of Rosencrantz and Guildenstern. He shows no remorse.

> Why, man, they did make love to this employment.
> They are not near my conscience, their defeat
> Does by their own insinuation grow.   (V,ii,57–59)

He is ready to "quit" the King with his own arm, Hamlet says in coldly impassioned words, and we can more readily accept his stated intention because of his tone.[29] Not only did Claudius kill Hamlet's father, his King, and whored his mother; he is also the man who "popp'd in between th' election and [his] hopes" and threw out an "angle" for his "proper life" (V,ii,63–70). He admits his desire, and so strong, I presume, is the effect of *his* change that Horatio ceases to be Hamlet's rhetorical foil and moves him to action with the news (however anemically put) that the death of Rosencrantz and Guildenstern will soon reach the King.

Osric enters. His mission, we learn, after many sweeps of his "bonnet" and hollow expressions of *politesse,* is from the King—to ask Hamlet to duel with Laertes. Osric is a burlesque of the courtier and his appearance, however comic, is a final reminder of the sham of court life. Horatio calls him a "lap-wing." Hamlet calls him a "waterfly." He forces him to spend of his "golden words" (V,ii,129–130). After Osric leaves, Hamlet remarks:

> 'A did comply with his dug before 'a sucked it. Thus has he—and many more of the same bevy that I know the drossy age dotes on—only got the tune of the time and, out of an habit of encounter, a kind of yeasty collection, which carries them through and through the most fanned and winnowed opinions; and do but blow them to their trial, the bubbles are out. (V,ii,184–191)

Hamlet's description of the courtier's speech may be an accurate indictment of the speech of the "drossy age," but it fails to recognize the dangers that such bubbly speech can carry when it is manipulated by those, like Claudius, who seem to have the power to do so. There can be no critical reflection, no meaningful resistance, when the (real) semantico-referential function of speech has been so reduced that speech becomes simply a promiscuously pragmatic marker of identity and allegiance to that—king, class, or cultural presumption—which cannot be "correctly" named.

The King is anxious. He has no faith in Osric. He sends a Lord to confirm the duel. Hamlet remains constant and even agrees to make up with Laertes. Horatio is also anxious. He offers to forestall the court's arrival. Hamlet refuses. He admits, however, an uneasiness (208–209) and dismisses it. "It is but foolery, but it is such a kind of gainsgiving as would perhaps trouble a woman," (V,ii,211–212). (Hamlet associates inaction with being a woman.) He quibbles.

> We defy augury. There is special providence in the fall of a sparrow. If it be now, 'tis not to come; if it be not to come, it will be now; if it be not now, yet it will come. The readiness is all. Since no man, of aught, he leaves, knows aught, what is't to leave betimes? Let be.   (V,ii,215–220)

Hamlet's fatalism is ominous. He cannot see the danger of the situation.[30]

The King's invitation seems ill-timed. Why ask Hamlet to fight a duel with the very man whom less than an hour earlier, we surmise (V,i,293–294), Hamlet would have killed on his own? Why would he invite a madman to fight a "harmless" duel with his enemy? What must the court think? What must the Queen think?[31] What *can* Hamlet think? We should consider the semantical condition of the court before we give psychological explanations (the King's desperation; Hamlet's self-destructiveness, resulting from Oedipal guilt or the death instinct) or characterological ones (Hamlet's fatalism). Is Hamlet, is any one in the court beside the King (and even he), in a position to know what is happening? Is such a position possible at Elsinore?

Hamlet's and Laertes' handholding before the duel, Hamlet's quibbling, Laertes' ponderous legalism make mockery of the rites of the duel. The two men fight as the King drinks to Hamlet. By accident—Claudius appears incapable of stopping her—the Queen drinks the poison that is destined for Hamlet. Laertes and Hamlet wound each other with the poisoned rapier, which Hamlet picked up in a scuffle. The Queen cries out she has been poisoned. Laertes tells Hamlet the rapier is poisoned. "The King—the King's to blame," he says. Hamlet stabs the King with the poisoned rapier and then forces him to drink the poisoned potion that killed his wife. The King dies. Laertes asks Hamlet's pardon. Hamlet bids adieu to his mother and asks Horatio (his name is derived from *orator*) to tell his story. "O

God, Horatio, what a wounded name, / Things standing thus
unknown, shall I leave behind me" (V,ii,349–351). He asks
Horatio to give his "dying voice" to the election of Fortinbras.

Fortinbras enters like a King reborn. Horatio promises to tell
him "truly" what happened.

> So shall you hear
> Of carnal, bloody, and unnatural acts,
> Of accidental judgments, casual slaughters,
> Of deaths put on by cunning and forc'd cause,
> And in the upshot, purposes mistook
> Fall'n on th' inventors' heads.   (V,ii,385–390)

He urges Fortinbras to accept the throne "even while men's
minds are wild, lest more mischance / On plots and errors happen" (V,ii,398–399). Fortinbras orders his captains to give Hamlet a proper burial. Order will be restored through appropriate
ritual.

It is remarkable that poison, the very substance that triggered
off the "carnal, bloody, and unnatural acts" in Denmark is also
the substance that restores order.[32] By poisoning the King
through the ear, by committing fratricide and regicide, Claudius
unsettled Denmark's moral and ritual order, creating thereby
semantic chaos, an evidential crisis, the seemingness of appearance. Words were no longer bound "naturally" to things. An
illegitimate King who had violated that order could not serve as
the guarantor of meaning. He could not hold things together;
he could not constrain perverted desire; he could not put a stop
to the chain of deaths and transgressions that ensued. Nor, for
that matter, could Hamlet. An insider, he was "benetted round
with villainies" in Denmark as he was on the ship that was to
carry him to his death in England. Through fooleries, feigned
madness, dumb shows, plays, and meta-linguistic commentaries, Hamlet was able perhaps to confirm the King's guilt, but he
could not act until signification was restored.

Despite the violent use of words, poison alone could restore
order and signification. It was only when the Queen acknowledged that she had been poisoned ("The drink, the drink, I'm
poisoned" [V,ii,316]), only when Laertes told Hamlet that the
rapier was "unbated" and "envenom'd," that signifier and signi-

fied, word and thing, were again meaningfully united.[33] It was then that Hamlet could kill the King, twice,—once for himself, Calderwood (1983:46) remarks, once to avenge his father. Claudius said nothing more. He could not have said more. But Hamlet was able to give his "dying voice" to Fortinbras, to give him legitimacy, and then Horatio was empowered to tell his tale and cure Hamlet of a wounded name. We never know how much those who died that day actually knew of what had happened. What Shakespeare shows us—and we do our best to deny—is that even when we are ignorant of the moral and ritual violations of people in power, we are affected by those violations, not directly perhaps but by indirection and semantical confusion.

Notes
References
Index

Notes

Introduction

1. Irony in anthropological writings has barely been studied. Krupat (1988) finds irony in the work of Franz Boas where I find contradiction. Clifford (1988:79) argues that the "history of ethnographic liberalism" can be seen as "an array of ironic positions." I would agree, were he to recognize that at least in the United States these positions tend to be masked by a moralistic seriousness. The ideologically repressed irony of ethnography has to be uncovered and the tyranny of its "seriousness"—its dogmatic realism—has to be exposed. For further discussion of the ironic mode, see White (1973).

2. Fabian (1983) stresses the allochronic (temporal distancing) dimension of the traditional anthropological vantage point. There is an aporetic relationship between the coeval time of field research and the allochronic time of exposition and analysis. I would argue that this aporetic relationship is inherent in all reflection. It is a consequence of the "politics" of complex dialogical engagements in which such reflection occurs. Fabian is quite correct in relating it to larger political (colonial, imperialist) arrangements, but his totalizing vision of society creates a fixity of vantage point that does not do justice to the "open-ended" nature of the deployment of power. It risks affirming precisely those "totalities" that are at stake in any power play.

3. Natural languages, as Silverstein (1985:225) points out, have "to a certain extent" their own pragmatic meta-language—a built-in meta-pragmatic function (for example, modes of talking about talk in a purposive way). They may also have more complex "indexical-denotationals" that "denote by virtue of instantiating an indexable configuration of speech-event components" (for example, in certain illocutionary predicates). Both meta-pragmatic functions (the built-in and instantiated) can be rendered more explicit meta-pragmatically—in a virtual way, as in the examples I have given. Considerably more research is required to discover how meta-

pragmatic functions are rendered explicit both linguistically and metaphorically in nonlinguistic terms.

4. In effect I will be expanding the argument set forth in Chapter 4.

5. I am referring here primarily to explicit and extensive descriptive paraphrases of such encounters and not to the meta-pragmatic dimension of such verbal qualifiers as "promise" or "assert" in "he promised that" or "she asserted that."

6. These characterological and socio-dramatic discussions may be expanded refractions of the meta-pragmatic verbal qualifiers of direct and indirect quotation in such paraphrases.

7. For a discussion of secondary dialogues, see Chapters 4 and 8.

8. Considerable controversy surrounds the exact meaning of Thucydides' words here (White 1960; Hogan 1980; Wilson 1982; Loraux 1986). Thucydides seems to be saying that the traditional evaluation (*axiosis*) of words (*onomaton*) changed during the factionalism on the island. What is of interest to us is Thucydides' emphasis on the evaluative dimension of the denotative act, not simply as a cognitive judgment but as a moral one. The axiological dimension of denotation appears to have escaped the notice of scientific linguists (reflecting perhaps their particular linguistic ideology, manifestly different from that of Thucydides) though, in a somewhat different way it is at least implicitly acknowledged by theorists of implicature (Grice 1975; Sweetser 1987). It would seem that during periods of civil strife, anomie, or ritual disorder the axiological dimension of denotation—the "morality of denotation"—can be perverted.

1. Centering

1. All references to *The Interpretation of Dreams* will be to the Strachey translation (London: George Allen and Unwin, 1954); they will be followed by a page reference to the German edition published by Fischer Taschenbuch Verlag in 1942 and reprinted in 1983.

2. It is interesting to speculate how "strong" centerings, like illness and cure, determine the dominant themes of ethnography. The ethnographer sometimes finds himself in the position of the man—or the woman—on a blind date who likes his partner, desperately tries to find a subject of interest that will "center" their relationship, and ends up talking about football. In fact he is not much interested in football, nor is she though she thinks he is. He is a man after all! They go on talking about football for months,

attending games, until they cannot stand it any longer. They are each in crisis. They can either break up or confess their lack of interest in the game and joke about it. The ethnographer, however, can neither risk "breaking up" with his informant nor afford to joke about his lack of interest in a particular subject (Rosaldo 1976; 1982). The informant is freer. He can break up with the ethnographer; he can joke about whatever it is that obsesses the ethnographer. Of course, he might actually take an interest in it. Is such an "interest" a cultural distortion?

3. I am not questioning here the validity of Freud's theory of the Oedipus complex or of the reality and pleasure principles; I am simply calling attention to their rhetorical function in establishing and legitimating the centrality of certain events, images, or constructs in psychoanalytic reports if not in psychoanalytic sessions themselves.

4. When Rat Man tells Freud, for example, about the rat punishment, he precipitates such a context. What preceded it discursively is now organized in terms of the punishment and what follows it will be so organized. *But* so is Freud's report. Rat Man's image is so symbolically powerful that it hides the interlocutory dynamics that privileged it (see Chapter 9).

5. "Eine grosse Halle—viele Gäste, die wir empfangen.—Unter ihnen Irma, die ich sofort beiseite nehme, um gleichsam ihren Brief zu beantworten, ihr Vorwürfe zu machen, dass sie die "Lösung" noch nicht akzeptiert. Ich sage ihr: Wenn du noch Schmerzen hast, so ist es wirklich nur deine Schuld.—Sie anwortet: Wenn du wüsstest, was ich für Schmerzen jetzt habe, im Hals, Magen, und Leib, es schnürt mich zusammen.—Ich erschrecke, und sehe an. Sie scheint bleich und gedunsen aus; Ich denke am Ende übersehe ich da doch etwas Organisches. Ich nehme sie zum Fenster und schaue ihr in den Hals. Dabei zeigt sie etwas Sträuben wie die Frauen, die ein künstliches Gebiss tragen. Ich denke mir, sie hat es doch nicht nötig.—Der Mund geht dann auch gut auf, und ich finde rechts einen grossen weissen Fleck, und anderwärts sehe ich an merkwürdigen krausen Gebilden, die offenbar den Nasenmuscheln nachgebildet sind, ausgedehnte weissgraue Schorfe.—Ich rufe schnell Dr. M. hinzu, der die Untersuchung wiederholt und bestätigt . . . Dr. M. sieht ganz anders aus als sonst; er ist sehr bleich, hinkt, ist am Kinn bartlos . . . Mein Freund Otto steht jetzt auch neben ihr, und Freund Leopold perkutiert sie über dem Leibchen und sagt: Sie hat eine Dämpfung links unten, weist auch auf eine infiltrierte Hauptpartie an der linken Schulter hin

(was ich trotz des Kleides wie er spüre) . . . M. sagt: Kein Zweifel, es ist eine Infektion, aber es macht nichts; es wird noch Dysenterie hinzukommen und das Gift sich ausscheiden . . . Wir wissen auch unmittelbar, woher die Infektion rührt. Freund Otto hat ihr unlängst, als sie sich unwohl fühlte, eine Injektion gegeben mit einem Propylpräparat, Propylen . . . Proprionsäure . . . Trimethylamin (dessen Formel ich fettgedruckt vor mir sehe) . . . Man macht solche Injektionen nicht so leichtfertig . . . Wahrscheinlich war auch die Spritze nicht rein" (Freud 1942:98).

6. I do not, however, want to overextend the use of transference and countertransference by suggesting that a transferential relationship develops between Freud and his readers. I suggest rather that the pragmatic strategies that are understood in psychoanalysis in terms of transference do occur on other occasions (facilitating perhaps the overextension of the terms "transference" and "countertransference"). I should note, however, that there is considerable variation in the relationship between author and reader and that today many readers of Freud seem to develop something like a transference with him. Such relations may be encouraged by various institutional practices, including psychoanalytic training itself. I remember talking to Jacques Lacan once about the thinkers who influenced him. He criticized his American translator, Anthony Wilden, explaining that Wilden had not understood that when he, Lacan, referred to Hegel, Heidegger, or Leenhardt, he was simply making use of "figures de pensée" (note the puns!) that his readers would recognize in order to convey his truths. He realized that there was an inherent danger in using such "figures" because they could lead his readers to an intellectual complacency—the last thing he wanted—by placing his thought in a familiar tradition. Such a placement (again a pun) would be a distortion. "Mais il faut commencer quelque part," he said resignedly. I asked, "What about Freud?" "Ah, ça, c'est autre chose," Lacan answered, acknowledging with a smile and a twinkle in his eye that even he had to accept someone's truths. I do not know whether he was also playing with the meaning of "ça"—as *that* and as the *id*.

7. I should note that my strategy for showing how an event like the Irma dream is centered and itself centers requires breaking the frame in which the event is placed. Here I follow a procedure ethnographers use in interpreting ritual: they refuse to frame the ritual as the native does, as the ritual "demands"—to succumb to the "ritual illusion" (see Chapter 12). Even in studies as linguisti-

cally sensitive as Maloney's (1977) study of the dream of Irma, the dream is separated from its surrounding verbal context (though not its biographical one). Of course Maloney's analysis like Erikson's (1954) and Anzieu's (1988) proceeds within the theoretical framework of psychoanalysis. He accepts, in other words, the meta-pragmatic (and, in the case in point, referentially explicated) "directions" for how the dream is to be interpreted.

8. In discussing the "dual nature" of *The Interpretation of Dreams*, the scientific and the personal historical, Schorske (1980:183–184) writes: "Imagine St. Augustine weaving his *Confessions* into *The City of God*, or Rousseau integrating his *Confessions* as a subliminal plot into *The Origin of Inequality:* such is the procedure of Freud in *The Interpretation of Dreams.* In the invisible personal narrative he takes us downward, dream by major dream into the underground recesses of his own buried self." Schorske finds three layers, the professional, the political, and the personal historical, in this "invisible personal narrative." It is the "professional" that dominates his reading of the Irma dream.

9. "Man hat eine begreifliches Scheu so viel Intimes aus seinem Seelenleben preiszugeben." ("One has an understandable timidity about exposing so many intimate [details] about one's psychic life.") Stratchy's translation fails to capture the somewhat pretentious, the heavy tone of the original. There there is a strong contrast between the German *Scheu* (timidity, shyness) and the French *Intimes. Preisgeben* suggests notions of abandonment and prostitution as well as exposure. *Seelenleben*, literally "soul life," always presents the English translator with difficulties, for it sounds too religious when translated literally and too scientific when translated as "mental life." *Man,* "one," is less impersonal than the English "there is." "Natural" is of course a weak translation of *begreifliches*.

10. Rousseau also had other motives, including revenge.

11. The English translation is awkward when compared to the more colloquial German. She "resisted," "bristled," "stiffened up," "struggled."

12. See Maloney (1977) for changes in the placement of ellipsis.

13. Maloney discusses the sexual connotations of the text in great detail, noting, for example, that *Wurf* in *Vorwurf* (reproach) means "brood," "litter," a "throw." *Lösung* (solution) can also mean "liquid solution" and a "firing (of guns)" and *leichfertig* may be translated as "wanton" as well as "lightly." Maloney gets carried away at times in his search for sexual connotations.

14. Maloney (1977:88) notes a general movement from outer to inner in the dream and in the associations.
15. Maloney (1977:90) suggests that Freud dominates Irma, women more generally, through grammar!
16. One characteristic of the associations is the peculiar status of the "I." It indexes at times Freud the external authority, at others Freud the dreamer, and at still others Freud the actor within the dream; it also indexes Freud the writer. Often it confuses two or more of these indexical referents. Such multiple indexing facilitates imaginary identifications and role plays.
17. It may also be interpreted in Lacanian terms as the ultimate object of desire that is precluded articulation insofar as desire has passed through the defiles of the signifier (Lacan 1966).

2. Hermes' Dilemma

1. In his commentaries on the Salon of 1846, Baudelaire (1846:634), who admired Catlin's work, wrote: "Le rouge, la couleur de la vie, abondait tellement dans ce sombre musée, que c'était une ivresse; quant aux paysages,—montagnes boisées, savanes immenses, rivières désertes,—ils étaient monotonement, éternellement verts; le rouge, cette couleur si obscure, si épaisse, plus difficile à pénétrer que les yeux d'un serpent—le vert, cette couleur calme et gaie et sóuriante de la nature, je les retrouve chantant leur antithèse mélodique." There is of course something of this melodic antithesis in Catlin's prose.
2. Gelley (1979:420) argues that ways of seeing in the realist novel can be understood "as a type of deictic at a phenomenological level, a sign important not so much on account of its content but because it is capable of identifying the instance of observation and tracing its modifications."
3. There is a revealing parallel between Catlin's disjunctive style and his jumpy speculations about the meaning of ceremony.
4. All translations are my own. The Auden and Mayer translation (Goethe 1982) is often very inaccurate.
5. See Michel (1976) for publication details.
6. It "fits in naturally with the Roman life style." ("Das Karneval ist . . . eigentlich nur eine Fortsetzung oder vielmehr der Gipfel jener gewöhnlichen sonn- und festtägigen Freuden; es ist nichts Neues, nichts Fremdes, nichts Einziges, sondern es schliesst sich nur an die römische Lebensweise ganz natürlich an" [1976a:642]).

7. "Auch wer nur die Dinge will und sonst nichts, erfasst sie in einer bestimmten Hinsicht, von einem bestimmten Gesichtspunkt aus. Dessen wird Goethe sich nicht bewusst. Er ist überzeugt, *die* ewig gültige Wahrheit entdeckt und begriffen zu haben, und traut sich zu, sie jedem, der Augen hat and sehen will, zeigen zu können. Da es sich um objektive Erkenntnisse handelt, gelingt das auch. Was Goethe darlegt, ist tatsächlich den wechselvollen Launen, der Stimmung, der Willkür der einzelnen Menschen entruckt und insofern zeitlos und uberall gültig. Es fragt sich aber, ob jedermann sich für diese Wahrheit interessiert, ob nicht mancher es vorzieht, die Dinge von einem andern Gesichtspunkt aus, in anderer Hinsicht wahrzunehmen. Darüber haben wir nicht zu rechten und ist ein Streit überhaupt nicht möglich" (Staiger 1956:17–18).

8. If there is no difference between actors and spectators in the carnival—a point made by Bakhtin (1965)—then any vantage point on the carnival would have to be "foreign," outside the carnival itself. I doubt, however, that there is no differentiation between actors and spectators. Goethe's "theatrical" description suggests there is, and I would argue that the absence of differentiation is, in fact, ideological—an expression of a defining alterity.

9. By his addressing the reader, the reader's function becomes, as Michael Andre Bernstein (1983) remarks, "akin to the function of the next day in a 'real' Saturnalia, the instant when everyone resumes his conventional roles, with the important distinction, however, that the reader's position represents a *continuously* present source of authority which even the most anarchic moments of the festival day do not succeed in suspending." Though I acknowledge the authoritative role of the reader in Goethe's *Römische Karneval*, Goethe's own authoritative position, far stronger than Catlin's, seems to be quite independent of his reader's.

10. It is interesting to note that Henry James (1873:139ff) also includes an Ash Wednesday meditation, "a Lenten peroration," in his description of the carnival in 1873. It is inspired by the view of a young priest praying by himself in a little church on the Palatine hill and continues as James, alone, keeps carnival "by strolling perversely along the silent circumference of Rome."

11. I am simplifying here. The ethnographer's "I" must be carefully examined in its specific occurrences, for it can serve multiple functions, even simultaneously. It may, for example, be descriptive, referring to a grammatically distorted interlocution ("I said"/"he said" or "I observed") or it may in fact refer to the context of

writing. There is also, as I argue in Chapter 3, an anaphoric potential to first and second person indexicals, particularly in "au-
thored" texts.

12. Ultimately one would have to consider the ontological status of
Balinese equivalents (if there are any) of these Western categories.

13. See my discussion in Chapter 5 of text and text metaphors. I argue
that despite a certain literary critical penchant to view texts abstractly, their rhetorical force rests on the concreteness, the tangible existence, of the text.

3. The Self, the Third, and Desire

1. I have given an explication of the Strachey translation. For the
purpose of my argument, insofar as the translation makes sense to
the reader, it reflects the implicit psychology to which I am referring. The German (Freud 1942:328) reads: "Dass das eigene Ich
in einem Träume mehrmals vorkommt oder in verschiedenen
Gestaltungen auftritt, ist im Gründe nicht verwündlicher, als dass
es in einem bewussten Gedanken mehrmals und an verschiedenen Stellen oder in anderen Beziehungen enthalten ist, z.b. im
Satz: wenn *ich* daran denke, was für gesundes Kind *ich* war." We
find the same fundamental distinction between dream (*Traum*)
and conscious thought (*bewusster Gedanke*). But in the German
there is not the same emphasis on appearance in the dream as in
the English translation. The ego *vorkommt*—comes forth, occurs,
appears (on the scene). Or it *auftritt*—steps forth, presents itself,
appears (on the scene). There is rather more emphasis on the
movement of the ego—coming or stepping forth—in the dream
than in conscious thought, which contains the ego (*enthalt das
Ich*). Both *vorkommen* and *auftreten* may be used in a theatrical
context to mean "to appear." This fits in well with Freud's reference to the dream as another stage (*ein anderer Schauplatz*). Conscious thought, insofar as it contains the ego, appears in any case
to have more control than the dream. The *ich* as ego and the *ich*
in the final phrase are of course homonyms in German and lend,
therefore, greater credence and panache to Freud's point.

2. For the distinction between implicit and explicit psychology, see
Chapter 11.

3. Strachey (1961) notes that Freud uses *das Ich* ("ego" here) in two
senses in his earlier writing: It may "distinguish a person's self as
a whole (including, perhaps, his body) from other people," or it

may denote a particular part of the mind characterized by special attributes and functions.

4. *Träume sind absolut egoistisch.* Note Freud's use of the Latin derivative *egoistisch* instead of the German *selbstisch.*

5. It is impossible in the context to determine whether the ego is synonymous with, or a referent of, the two "I"s. At the time, Ferdinand de Saussure's work on the sign had not yet been elaborated—or at least not yet published.

6. It is reflected, for example, in the frequent confusion (or blending) of self-awareness with self-conceptualization and of the phenomenological approach with a conceptual one.

7. Compare Mauss's (1973:362) question at the end of his lecture: "Qui sait ce que seront encore le progrès de l'Entendement sur ce point [the development of the concept of the self]? Qui sait même si cette 'catégorie' que tous ici nous croyons fondée sera toujours reconnue comme telle?"

8. Compare Aristotle (1941, *De Interpretatione* 16 Al): "Spoken words are the symbols of mental experience and written words are the symbols of spoken words. Just as all men have not the same writing, so men have not the same speech sounds, but the mental experiences, which these directly symbolize, are the same for all, as also are those things of which our experiences are the images."

9. Mead's stages seem to be at times situationally determined (in play, in a game) and at times developmental.

10. Benveniste's argument in fact proceeds in two directions at once. He is concerned with the emergence of subjectivity through discourse. He is implicitly concerned with the denotations of subjectivity: *subject, ego, subjectivity, person,* and so on. Despite the rigor of his argument, Benveniste's use of the terms reflects the same (symptomatically) "promiscuous" usage we have observed in the treatment of the self in the other authors we have considered.

11. Compare with Freud's notion of the ego in our first quotation.

12. Note the question Benveniste (1966:251–257) poses in his article "The Nature of Pronouns": "What then is the reality to which *I* or *you* refers?"

13. Compare Leenhardt's (1979) understanding of the dual.

14. We should note that in asking what the *I* refers to—a question that is from Benveniste's own perspective meaningless—he (1966:252; 1971:219) is forced to posit a reality, which he identifies with "objective positions in space and time" Of course the *I* and *you*, he argues, do not always refer to the same objects in the spatio-

temporal continuum but rather to "utterances unique each time." Aside from considering the obvious point that such utterances are also objective occurrences in *reality,* Benveniste fails to consider that the speaker who uses *I* and *you* and his interlocutor who understands *I* and *you* would be unwilling to limit their reference to such instances of discourse.

15. Many obscure passages in Lacan are the result of his insistence on a referential model of language. The *béance,* to play on Lacan's term, between reference and index affords him the space for much of his language play.

16. Lacan uses this awkward phrase to stress that it is the father-qua-symbol that is in question here. *Nom* in *nom-de-père* is also more or less homonymous with *non-de-père,* the father's "no."

17. In Freudian thought, *father,* and *mother* serve as full stops in the otherwise unending chain of symbolic references and cross-references. Their special position within the psychoanalytic hermeneutic is rationalized by chronological and developmental priority.

18. Mead himself does not explicitly recognize the generalized other as a Third in the relationship between self and other.

19. My use of the *Third* is probably not altogether dissimilar to Peirce's (1931) notion of *thirdness,* at least in certain of his usages. I am thinking specifically of where he relates thirdness to meaning, thought, and law—and to the possibility of generality. He (1931:173) notes, interestingly, that "the dream itself has no prominent thirdness; it is, on the contrary, utterly irresponsible; it is whatever it pleases. The object of experience as a reality is a second recant. But the desire in writing to attach the one to the other is a third, or medium." The third, I suppose, enters the dream with the question of meaning. Peirce's observation that genuine triadic relations can never be built out of dyadic relations is of singular importance to my argument. It is reflected in the Oedipus myth and other myths having to do with the genesis of the genuine triad.

20. Lacan's Hegelianism is apparent.

4. Self-Characterization

1. I cannot elaborate on secondary, or shadow, dialogues here. They are a model for thought that accompanies primary dialogues. I am, of course, indebted to theorists who have conceived of thought as inner speech (Vygotsky 1962; Wertsch, 1985) or more specifically

as dialogue (Bakhtin 1977; Emerson 1983). The interlocutors in such secondary dialogues are highly symbolic and unstable (despite whatever fantasized determinations they may have). They may be within these terms determinate, as for example when one maintains an inner conversation with an enemy, or when one suffers from what Diderot called *esprit d'escalier*. Or they may be indeterminate—unspecified, generalized partners of the sort that psychoanalysts would see as introjects of important (parental) figures in one's biography; or they may be abstract like "the voice of conscience."

2. I am indebted to Michael Silverstein for this formulation.

3. I use the word "ascriptor" to stress a certain presumption in such characterizations—a presumption that has moral and political force. Although I do not wish to engage in the debate between descriptivists and ascriptivists (see Geach 1960, for example) which is only tangential to my argument, I do want to call attention to the fact that characterizations of *self and other* are rarely "neutral," empirically verifiable descriptions; they figure within the plays of power and desire that occur in every verbal exchange and are thus morally and politically resonant ascriptions.

4. The static, empirical view also provides the basis for critical views that so strongly assert the creative dimension of language that any empirical certainty, other than at the level of language, is precluded.

5. When someone says, for example, "I'm timid" or "I'm an introvert," only a naive interlocutor would accept such self-characterizations at face value. The sophisticated interlocutor might use them as evidence for whatever characterization he might make in roughly the following way: X is the sort of person who says "I'm timid" or "I'm an introvert" in context B when talking to Y. In other words the referentiality of such characterizations is less diagnostic than its pragmaticity. (See below in text.)

6. See note 5. The acceptability of self-characterizations is, in fact, considerably more complicated than I have indicated here. It depends, in part, on the distance the speaker creates between himself in some seemingly extra-discourse sense and himself in an intra-discourse sense—between what Goffman (1981) calls the "animator" of the statement and the "figure" in the animator's statement. There seems to be some sort of split between the I of any utterance that indexes the speaker as outside, independent, and master of the utterance and the I that is indexed as internal to, controlled by, and qualified through the utterance—through

predication, style, and attribution. See Silverstein (1985:225) for an elaboration of the functional laminations of pronomial usage. He notes, for example, that the objects *I* and *you* pick out are characterized as parts of the speech situation indexed in and by the pragmatics of use, independent of the fact that these objects are also the referents of the expression *I* and *you*. A self-characterization in the present tense uttered with irony may on certain occasions be taken at face value while the same self-characterization, in the same tense, uttered on an identical occasion in a nonironic serious mode would be completely unacceptable. Self-characterizations in the past tense or in narratives of the past are at times acceptable at face value within their explicit or implicit narrative context in part at least because of the "distance" between the speaker and the I embedded in his discourse. Other conventions are probably operative as well. A reader of Conrad's *Heart of Darkness*—Marlowe's silent audience—might accept Marlowe's characterizations of himself as a younger man trying to find a job on an African steamer by "worrying" his Continental relations. "I am sorry to own I began to worry them. This was already a fresh departure for me. I was not used to get things that way, you know. I always went my own road and on my own legs when I had a mind to go. I wouldn't have believed it of myself" (1899:8). But pragmatically, by characterizing his past self in this rhetorically and stylistically complex passage with its avowals and disavowals and its pleas to an audience, Marlowe is in fact casting his present self—as an old tar, a storyteller, an adventurer with an introspective bent. Sophisticated interlocutors have to ask: what kind of a man is Marlowe such that he would characterize himself as a young man in the way he does?

7. Depth metaphors in psychoanalysis and other psychologies often serve to mediate or even to fudge theoretical contradictions existing at their deepest level.

5. Text, Transference, and Indexicality

1. In the original version of this essay I used "referential" for what I have chosen to call here the *semantico-referential* or at times the *symbolic* (roughly equivalent to Silverstein's [1976] "semantic") in order to avoid confusing pure reference with the referential dimension of such indexicals as shifters. My use of "symbolic" should not be confused with either the Freudian or the Lacanian use of the term. For me, the symbolic refers to the purely referen-

tial dimension of a sign's meaning, its descriptive capacity that is taken (meta-pragmatically) to be quite independent of any specific context. The symbolic function contrasts, therefore, with the context-dependent indexical or pragmatic function of a speech event.

2. I am using "text" here, as Freud does, to refer to the transcript of the account of the dream. Freud also has another metaphorical use of "text" and other writing and printing terms. These terms "describe" the psychical apparatus, in particular memory and the "contents" of the unconscious and their passage—their translation (*Ubersetzung*) or "inscription" (*Umschrift*)—into consciousness (Derrida 1967a).

In Derrida's words, "Ici encore, le concept métaphorique de traduction (*Ubersetzung*) ou de transcription (*Umschrift*) n'est pas dangereux en ce qu'il fait reférence a l'écriture mais en ce qu'il suppose un texte déjà là, immobile, presence impassible d'une statue, d'une pierre écrite ou d'une archive dont on transporterait sans dommage le contenu signifié dans l'élément d'un autre langage, celui du préconscient ou du conscient. Il ne suffit donc pas de parler d'écriture pour être fidèle à Freud, on peut alors le trahir plus que jamais," (1967:312–313).

The question is not, I suspect, whether or not the reader betrays Freud but whether or not the "betrayal" is inherent in Freud's metaphors. The text, writing, and printing metaphors reflect an epistemological tentativeness in Freud's meta-psychological speculations.

3. See Introduction for a discussion of semantico-referential and pragmatic. I am using "deictic" and "indexical" interchangeably for the pragmatic function of language. My use of "symbolic" ("semantico-referential") and "indexical" or "deictic" is broader than in scientific linguistics. I hope this extended usage will point to what can be called the linguistic facilitation of "psychological" interpretation. My usage reflects the same language and highlights the same linguistic ideology that are projected and objectified in our "psychological" understanding and interpretation. See Silverstein (1979) for an extended discussion of linguistic ideology and for a radical rereading of Whorf. Silverstein avoids addressing himself fully in this paper to the status of scientific linguistics. Is "scientific" linguistics also caught in the same closure as "ideological" linguistics?

4. Marcus (1974:104) notes that the early Freud, the Freud of *The Interpretation of Dreams* and the "Fragment" "is the servant of

his *daimon"*—"the spirit of science, the truth, or reality" which, according to Marcus, are all the same for Freud. Freud, self-cast as the Victorian man of science, is "the relentless investigator pushing on no matter what."

5. My debt to Derrida (1967a;1967b) should be obvious.

6. Derrida's deconstruction of Western metaphysical thought, is not alien to self-reflective anthropology—to an anthropology that recognizes its own closure (*clôture*). To attack Derrida's insistence on the priority of writing on empirical grounds, for instance, is to miss his point entirely. What he attempts to expose is the "construction" of our "written" thought. What is of significance to us here is the limitation of Derrida's own (Saussurian) approach to language; he drives this approach to the limit. We are reduced to writing *sous rature;* under erasure the word is both printed and deleted: present and absent, legible and illegible, for words (particularly those governing words of Western thought: "~~presence~~," "~~being~~," and "~~psyche~~") are both inaccurate and necessary. ("~~Word~~" too should be written under erasure.) Any anthropology that attempts to "~~capture~~" the "~~world~~" of the "~~other~~" is, I suppose, ideally written *sous rature!* Is that not the function of our rather promiscuous use of quotation marks, italicized words from exotic tongues, and confessions of the inadequacy of translation? And yet here, as in so much structuralist and post-structuralist thought, the reader, even the sympathetic one, who recognizes the limitation of his own language and the tyranny of his own metaphysical closure, feels that the system founders on its own (symptomatic) understanding of language, its own conceit (see also Tedlock 1979).

7. The "we" relationship, with the collusive (ideological/experiential) denial of the differing perspectives of the participating "I," predominates in those privileged moments Turner (1969) calls *communitas.*

8. "Lebt her mit einiger Ruhe, Sicherheit und Konsequenz" (Nietzsche 1966:316).

9. Although Freud's later thinking shifts away from the "historical reality" of remembered events and analytic reconstructions, a close reading reveals a continued ambivalence in his attitude toward the historicity of such events. In any social encounter, including the psychoanalytic, there is always a *push* toward accepting the reality of what is narrated. The *real,* Lacan (1966) notes, is not autonomous but always a function of the Imaginary and the Symbolic.

10. This is why, in Freud's terms, transference is a repetition and not a memory. Is it possible that the linguistic ground for memory is the symbolic and that of repetition (not imitation) is deixis? What is indexed can of course be symbolically described and remembered.

11. "Die Krankengeschichte selbst habe ich erst nach Abschluss der Kur aus meinem Gedächtnisse niedergeschrieben so lange meine Erinnerung noch frisch und durch das Interesse an der Publikation gehoben war" (Freud 1942a:166–167).

    Freud's language in this passage is revealing of the role of writing, of the text, in his quest for certainty. The case history was "committed to writing from memory." Memory, a continual subject of Freud's speculation, is conceived in terms of writing and printing. The possibility of "publication" "heightens" Freud's memory, giving it a greater trustworthiness, authority, and repetitive capability than a mere transcription would achieve. The passage reminds one of the opening paragraphs of "Notes upon the 'Mystic Writing Pad' " (1959c), which was written in 1925 and attests to the continuity of Freud's metaphorical repertoire and a certain anxiety before the distortions of memory.

    > If I distrust my memory—neurotics, as we know, do so to a remarkable extent, but normal people have every reason for doing so as well—*I am able to supplement and guarantee its working by making a note in writing.* In that case the surface upon which this note is preserved, the pocket book or sheet of paper, is as it were a materialized portion of my mnemonic apparatus, the rest of which I carry about with me invisible. I have only to bear in mind the place where this "memory" has been deposited and I can then "reproduce" it at any time I like, *with the certainty that it will have remained unaltered and so have escaped the possible distortions to which it might have been subjected in my actual memory* (Freud 1959c:175, emphasis added).

    That Freud considered the publication of Dora's case history from an early stage and that he postponed its publication for several years suggests that the "Fragment" is indeed an attempt to master the countertransference and his memory. "Phonographically" reflects clearly the position of the spoken word in Freud's and our own chirographic-typographic culture. Derrida would doubtless note that "phonographically" is derived from both the Greek *phone* ("sound" or "voice") and *graphien* ("to write," "to scratch," or "to draw").

12. I have suggested in Chapter 3 that the dialogical process reflects or facilitates the conceptualization of dialectical thought.

13. Lacan (1966:216) writes: "Dans une psychanalyse en effet, le sujet, à proprement parler, se constitue par un discours où la seule présence du psychanalyste apporte, avant toute intervention, la dimension du dialogue."

14. It is possible to argue that the patient-doctor relationship is indexically presupposed and that the transference and countertransference are indexically created or entailed. This argument would, however, oversimplify the play of presupposition and creativity (reality and fantasy) that transpires in the psychoanalytic and other encounters. Such a complete splitting of the two indexical functions would preclude the possibility of studying, for example, the development of shared fantasies. Despite his or her "understanding" of the countertransference, the psychoanalyst is not immune to the effects of the patient's indexical intriguing. The very language by which the analyst understands the transference and the countertransference is itself a precipitate—an objectification or projection (see Silverstein 1979 on Whorf)—of that intrigue and implicates the analyst inevitably in it. It is not just on psychological grounds that the analyst cannot achieve complete lucidity but, I would argue, on linguistic grounds as well.

15. I am simplifying the interpretation here. My aim is not to enter *directly into* the psychoanalytic discourse—to offer an interpretation of the transference and countertransference—but to comment on the discourse and its facilitation. Lacan (1966:215–226) suggests, for example, that Freud's countertransference is to Herr K; Gearhart (1979) argues that Freud's countertransference is essentially more complex. It is directed to Herr K, to Dora's father, and to Dora herself. Indeed, if I understand the implications of Gearhart's argument correctly, any interpretation of transference gives an illusory textual coherence. I would argue that the particularizing indexical movement is countered by the generalizing movement of the symbolic interpretation; the illusion of real continuity, coherence, and consistency—identity over time and place—is produced. This generalizing movement is rendered possible by the anaphoric potential of the first and second person pronouns.

16. Brown and Gilman (1960) point out two dimensions of second person pronoun usage in Indo-European languages. One relates

to the relations of power and the other to relations of solidarity. Both dimensions are embedded in the use of "formal" and "informal" forms of the pronouns of address, such as *vous* and *tu* in French or *Sie* and *du* in German. The informal ones are associated with "condescension" and "intimacy" and the formal with "reverence" and "formality." Despite a marked shift from the "power semantic" to the "solidarity semantic," associated by Brown and Gilman with a shift from a more hierarchical to a more egalitarian ideology, the power dimension is still embedded in the pronominal system of address. It affects, I would argue, the indexical play that occurs between speakers and the interpretation of that play (for example, in the interpretation of transference and counter-transference). "Condescension," "intimacy," "reverence," and "formality," to use Brown and Gilman's glosses, become relevant dimensions in both the rhetoric of Indo-European social existence and in its interpretation. Would these be significant elements in differently constituted pronominal systems?

17. Gearhart (1979) argues that Freud's case not only reflects a particular view of man and woman but his own paternal position. Even Freud's critics continue "to privilege the principle of paternity according to which Freud is the author, the master, the sovereign subject, and ultimately the father of his work" (Gearhart 1979:114). For Lacan himself, Gearhart (1979:126) insists, the place designated by Freud's name, however empty, "comports all the guarantees of the formal coherence of the work that the classical subject does." "Freud" is the guarantor of "Dora" of the Case of Dora.

6. Talking (about) Psychoanalysis

1. Anthropology and psychology differ in important ways with respect to their positions and evaluations within larger socio-economic arrangements. Anthropologists, for example, are usually attached to academic or research organizations and subject to all of the constraints—and the freedoms too—that come with such institutional affiliation. Psychoanalysts have for the most part less "consuming" institutional affiliations. Anthropologists are salaried, and like most academics receive lower wages than other professionals with whom they are symbolically equated. Psychoanalysts, most often in private practice, receive a remuneration that is more commensurate with the professionals with whom they are associated, though they have an ambiguous status within the medical establishment. (Anthropologists also have an ambiguous status

within university circles.) Despite the claims of applied anthropology, anthropologists are generally considered to be researchers and teachers while psychoanalysts, despite their research claims, are considered to be therapists. Anthropologists are evaluated in terms of the quality of their research, their publications, and the status of the institution to which they are affiliated. The esteem of a psychoanalyst is less institutionally bound and is usually a matter of "reputation," the criteria for which are vague. They may include the quality of research and publications as well as therapeutic success. Reputation in both fields is also determined by the role that practitioners play—politically—in various professional organizations. See also Crapanzano (1986).

2. For a discussion of Lacan's expulsion from the International Association of Psycho-Analysis see the *International Journal of Psycho-Analysis* 35 (1954):267–278; and 37 (1956):122.

3. For a history of hermeneutics see Gadamer (1975) and Mueller-Vollmer (1985), who includes an extensive bibliography.

4. I do not deny that "an unresolved Oedipal conflict" can govern a particular patient's response to torture and its aftermath. What I find objectionable is giving infantile fantasms governing priority over political reality and thus facilitating a complacency before, if not an actual denial of, such a political reality. So long as psychoanalysis fails to question its own praxis, so long as it does not attempt to integrate social and political reality into its theoretical perspective (and not simply incorporate it), it lends itself to the political and social misuse of the sort that was seen in Argentina and Brazil. For at least one important discussion of psychoanalytic understanding and political reality (by a psychoanalyst) see Paul Parin. Parin (1978:3) writes: "Die Aussage, dass ein politisches Engagement *nichts anderes* sei als der Versuch, persönliche Konflicte zu lösen, ist ebenso unsinnig wie jene andere, dass die Beteiligung an einer politischen Bewegung aus rein objektiven oder rationalen Motiven ohne die Mobilisierung individueller Konflicte zustande kommen konnte."

5. Put another way, the field or therapeutic exchange between partners who call one another I and you, that is, use indexical first and second person personal pronouns, is transformed into exchanges described minimally by one anaphoric pronoun—he, she, or they—for the informant or patient, or by two such pronouns, one for the informant or patient and the other for the ethnographer or therapist (that is if the ethnographer or therapist resists even more impersonal, though perhaps more authoritative, passive locutions).

There can under normal circumstances be no dialogue between an I and a he or she or they.

6. The metaphor of depth is related to the notion of origin. The deeper one probes, so the argument goes, the closer to an origin one comes. Depth so understood, like origin, is a distinctly romantic preoccupation (de Man 1979).

7. I am not suggesting that all transactions have a transferential dimension. I believe that "transference" and "countertransference" should be restricted to psychoanalytic and possibly other psychotherapeutic encounters in which an identity play has been granted a conventional freedom of expression whose very conventionality is barred from consideration. Rather I am stressing that all social encounters, including the psychoanalytic and psychotherapeutic, always involve a pragmatic negotiation of identity that is rarely subject to immediate reflection and discussion. Psychoanalysis differs from other such encounters in that it promotes such immediate discussion, but like other such encounters, it does not usually question how the pragmatic features of the encounter are to be discussed.

7. Mohammed and Dawia

1. Although Wallace (1959), Bourgignon (1968), and others have correctly pointed out that possession is not a single, distinct psychophysiological syndrome but an interpretation of a number of possible syndromes, they have failed to consider adequately the role that interpretation as possession plays in the symptomatology and cure of the syndrome and in other facets of the possessed individual's subjective experience.

2. The distinction between a follower and a husband of 'A'isha Qandisha is not clear cut. A follower may become a husband, a husband a follower. Relations with the she-demon change over time.

3. *Hamdushi* is the masculine singular of *Hamadsha; Hamdushiyya* is the feminine singular.

4. 'A'isha Qandisha and the other *jnun* may take the form of a scorpion.

5. In conversation Mohammed once implied that it was not Dawia's but the demon's volition that made her slap the *fqih*. For Mohammed, who prefers to think of Dawia as struck by the she-demon and not her husband, it was 'A'isha Qandisha who struck the fqih.

6. The oboe, or *ghita,* is one of the Hamadsha instruments.

7. Note that Mohammed refers to an oven fire in his account and

Dawia to the fire in a brazier in hers. Gueddar was scalded by water boiling in a brazier.

8. Dawia sometimes identifies the Feast of the Sheep with Khadija's name-day celebration during which the Hamadsha were invited. Detailed questioning revealed that the Feast of the Sheep was in fact after Khadija's name day. The exact chronology is not clear.

9. Dawia explained that she did not want to go to her mother's house because she was afraid there would be a fire there. She claims that when she arrived there, there was in fact a fire. One of her younger sisters had been playing with matches.

10. Unsalted meat is frequently given to the victims of the jnun. The jnun are said not to like salt. Many Moroccans sprinkle salt on places where the jnun are said to congregate before they go to bed.

11. Note the transformation of 'A'isha Qandisha and her husband from Jews to Muslims, from aliens to friends. This mirrors visually the transformation of the jnun during the cures from malevolent to benevolent spirits (Crapanzano, 1971). Note also that Dawia does not at first understand Shaykh al-Kanun because he speaks the Jews' language.

12. Dawia implies not only that Mohammed does not mean what he says but also that he is not responsible for his words. Her observation must not be considered "insight" in the psychoanalytic sense of the word, for she is not aware of the underlying dynamic of her "symptom formation."

13. 'A'isha Qandisha is said to force her husbands and some of her followers to let their fingernails grow. Mohammed resists; he does the opposite. He keeps them short. As a child he bit his nails and was punished by his father.

14. On at least one occasion, Mohammed tied up his daughter Khadija and beat her with a stick. On another, he beat Dawia up so badly for having given a loaf of bread to a neighbor that she went to court. Mohammed was found guilty, and Dawia then withdrew her charges. Khadija explained her father's anger in the following words:

> He flies into a rage and turns pale and does not know what he is doing. It comes on him from time to time. There is no reason for it. When I saw him starting to get mad, I used to go into the toilet and lock the door. Once, he was suddenly not himself. He turned pale and started saying things and looked around in all directions at once. He

wanted his stick to beat me. I went into the toilet and stayed for hours. Then, when it was night, he turned off the lights so that I would come out. I was very scared but I stayed until he fell asleep. Then I came out and tiptoed into the bedroom and lay down. In the morning he had forgotten his anger and said, "I wasn't myself."

Upon questioning, Khadija implied that 'A'isha Qandisha was responsible. Khadija and her father have frequently fought. Sometimes they tickle each other until they cannot laugh anymore. Khadija was thirteen or fourteen at the time.

15. When Mohammed finished telling me about his circumcision, I asked him to tell me any story that occurred to him. He told me a long, rambling one about a beggar who overcame a king and married a beautiful woman. The beggar then became king.

16. On one occasion I told Mohammed about *vagina dentata* myths. He was frozen for a moment, then duly denied the existence of women with toothed vaginas. Finally he asked if such women existed in Europe and America.

17. Dawia claims that with Mohammed's help she is now employing magical birth control techniques.

18. These are Hamadsha instruments.

19. One of these melodies is the same as Dawia's. They do not, however, share the same colors or incense.

20. Mohammed always expressed considerable interest in my car.

21. That is, his jinn was not satisfied. Mohammed is usually anxiety-ridden when he has not had enough. He is distracted and moody, given to depression. His body is sore, and he has difficulty breathing. He suffers from tingling in his joints.

22. Mohammed was still not a *shuwwaf* in 1973.

23. Moroccans, like other Muslims, believe that there are two angels always at the side of every human being. The angel on the right keeps account of the human being's good deeds, the one on the left of his bad deeds. These are weighed on Judgment Day.

24. 'A'isha Qandisha's favorite colors are red and black.

25. During the trance dance, women let their hair fall.

26. Mohammed has not smoked *kif* in years.

27. This is one of the more idiosyncratic rules that Dawia follows. It is by no means universally accepted by the Hamadsha.

28. 'A'isha Qandisha is said to like henna. Henna is often symbolic of blood. Just as Dawia drank the goat's blood, so she drinks henna.

29. I was not able to discover any other problem between Mohammed

and Dawia at this time. They argued over whether or not they should spend the money for the ceremony after having spent so much for their house. Dawia did not want to. She was struck. Then Mohammed refused to sponsor the ceremony for her. He was struck. The ceremony was given. Their relationship was restored. To look at the cause of the illness only in terms of a breach of ritual obligation, as Wittkower (1971) does, is to miss the role that rituals play in reconstituting interpersonal relations on the verge of collapse. The breach is a symbol for the interpersonal defect.

30. Shaykh al-Kanun and Musawi may parallel the two manifestations of 'A'isha Qandisha. The theme of transformation may be hidden here.

31. Our field assistant was present at most of our interviews with Mohammed and Dawia.

32. The following associations were elicited when I asked him to tell me what occurred to him when I said "white." "It is good, the white, because everyone dresses in white on Fridays. They say their prayers in white. White is a favorite color. White is worn by pious people. It is the color one should wear. There are many people who like it. In Morocco one wears all kinds of colors: white, black, and yellow. It reminds me of the Friday flag."

33. Mohammed's ambiguous sexual identity is illustrated in a self-portrait I asked him to draw in which he combined male and female genitals. He had carefully distinguished these in his earlier drawings of a man and a woman. For reproductions of the drawings, see Crapanzano 1973c:174.

34. There is an irony in the names of Mohammed's mother and stepmother, Dawia and 'A'isha. He is married to a Dawia and *maqius* to an 'A'isha. One cannot help but wonder whether his desire to marry Dawia was not in a sense symbolic of his desire to recover his "good" mother. Of course, Dawia was so young—ten at his first proposal—that she was probably less threatening than an older woman.

35. His potency may well be a defense against castration fears. The "phallic orientation" of Mohammed's sexuality is not untypical of other Hamadsha.

36. Its reality is perhaps too painful for him. Gueddar is more than just a son; he is proof of Mohammed's manhood. His death is in a sense the death of Mohammed, Mohammed qua man.

37. It should be noted that years later, in March 1968, when Dawia was again struck, she saw a tea tray, a kettle of boiling water, and a brazier. Mohammed was praying.

38. When she was struck in March 1968, Mohammed was also struck.

8. *Dialogue*

1. In discussing the ideology of dialogue, I find it difficult, symptomatically, to decide when to put *dialogue* in quotation marks, for much of the time I am not talking about the word "dialogue" nor a dialogical event but the symbolic connotations of the event conceived as a dialogue.
2. Tedlock and other dialogue theorists, especially the phenomenologists, uses "dialogue" and "conversation" interchangeably. I have followed their example, although at a simple empirical level I think a case can be made for distinguishing between the dyadic relations of dialogue and the polyadic relations of conversation. Given my own concern with shadow dialogues, the distinction is perhaps less significant because all dialogues are polyadic.
3. See Theunissen (1986) for detailed review and discussion of the dialogue in phenomenology.
4. "Die Partner können aber auch teilweise oder ganz getrennt bleiben: weil sie einem Kurzschluss erliegen, weil sie sich damit benügnen, etwas nur approximativ zu verstehen, oder weil die geäusserten Gedanken und die verwendete Sprachform mindestens in ihrer Wirkung voneinander abweichen" (Bauer 1969:3).
5. See Maranhao (1986) for a discussion of three operations of understanding—comprehension, acceptance, and appropriation—and the fragility of understanding within a dialogical context. For Maranhao, understanding is never complete without appropriation, and insofar as dialogue does not aim at producing texts, which are easily appropriated, understanding in a dialogical context remains always incomplete and critical. I would argue, more cynically perhaps, that many verbal transactions that pass for dialogue, are in fact a struggle for—and insistence on—a particular, potentially textualized understanding that can and must be appropriated by each of the partners to the dialogue.
6. See the discussion below on changing perspectives and contexts.
7. Memory "is not properly understood if it is regarded as merely a general capacity or aptitude," Gadamer (1975:16) argues. It is "an essential element of the finite historical being of man."
8. In *Hölderlin and the Essence of Poetry* Heidegger (1949) sees conversation—a single conversation that is the essential mode and actualization of language—as a support for man's existence. "We are a conversation—and that means: we can hear from one another.

We are a conversation, that always means at the same time: we are a *single* conversation. But the unity of conversation consists in the fact that in the essential word there is always manifest the one and the same thing on which we agree, and on the basis of which we are united and so are essentially ourselves. Conversation and its unity support our existence."

9. It is, nevertheless, important not to confuse understanding with identification, as Bakhtin (1977:100ff) points out. One decodes a sign but one only identifies a signal. MacIntyre does not elaborate on how exactly allocation of a conversation to a particular genre works.

10. See Bauer (1969), for discussion and bibliography.

11. One particularly evident area in which this learning takes place is psychotherapy. It does not take a particularly perspicacious observer to recognize a speaker who is in psychotherapy, particularly group therapy. Often they direct attention to the pragmatic dimensions of the discourse in which they are engaged.

12. Although Dwyer tries to distinguish his conversations with Mohammed from the standard ethnographic interview (however that is understood), he seems to have conducted his exchanges the way anthropologists always do—posing short, disengaged questions and awaiting long, committed answers—that is, until the final interview.

13. The tape recorder can also have the opposite effect. In my research in South Africa, whites preferred to talk, and talked more freely, when I used a tape recorder. Janet Malcolm (personal communication) found that in several interviews with psychoanalysts the tape recorder seemed to free them, becoming, as it were, a mediator.

14. The autobiographical illusion is socially necessitated. Imagine the havoc our legal system would be in were we to acknowledge the quotation marks around witnesses and the people they talk about in their testimonies! We would then have to recognize them as *characters* in highly conventionalized, dramatic performances that are taken to be merely representations of what occurred. Rather than judge them in terms of their "truth value," as we normally do, we would have to judge them in terms of their persuasiveness. It would seem, however, that the quotation marks have to be recognized in any endeavor that pretends to science even if that recognition risks subverting its traditional scientific claim.

15. Of course each dialogue is elaborately contextualized in terms of Dwyer's theoretical reflections. It is never altogether clear when and where these reflections occurred.

16. In the theater, the context of utterance is created or recreated

through the performance and its setting. In many novels, the contextual deficiency of mere dialogue is made up by the narrator's commentary: "He said nervously," "I detected a slight tremor in his voice as he confessed his love," "As she uttered the words the old hag had given her, the sky darkened." Such commentary is out of bounds in most scientific writing.

17. Banality may of course have the opposite effect. How often has a romance ended because of a "revealing" cliche?

   I should also note that people who work with the mentally ill often experience a vulnerability similar to that of the ethnographer. Theirs may come, however, from their patients' calling attention to the hidden pragmatic dimensions of their discourse, as do certain schizophrenics, or from their own therapeutic techniques, which in various guises (for example, the analysis of transference or the breaking up of traditional relationships by questioning them in family therapy) call attention to the way the "therapeutic" relationship is constituted.

18. In Chapter 4 I suggest that a similar struggle occurs between a character in a novel and the narrator, who needs to be responsive to the character he has created.

9. Symbols and Symbolizing

1. Eliade does not always clearly differentiate between "symbols" and "religious symbols."
2. This evaluation of the "perfect version" parallels the evaluation of the "original" in the representational arts. See Walter Benjamin's (1969; 217–251) famous essay "The Work of Art in the Age of Mechanical Reproduction." Is the notion of "perfect version" a precipitate of a particular capitalistic economic arrangement?
3. In his Case Notes of November 30, 1909, Freud (1955b; 289) wrote: "More rat-stories; but as he admitted in the end, he had only collected them in order to evade the transference phantasies which had come up in the meantime." Neither Freud nor his patient considered the full implication of this observation.
4. Note the parallel between Nietzsche's coin imagery and that of Mallarmé and Lacan.

10. Glossing Emotions

1. De Sousa (1980) argues that attitudes concerning emotions—an ideology of emotions—affect their emotional content. He is particularly concerned with gender and the content of emotions.

Whether such attitudes or ideologies affect the content of emotions or not, they do affect the expression and the glossing of emotions. De Sousa (1980:291) suggests that love "whose characterization involves whole complexes of particular feelings, expectations, long term patterns of intercourse, and social sanctions," is "arguably too complex to be called an emotion." The point is that it *is* considered an emotion—an exemplary one. The duration of an emotion becomes a problem when its ontological status is questioned, but it does not appear to me to be a problem when its expression or glossing is considered rhetorically.

See Lakoff and Kovecses (1987) for a referentially based discussion of the "conceptual structure" of anger in American English. Their attempt to relate the metaphors of anger to "actual physiology" conforms to the prevalent American essentializing attitude toward emotions.

2. Although there are undoubtedly important differences in nuance between feelings and emotions, not to mention between feelings and emotions and sentiments, they are easily substituted for one another in most casual conversations. See Ryle (1949) and Solomon (1980) for a discussion of the distinction; Lutz (1986) for a discussion of emotion as a cultural category.

3. See Lutz and White (1986) for a comprehensive review of anthropological studies of emotion.

4. Compare to Searle (1983), who argues that one has to distinguish carefully between the ontological category of Intentionality and its logical properties (to these I would add, in accordance with my own conversational approach, its rhetorical properties or uses). See Bedford (1962) for an interesting but somewhat restricted discussion of the judicial function of emotional utterances. For Bedford, statements about emotion do not describe behavior but interpret it. It is, he argues, a logical mistake to treat emotion words as names; it masks their other—their judicial—functions. "Emotion words form part of the vocabulary of appraisal and criticism, and a number of them belong to the more specific language of moral criticism" (119). Like so many arguments advanced by Anglo-American analytic philosophers, Bedford's reflects, uncritically, the linguistic and psychological values of his culture. He does point, however, to the nonreferential function of emotion words.

5. In Freudian psychology the deepest recesses of being—of character—are given some transactional basis. Character is said to be determined in part at least by early childhood experiences of parental and other family figures or their surrogates, though at

times Freud and other analysts speak as though these experiences were somehow predetermined.

6. I am of course concerned here primarily with social relations, that is, with relations between human beings. Relations with the environment, with the animal world, the plant world, with the supernatural, however understood, also give rise to emotions of all sorts. Often these nonhuman worlds are anthropomorphized when they are the source of emotion, particularly intense emotion.

7. I use the expression "to call the context" to stress the fact that all pragmatic locutions are not only reflective of a given context but, to varying degrees, create, or at least highlight, that context.

8. We ought of course to write "self," "experience," "social," "interaction," with a tentativeness that indicates if not a real then a potential break with our own, logocentric or not, metaphysical tradition. It is noteworthy that anthropologists have been unwilling to use and even to discuss Derrida's (1976) *sous rature* convention (Crapanzano 1990a).

9. The two are of course related; for performatives, tenseless as they are, are immediately linked indexically to their context of utterance since they create what they index. As such, they replicate the indexical function of such utterances as "I love you" and "I am angry at you." See Lee (1985) for a discussion of the indexical dimension of performatives and for an interesting derivation of the mind-body dichotomy through the projection of the (external) indexicality of performatives onto the (internal) indexicality of mental state verbs that share many of their grammatical features. Lee's argument can probably be applied to the first person (nonprogressive present tense) utterances of emotion that we are treating here.

10. Throughout this chapter I use "symbolicity" and "semanticity" interchangeably to refer to abstract reference or description that is considered to be context-independent.

11. See Taylor (1987) for an interesting example of this disjunction among dancers of the tango in Argentina.

12. There may also be contradictions in the glossing of the emotions themselves. This is particularly true in cases of special vocabularies and other locutionary forms, for example, the brief poems (*ghinnawas*) among the Bedouin women of western Egypt (Abu Lughod 1986), for referring to emotions that are not permitted in ordinary discourse. See Kondo (1987) for a discussion of the relationship between the "expression" of emotion and levels of formality in Japanese.

13. Obviously, in such circumstances disjunction has to be understood rhetorically. When doublebinding occurs, it becomes pathogenic if it is not understood, at some level, as a rhetorical strategy; that is, if there is a failure to communicate, or to understand, how the doublebinding utterance is to be read.

11. Saints, Jnun, and Dreams

1. I am indebted to the works of Alfred Schutz (1967), Peter L. Berger and Thomas Luckmann (1967), and Ludwig Binswanger (1960) for much of my argument.
2. Lacan (1966) has stressed the importance of distinguishing between the verbal texts the analyst analyzes and the "reality" of the experience reported.
3. The dreams and other life-history material reported here were told to me by members or devotees of the Hamadsha. I worked with the three principal dreamers in this paper for at least six months. We were friends. My knowledge of Moroccan dream theory resulted from direct questioning; the dreams themselves were reported in the course of interviews in which free association was encouraged. Although I expressed a strong interest in dreams, I never made it a center of focus. I was learning about the brotherhood, the life of my informants, and, more generally, about Morocco. That I would be interested in dreams was taken for granted by my informants. The dreams reported here are but a few of many dreams that were told to me in my interviews; they were all considered by the dreamers to be of central importance to them. The dynamics discussed in terms of the three principal informants occur also in the dream-life of other Moroccans with whom I worked.
4. It should be pointed out that the practices of popular religious brotherhoods like the Hamadsha were well-known. They provided many of the symbolic-interpretive elements for the articulation of experience. The extent to which these are primary elements of articulation outside their immediate milieu remains an open question. The importance of such brotherhoods, even today, must not be underestimated.
5. A discussion of demons and demonic possession appears in Chapter 7.
6. Some Moroccans argue that the soul (*ruh*) could not leave the body during sleep for then the sleeper would die; they associate the ruh with the *nafs*, or breath. Others suggest that one dreams what

one desires; the heart, *qalb,* the seat of desire, is thus considered responsible for dreams. The dreamer is thought to be in a potentially dangerous state and is not to be disturbed when visibly dreaming.

7. Hypnopompic images are considered to be the work of Shitan too. A person who is late for work may say, "I have been covered by Shitan" *(ratani iblis),* meaning that he had been overcome by dreams or early morning imagery and could not get up.

8. For a more general account of *stikhara* (classical Arabic *istikhara),* see Lecerf (1966).

9. Dreams, at least good dreams, are said to have *baraka,* and baraka is said to be contagious.

10. On the few occasions when I was told the dream that "announced" my arrival, I was unable to see any immediate relationship between the content of the dream and my visit. The dreamer himself was often hard-pressed to find a connection. The fact of the dream appeared to be more important than its content; it provided, perhaps, the occasion for an optional but conventional expression of hospitality.

11. Strictly speaking, it is necessary to recognize here, and elsewhere in this paper, that "real life context" and "the real" are also subject to idiomatic structuralization and evaluation—to what Lacan (1966) calls symbolic and imaginary functions. See Leclaire (1958) and Laplanche and Pontalis (1967).

12. Since the publication of "Saints, Jnun, and Dreams," I have written about this dreamer in some detail (1988).

13. Moulay Abedsalem was in his late seventies or early eighties when he reported his dream to me. He was a very lucid, intelligent man who was considered to have great baraka and wisdom. He treated me as both a son and a student.

14. Biting or chewing fingernails is often regarded as a symptom of separation anxiety!

15. Mohammed was in his middle or late forties. He had sponsored the first private Hamadsha ceremony I had attended and considered himself responsible for my learning the truth about the brotherhood. My wife and I, and my Moroccan field assistant and his wife were all very close to Mohammed and his family. Like other Moroccans of his background, Mohammed was quick to form dependency relationships with those whom he considered his superiors. My wife and I did our best to discourage such a relationship. For more details, see Chapter 7.

16. Mohammed, who spent several years in the French army, is much

more conscious of age and chronology than the average Moroccan of his background.

17. Somatization is a frequent response to anxiety among Moroccans of Mohammed's milieu. Note that even Moulay Abedsalem's response to his dream, at least figuratively, was that he "couldn't even get up until the sun rose."

18. Moroccan women during pregnancy often demand special foods which their husbands—or other members of their families must give them. If such demands are not fulfilled, their children, they say, will suffer dire consequences.

19. Hamid, a fellah, was in his middle thirties when he recounted this experience which had occurred several years earlier. He was an intelligent man who appeared to be quite well adjusted. He was not one of my principal informants.

20. Tuhami was perhaps my most interesting informant. I met with him an average of three hours a week for about six months. My interviews, which he looked forward to, soon took on a therapeutic cast. He was a desperately lonely man caught in a bind from which he could not escape. He died a bachelor, a year after I left Morocco. He is the subject of my book *Tuhami*.

21. Judging from Tuhami's symptoms and from the hospital to which he was admitted, it seems likely that he was suffering from a physical ailment.

22. Tuhami was not always so confused as in this early interview. Indeed, as our interviews continued, he seemed to have succeeded in relating his fantasies and dreams to real-life contexts.

12. Rites of Return

1. A similar criticism may be advanced for Victor Turner's (1967) use of "state" in his discussion of rites of passage. Turner argues that such rites "indicate and constitute transitions between states." *State* he defines as "a relatively fixed or stable condition." He includes in its meaning "such social constancies as legal status profession, office or calling, rank or degree"; he includes in it too the "culturally recognized degree of maturation" of an individual as well as his physical mental or emotional condition. Such broad usage can only serve to mask ritual intricacy.

2. I do not use "experiential vantage point" here in a strictly phenomenological sense but rather in the sense of a "construct" as it is frequently used in psychoanalysis.

3. The rite of circumcision, like all rituals, is of significance to all the participants from their specific vantage points. Frequently, the choice of a central figure—the boy or the father in the circumcision rite—masks the significance of the rite for other participants—the mother, brothers, or sisters. The ritual must be understood not simply in terms of enactment or reenactment by any of its participants, but also as a live act or a reliving—a remembering. See below.

4. Whatever validity Cohen's (1964) distinction between two stages of puberty may have would not affect my experiential argument here. Unless these two stages are culturally distinguished, they would not affect the perception of disjunction.

5. Female excision is less common and is not found in Morocco (Dostal n.d.). A spurious saying of the Prophet condones the practice: circumcision is a *sunna* (commendable act) for men and an honor for women (Margoliouth 1911).

6. Many of the women in the area in which I worked did not believe that Jews were circumcised. This is apparently true for some of the men as well (Rosen 1970).

7. Westermarck (1926) found that most circumcisions took place between the ages of two and seven in Morocco.

8. Doughty (1964) heard tales of this practice for the Harb. When he came to them and asked about it, they answered: "Lord! That so strange things should be reported of us poor people! but Khalil, these things are told of 'el-Kahtan'—that is, of a further nation and always far off."

9. Frequently, circumcision is translated by North Africans into French as *baptême* (baptism) (Tillon 1966).

10. Here I encountered great resistance until I explained that I was circumcised—and then surprise and fraternal openness.

11. Berber tribes in the area such as the Majatte have essentially the same rite; the barbers who perform their circumcisions are usually the same as those who perform the rite for the Arabs. The Berbers say the Arab circumcisions are less joyous and couched in more secrecy. They criticize the Arabs for not explaining the operation to the boy ahead of time.

12. The serving of tea in Morocco provides an idiom for the articulation of social relations. The most honored guest is asked—encouraged, forced even—to prepare tea by the host and other guests who in round-robin fashion politely refuse to prepare it. Special attention is paid to the level of tea in each glass. I have

heard stories told of men being killed for having failed to serve equal amounts of tea. The preparer of tea always tastes the tea before serving it "to show that it is not poisoned."

13. The wealthy frequently sponsor circumcisions for the poor; the sponsor obtains a great blessing for such an act (Le Tourneau 1949). Westermarck (1926; Talha 1965) claims that some families are prevented by magical fright (*tera*) from sponsoring circumcisions for their sons. The sons must be carried off in secret by another family to be circumcised. In the cities there are yearly public circumcisions for the poor; these are usually held in a saint's sanctuary.

14. Ali is the Prophet's son-in-law. I have heard numerous tales of his bravery, his sexual prowess, and of course, his spirituality. He is, in a sense, the ideal man.

15. Boys frequently catch a bird, tie a long string to one of its legs, and let it fly off, only to pull it back again. They repeat this letting go and pulling back until the bird dies.

16. Mothers frequently carry children on their backs.

17. The quality of such conversation is revealed in the following abbreviated excerpts from my field notes. The conversation occurred at breakfast before a circumcision. The prostitute and the musicians had arrived the previous night. There had been dancing after the application of henna. The prostitute, who was about fifteen, had slept in bed with the men but had not made love to them.

> There was joking about how the prostitute had sneaked off to bed before the men in order to have the most comfortable place. One man could not even find a place to sleep. She had taken up so much room! She flirted a lot with Driss (one of the musicians) and touched him and the other men a lot. She said, "Europeans eat only a little biscuit for breakfast. Moroccans will eat anything you put in front of them—a whole bowl of butter even. I have a girlfriend who lives with me. When we eat, I take all the meat and stick it in my mouth and then I take it out again. She can't eat any of the meat that way. Then my girlfriend sticks her hand in the food and messes it all up so that I can't eat it. Then we laugh and share it anyway. I wouldn't do this with anyone but her because she is my girlfriend." The prostitute thought all this very interesting; it was sexually loaded. The men didn't pay much attention to details; they just enjoyed listening to her talk. The prostitute

then began to flirt with Hasan (a shy villager). There was much joking about who would go into the backroom with her alone. Everyone said Hasan would not go with her because he was afraid he would be circumcised again. The prostitute gave Hasan a choice: He could go in with her alone or wait for the barber. Everyone laughed. Then several men suggested Hasan should hold the boy who was going to be circumcised. Hasan blanched.

18. There are other unmarked transitions. Among these I would include not only the boy's first heterosexual experience but also his homosexual adventures, especially his taking the dominant position. Younger boys play a passive part with older boys and later, when they get older, they turn dominant and enter the younger boy. I would also include a second, unmarked transition in which the son, especially the eldest, takes his father's "place" upon his father's death. Adult sons tend to avoid their fathers, do not smoke in front of them, do not talk about sex with them, and do not engage in flirtations in front of them. They do not show anger toward them (but often deflect anger to their brothers). The sons are generally submissive to their fathers and their fathers' authority.

13. Maimed Rites and Wild and Whirling Words

1. It was only after completing the first draft of this essay that I came across Gorfain's (1986). Although I do not share many of her premises about "texts," "fictions," or "play," which have to be considered as historically and culturally specific notions, I do find striking parallels between our two readings of the play. Gorfrain focuses on Hamlet's moral and epistemic dilemma, while I stress the moral and epistemic crisis at Elsinore. Hamlet's antics are, in my understanding, the consequence of this crisis.

2. Mahood (1957:115) notes that "cloak," "suits," "forc'd," "forms," "moods," and "shapes" are ambiguous and suggest "an assumed disguise as well as an outer manifestation of genuine qualities." Message and figuration parallel each other here.

3. Paterson (1951), also notes the "breakdown and prostitution of language" at Elsinore, and emphasizes an "intensely critical, almost disillusionist attitude of the play toward language itself." He argues that at the end of the play the validity of the word has been

re-established. He does not examine the nature of the linguistic crisis, however, and fails to consider the ironic implications of Horatio's newfounded ability to narrate (not to perform) what has taken place in Denmark. Ewbank (1979), who recognizes the way in which morality and a sensitivity to language are tied up with each other in *Hamlet,* suggests that the loss of faith in language for Hamlet and other characters in the play has to be seen against a background of faith in the power of the word. For Ewbank, it is a question of a character's finding the appropriate language. Sacks (1982) sees a marked change in Hamlet's attitude toward language; he learns "to recognize the efficacy of the mediating shows and forms which he had rejected at the opening of the play" (Sacks 1982:597). Hamlet's changing attitude parallels a change from vengeful to elegiac pursuits, from action to language. Sacks, like Ewbank, focuses on the meaning of language for Hamlet and not on the semantical condition of Elsinore. See also Calderwood's (1983) discussion of court speech as noise.

4. My language will inevitably betray this intentional problematic, for it is embedded in an intentional psychology I cannot escape.

5. Burckhardt (1968) suggests that Shakespeare's plays explore the consequences of the "disintegration of language" that results from the disintegration of social order.

6. Contrast Parmentier (1987) who questions this traditional wisdom. I would argue that conventions are still deemed "necessary," "inevitable," "required," "prescribed," or "logical," whether or not they are understood in terms of "nature."

7. Mahood (1957:170) writes that for the Elizabethans the right names of things were given by God and discovered by Adam. "Names, then, seemed true to most people in the sixteenth century because they thought of them as at most the images of things and at least the shadows of things, and where there was a shadow there must be a body to cast it." It is not clear what Mahood's evidence for this observation is. But he does go on to note that alongside the "dominant linguistic realism" was a linguistic skepticism. See also Ewbank (1986:50) and Trousdale (1982). Shakespeare was certainly aware of the tension between these two positions. In *Julius Caesar,* for example, words are arbitrary symbols for Cassius and Brutus, but for the excited masses the word can substitute for the thing. Although the poet Cinna tells them that he is not Cinna the conspirator, they turn on him: "It is no matter, his name is Cinna; pluck but his name out of his heart, and turn him going" (III,iii,33–34).

8. Ewbank (1979:92) argues that oxymorons cancel each other out; this creates a false sense of legitimacy for his argument.

9. A younger brother's marriage to an elder brother's widow was considered incestuous in Elizabethan England if the elder brother left a surviving son (Rosenblatt 1978). Gorfain (1986:219) notes that Claudius's marriage to Gertrude "was tantamount to declaring Hamlet dead, since his existence should have outlawed the marriage."

10. Gorfain (1986:222) argues that the ghost puts Hamlet in a double-bind by insisting that he revenge his murder when only God may exact such vengeance. I do not find sufficient internal evidence to support this argument.

11. The ghost cries from under the stage for the friends to swear, and Hamlet in what Empson (1953:23) calls a "recklessly comic throw-away of illusion" remarks: "Come on, you hear this fellow in the cellarage" (I,v,159). "Cellarage" refers technically to the understage. In an unexpected, frenzied colloquialism that prefigures his mad scenes ("Ah ha, boy, say'st thou so? Art thou there, truepenny?" [I,v,158]), Hamlet calls attention to the "reality" behind the play as he is semantically unsettled. Is Shakespeare playing with "reality" here (paradoxically through an "unreal" or a "differently real" being—the ghost) the way Hamlet will play with "reality" through his play within the play? Hungerford (1967) suggests that Shakespeare frequently blends Hamlet the person with Hamlet the character in the play. He notes that among Hamlet's last words (V,iii,340) is a crossing over through a pun on the word "act" from the inner world of the play to the theatrical performance. He argues that the many theatrical terms in the last lines of *Hamlet*—"shows," "plots," "stage," "performed"—indicate that Shakespeare was directing his audience to his theater as theater and to his play as artifice. (See also Calderwood 1983 for further discussion of the theatrical illusion.) Certainly *Hamlet* cannot be totally divorced from the political realities of Shakespeare's England. But more important for our purposes is the fact that just as a translation has at some level to mark itself as a translation in order to work, so a theatrical performance has to mark itself as such to succeed. Usually this marking occurs pragmatically in complex ways, but here (and elsewhere in *Hamlet*, for comic effect) Shakespeare calls attention to that other reality referentially. His audience is of course free to laugh at the confounding of realities in a way in which Hamlet's audience is not. Shakespeare's political references, to Essex's plot, for example, are never so specific.

12. Attention to the pragmatic dimensions of language coordinates with what Elias (1983) calls "court rationality"—the calculated planning to increase one's status, prestige, and power in the never certain circumstances of the court. Attitudes are carefully measured, gestures meticulously calculated, and speeches subtly nuanced; for they are all indicators of position and power. The courtier "is always observed in court society in his social context, as a *person in relation to others*" (Elias 1983:104). Interestingly, a form of self-observation develops—so Elias (1883:105) maintains—with a view to self-discipline. "Just as he [the courtier] is forced to seek the true motives of others behind their controlled outward behaviour, just as he is lost if he is unable to unmask the affects and interests of his rivals behind their dispassionate facades, he must know his own passions if he is to conceal them effectively." Hamlet's self-observation seems to deviate from this pattern in contradictory ways. Of course the etiquette and ceremony at Elsinore—or in Elizabeth's court—were never so formally elaborated as in the French court Elias discusses.

13. Technically speaking, the meta-pragmatic regimentation of an utterance, and even better, of an exchange, no longer functions in a determinable fashion. The courtier does not know how to take a particular utterance, literally or figuratively.

14. Calderwood (1983:81) also notes that Hamlet's word play is aimed at restoring meaning—*his* own—to the vacuous speech of the court. He sees Hamlet's word play as an attempt to negate, to erase, courtly inanities. "By offering him the eraser of negation, word play also enables Hamlet to purge words of their pretense to meaning—their bland and unctuous vacuity, their false shows and received smugness, their urbane noise—and invest them with meanings of his own." I would stress "meanings of *his* own" along with Hamlet's attempt to regain a meaning-giving context.

Calderwood (1983:82) argues, not altogether convincingly, that Hamlet's puns are rarely heard by anyone except himself and the audience. A form of "cross-erasure" occurs: "Hamlet's wordplay erases courtly inanities wittingly, and the court erases Hamletic ironies unwittingly." The parallel is too neat for so rough and tumbling a play as Shakespeare's. But, more important, word play ("heard" or not) can have an effect on the word player's interlocutor. Calderwood (1983:91) is undoubtedly correct in noting the isolating effect of Hamlet's word games, but I cannot accept his observation that word play "as a form of not-saying" shields him "against the verbal contamination of Elsinore." It may give him an illusion of being shielded (who knows?), but it has to be seen, so I argue, as a response to that contamination, (see Note 15).

15. See Mahood (1957), Burckhardt (1968), and Calderwood (1983) among others on punning in *Hamlet*. Mahood notes that Hamlet quibbles some ninety times in the play (see Note 14).

Puns and other forms of word play are a bit like shifters; they call attention to (the foibles of) language and may even offer an evaluation of a particular utterance. Insofar as they focus on language, they reframe conversation, momentarily at least. Whatever the subject matter was, it is now the words in which the subject matter is cast. One moves from a naive, referential understanding of words as transparent indicators of things, to a more sophisticated understanding: the web of signification that transcends any particular referential moment is acknowledged. Put somewhat differently, word play calls attention to the arbitrariness of the sign in a context in which it has been taken, or risks being taken, as "natural." Punning, Sigurd Burckhardt (1968:25) suggests in another vein, "denies the meaningfulness of words and so calls into question the genuineness of the linguistic currency on which the social order rests." For Burckhardt punning is an act of verbal violence which, tearing the close bond between word and its meanings, asserts the phonetic aspect, the materiality of the word. "The pun gives the word as entity primacy over the word as sign."

16. In my terms Hamlet embodies the unstable third: a guarantor of meaning who can offer no guarantee. As such he is the opposite of the legitimate king. Burckhardt (1968:262) argues that the social order is "a silent but essential partner" in every dialogue.

Gorfain (1986:222) notes: "the antic disposition creates endless puzzles about how to assess the truth of what is said within a metamessage that denies itself as well as the member of the class to which it belongs."

17. Note Mack's (1952) stress on the riddle. Alexander (1971:113) suggests that the entire action of *Hamlet* "may be viewed as a series of traps and stratagems."

18. Rosencrantz and Guildenstern will describe the scene retrospectively to the King and Queen at the beginning of Act III. The King is of course interested in the cause of Hamlet's lunacy; the Queen in his manner. The frequent anticipatory and retrospective accounts and asides in *Hamlet* of scenes witnessed by the audience suggest the untrustworthiness of language and indicate that description and other observations are permeated by selfish and unconstrained desire. Such accounts textualize the event, removing

it as it were from reality and permitting its manipulation for personal ends. Once textualized the events become representations, the equivalent of spectacles—scenes secretly observed from behind the arras, the play within the play.

19. Alexander (1971) stresses the mnemonic functions of the play within the play—a bringing forth of memory.

20. When he thinks of women, Alexander (1971:153) observed, he can "only see the unrestrained figure of *Voluptas.*"

21. Compare II,ii,578–583.

22. As so often in *Hamlet,* the following scene serves as a comment on the implicit assumptions about court language in the preceding scene. Hamlet tells Horatio that he is not flattering him. "Why should the poor be flatter'd?" He asks.

> No, let the candied tongue lick absurd pomp,
> And cook the pregnant hinges of the knee
> Where thirst may follow fawning.   (III,ii,59–62)

23. Calderwood (1983:95) remarks: "By substituting 'nephew' for 'brother,' Hamlet makes his own future murder of Claudius issue causally from Claudius' murder (both real and theatrical) of Hamlet's father."

24. I do not believe that the difference in punctuation in Q2 and F1 affect my argument. In Q2 Hamlet says "a Rat" and in F1 "a Rat?"

25. There is a third letter, to Gertrude, the contents of which we never learn.

26. There is an extraordinary irony in Ophelia's choice of flowers and herbs; for, as Newman (1979) points out, several of them—rosemary, fennel, rue, pansies, and violets—were thought to be abortifacients and emmenagogues. Rue was also said to diminish desire. The "naturalization" of the relation between word and thing operates here at the manifest—the literal—level, and it is subverted at the latent—the connotative—level. The parallel with the sham of court life, with the seemingness that covers up the corruption, is striking.

27. "Lay" may also have sexual connotations. It could be argued that sexual intercourse, as the coupling of two distinct beings, mediates between the articulate and the inarticulate, between signifier and signified, sign and reality. It could be argued further that this mediation is precluded by the King's "incestuous" violation of marriage relations. Death would then be the only possible way of restoring the "natural" bond of signification.

   I should also note that Ophelia's death occurs in a stream, in moving water. Her death in the stream collapses the immobile and the mobile, eternity (or nontime) and time. It would be, in Derrida's understanding, the timeless time of *differance*. "Lay," it should be remembered, can also mean a "pond."

28. Gorfain (1986:225) suggests that it "encapsulates the agonistic acts of the court which thus far have been masked as playful interrogation." She also notes that, unlike Hamlet's freeplay, which has no consequences (!), the game is irreversible. I would argue that *play*, however playful, is never without consequences, if only those that result from the delay—the time of play.

29. We may also be better prepared to accept Hamlet's stated intent because we experience his departure for England, his arranging for the death of Rosencrantz and Guildenstern, his struggle and escape, his return to Denmark, and perhaps even his fight with Laertes in Ophelia's grave as a passage of ritual dimension into determined manhood. He does admit that he is sorry he forgot himself in front of Laertes. "For by the image of my cause I see / The portraiture of his" (V,ii,76–78).

30. Earlier (V,ii,75ff), when Hamlet told Horatio that he forgot himself before Laertes because he saw in Laertes the image of his own cause, he did not seem to recognize that he was the object of Laertes' revenge (Jenkins 1982).

31. To be sure, the Queen has come to know the course of her son's fits of madness. In an odd metaphor, evoking, however perversely, maternity, she equates the end of his mania with what we have come to call a post-partum depression even if we do not, to my knowledge, use it for doves.

> This is mere madness
> And thus awhile the fit will work on him
> Anon, as patient as the female dove
> When that her golden couplets are disclos'd
> Her silence will sit drooping.   (V,i,279–283)

It is not clear how such a pathography could blind the Queen to the precipitousness of the King's invitation and of her son's willingness to engage in "gentle entertainment" with Laertes (V,ii,202–203). (She does not know that Hamlet is sorry that he forgot himself in front of Laertes.) But then, we never know what the Queen permits herself to know.

32. Alexander (1971:24) notes the symmetry of the poisonings but he does not recognize their separate functions: producing disorder and restoring order. Derrida (1972) has discussed the meaning of

pharmakon—poison and remedy in Greek. It would seem that the double meaning—or should I say "double function"?—of poison transcends philology, for poison in *Hamlet* is both death-dealing and curative.

33. Claudius tries desperately to preserve the sham of signification. When the Queen falls, he says, "She swoons to see them bleed" (V,ii,314).

References

Abu-Lughod, Lila. 1986. *Veiled Sentiments: Honor and Poetry in a Bedouin Society.* Berkeley: University of California Press.

Alexander, Nigel. 1971. *Poison, Play, and Duel.* Lincoln: University of Nebraska Press.

Anzieu, Didier. 1988. *L'auto-analyse de Freud et la découverte de la psychanalyse.* Paris: Presses Universitaires de France.

Apel, Karl-Otto. 1987. The Problem of Philosophical Foundations in Light of a Transcendental Pragmatics of Language. Pp. 250–290. *Philosophy: End of Transformation,* ed. Kenneth Baynes, James Bohman, and Thomas McCarthy. Cambridge, Mass.: MIT Press.

Aristotle. 1941. De Interpretatione. Pp. 40–61. *The Basic Writings of Aristotle.* New York: Random House.

Ashley-Montagu, M. F. 1946. Ritual Mutilation among Primitive People. *Ciba Symposium* 8:421–436.

Austen, Jane. [1816.] *Emma.* New York: Norton, 1972.

Austin, J. L. 1970. *How to Do Things with Words.* New York: Oxford University Press.

Bachofen, J. J. 1967. *Myth, Religion, and Mother Right.* Princeton: Princeton University Press.

Bacon, Francis. 1937. Of Simulation and Dissimulation. Pp. 16–19. *Essays, Advancement of Learning, New Atlantis, and Other Pieces.* New York: Odyssey Press.

Bakhtin, Mikhail. 1965. *Rabelais and His World.* Cambridge, Mass.: MIT Press.

—— [V. N. Voloshinov, pseud.] 1977. *Le Marxisme et la philosophie du langage.* Paris: Minuit.

—— 1981. *The Dialogic Imagination.* Austin: University of Texas Press.

—— 1986. *Speech Genres and Other Late Essays.* Austin: University of Texas.

Banfield, Ann. 1985. Ecriture, Narration, and the Grammar of French. Pp. 1–24. *Narrative from Malory to Motion Pictures,* ed. Jeremy Hawthorn. London: E. Arnold (Stratford-upon-Avon Studies, 2nd Series).

Bar-Hillel, Yehoshua. 1970. Indexical Expressions. Pp. 69–88. *Aspects of Language: Essays and Lectures on Philosophy of Language, Linguistic Philosophy, and Methodology of Linguistics.* Jerusalem: Magnes Press.

Barre, Tolkein. 1969. The "Pretty Languages" of Yellowman: Genre, Mode, and Texture in Navaho Coyote Narratives. *Genre* 2:211–235.

Barthes, Roland. 1953. *Le degré zero de l'écriture.* Paris: Seuil.

——— 1977. From Work to Text. Pp. 155–164. *Image-Music-Text.* New York: Hill and Wang.

Basset, H. 1929. *Le culte des grottes au Maroc.* Algiers: Ancienne Maison Bastide-Jourdan.

Bateson, Gregory. 1972. *Steps to the Ecology of Mind.* New York: Ballantine.

Baudelaire, Charles. [1846.] Salon de 1846. Pp. 605–680. *Oeuvres complètes.* Paris: Editions de la Pléiade, 1954.

Bauer, Gerhard. 1969. *Zur Poetik des Dialogs: Leistung und Formen der Gesprachsfuhrung in der neueren deutschen Literatur.* Darmstadt: Wissenschaftliche Buchgesellschaft.

Bedford, Errol. 1962. Emotions. Pp. 110–126. *The Philosophy of Mind,* ed. V. C. Chappell. Englewood Cliffs, New Jersey: Prentice-Hall.

Béguin, Albert. 1939. *L'âme romantique et le rêve.* Paris: Corti.

Benjamin, Walter. 1969. *Illuminations.* New York: Schocken.

Benveniste, Emile. 1966. *Problèmes de linguistique générale,* vol. 1. Paris: Gallimard.

——— 1971. *Problems in General Linguistics.* Coral Gables, Florida: University of Miami Press.

Berger, Peter and Hansfried Kellner. 1970. Marriage and the Construction of Reality: An Exercise in the Microsociology of Knowledge. Pp. 50–72. *Recent Sociology, No. 2: Patterns of Communicative Behavior,* ed. H. P. Dreitzel. New York: Macmillan.

Berger, Peter L. and Thomas Luckmann. 1967. *The Social Construction of Reality: A Treatise in the Sociology of Knowledge.* Garden City, New York: Anchor Books.

Bernstein, Michael Andre. 1983. When the Carnival Turns Bitter: Preliminary Reflections upon the Abject Hero. *Critical Inquiry* 10:283–305.

Bettelheim, Bruno. 1955. *Symbolic Wounds: Puberty Rites and the Envious Male.* London: Thames and Hudson.

Binswanger, L. 1960. *Being in the World: Selected Papers.* New York: Doubleday.

Black, Mary B. 1969. Eliciting Folk Taxonomy in Ojibwa. Pp. 165–189.

Cognitive Anthropology, ed. S. Tyler. New York: Holt, Rinehart, and Winston.

Booth, Wayne. 1961. *The Rhetoric of Fiction.* Chicago: University of Chicago Press.

Bourdieu, Pierre. 1977. *Outline of a Theory of Practice.* Cambridge: Cambridge University Press.

Bourgignon, Erika. 1968. Divination, transe, et possession en Afrique transsaharienne. Pp. 331–358. *La Divination,* vol. 2, ed. A. Caquot and M. Leibovici. Paris: Presses universitaires de France.

Bowers, Alfred W. 1950. *Mandan Social and Ceremonial Organization.* Chicago: University of Chicago Press.

Briffault, Robert. 1927. *The Mothers: A Study of the Origins of Sentiments and Institutions.* New York: Macmillan.

Brown, Norman O. 1969. *Hermes the Thief: The Evolution of a Myth.* New York: Random House.

Brown, Roger and A. Gilman. 1960. The Pronouns of Power and Solidarity. Pp. 253–276. *Style in Language,* ed. T. A. Sebeok. Cambridge, Mass.: MIT Press.

Brunel, René. 1926. *Essai sur la confrérie religieuse des 'Aissaoua au Maroc.* Paris: Paul Geuthner.

Bryk, Felix. 1934. *Circumcision in Man and Woman: Its History, Psychology, and Ethnology.* New York: American Ethnological Press.

Burkhardt, J. [1867.] *Die Kultur der Renaissance in Italien.* Leipzig: Alfred Kroner, 1962.

—— 1955. *The Civilization of the Renaissance in Italy.* London: Phaidon.

Burckhardt, Sigurd. 1968. Notes on a Theory of Intrinsic Interpretation. Pp. 285–313. *Shakespearean Meaning.* Princeton: Princeton University Press.

Calame-Griaule, Geneviève. 1965. *Ethnologie et langage: La parole chez les Dogon.* Paris: Gallimard.

Calderwood, James L. 1983. *To Be and Not To Be: Negation and Metadrama in Hamlet.* New York: Columbia University Press.

Cansever, Gock. 1965. Psychological Effects of Circumcision. *British Journal of Medical Psychology* 38:321–331.

Carroll, Lewis [Charles Lutwidge Dodgson]. [1865.] *The Annotated Alice: Alice's Adventures in Wonderland and Through the Looking Glass.* New York: Bramhall House, 1960.

Catlin, George. [1841.] *Letters and Notes on the Manners, Customs, and Conditions of the North American Indians,* vol. 1. New York: Dover Publications, 1973.

———— [1867.] *O-Kee-Pa: A Religious Ceremony and Other Customs of the Mandan.* New Haven: Yale University Press, 1967.

Charney, Maurice. 1969. *Style in Hamlet.* Princeton: Princeton University Press.

Clifford, James. 1983. On Ethnographic Authority. *Representations* 1:118–146.

Codignola, E. 1977. *Il vero e il falso.* Turin: Paolo Boringhiere.

Cohen, Yehudi. 1964. *The Transition from Childhood to Adolescence: Cross-Cultural Studies in Initiation Ceremonies, Legal Systems, and Incest Taboos.* Chicago: Aldine.

Conrad, Joseph. 1971 [1899]. *Heart of Darkness.* New York: Norton.

Crapanzano, Vincent. 1971. The Transformation of the Eumenides: A Moroccan Example. Paper read at the annual meetings of the American Anthropological Association.

———— 1972. The Hamadsha. Pp. 327–348. *Saints, Scholars, and Sufis,* ed. Nikki Keddie. Berkeley: University of California Press.

———— 1973a. *The Hamadsha: A Study in Moroccan Ethnopsychiatry.* Berkeley: University of California Press.

———— 1973b. Popular Anthropology. *The Partisan Review* 40:471–482.

———— 1977a. Introduction. Pp. 1–40. *Case Studies in Spirit Possession,* ed. V. Crapanzano and V. Garrison. New York: John Wiley.

———— 1977b. The Life History in Anthropological Field Work. *Anthropology and Humanism Quarterly* 2:3–4.

———— 1977c. The Writing of Ethnography. *Dialectical Anthropology* 2:69–73.

———— 1978. Lacan's *Ecrits. Canto* 2:183–191.

———— 1979. Preface. Pp. vii–xxix. *Do Kamo: Person and Myth in the Melanesian World,* by M. Leenhardt. Chicago: University of Chicago Press.

———— 1980. *Tuhami: A Portrait of a Moroccan.* Chicago: University of Chicago Press.

———— 1981. Review of *Meaning and Order in Moroccan Society: Three Essays in Cultural Analysis* by C. Geertz, H. Geertz, and R. Rosen. *Economic Development and Cultural Change* 29:851–860.

———— 1985. *Waiting: The Whites of South Africa.* New York: Random House.

———— 1986. Some Thoughts on Hermeneutics and Psychoanalytic Anthropology. Paper delivered at the Annual Meetings of the American Anthropological Association.

———— 1987. Editorial. *Cultural Anthropology* 2:179–189.

———— 1988. Moulay Abedsalem: An Ethnographic Fiction. Pp. 288–310. *Dialectics and Gender: Anthropological Approaches,* ed.

R. R. Randolph, D. M. Schneider, and M. N. Diaz. Boulder, Colorado: Westview.

—— 1990. Afterword. Pp. 300–308. *Modernist Anthropology: From Fieldwork to Text*, ed. M. Manganaro. Princeton: Princeton University Press.

Crawley, E. 1927. *The Mystic Rose.* New York: Boni and Liveright.

Daly, C. D. 1950. The Psycho-Biological Origins of Circumcision. *International Journal of Psychoanalysis* 31:217–236.

Darnell, Regna. 1974. Correlates of Cree Narrative Performance. Pp. 315–336. *Explorations in the Ethnography of Speaking*, ed. R. Bauman and J. Scherzer. Cambridge: Cambridge University Press.

Deakins, Roger. 1980. The Tudor Prose Dialogue: Genre and Anti-Genre. *SEL* 20-5-25.

de Man, Paul. 1979. *Allegories of Reading.* New Haven: Yale University Press.

Dermenghem, E. 1954. *Le culte des saints dans l'Islam maghrébin.* Paris: Gallimard.

Derrida, Jacques. 1967a. Freud et la scène de l'écriture. Pp. 293–340. *L'écriture et la difference.* Paris: Seuil.

—— 1967b. *De la grammatologie.* Paris: Minuit.

—— 1972a. La double séance. Pp. 199–318. *La dissemination.* Paris: Seuil.

—— 1972b. La pharmacie de Platon. Pp. 69–198. *La dissemination.* Paris: Seuil.

de Sousa, Ronald. 1980. Self Deceptive Emotions. Pp. 283–297. *Explaining Emotions*, ed. Amelie Rorty. Berkeley: University of California Press.

Devereux, George. 1967. *From Anxiety to Method in the Behavioral Sciences.* The Hague: Mouton.

Dieterlin, G. 1973. *La notion de personne en Afrique noire.* Paris: Editions C.N.R.S.

Dostal, Walter. n.d. Zum Problem der Mädchenbeschneidung in Arabien. *Wiener Völkerkündliche Mitteilungen* 11:83–89.

Doughty, Charles M. 1964. *Travels in Arabia Deserta.* London: Jonathan Cape.

Doutté, E. 1909. *Magie et religion dans l'Afrique du Nord.* Algiers: Jourdan.

Dupre, W. 1975. *Religion in Primitive Cultures: A Study in Ethnophilosophy.* The Hague: Mouton.

Durkheim, E. [1914.] The Dualism in Human Nature. Pp. 325–340. *Essays on Sociology and Philosophy*, ed. K. Wolff. New York: Harper and Row, 1964.

——— 1915. *The Elementary Forms of the Religious Life.* New York: Free Press, 1965.

Durkheim, E. and M. Mauss. [1903.] *Primitive Classification.* Chicago: University of Chicago Press, 1963.

Dwyer, Kevin. 1982. *Moroccan Dialogues: Anthropology in Question.* Baltimore: Johns Hopkins University Press.

Eikelman, Dale F. 1977. Time in a Complex Society: A Moroccan Example. *Ethnology* 16:39–55.

Eliade, Mircea. 1962. Remarques sur le symbolisme religieux. Pp. 277–312. *Mephistophèles et l'androgyne.* Paris: Gallimard.

——— 1971. *La nostalgie des origines.* Paris: Gallimard.

——— 1972. *Shamanism: Archaic Techniques of Ecstasy.* Princeton: Princeton University Press.

——— 1975. *Traité d'histoire des religions.* Paris: Payot.

Elias, Norbert. 1983. *The Court Society.* New York: Pantheon.

Eliot, T. S. 1960. Hamlet and His Problems. Pp. 121–126. *Selected Essays.* New York: Harcourt, Brace, and World.

——— 1963. The Four Quartets (East Coker). *Collected Poems.* New York: Harcourt, Brace, and World.

Emerson, C. 1983. The Outer Word and Inner Speech: Bakhtin, Vygotsky, and the Internalization of Language. *Critical Inquiry* 10:245–264.

Empson, William. 1953. Hamlet When New. *Sewanee Review* 61:15–42.

——— 1964. *The Structure of Complex Words.* London: Chatto and Windus.

Erasmus, Desiderius. 1958. *The Praise of Folly.* Ann Arbor: University of Michigan Press.

Erikson, Erik H. 1954. The Dream Specimen of Psychoanalysis. Pp. 131–170. *Psychoanalytic Psychiatry and Psychology,* ed. R. P. Knight and C. R. Friedman. New York: International Universities Press.

Evans, B. I. 1952. *The Language of Shakespeare's Plays.* London: Methuen.

Ewbank, Inga-Stina. 1979. "Hamlet" and the Power of Words. Pp. 84–101. *Aspects of Hamlet,* ed. K. Muir and S. Wells. Cambridge: Cambridge University Press.

——— 1986. Shakespeare and the Arts of Language. Pp. 46–66. *The Cambridge Companion to Shakespeare Studies,* ed. S. Wells. Cambridge: Cambridge University Press.

Ewers, John C. 1967. Introduction to *O-Kee-Pa: A Religious Ceremony and Other Customs of the Mandan,* by George Catlin. New Haven: Yale University Press.

Fairley, Barker. 1947. *A Study of Goethe*. Oxford: Clarendon Press.

Fajans, J. 1985. The Person in Social Context: The Social Character of Baining "Psychology." Pp. 367–397. *Person, Self, and Experience: Exploring Pacific Ethnopsychologies*, ed. G. M. White and J. Kirkpatrick. Berkeley: University of California Press.

Farrar, Reginald. 1917. Jane Austen, *ob* July 18, 1817. *Quarterly Review* 128:23–25.

Firth, Raymond. 1963. *We, the Tikopia: Kinship in Primitive Polynesia*. Boston: Beacon Press.

Fitzgerald, F. Scott. 1956. *The Crack Up*. New York: New Directions.

Foakes, R. A. 1956. *Hamlet* and the Court of Elsinore. *Shakespeare Survey* 9:35–43.

Foucault, M. 1965. *Madness and Civilization*. New York: Vintage.

—— 1966. *Les mots et les choses*. Paris: Gallimard.

Frazer, J. G. 1922. *Balder the Beautiful*. London: Macmillan.

Freud, Sigmund. [1912.] Totem and Taboo. *Standard Edition* 13:9. London: Hogarth, 1938.

—— [1925 (rev).] *Traumdeutung. Gesammelte Werke*, vols. 2 and 3. Frankfurt/Main: Fischer, 1942.

—— [1930.] Civilization and Its Discontents. *Standard Edition* 21:59. London: Hogarth, 1961.

—— [1933.] New Introductory Lectures on Psychoanalysis. *Standard Edition* 22:3. London: Hogarth, 1957.

—— [1939.] Moses and Monotheism. *Standard Edition* 23:3. London: Hogarth Press, 1967.

—— 1941. Bemerkungen über einen Fall von Zwangsneurose. Pp. 379–463. *Gesammelte Werke*, vol. 7. Frankfurt/Main: Fischer.

—— 1942a. Bruckstruck einer Hysterie-Analyse. Pp. 161–286. *Gesammelte Werke*, vol. 5. Frankfurt/Main: Fischer.

—— 1945a. Ratschlage für den Arzt bei der Psychoanalytischen Behandlung. Pp. 376–387. *Gesammelte Werke*, vol. 8. Frankfurt/Main: Fischer.

—— 1945b. Zur Dynamik der Ubertragung. Pp. 363–374. *Gesammelte Werke*, vol. 8. Frankfurt/Main: Fischer.

—— 1946a. Bermerkungen über die Ubertragungsliebe. Pp. 305–322. *Gesammelte Werke*, vol. 10. Frankfurt/Main: Fischer.

—— 1946b. Erinnern, Wiederholen und Durcharbeiten. Pp. 125–136. *Gesammelte Werke*, vol. 10. Frankfurt/Main: Fischer.

—— 1948. Notiz über den 'Wunderblock.' Pp. 1–8. *Gesammelte Werke*, vol. 14. Frankfurt/Main: Fischer.

—— 1950. *Aus den Anfangen der Psychoanalyse: Briefe an Wilhelm Fliess, Abhandlungen und Notizen aus den Jahren 887–1901*. London: Imago.

——— 1954a. *The Interpretation of Dreams*, trans. James Strachey. London: George Allen and Unwin.

——— 1954b. *The Origins of Psychoanalysis: Letters to Wilhelm Fliess, Drafts and Notes: 1887–1902*. New York: Basic Books.

——— 1955a. Notes upon a Case of Obsessional Neurosis. Pp. 153–249. *Standard Edition* 10. London: Hogarth.

——— 1955b. Original Record of the Case. *Standard Edition* 10:251–318. London: Hogarth.

——— 1959a. The Dynamics of Transference. Pp. 312–322. *Collected Papers*, vol. 2. New York: Basic Books.

——— 1959b. Fragment of an Analysis of a Case of Hysteria. Pp. 13–146. *Collected Papers*, vol. 3. New York: Basic Books.

——— 1959c. From the History of an Infantile Neurosis. Pp. 473–605. *Collected Papers*, vol. 3. New York: Basic Books.

——— 1959d. A Note upon the 'Mystic Writing-Pad.' Pp. 175–180. *Collected Papers*, vol. 5. New York: Basic Books.

——— 1959e. Notes Upon a Case of Obsessional Neurosis. Pp. 291–383. *Collected Papers*, vol. 3. New York: Basic Books.

——— 1959f. Observations on Transference-Love. Pp. 377–391. *Collected Papers*, vol. 2. New York: Basic Books.

——— 1959g. Recollection, Repetition and Working-Through. Pp. 366–376. *Collected Papers*, vol. 2. New York: Basic Books.

——— 1959h. Recommendations for Physicians on the Psychoanalytic Method of Treatment. Pp. 323–333. *Collected Papers*, vol. 2. New York: Basic Books.

Fromm-Reichman, Frieda. 1955. *An Outline of Psychoanalysis*. New York: Random House.

Gadamer, Hans-Georg. 1975. *Truth and Method*. New York: Seabury.

Gardiner, Muriel. *The Wolf-Man by the Wolf-Man*. New York: Basic Books.

Geach, P. T. 1960. Ascriptivism. *Philosophical Review* 69:221–225.

Gearhart, Suzanne. 1979. The Scene of Psychoanalysis: The Unanswered Question of Dora. *Diacritics* 9:114–126.

Geertz, Clifford. 1968. *Islam Observed: Religious Development in Morocco and Indonesia*. New Haven: Yale University Press.

——— 1973. *The Interpretation of Cultures*. New York: Basic Books.

Gelley, Alexander. 1979. The Represented World: Toward a Phenomenological Theory of Description in the Novel. *Journal of Aesthetics and Art Criticism* 37:415–422.

Gellner, Ernest. 1988. The Stakes in Anthropology. *American Scholar*: 17–30.

Girard, Rene. 1961. *Mensonge romantique et vérité romanesque.* Paris: Grasset.

Gluckman, Max. 1962. *Essays on the Ritual of Social Relations.* Manchester, Eng.: Manchester University Press.

Goethe, J. W. von. 1973. *Wilhelm Meisters Lehrjahre.* Munich: Beck.

——— 1976a. *Italienische Reise,* 2 vols. Frankfurt/Main: Insel.

——— 1976b. *Tagebuch der Italienische Reise: 1786.* Frankfurt/Main: Insel.

——— 1982. *Italian Journey: 1786–1788.* San Francisco: North Point Press.

Goffman, Erving. 1981. *Forms of Talk.* Philadelphia: University of Pennsylvania Press.

Gorfain, Phyllis. 1986. Play and the Problem of Knowing in *Hamlet:* An Excursion into Interpretive Anthropology. Pp. 207–238. *The Anthropology of Experience,* ed. Victor Turner and E. M. Bruner. Urbana: University of Illinois Press.

Gray, L. H. 1911. Circumcision. *Encyclopaedia of Religion and Ethics,* vol. 3, ed. J. Hastings. New York: Charles Scribner's Sons.

Griaule, Marcel. 1970. *Conversations with Ogotemmeli.* New York: Oxford University Press.

Greenson, Ralph. 1965. The Working Alliance and the Transference Neurosis. *Psychoanalytic Quarterly* 34:155–181.

——— 1967. *The Technique and Practice of Psychoanalysis,* vol. 1. New York: International Universities Press.

Greenson, Ralph and M. Wexler. 1969. The Non-Transference Relationship in the Psychoanalytic Situation. *International Journal of Psychoanalysis* 50:27–39.

Halliday, M. A. K. and R. Hasan. 1976. *Cohesion in English.* London: Longman.

Hallowell, A. I. 1967. The Self and Its Behavioral Environment. Pp. 75–110. *Culture and Experience.* New York: Schocken.

Hallpike, C. R. 1979. *The Foundations of Primitive Thought.* Oxford: Clarendon Press.

Hegel, G. W. F. 1975. *Aesthetics: Lectures on Fine Art.* Oxford: Clarendon.

——— 1979. *The Phenomenology of the Spirit.* Oxford: Oxford University Press.

Heidegger, Martin. 1949. Hölderlin or the Essence of Poetry. Pp. 270–291. *Existence and Being.* South Bend, Indiana: Regnery/Gateway.

——— 1967. *Being and Time.* Oxford: Basil Blackwell.

——— 1971. *On the Way to Language.* New York: Harper and Row.

Herber, J. 1923. Les Hamadcha et les Dghoughiyyin. *Hespéris* 3:217–235.

Hungerford, Edward B. 1967. Hamlet: The Word at the Center. *Tri-Quarterly* 8:69–89.

Irving, Judith T. 1982. Language and Affect: Some Cross-Cultural Issues. Pp. 31–47. *Contemporary Perceptions of Human Language: Interdisciplinary Dimensions*, ed. H. Byrnes. Washington, D.C.: Georgetown University Press.

Jakobson, Roman. 1960. Closing Statement: Linguistics and Poetics. Pp. 350–377. *Style in Language*. Edited by T. Sebeok. Cambridge, Mass.: MIT Press.

—— 1963. Les embrayeurs, les catégories verbales et le verbe russe. Pp. 176–196. *Essais de linguistique générale*. Paris: Minuit.

—— 1981. Ein Blick auf *Die Aussicht* von Hölderlin. Pp. 388–446. *Selected Writings III: Poetry of Grammar and Grammar of Poetry*. The Hague: Mouton.

—— 1987. The Dominant. Pp. 41–46. *Language in Literature*. Cambridge, Mass.: Harvard University Press.

Jakobson, Roman and M. Halle. 1971. *Fundamentals of Language*. The Hague: Mouton.

James, Henry. [1873.] A Roman Holiday. Pp. 136–154. *Italian Hours*. New York: Grove Press, 1959.

—— 1983. *Confidence*. Pp. 1039–1252. *Novels: 1871–1880*. New York: Library of America.

James, William. [1890.] *The Principles of Psychology*, vol. 1. New York: Dover, 1950.

Jeanmaire, H. 1949. Le traitement et la mania dans les "mystères" de Dionysios et des Corybantes. *Journal de Psychologie* 45:64–82.

Jenkins, Harold. 1982. Notes to the Arden Edition of *Hamlet*. London: Methuen.

Jensen, A. E. 1933. *Beschneidung und Reiferzeremonien bei Natürvölkern*. Stuttgart: Strecken und Schroeder.

Joseph, Sister Meriam. 1947. *Shakespeare's Use of the Arts of Language*. New York.

Kantorowicz, Ernest H. 1957. *The King's Two Bodies: A Study in Medieval Political Theology*. Princeton: Princeton University Press.

Kardiner, A. 1945. *The Psychological Frontiers of Society*. New York: Columbia University Press.

Kay, Paul. 1987. Linguistic Competence and Folk Theories of Language: Two English Hedges. Pp. 67–77. *Cultural Models in Language and Thought*, ed. D. Holland and N. Quinn. Cambridge: Cambridge University Press.

Khan, M. 1965. Foreskin Fetishism and Its Relation to Ego Psychology in a Male Homosexual. *International Journal of Psycho-Analysis* 46:64–80.

Kitahara, Michio. 1976. A Cross-cultural Test of the Freudian Theory of Circumcision. *International Journal of Psychoanalytic Psychotherapy* 5:535–546.

Kittay, Jeffrey and W. Godzich. 1987. *The Emergence of Prose: An Essay in Prosaics*. Minneapolis: University of Minnesota Press.

Klein, Melanie. 1932. *The Psycho-Analysis of Children*. London: Hogarth.

Kondo, Dorinne K. 1987. Creating an Ideal Self: Theories of Selfhood and Pedagogy at a Japanese Ethics Retreat. *Ethos* 15:241–272.

Kracke, Waud and G. Herdt. 1987. Interpretation in Psychoanalytic Anthropology. *Ethos* 15:3–143.

Kramer, Jane. 1971. *Honour to the Bride like the Pigeon That Guards Its Grain under the Clove Tree*. London: Collins.

Kuhn, T. S. 1970. *The Structure of Scientific Revolutions*, 2nd ed. Chicago: University of Chicago Press.

LaBarre, Weston. 1970. *The Ghost Dance: The Origins of Religion*. New York: Doubleday.

La Bruyère. 1963. *Les caractères*. Paris: Flammarion.

Lacan, Jacques. 1966. *Ecrits*. Paris: Seuil.

———— 1966. La direction de la cure et les principes de son pouvoir. Pp. 585–645. *Ecrits*. Paris: Seuil.

Lakoff, George and Z. Kovecses. 1987. The Cognitive Model of Anger Inherent in American English. Pp. 195–221. *Cultural Models in Language and Thought*, ed. D. Holland and N. Quinn. Cambridge: Cambridge University Press.

Lamprecht, K. 1900. *Die Kulturhistorische Methode*. Berlin: Gaertner.

Lane, Edward. 1963. *The Manners and Customs of Modern Egyptians*. London: J. M. Dent.

Lanham, Richard A. 1969. *A Handlist of Rhetorical Terms*. Berkeley: University of California Press.

Laplanche, J. and Pontalis, J. P. 1967. *Vocabulaire de la Psychanalyse*. Paris: Presses Universitaires de France.

Lecerf, J. 1966. The Dream in Popular Culture: Arabic and Islamic. Pp. 365–379. *The Dream in Human Societies*, ed. G. E. von Grunebaum and R. Caillois. Berkeley: University of California Press.

Leclaire, S. 1958. A la recherche des principes d'une psychothérapie des psychoses. Pp. 377–411. *L'Evolution psychiatrique*. Paris: Payot.

Lee, Benjamin. 1985. Peirce, Frege, Saussure, and Whorf: The Semiotic Mediation of Ontology. Pp. 99–128. *Semiotic Mediation: Sociocultural and Psychology Perspectives,* ed. E. Mertz and R. Parmentier. Orlando, Florida: Academic Press.

Leenhardt, M. 1953. Quelques éléments communs aux formes inférieures de la religion. *Histoire des religions* 1:83–110.

——— 1979. *Do Kamo: Person and Myth in the Melanesian World.* Chicago: University of Chicago Press.

LeTourneau, Roger. 1949. *Fèz avant le protectorat: Etude économique et sociale d'une ville de l'occident musulman.* Rabat: Publication de l'Institut des Hautes Etudes marocaines, No. 45.

Lévi-Strauss, C. 1958. *Structural Anthropology.* New York: Basic Books.

——— 1963. *Totemism.* Boston: Beacon Press.

Levy, R. 1962. *The Social Structure of Islam.* Cambridge: Cambridge University Press.

Lewes, George Henry. [1855.] *The Life and Works of Goethe.* London: J. M. Dent, 1949.

Lieberson, Jonathan. 1984. Review of *Local Knowledge: Further Essays in Interpretative Anthropology,* by Clifford Geertz. *New York Review of Books* 31:39–46.

Lienhardt, G. 1961. *Divinity and Experience: The Religion of the Dinka.* Oxford: Clarendon.

Lubbock, J. 1870. *The Origin of Civilization and the Primitive Condition of Man.* London: Longmans, Green.

Lutz, Catherine. 1986. Emotion, Thought, and Estrangement: Emotion as a Cultural Category. *Cultural Anthropology* 1:287–309.

Lutz, Catherine and G. M. White. The Anthropology of Emotion. *Annual Review of Anthropology* 15:405–436.

Lyotard, J. F. 1979. *The Postmodern Condition: A Report on Knowledge.* Minneapolis: University of Minnesota Press.

MacIntyre, Alasdair. 1984. *After Virtue,* 2nd ed. Notre Dame, Indiana: Notre Dame University Press.

McLaughlan, Juliet. 1979. The Prince of Denmark and Claudius's Court. Pp. 49–63. *Aspects of Hamlet,* ed. K. Muir and S. Wells. Cambridge: Cambridge University Press.

McLennan, J. F. 1865. *Primitive Marriage.* Edinburgh: Adam and Black.

MacLeod, R. B. 1947. The Phenomenological Approach to the Social Psychology. *Psychological Review* 54:193–210.

Mack, Maynard. 1952. The World of Hamlet. *Yale Review* 41:502–523.

Mahood, M. M. 1957. *Shakespeare's Wordplay.* London: Methuen.

Maine, H. S. 1861. *Ancient Law*. London: Murray.

Maloney, Patrick. 1977. Toward a Formalist Approach to Dreams. *International Review of Psychoanalysis* 2:83–98.

Mannoni, O. 1969. *Clèfs pour l'imaginaire ou l'autre scène*. Paris: Seuil.

Maranhao, Tullio. 1986. *Therapeutic Discourse and Socratic Dialogue*. Madison: University of Wisconsin Press.

Marcus, George. 1980. Rhetoric and Ethnographic Genre in Anthropological Research. *Current Anthropology* 21:507–510.

Marcus, George and D. Cushman. 1982. Ethnographies as Texts. *Annual Review of Anthropology* 11:25–69.

Marcus, Steven. 1974. Freud and Dora: Story, History, Case History. *Partisan Review* 41:12–23, 89–108.

Margoliouth, D. S. 1911. Circumcision (Mohammadan). *Encyclopaedia of Religion and Ethics*, vol. 3, ed. J. Hastings. New York: Charles Scribner's Sons.

Matthews, Washington. 1873. *Grammar and Dictionary of the Language of the Hidatsa*. New York: Shea's American Linguistics, series 2, no. 1.

Mauss, M. 1973. *Sociologie et anthropologie*. Paris: Presses Universitaires de France.

Mead, G. H. 1934. *Mind, Self, and Society from the Standpoint of a Social Behavioralist*. Chicago: University of Chicago Press.

—— 1964. *On Social Psychology*. Chicago: University of Chicago Press.

Michel, Christoph. 1976. Nachwort. Pp. 737–53. *Italienische Reise*, vol. 2, by J. W. von Goethe. Frankfurt/Main: Insel.

Morgan, L. H. 1877. *Ancient Society*. New York: World Publishing.

Mueller-Volmer, Kurt. 1985. Introduction. Pp. 1–53. *The Hermeneutic Reader*. New York: Continuum.

Mukarovsky, Jan. 1977. *The Word and Verbal Art*. New Haven: Yale University Press.

Newman, Lucile F. 1979. Ophelia's Herbal. *Economic Botany* 33:227–232.

Nietzsche, Friedrich. 1956. *The Genealogy of Morals*. New York: Anchor.

—— 1965. Truth and Falsity in an Ultramoral Sense. Pp. 503–515. *The Philosophy of Nietzsche*, ed. G. Clive. New York: Mentor.

—— 1966. Über Wahrheit und Lüge im aussermoralischen Sinn. Pp. 309–322. *Werke in Drei Banden*, vol. 3. Munich: Carl Hanser.

Nilsson, M. P. 1949. *History of Greek Religion*, 2nd ed. Oxford: Oxford University Press.

Noyes, Arthur F. and L. C. Kolb. 1963. *Modern Clinical Psychiatry*, 6th ed. Philadelphia: W. B. Saunders.

Nunberg, Hermann. 1965. Problems in Bisexuality as Reflected in Circumcision. Pp. 13–93. *Theory and Practice of Psychoanalysis*, vol. 2. New York: International Universities Press.

Ong, Walter J. 1970. *The Presence of the Word: Some Prolegomena for Cultural and Religious History*. New York: Clarion.

Onians, Richard B. 1951. *The Origins of European Thought about the Body, the Mind, the Soul, the World, Time, Fate*. Cambridge: Cambridge University Press.

Orgel, S. Z. 1956. The Problem of Bisexuality as Reflected in Circumcision. *Journal of the Hillside Hospital* 5:375–383.

Ortega y Gasset, J. 1961. *The Modern Theme*. New York: Harper Brothers.

Ozturk, Orhan M. 1973. Ritual Circumcision and Castration Anxiety. *Psychiatry* 35:49–60.

Parin, Paul. 1978. Freiheit und Unabhängigkeit: Zur Psychoanalyse des politischen Engagements. Pp. 22–33. *Der Widersprüch im Subjekt: Ethnopsychoanalytische Studien*. Frankfurt/Main: Syndikat.

Parmentier, Richard J. 1987. Naturalization of Convention. *Working Papers and Proceedings of the Center for Psycho-social Studies* 17.

Patai, Raphael. 1969. *Golden River to Golden Road: Society, Culture, and Change in the Middle East*, 3rd ed. Philadelphia: University of Pennsylvania Press.

Paterson, John. 1951. The Word in Hamlet. *Shakespeare Quarterly* 2:47–55.

Peirce, C. S. [1931.] Principles of Philosopy. Pp. 3–363. *Collected Papers*, vol. 1. Cambridge, Mass.: Harvard University Press, 1974.

Pfander, A. 1967. *Phenomenology of Willing and Motivation*. Evanston, Illinois: Northwestern University Press.

Puttenham, George. 1936. *The Arte of English Poesie*. Cambridge: Cambridge University Press.

Radin, Paul. 1957. *Primitive Religion: Its Nature and Origin*. New York: Dover.

Rasmussen, K. 1929. *Report of the Fifth Thule Expedition, 1921–1924: Intellectual Culture of the Iglulik Eskimos*, vol. 7, no. 1. Copenhagen: Gyldendalske Boghandel, Nordisk Forlag.

Reik, Theodor. 1946. *Ritual: Psychoanalytic Studies*. New York: International Universities Press.

Ricoeur, Paul. 1965. *De l'interprétation: essai sur Freud.* Paris: Seuil.

Rilke, Rainer Maria. 1972. *Letters of Rainer Maria Rilke, 1892–1910.* New York: W. W. Norton.

Rimbaud, Arthur. 1954. Ophélie. Pp. 51–52. *Oeuvres complètes.* Paris: Bibliothèque de la Pléiade.

Roheim, Geza. 1942. Transition Rites. *Psychoanalytic Quarterly* 11:336–374.

—— 1945. *The Eternal Ones of the Dream: A Psychoanalytic Interpretation of Australian Myth and Ritual.* New York: International Universities Press.

—— 1972. *Animism, Magic, and the Divine King.* New York: International Universities Press.

Rosaldo, Renato. 1976. The Story of Tukbaw: 'Listen as He Orates.' Pp. 121–151. *The Biographical Process,* ed. F. E. Reynolds and D. Capps. The Hague: Mouton.

Rosen, L. 1970. A Moroccan Jewish Community during the Middle Eastern Crisis. Pp. 308–404. *Peoples and Cultures of the Middle East,* vol. 2, ed. L. P. Sweet. New York: The Natural History Press.

Rosenblatt, Jason. 1978. Aspects of the Incest Problem in *Hamlet. Shakespeare Quarterly* 29:349–364.

Rosenfeld, H. A. 1965. *Psychotic States: A Psychoanalytic Approach.* London: Hogarth.

Ryle, Gilbert. 1949. *The Concept of Mind.* New York: Barnes and Noble.

Sacks, Peter. 1982. Where Words Prevail Not: Grief, Revenge, and Language in Kyd and Shakespeare. *ELH* 49:576–601.

Sartre, Jean-Paul. 1945. *Huit Clos.* Paris: Gallimard.

—— 1956. [1943.] *Being and Nothingness: An Essay in Phenomenological Ontology.* New York: Philosophical Library.

—— 1964. *Saint-Genet: Actor and Martyr.* New York: Mentor.

Schlossman, Howard H. 1966. Circumcision as a Defense: A Study in Psychoanalysis and Religion. *Psychoanalytic Quarterly* 35: 340–356.

Schoolcraft, H. R. 1851–57. *Historical and Statistical Information Respecting the History, Condition, and Prospects of the Indian Tribes of the United States.* Washington, D.C.: Bureau of Indian Affairs.

Schorske, Carl E. 1980. *Fin-de-Siècle Vienna: Politics and Culture.* New York: Alfred A. Knopf.

Schutz, A. 1967. *The Phenomenology of the Social World.* Evanston, Illinois: Northwestern University Press.

Scott, Walter. 1815. Review of *Emma*. *Quarterly Review* 14:188–201.

Searle, John R. 1983. *Intentionality: An Essay in the Philosophy of Mind*. Cambridge: Cambridge University Press.

——— 1985. *Expression and Meaning*. Cambridge: Cambridge University Press.

Silverstein, Michael. 1976. Shifters, Linguistic Categories, and Cultural Description. Pp. 11–55. *Meaning in Anthropology*, ed. K. Basso and H. Selby. Albuquerque: University of New Mexico Press.

——— 1979. Language Structure and Linguistic Ideology. Pp. 193–247. *The Elements: A Parasession on Linguistic Units and Levels*, ed. P. Clyne, W. Hanks, and C. Hofbauer. Chicago: Chicago Linguistic Society.

——— 1985. The Functional Stratification of Language and Ontogenesis. Pp. 205–235. *Culture, Communication, and Cognition: Vygotskian Perspectives*, ed. J. V. Wertsch. Cambridge: Cambridge University Press.

——— 1987. The Three Faces of "Function": Preliminaries to a Psychology of Language. Pp. 17–38. *Social and Functional Approaches to Language and Thought*. New York: Academic Press.

Solomon, Robert C. 1980. Emotions and Choice. Pp. 251–281. *Explaining Emotions*, ed. Amelie Rorty. Berkeley: University of California Press.

Spurgeon, Caroline. 1935. *Shakespeare's Imagery and What It Tells Us*. Cambridge: Cambridge University Press.

Staiger, Emil. 1956. *Goethe*, vol. 2. Zurich: Atlantis.

Steegmuller, F. 1972. *Flaubert in Egypt*. London: Bodley Head.

Stewart, E. 1969. Dream Theory in Malaya. Pp. 159–167. *Altered States of Consciousness*, ed. C. T. Tart. New York: John Wiley.

Strachey, J. 1961. Editor's introduction to S. Freud's *The Ego and the Id. Standard Edition* 19:3–11. London: Hogarth.

Strawson, P. F. 1959. *Individuals*. London: Methuen.

Sweetser, Eve E. 1987. The Definition of *Lie*: An Examination of the Folk Models Underlying a Semantic Prototype. Pp. 43–66. *Cultural Models in Language and Thought*, ed. D. Holland and N. Quinn. Cambridge: Cambridge University Press.

Talha, Abdelouahed ben. 1956. *Moulay Idriss du Zerhoun: Quelques aspects de la vie sociale et familiale*. Rabat: Editions Techniques Nord-Africaines.

Tambiah, Stanley. 1985. *Culture, Thought, and Social Action! An Anthropological Perspective*. Cambridge, Mass.: Harvard University Press.

Taylor, Julie. 1987. Tango. *Cultural Anthropology* 2:481–498.

Tedlock, Dennis. 1969. Beyond Logocentrism: Trace and Voice among the Quiche Maya. *Boundary* 8:321–333.

——— 1983a. The Analogical Tradition and the Emergence of a Dialogical Anthropology. Pp. 321–338. *The Spoken Word and the Work of Interpretation*. Philadelphia: University of Pennsylvania Press.

——— 1983b. *The Spoken Word and the Work of Interpretation*. Philadelphia: University of Pennsylvania Press.

——— 1983c. The Story of How a Story Was Made. Pp. 302–311. *The Spoken Word and the Work of Interpretation*. Philadelphia: University of Pennsylvania Press.

Theunissen, Michael. 1986. *The Other: Studies in the Social Ontology of Husserl, Heidegger, Sartre, and Buber*. Cambridge, Mass.: MIT Press.

Thucydides. 1954. *The Peloponnesian War*. Harmondsworth, Eng.: Penguin.

Tillon, Germaine. 1966. *Le harem et les cousins*. Paris: Seuil.

Todorov, Tzvetan. 1984. *Mikhail Bakhtin: The Dialogical Principle*. Minneapolis: University of Minnesota Press.

Trousdale, Marion. 1982. *Shakespeare and the Rhetoricians*. Chapel Hill: University of North Carolina Press.

Turner, Victor W. 1962. Three Symbols of Passage in Ndembu Circumcision Ritual: An Interpretation. Pp. 124–173. *Essays on the Ritual of Social Relations*, ed. M. Gluckman. Manchester, Eng.: Manchester University Press.

——— 1967. *The Forest of Symbols: Aspects of Ndembu Ritual*. Ithaca, New York: Cornell University Press.

——— 1969. *The Ritual Process: Structure and Antistructure*. Chicago: Aldine.

Tyler, S. A. 1981. Words for Deeds and the Doctrine of the Secret World. Pp. 34–57. *Proceedings of the Chicago Linguistic Society*. Chicago: University of Chicago Press.

——— 1986. On Being Out of Words. *Cultural Anthropology* 1:131–137.

——— 1987. *The Unspeakable: Discourse, Dialogue, and Rhetoric in the Postmodern World*. Madison: University of Wisconsin Press.

Tylor, E. B. 1958. *Primitive Cultures*, vols. 1 and 2. New York: Harper Torchbooks.

Urban, Greg. 1986. Ceremonial Dialogues in South America. *American Anthropologist* 88:371–386.

van den Abbeele, George Y. 1984. Cartesian Coordinates: Metaphor,

Topography, and Presupposition in Descartes. Pp. 3–14. *Voyages: récits et imaginaires,* ed. Bernard Beugnot. Paris: Biblio 17.

van den Berg, J. H. 1955. *The Phenomenological Approach to Psychiatry: An Introduction to Recent Phenomenological Psychopathology.* Springfield, Illinois: Charles C. Thomas.

van Gennep, Arnold. 1960. *The Rites of Passage.* Chicago: University of Chicago Press.

Veltrusky, J. 1976. Basic Features of Dramatic Dialogue. Pp. 130–133. *Semiotics of Art: Prague School Contributions,* ed. L. Matejka and I. R. Titunik. Cambridge, Mass.: MIT Press.

von Grunebaum, C. E. 1951. *Muhammadan Festivals.* New York: Henry Schuman.

———— 1966. The Cultural Function of the Dream as Illustrated by Classical Islam. Pp. 3–21. *The Dream and Human Societies,* ed. G. E. von Grunebaum and R. Caillois. Berkeley: University of California Press.

Vygotsky, L. S. 1962 [1934]. *Thought and Language.* Cambridge, Mass.: MIT Press.

Wallace, A. F. C. 1958. Dreams and Wishes of the Soul: A Type of Psychoanalytic Theory among the Seventeenth Century Iroquois. *American Anthropologist* 60:234–248.

———— 1959. Cultural Determinants of Response to Hallucinatory Experience. *A.M.A. Archives of General Medicine* 1:74–85.

Weber, Max. 1968. *On Charisma and Institutional Building.* Chicago: University of Chicago Press.

Webster, Steven. 1982. Dialogue and Fiction in Ethnography. *Dialectical Anthropology* 7:91–114.

Weiman, Robert. 1985. Mimesis in *Hamlet.* Pp. 275–291. *Shakespeare and the Question of Theory,* ed. P. Parker and G. Hartmen. New York: Methuen.

Weintraub, K. J. 1966. *Visions of Culture.* Chicago: University of Chicago Press.

Wertsch, James V. 1985. *Vygotsky and the Social Formation of Mind.* Cambridge, Mass.: Harvard University Press.

Westermarck, Edward. 1914. *Marriage Ceremonies in Morocco.* London: Macmillan.

———— 1926. *Ritual and Belief in Morocco,* vols. 1 and 2. London: Macmillan.

Whiting, J. W. M. 1964. Effects of Climate on Certain Cultural Practices. Pp. 511–544. *Explorations in Cultural Anthropology,* ed. W. Goodenough. New York: McGraw Hill.

Wilden, Anthony. 1968. *Language of the Self.* Baltimore: Johns Hopkins University Press.

Wittgenstein, L. 1971. Remarks on Frazer's *Golden Bough. Human World* 3:18–41.

——— 1978. *Philosophical Grammar.* Berkeley: University of California Press.

Wittkower, E. D. 1971. Transcultural Psychiatry. Pp. 697–712. *Modern Perspectives in World Psychiatry,* ed. J. G. Howells. New York: Brunner/Mazel.

Woolf, Virginia. 1942. *Death of a Moth.* London: Hogarth.

Wylie, Laurence. 1974. *Village in the Vaucluse.* Cambridge, Mass.: Harvard University Press.

Zetzel, E. R. 1956. Current Concepts of Transference. *International Journal of Psycho-Analysis* 37:369–376.

Index

Heart of Darkness (Conrad), 328n6
Hegel, G. W. F., 89, 91, 122, 289
Heidegger, Martin, 3, 147–148, 150, 198
Hemingway, Ernest, 18
Heraclitus, 74
Hermeneutics, 7, 116–117, 121, 133–134, 137, 141, 148, 150
Hermes, 2–4, 24, 43–45, 60, 69, 140, 150–151
Heuristic relativism, 5
Hippies, 4–5
Historical and Statistical Information Respecting the History, Condition and Prospects of the Indian Tribes of the United States (Schoolcraft), 53
Hölderlin, Friedrich, 198
Hölderlin and the Essence of Poetry (Heidegger), 339n8
Holy Writ, 147–148
Hopi, 71, 148, 211
Horatio, 24, 290–291, 294, 299–300, 304–305, 307, 309, 312–314
Hugo, Victor, 27, 93
Humboldt, Alexander von, 53
Hungerford, Edward B., 351n11
Hypostatization of self, 12

Ideology of dialogue, 189–190
Ideology of texts, 119–124
Illyricus, Matthis Flacius, 148
Incubation dreams, 244
Indexicals, 15–16, 119, 126, 130–135, 235–236
Indians, American, 7, 45–53, 55, 60, 65, 68–69, 76, 145, 200, 211–212
Indonesia, 220
Interiority, 104
Interlocutions, 28
Interpretation of Dreams, The (Freud), 28, 31, 34–35, 39, 41, 70, 115, 117, 121, 126, 132, 151, 318n1, 321n8
Interpretations, 43–45, 121, 129–130, 145–148; dialogue as model for, 196–197; of dreams, 27,

30–31, 34–42, 70–71, 117, 127–129, 131–134, 145–146
Interviews, 201–202, 205–206
Ionesco, Eugene, 201
Irma, dream of, 27, 31–42
Irony, 317n1
Iroquois, 145, 241
Irvine, Judith, 236
'Isa, M'hamed ben, 161, 164, 246–247, 253–254
Isaac, 31
'Isawa brotherhood, 246, 280
Islam. *See* Muslims
Italian, 13
Italian Journey (Goethe), 45, 54–57
Italy, 74–75, 147

Jakobson, Roman, 15–16, 145, 206
James, Henry, 28–29, 31, 58, 149, 207, 323n10
James, William, 71, 89
Japan, 343n12
Jenkins, Harold, 292, 308
Jews, 165, 270–271
Jidba, 159–160, 172, 248, 280
Jilala brotherhood, 280
Jnun, 158–160, 165, 171–173, 175, 177–186, 240–259, 279
Joyce, James, 103
Julius Caesar, 286, 290, 299
Julius Caesar (Shakespeare), 350n7
Jung, Carl C., 144, 222, 227
Justinian, Code of, 147

Kafka, Franz, 38
Kamerastücke (Schnitzler), 126
Kamo, 77–78
Kant, Immanuel, 8, 74, 223
Kardiner, Abram, 136–138, 140
Kauffmann, Angelica, 56
Keller, Gottfried, 27
Kellner, Hansfried, 157, 185–186
Khadija (daughter of Mohammed), 160, 162, 164–166, 171, 177, 185–186
Khalifi, 164
King Lear (Shakespeare), 65–66
Kipp, James, 53